Assistive Technologies and Other Supports for People With Brain Impairment

Marcia J. Scherer, PhD, MPH, FACRM, is President of The Institute for Matching Person and Technology, NY; Professor of Physical Medicine and Rehabilitation, University of Rochester Medical Center, and Project Director at the Burton Blatt Institute, Syracuse University. Dr. Scherer has authored, co-authored or edited nine books, including *Assistive Technology, Connecting to Learn, and Living in the State of Stuck.* She is a Fellow of the American Psychological Association, American Congress of Rehabilitation Medicine, and Rehabilitation Engineering and Assistive Technology Society of North America (RESNA). She is Editor of *Disability and Rehabilitation: Assistive Technology,* an international multidisciplinary journal.

Dr. Scherer lives on the shore of Lake Ontario in the Rochester, NY, area with John Scherer, an electrical engineer and her husband of thirty-five years.

Assistive Technologies and Other Supports for People With Brain Impairment

by

Marcia J. Scherer, PhD, MPH, FACRM

SPRINGER PUBLISHING COMPANY
NEW YORK

Springer Publishing Company, LLC
11 West 42nd Street
New York, NY 10036
www.springerpub.com

Acquisitions Editor: Sheri W. Sussman
Production Editor: Dana Bigelow
Composition: Absolute Service, Inc.

ISBN: 978-0-8261-0645-2
E-book ISBN: 978-0-8261-0646-9

11 12 13/ 5 4 3 2 1

The author and the publisher of this Work have made every effort to use sources believed to be reliable to provide information that is accurate and compatible with the standards generally accepted at the time of publication. The author and publisher shall not be liable for any special, consequential, or exemplary damages resulting, in whole or in part, from the readers' use of, or reliance on, the information contained in this book. The publisher has no responsibility for the persistence or accuracy of URLs for external or third-party Internet websites referred to in this publication and does not guarantee that any content on such websites is, or will remain, accurate or appropriate.

Library of Congress Cataloging-in-Publication Data

Scherer, Marcia J. (Marcia Joslyn), 1948–
  Assistive technologies and other supports for people with brain impairment / by Marcia J. Scherer.
      p. ; cm.
  Includes bibliographical references and index.
  ISBN 978–0–8261–0645–2—ISBN 978–0–8261–0646–9 (E–book)
  I. Title.
  [DNLM: 1. Brain Diseases—rehabilitation. 2. Cognition Disorders—rehabilitation. 3. Self–Help Devices. WL 348]
  LC classification not assigned
  616.8—dc23

2011045283

Special discounts on bulk quantities of our books are available to corporations, professional associations, pharmaceutical companies, health care organizations, and other qualifying groups.

If you are interested in a custom book, including chapters from more than one of our titles, we can provide that service as well.

For details, please contact:
Special Sales Department, Springer Publishing Company, LLC
11 West 42nd Street, 15th Floor, New York, NY 10036-8002
Phone: 877-687-7476 or 212-431-4370; Fax: 212-941-7842
E-mail: sales@springerpub.com

Printed in the United States of America by Bang Printing.

For individuals with brain impairments,
their families, caregivers, and health care providers.
The causes of brain impairment are many,
each course unique, and support needs diverse.
Keep looking forward!

Contents

Foreword

Visualize, if you will, an ornate hearing room in a United States Senate Office Building. It's 24 years ago and Al Cavalier is presenting testimony before what was then called the United States Senate Subcommittee on the Handicapped. Mr. Cavalier headed the Arc-United States' Bioengineering Program at the time, and in his testimony he emphasized an unfortunate but widely prevailing belief in the assistive technology field and across society generally, that people with cognitive disabilities such as intellectual disability, were simply not "appropriate consumers" of assistive technology or of any other technology for that matter.

He argued in his testimony that because of this unfortunate misconception they should be designated by the Federal Government as a *traditionally underrepresented group* and that affirmative action was necessary in the implementation of the then proposed 1987 Technology Act legislation to insure their right to inclusion in its benefits. Unfortunately, that affirmative designation didn't happen and it has been up to leaders in clinical applications of rehabilitation technology like Professor Marcia Scherer to advance the field by "Scherer determination," pun intended.

But dramatic and unforeseen general advances in technology soon followed Cavalier's testimony—in semiconductors, personal computers, and server technology, and in smart phones, web services, and wireless networks, to name a few. Information accessibility for people with and without cognitive disabilities also improved as dependence on rote memory decreased, more complementary visual, audio, and multi-graphic formats were developed, and user complexity was reduced in requisite vocabulary and organizational skills. On the hardware side, according to Kurzweil, there were 22 doublings of price-performance in raw computing capacity between 1967 and 2003, and processor speeds increased from .25 MIPS to 1,000 MIPS. An MIP is one million instructions per second.

In this exceptional book, Professor Scherer displays a deep understanding of the potential capacity of technology to improve the quality of life of people with cognitive disabilities in our society and throughout the world. However, she does not underestimate the intense discrimination faced by people with cognitive disabilities when she remarks that "you can legislate community re-entry, but you cannot legislate community re-integration or acceptance." Fear, distrust and rejection impact self esteem and have emotional and behavioral consequences. Her grasp of the present state of the disability field, from both clinical and assistive technology perspectives, is impressively broad and deep. Her "Matching Person and Technology Model," so capably described in this book and in a stream of her earlier works dating back to 1986, remains a foundational contribution to the clinical application of assistive technology.

Scherer's multidisciplinary knowledge base also stems from her extensive experience as a practicing, doctoral trained, clinical psychologist. That experience includes extensive work directly with people with mental health disorders, developmental disabilities, and physical disabilities. She writes movingly in this book, most touchingly so when describing her lived experience as the daughter of a beloved family member with a brain disorder. I palpably felt the author's deep compassion throughout the book. I admired her clinical competence and commitment as she provided detail about her close working partnerships with numerous people with varied abilities to use technology to help themselves achieve greater independence and self-confidence.

Dr. Scherer skillfully guides us in how to develop and apply reasonable, measureable clinical goals using assistive technology, and to step back frequently and revise those goals as deeper insights about what works with a given client are more fully recognized and understood. My familiarity with Dr. Scherer's work has stemmed in part from her productive participation in the research and development activities of the University of Colorado's Rehabilitation Engineering Research Center on Cognitive Technologies and in the Coleman Institute for Cognitive Disabilities' 11 annual technology conferences to date, I know her to be a thoughtful and uncommonly creative writer and presenter. Her new book does not disappoint.

The most powerful insights she offers students, clinical colleagues, and general readers in this book flow directly from the several excellent case study presentations she offers. They display her extensive clinical experience, compassion, and realism in setting goals and evaluating attainment of those goals collaboratively with the consumer. But I am most impressed by two powerful ideas that rush to mind after reading this book: that cognitive technology is a byproduct of the human spirit and imagination and it will continue to surprise us in ways we cannot now fully envision; secondly, thanks to Marcia Scherer and this book, we have a new compass to inspire and guide us on this exciting journey of the imagination. Bon voyage....

David Braddock, PhD
Coleman-Turner Chair and Professor in Psychiatry
Executive Director, Coleman Institute for
    Cognitive Disability
Associate Vice President, University of Colorado

Acknowledgments

Writing a book of this depth and breadth required that I have my own supports. Mary Brownsberger, a rehabilitation neuropsychologist affiliated with Bancroft Brain Injury Services in New Jersey, and Lauren Taylor, holder of a graduate degree from the London School of Hygiene & Tropical Medicine, served as my "development editors." They kept a close eye on each chapter's structure, content and tone, and pointed out where there needed to be better bridges within or between chapters. Dan Davies, founder and president of AbleLink Technologies Inc. in Colorado; Ed Lopresti, president of AT Sciences in Pittsburgh, Pennsylvania; Clayton Lewis, professor of Computer Science, University of Colorado at Boulder; and Cathy Bodine, associate professor in the Department of Physical Medicine and Rehabilitation, University of Colorado Health Sciences Center and Co-Principal Investigator of the Rehabilitation Engineer Research Center for Advancing Cognitive Technologies, all contributed information and insights on specialized and everyday technologies for individuals with cognitive disabilities. Steve Lowe, associate project manager of AbleData; and Yvonne Heerkens, program manager of Terminology & Technology for the Dutch National Institute of Allied Health Care, provided invaluable help with the classification of assistive technology products and its fit with the World Health Organization's International Classification of Functioning, Disability, and Health. Colleagues in the University of Rochester Medical Center's Department of Physical Medicine and Rehabilitation and in the university's computer science department, were generous with time and support as were colleagues affiliated with the Burton Blatt Institute at Syracuse University.

I am grateful to all the professionals at Springer Publishing Company, especially Sheri Sussman, executive editor, who always knew when and how to best nudge me along to the book's completion. I am proud to be an author with this venerable publishing house.

Much of my work would not have been accomplished without the support I received through grant funding. I am honored to acknowledge the following support over the years:

National Institute for Disability and Rehabilitation Research. Co-Principal Investigator for grant number H133A090004 to the Burton Blatt

Institute at Syracuse University and the Institute for Matching Person & Technology for the DRRP *Center of Effective Rehabilitation Technology (CERT)*.

Centers for Disease Control and Prevention, Grant number DD000219 to the The Institute for Matching Person & Technology, Inc. for the project, *Matching Assistive Technology and Child (MATCH)*.

National Institutes of Health, National Institute of Child Health and Human Development, National Center for Medical Rehabilitation Research. Grant number HD052310 to The Institute for Matching Person & Technology, Inc. for the project, *Improving the Match of Person and Assistive Cognitive Technology*.

National Institutes of Health, National Institute of Child Health and Human Development, National Center for Medical Rehabilitation Research. Grant number HD38220 to The Institute for Matching Person & Technology, Inc. for the project, *Improving the Match of Person and Mobility Technology*.

National Science Foundation, Ethics and Values in Science and Technology and Biotechnology & Research to Aid the Handicapped. Grant number RII-8512418 for dissertation research project, *Improving Technological Innovations for People with Physical Disabilities*.

NIDRR Projects Contracting with the Institute For Matching Person & Technology

Rehabilitation Engineering Research Center for the Advancement of Cognitive Technologies (RERC-ACT), University of Colorado Health Sciences Center, Project Number: H133E090003.

Rehabilitation and Research Training Centers: Developing Strategies to Foster Community Integration and Participation for Individuals with Traumatic Brain Injury. Memorial Hermann Clinical Innovation & Research Institute, Project Number: H133B090023.

The TATE Project: Training Assistive Technology in the Environment. Western Oregon University.

Rehabilitation Engineering Research Center for the Advancement of Cognitive Technologies (RERC-ACT), University of Colorado Health Sciences Center, Project Number: H133E040019.

Last but foremost, I owe much more than words can convey to John Scherer, who as an electrical engineer and loving husband, provided me with substantive assistance as well as moral support and encouragement. He endured without complaint many take-out dinners and lonely evenings while I worked at the computer. Thank you, John—you are truly the love of my life.

Introduction

Brain injuries have been in the news a lot lately. We've read news coverage of professional football legend Terry Bradshaw's rehabilitation efforts for traumatic brain injury, numerous reports of young people with sports-related concussions, the brain injury recovery process of U.S. Representative Gabrielle Giffords (D-Arizona) after she was shot in Tucson, and accounts of scores of wounded service members returning from wars in Afghanistan and Iraq with brain impairments. What doesn't get as much press are the thousands of people with other forms of brain impairment—those who have survived a stroke, who struggle in school because of autism or an intellectual disability, who live with an emotional or behavioral disability, or who are living their last years with dementia or Alzheimer's disease. The term *brain impairment*, thus, refers to the consequences of damage to the functions and structure of the brain as an outcome of a wide range of causes.

Enter technology to the rescue. Advances in injury diagnosis and emergency treatment, imaging, and medical and rehabilitation interventions have not only saved lives, but also made recovery and community living possible.

Ah, technology! It can be frustratingly complex at times, confuse and overwhelm us, but we can't seem to live without it. Or even want to. On a recent flight, as I walked from row 10 to the back of the plane to use the lavatory, I saw people:

Reading newspapers and magazines
Reading paperback and hardcover books
Reading Kindle
Doing crossword puzzles in the airline magazine
Playing computer games
Watching the airline's movie
Watching movies on their iPad
Doing work on their PCs
Talking with a seatmate
Sleeping.

Just how does technology affect the way we work, accomplish tasks, and relate to other people? How has it helped our quality of lives? These topics have been my area of research for the past 20 years, but particularly in the ways technology has affected those living with disabilities. No one is more affected in a personal way than people who must use technology to accomplish a task or get from place to place.

In the late 1970s and throughout the 1980s, there was an explosion of technologies being developed as a result of technology transfer from aerospace and other science and engineering achievements. The ability to miniaturize components led to smaller and more powerful computers. One outcome was a burgeoning of products developed for the specialized needs of persons with disabilities. Unfortunately, designers of the products had not fully taken consumer goals, priorities and preferences and product usability into account. Thus, what was a brilliant engineering design was not always viewed by the user as a desirable form of support. Many had fear of use and avoided it altogether. Many devices were used for a time, but then were determined to be too complicated or uncomfortable to use and were relegated to the basement, closet, or drawer to never again see the light of day. Today, we see more common platforms that are customizable in order to present options. For example, to enter many hotels, you can use a revolving door, a levered door, or a door that automatically swings open with the push of a button.

It was in the context of rapidly evolving technology supports for people with disabilities that I developed my PhD dissertation proposal and grant application to the National Science Foundation. Up to that point, few had studied the myriad characteristics differentiating adults with disabilities who did use various technologies from those who did not use them. The characteristics identified in my research fell into three broad areas: characteristics of the person, environments of use, and the devices themselves. The influences were then organized into a format where they could be used to guide the match of person and technology as well as assess outcomes of the device selection and procurement process. The influences have been presented and discussed in earlier books, which are also biographical accounts of the lives and experiences of persons with disabilities and include those who can't hear or see, can't walk or talk, and can't even sip a cup of coffee independently. These individuals must depend on other people, depend on technologies, or be stuck.

As time has progressed to 2011, there is much less fear of technology. Rather, for many devices, there is increasing reliance and, some might say, overreliance or dependence. We have evolved to the point where embracing technology is not an issue, but knowing how to choose the best of it and ignore what is distracting or useless is a growing concern.

For many products, the operations needed to control them have been streamlined. For others, there is more cognitive complexity because of increased choice. For example, to operate early microwave ovens, one just turned a dial to the desired number of minutes. Now, one needs to decide if high or low wattage is best, operate the numeric keypad, and determine if one wants convection cooking, grilling, and browning.

How the power of today's technologies is being harnessed to support people with brain impairments, and how people can best select the most appropriate support from a wide array of options, is a key reason for my writing this book. Assistive and cognitive support technologies are discussed along with an array of accommodations and resources as well as individualized blends of different forms of support. Examples are provided to base the points and ideas made in real-life situations with actual support users. Here are the individuals you will read about and their particular form of brain impairment along with the age when it typically occurs or becomes apparent:

INFANCY	CHILDHOOD	OLDER AGE	ANY AGE
Intellectual disability including Down syndrome *Theresa* (Chapter 2)	Learning disability *Louisa* (Chapter 6)	Dementia, including Alzheimer's disease *Marjorie* (Chapter 1) *James* (Chapter 6)	Traumatic and acquired brain injury *Delmar* (Chapter 3)
Cerebral palsy *Maggie* (Chapter 2)	Asperger syndrome *Ryan* (Chapter 3)	Stroke *Marjorie* (Chapter 1)	Mental, emotional, and behavioral disabilities *Louisa* (Chapter 6)

Their experiences are told in their own words, or those of the professionals with whom they worked. In the example of Marjorie, conversations were not recorded or noted at the time they occurred, but have been reconstructed based on my recall and the concurrence of family members. Ryan's experiences are related by his sister.

Now, on to the subject of the book: How to best match individuals who have a variety of forms of brain impairment with the most appropriate supports so that they lead productive and satisfying lives and achieve a high quality of life.

1

The Aging Brain—When The Mind Dissolves

I exist as I am, that is enough.
—Walt Whitman

Working with individuals with cognitive disability of any age, and their families, can be very rewarding, exhilarating, challenging, frustrating, the whole package—usually within the same day. Even the best of professionals find this to be true. Families, caregivers, and individuals with cognitive disability themselves experience this, plus other factors can come into play such as denial, being unaware of needs, and emotional distress. Let me provide an actual example.

Back in the winter of 2008, I lingered outside of Marjorie's room for just a minute. Just enough time to prepare myself, I made sure my demeanor conveyed confidence and my face had a smile. The day before, when I walked into her room, my eyes were still watering from the cold air (it was, after all, February in Western New York) and Marjorie noticed that right away. "Why are you crying?" she inquired. I told her I wasn't, that my eyes were watering from the cold. She looked at me skeptically and asked, "Are you sure? You're not crying because of some news about me, are you?" I assured her I was not. Then she looked me directly in the eye and snapped, "You need to be very careful, you know. You should never go into a patient's room with watery eyes. It makes them think . . . it made me think . . . something is wrong." Her next words were spat out. "Some PhD . . . jeez!" As a former nurse, Marjorie had no qualms about dressing down the "younger generation." I felt as helpless as Marjorie believed me to be.

A week later, I visited Marjorie again. When I walked into her area, I reminded myself to be aware of what I saw and heard, and also what I did *not* see and hear. People socializing? Crying or screaming? Too many TVs on? To be aware of what I smelled, and what I did *not* smell. Food? Cleaning fluid? Urine? Then I put all these bits of information together to form my impression of the entire place that day, assessing its general atmosphere and character. I used a gestalt perspective, where the whole is greater than the sum of its parts; a big picture beyond mere details, where one sees the forest for the trees.

When I walked into Marjorie's room at noon, she was lying in bed and greeted me with a nonchalant look and with a chill in her greeting. There it was, that glob of anger creeping up my chest, up my neck, and into my throat and in place for a snippy retort. I swallowed the glob back down, made myself focus solely on her. I asked, "How is your pain today?"

"Awful. Awful . . . oh, just awful." She shook her head slowly back and forth.

Awful was becoming her most frequently used word.

"Did they give you your pain medication yet?"

"Yes. I guess so. I think so. It doesn't do much good, though."

"And did you walk this morning?"

"Not yet. Maybe later. My back hurts too much now."

At this, she closed her eyes, wiggled a bit, and winced as if to provide physical proof of what she had just told me.

I wanted to say, scream it, actually, "Maybe your back would feel better if you walked. *Don't you care anymore?* If you don't walk now, eventually you won't be able to walk at all. The less you do, then the less you *can* do. *Don't you want to get better?*" Instead, I said what I always said to her. "Well, that's too bad. I understand. Later then."

Marjorie's hair was snow-white, but you could never tell from her face that she was 94 years old, even though over the years, she had gone from 150 pounds to less than 100 and had shrunk several inches to 5'2". In a few minutes, a tall, large-boned nursing assistant came in to help Marjorie into her wheelchair to go to the small dining room for lunch. This was an agonizing experience for all—Marjorie, who found it painful; the assistant, who could think of nothing else to try to make it easier; and anyone nearby watching and listening. Marjorie's loud groaning was the worst part of it, even though to my trained eye, I could see nothing that would cause such a sudden onset of excruciating pain. I asked Marjorie about it once she had settled physically and emotionally into her wheelchair.

"Oh, it's not that bad really. Tawny [the assistant] knows, don't you, Tawny?" And she gave Tawny a conspiratorial look and a small smile.

Tawny gave a truly good-natured laugh and replied, "I know Marjorie. It's just our routine."

Marjorie was behaving like a manipulative and spoiled child, with some complicity from Tawny who believed that anyone "of a certain age" earned the right to do just as they pleased even if that meant staying in bed all day. In other words, in my mind, that they had the right to give up.

Marjorie believed that she could moan and groan any time she wanted and everyone would understand. If they knew who she was and what she had endured over the past few months, they would surely excuse any behavior. The trouble was, they didn't, and they wouldn't.

MARJORIE'S RECENT MEDICAL HISTORY

Marjorie had broken her hip almost 3 months previously on Thanksgiving Day. Her sister had picked her up to bring Marjorie over to her house for the afternoon and dinner. They drove into the garage and Marjorie got out and stood waiting under the open door. Then her sister, not knowing where Marjorie was standing, pushed the button to close the garage door, which hit Marjorie on the shoulder and slammed her down onto the concrete floor. An emergency hip replacement was done that night.

How quickly life changes!

Back at Marjorie's house, where she lived alone, her cup and saucer sat ready for the next morning's coffee. Beside it was a banana leftover from the lunch brought the day before by Meals on Wheels. The Thanksgiving Day morning paper was by her chair for reading when she returned back home that evening.

But Marjorie would never return to her home again. Prior to breaking her hip, Marjorie had gotten very thin, but her primary care physician had said she was in good health otherwise—strong heart, lab results came back just fine, blood oxygen level was high. This was excellent news, especially because she had been hospitalized 6 years earlier for severe bronchitis and now had chronic obstructive pulmonary disorder (COPD), which is a progressive lung disease affecting breathing.[1] She only rarely needed to use the inhaler her doctor prescribed for her.

She was admonished to eat more and to put on some weight for "cushioning," for if she should fall and break a hip, that would be very serious. This she said she knew, and to prove it, she had widened her eyes and affirmatively nodded her head. But still she didn't eat enough.

Then, there was the fall in the hospital after her hip replacement surgery when she woke up in the middle of the night and walked to the bathroom. An X-ray confirmed all was fine with her hip. But she had to stay in bed and this led to the development of decubitus ulcers.

In popular parlance, a decubitus ulcer is termed a *bed* or *pressure sore*. It is an ulcer in the skin caused by sitting or lying in one position too long. Blood circulation in the skin is reduced by pressure, particularly pressure over skin that is over bony prominences in the back and hips. At greatest risk are those who are older adults and those who have diabetes, dementia, or conditions that weaken the immune system. Thus, a decubitus ulcer is a serious medical condition; when it doesn't heal, it may get larger and deeper, cause considerable pain, become infected, and become life threatening.

Marjorie's small frame and low weight contributed to this to a large extent. When she left the hospital for subacute rehabilitation, she had to spend time in bed to ease the pressure off her buttocks. By becoming more sedentary, she got weaker and she required assistance to go to the toilet and shower.

She resisted walking more and more in physical therapy because she said that it was too painful to walk. Her lack of progress meant that she could no longer remain in that status even though they did give her more time. Marjorie was then placed on nursing home status. Shortly thereafter, she developed pneumonia that required a return stay in the hospital. From that time on, she required the continual use of oxygen, which meant a large oxygen tank had to accompany her everywhere. This she hated.

MARJORIE'S PSYCHOSOCIAL HISTORY AND LIFE COURSE

Marjorie was born in 1913, just before World War I, the first child of four. She was pampered by her parents as well as her paternal uncle, a physician; aunt; and grandmother. She always presented it as an idyllic childhood until tragedy struck one sunny autumn day when she was 7. She and her younger brother were playing in a curbside pile of leaves with several other neighborhood children when a milk truck came along. The milk truck driver didn't see the children playing so close to the edge of the road, and when he pulled alongside the curb, he ran over Marjorie's brother who died instantly. She was then an only child until a sister was born 12 years later and then another brother.

During the Depression, she enrolled in nursing school. She often talked about her memories of different patients on the wards, what medicine and health care was like then, and how the leftover food from the kitchen was taken outside to spoon into the dishes of those who had learned to patiently gather and wait for this daily occurrence. She told me that only 50% of those in her class actually passed and returned for their second year of study. They knew they had passed when they went to their classroom and they saw a cape draped on the back of their chair. No cape and you turned around, went back to the dorm room, and packed.

As a registered nurse, Marjorie was the first to administer sulfa in the hospital where she worked. She was very proud of this because sulfa was an early antibiotic that made it possible to control bacterial infections that up to that time had taken the lives of many of her patients. As much as she loved nursing, she quit her profession when she married a mechanical engineer who owned a business, and only returned to nursing when he was drafted into the Army during World War II. Less than a year after her husband returned from the war, Marjorie's father died of a cerebral hemorrhage, one more loss in her life. But then, things again became steady and calm. After several miscarriages, Marjorie and her husband had one child and settled into small town community life. It was a love-filled home, and Marjorie willingly made it her full-time job to care for the house, her husband, and their child.

Marjorie was never particularly outgoing and didn't pursue an active social life. Even as a nurse, she had preferred night duty and the hours when most were sleeping and the typical buzz of the hospital was at its most quiet. She wasn't shy or a loner, she just preferred things to be calm and steady, which they were until her husband died in 1972.

MARJORIE'S PAST MEDICAL HISTORY

Two years after her husband's death, when she was 60 years old, Marjorie had a stroke.

A Stroke Is a Brain Attack

Stroke (or brain attack) is the third leading cause of death in the United States and a leading cause of adult disability. According to the National Institute of Neurological Disorders and Stroke (NINDS), National Institutes of Health (2010c), a stroke occurs when the blood supply to a part of the brain is suddenly interrupted, such as when a blood clot blocks a blood vessel to an area of the brain. This is called an *ischemic* form of stroke. A stroke may also be the result of a blood vessel in the brain bursting, thus spilling blood into the spaces surrounding brain cells; this is called a *hemorrhagic* form of stroke. Brain damage occurs when brain cells die because they no longer receive oxygen and nutrients from the blood (ischemic), or when there is sudden bleeding into or around the brain (hemorrhagic).

Stroke can occur at any age (even in utero), although it is most commonly seen in adults older than the age of 55 years. Both the American Stroke Association and the National Stroke Association (2010) list lifestyle risk factors for stroke such as substance abuse, obesity, as well as genetics, medical conditions (high cholesterol, high blood pressure, heart and circulatory disease), and injury to the head or neck. A stroke can also be a consequence of surgery, infection, or other health conditions.

To better describe the outcomes of stroke or brain attack, we could benefit from some visualization to accompany the text. Let's use Leonardo da Vinci's *Vitruvian Man* (Figure 1.1).[2] It is a familiar image and useful for

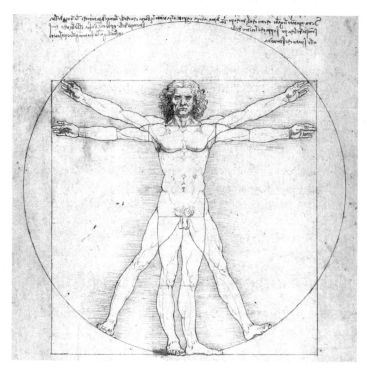

FIGURE 1.1   Leonardo da Vinci's Vitruvian Man, 1490.

describing general aspects of what happens when there is a brain attack or stroke.

The consequences of a stroke are largely dependent on the side of the brain in which the stroke occurs. For example, if it occurs in the left hemisphere, the opposite or right side of the body is generally affected. This is known as the contralateralization of brain function (Figure 1.2).

There may be *paralysis*, typically on one side of the body, which is called *hemiplegia*, or *hemiparesis* if there is muscle weakness without paralysis. Thus, stroke results in brain damage which, in turn, can lead to difficulties with upper extremity control (fingers, hands, arms, shoulders) on the affected side. Lower extremity control can also be affected, resulting in difficulty with walking and mobility.

Stroke survivors may also have numbness or strange sensations. When present, the pain is often worse in the hands and feet and can be made worse by movement and temperature changes, especially cold temperatures. Compounding difficulties with such activities as walking, eating, reading, and writing are neurological and neuropsychological consequences such as spatial neglect and proprioceptive sense.

Spatial neglect typically occurs from injury to the right hemisphere (Bowen, McKenna, & Tallis, 1999). This causes the individual to "neglect"

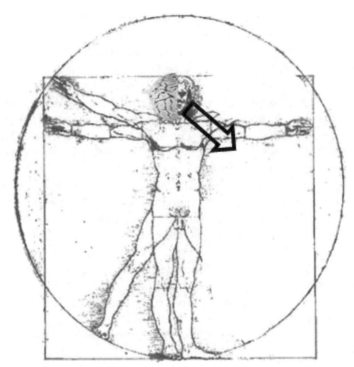

FIGURE 1.2   Contralateralization of brain function. Right hemisphere injury can cause neglect of the left side of space.

sensory input from the left and treat as nonexistent what is on the left side of space (as shown in Figure 1.2). When, for example, individuals are asked to draw a clock, they may not include the numbers 6–12.[3] They may neglect sounds coming into the left ear, not eat food from the left side of the plate, or fail to put a glove or mitten on their left hand.

Another possible outcome of stroke is the effect on the sense of proprioception, or the sense of where a particular body part (such as an arm or foot) is in space. It is related to kinesthesia or the perception of whether or not that body part is moving in space. Smith, Akhtar, and Garraway (1983) studied spatial neglect and proprioception in 287 stroke survivors and they found that proprioceptive loss indicated a more extensive lesion, more impaired intellectual function, and greater loss of upper and lower extremity motor power. Whereas proprioceptive loss had an adverse effect on the level of independence achieved and length of stay in the hospital, significant spatial neglect was associated with higher mortality and poor outcome for functional recovery.

Depending on the extent and side of damage, cognition, including remembering and learning as well as awareness, attention, and judgment, can be mildly to severely affected. Hearing and eyesight loss may be involved and stroke survivors may have problems understanding speech (receptive communication) or speaking (expressive communication). A stroke can lead to emotional lability (instability) and other mental, emotional, and behavioral problems. Stroke patients may be less able to control their emotions or may express them inappropriately. Many stroke patients experience depression; in fact, depression is considered the number one consequence of stroke because approximately one third of stroke survivors experience it (Andersen, Vestergaard, Riis, & Lauritzen, 1994; Hackett, Yapa, Parag, & Anderson, 2005). It is thought in the medical and scientific community that depression can also be a contributor to the onset of stroke (Ostir, Markides, Peek, & Goodwin, 2001; Salaycik et al., 2007) as well as a leading consequence of it. Because depression can affect a person's thinking, remembering, and learning as well as functional recovery and motivation to participate in rehabilitation, there have been efforts to identify the factors associated with depression in stroke survivors (Hackett & Anderson, 2005). There is some evidence to suggest that loss of functioning and expressive communication are predictors of emotional distress post-stroke (Thomas & Lincoln, 2008).

We can use the Vitruvian Man to further illustrate aspects of functioning affected by stroke (Kelly-Hayes et al., 1998):

Around the Head
- Impairments in memory, attention, orientation, calculation abilities, visual–motor coordination
- Spatial neglect and proprioception
- Depression is common; emotional lability
- Monocular visual loss, homonymous hemianopia, or cortical blindness
- Loss of smell
- Increased sensitivity to light or sound
- Hearing loss
- Difficulty swallowing or speaking clearly (caused by disruption of facial nerves and muscles)
- Language difficulties include dysphasia or aphasia that may be exhibited by disturbances in comprehension, naming, repetition, fluency, reading, or writing

Trunk, Arms, and Hands
- Difficulty with precise motions, such as writing or buttoning a shirt
- Numbness, tingling, or altered sensitivity

Legs and Feet
- Balance, disruption of walking and gait, coordination

Marjorie's stroke resulted from a hyperextension injury to the neck caused by a fall because of high alcohol consumption. Her type of stroke did not originate in a hemisphere of the brain. Rather, it came from a neck injury that affected the vertebrobasilar arterial system when the vertebral or carotid arteries became torn. The clinical features are different from those of hemispheric strokes; cerebellar signs are frequent (e.g., uncoordinated movement or dysmetria and poor coordination or ataxia) and aphasia and cognitive impairment are generally absent (Bogousslavsky & Caplan, 2008; Okawara & Nibbelink, 1974). Many such tears or lesions are small and specific, resulting in focal neurologic deficits. In general, the prognosis for functional recovery is better than with a stroke originating in the brain itself.

Mental Status: When the Mind Melts Away

After her stroke, Marjorie's speech, thinking, and memory remained unaffected, but preexisting (and less than desirable) personality traits became amplified. For example, she became more judgmental and self-focused. This could be caused by stroke or undiagnosed depression. She had some weakness in her left hand, but her arm functioning and strength was good. Then her only child married and didn't spend as much time with Marjorie as before. Marjorie, however, was determined to muster her "Yankee spirit" and be independent. She remained in her two-story home, mowed her acre of lawn herself, and would spend many summer hours in her flower garden and winter hours at the sewing machine. Marjorie enjoyed game shows on television and reading. She practically memorized the newspaper and knew all about every current event that was deemed fit to print.

Because it happens with everyone, as Marjorie aged, so, too, did all her organs and body structures. Marjorie adapted to small changes in her capabilities by using good strategies. For example, she used only lower shelves when she could no longer reach high ones instead of standing on her step stool.

And so life went on until she had bronchitis about 6 years before she broke her hip, the gradual loss of hearing, and weight loss that eventually resulted in her being enrolled in Meals on Wheels. By the time she was in her 90s, when she broke her hip, she had become reclusive. Her grooming deteriorated (she had a "falling out" with her hairdresser of 60 years and stopped going). One day her phone was shut off. The phone company said she hadn't paid her bill.

What was happening? I quickly went to Marjorie's house, an 80-mile drive, to try to determine what was going on.

I could see her through the window in the front door. Her head was on her chest and she was sound asleep in spite of the TV turned up to about 100 decibels. My knocking did rouse her, and when she saw my face, she smiled and came to the door, a bit surprised at this unannounced visit. The knot in my stomach told me this was not going to be easy.

I said in a calm and loving voice, for she was much loved, "Hey, Mom, how are you? What's going on? I tried calling you but the phone company said they turned your phone off because you didn't pay your bill."

Yes, Marjorie is my mother.

The Insidious Nature of Deterioration

How could I so utterly fail to see what was going on with my own mother, and had been? What kind of a psychologist am I, anyway?

There had been another recent warning. The Meals on Wheels volunteer had reported that "Marjorie doesn't seem to be taking proper care of herself." I checked, the social worker checked, all seemed to be okay. Clearly, though, it wasn't. Yet, when talking to Mom, it was difficult to notice that anything was wrong or needed attention. She stayed up on current events, always knew who she was speaking with and when and where she had been and was going. She was engaged and fully involved in conversations. Her physician never suspected anything was awry because there were no structural or biological indications. How would anyone know that she could no longer properly concentrate on tasks? Her strategies had worked so well that everyone was deceived into believing she was managing just fine.

It was the incident of the phone being cut off that finally did it. I went to get Mom's checkbook and saw how many checks she had written, and then crossed off, and then written again. There was a sheet of paper with her record of additions that looked more like a third grader's struggle than the work of an adult balancing her account. The mail was piled up on the table—bills, magazines, thank-you gifts including quite expensive ones from the World Wildlife Federation. Clearly, she had been giving the World Wildlife Federation substantial donations. The entire time I was going around the house assessing her state of affairs, Mom just stayed in her chair with her head down, looking both chagrin and whipped, knowing something was wrong but not exactly sure what it was. I knew now that something had to be done and stepped up my efforts to get more help for her. This was a month almost to the day before Thanksgiving.

Unlike the sudden onset of her stroke with the immediate visible signs that something was wrong, her dementia was so slow and progressive that the small changes it brought weren't all that discernable. They were easy to miss—or rather, deny.

Advanced Dementia

Dementia is a general term used to connote changes in personality, behavior, thinking, remembering, and learning because of declining brain functioning, and it is usually associated with advanced age. There are many different types of dementia, of which Alzheimer's disease and Lewy body dementia are two, and dementia involves multiple parts of the brain. Dementia can be caused by several factors, including aging, brain injury, vascular problems, exposure to toxic substances such as lead or chemicals, and substance abuse. Individuals with earlier brain injury, for example, from a stroke, are more likely to experience degenerative dementia. The diffuse and slow onset of dementia often leads to difficulties in recognizing it.

Separate surveys have come up with different prevalence figures because of variation in the criteria used to define dementia. In an attempt to directly determine the dementia prevalence rate in the United States, the *Aging, Demographics, and Memory Study (ADAMS)* was funded as the first population-based study of dementia to include individuals from all regions of the country (Plassman et al., 2007). The researchers state that their ADAMS sample was composed of 856 individuals aged 71 years and older from the nationally representative Health and Retirement Study (HRS). Participants were evaluated for dementia using an in-home assessment. An expert consensus panel used the assessment data to assign a diagnosis of normal cognition, cognitive impairment but not demented, or dementia (and dementia subtype). Using sampling weights derived from the HRS, they estimated the national prevalence of dementia, including Alzheimer's disease and vascular dementia, by age and gender. The results of the ADAMS project showed that the proportion of persons with dementia increased by age; 37.4% of individuals aged 90 and older had dementia and 70% of this group had Alzheimer's disease.

Internationally, the prevalence of dementia varies by country. A team of 12 experts (Ferri et al., 2005) reviewed data from all world regions and all types of dementia (i.e., they didn't separately look at Alzheimer's disease, Lewy body dementia, vascular dementia, etc.). They reached consensus on the proportion of the older population likely to be affected by dementia in each region and then used United Nations population estimates to produce prevalence figures for both men and women in five age groups (the oldest being "85 and older"). In the international comparison, the United States came in with the third highest proportion of its citizens with dementia. China was first, followed by the European Union. Overall, the experts estimated a prevalence of 24.3 million people with dementia in the world, with 4.6 million new cases of dementia annually (or annual incidence), and with Alzheimer's disease being the most prevalent. This means that approximately every 7 seconds, someone in the world receives a new diagnosis of dementia.

Ferri, Ames, and Prince (2004) studied the behavioral and psychological symptoms of dementia (BPSD) in a sample of 555 individuals with known dementia in developing countries (low- and moderate-income countries). They found that at least one BPSD was reported in 70.9% of their sample. Depression syndromes (43.8%) were most common, followed by anxiety disorders (14.2%). However, depression (pseudodementia) can produce similar symptoms as dementia in an older person. Thus, a careful examination is needed as the treatment of depression in older adults can be quite effective—and ameliorate cognitive effects associated with depression. The key distinguishing factor is self-awareness; someone with depression is more likely to notice and complain about cognitive issues. A person with Alzheimer's disease is less likely to be aware of one's own cognitive decline.

Behavioral and psychological symptoms are significant contributors to caregiver strain and require much further study and intervention. These and other functional impacts of dementia include the following:

Around the Head
- Depression and poor outlook
- Anxiety
- Loss of motivation to do activities
- Memory loss
- Disorientation in time and place
- Loss of skill in reasoning and judgment
- Communication difficulties
- Inadequate amount of food consumed

Trunk, Arms, and Hands
- Inability to perform routine tasks such as self-care and preparing a meal
- Congestive heart failure
- Shortness of breath
- Need for oxygen therapy
- Bowel incontinence

Legs and Feet
- Physical inactivity
- Difficulty walking without support

As dementia advances, there is increasing memory loss, communication difficulties, disorientation to time and place, loss of skill in reasoning and judgment, and a steady decline in the ability to perform such routine tasks as shopping, preparing a meal, and various self-care activities. Motivation to do these activities also diminishes. The rate at which dementia progresses is highly variable but is often exacerbated by a change in living situation or family circumstances, medical conditions, surgical interventions, a hospital stay, and so on.

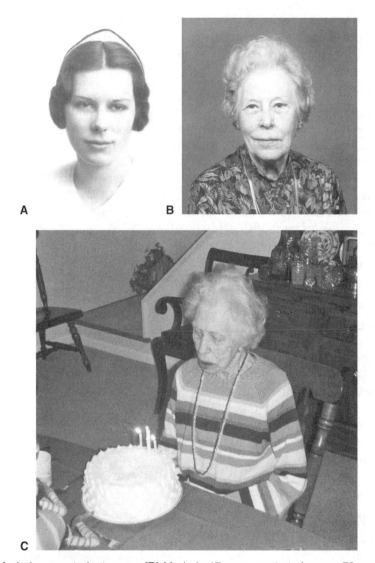

(A) Marjorie as a student nurse, **(B)** Marjorie 17 years post-stroke, age 78, and **(C)** Marjorie's 93rd birthday.

Four months before Marjorie's death, 2 months after her hip fracture, she lost interest in everything: her favorite television shows, reading, and sewing. Her cognitive world had become so small that it was difficult to carry on any semblance of a conversation. News about the people back home, even the family, was met with "Oh, so what?" "Current events?" "Who cares?"

Although it can be difficult to discern what loss of functioning is because of pain, medications, the underlying disease, and the disruption in lifestyle from nursing home placement, there are effective interventions. Treating the aging adult with dementia is very complex and requires both medical and psychological care and attention.

Dementia and Mortality

One thing I recall very clearly after my mother's hip replacement was the surgeon calling me into the recovery room and cautioning that, although my mother came through the surgery just fine, "You should know that the 1-year mortality rate is 30%." He said no more about why this was so and I didn't ask. At the time, I felt resentment toward him for saying this and immediately thought to myself, "Oh yeah? Well then, you'll be pleased and perhaps surprised to see that we're in that 70% group of survivors."

Indicators of mortality in those with advanced dementia have indeed been studied. One group of researchers longitudinally followed a group of newly admitted nursing home residents (Mitchell et al., 2004). They derived what they called 12 indicators of 6-month mortality:

- Significant impairment of activities of daily living
- Male gender
- Age older than 83 years
- Cancer
- Congestive heart failure
- Shortness of breath
- Need for oxygen therapy
- No more than 25% of food eaten at most meals
- Unstable overall condition
- Bowel incontinence
- Bedfast
- Sleeping most of the day

Using these variables, a risk for mortality is calculated. The more variables that apply and the more severe they are, the higher the risk of death. Please note, however, the absence of explicit behavioral and psychological indicators.

Let's see how Marjorie fared on these criteria 1-month preinjury, before her hip facture (exactly 6 months before her death), and then 1-month posthip replacement. Significant impairment of daily activities? Preinjury, not really. She got up every day, dressed and bathed, fixed herself a small breakfast, and had an established daily routine. She walked more slowly now and got out of breath quite often, but she still drove her car—and not badly either. I had actually witnessed her driving from the passenger seat when I asked her to drive us to the grocery store and the post office for exactly the purpose of assessing her driving skills.

There is a home movie of me as a toddler trying not to lag too far behind my mother as we were walking in the yard and garden. On my face is a look of plucky, good-natured determination to catch up to her. A look that said, "Don't worry, I'm coming." Her face, turned back to see just where I was, had a smile of loving patience. I recalled that moment vividly when we went grocery shopping that day. I had gotten ahead of her to get the shopping cart, and when I turned around to see where she was, she had that same plucky, good-natured look of determination to catch up to me. I so hope I looked at her with the same patience and love she had shown me.

Post hip replacement, Marjorie's entire lifestyle and daily routine changed, which represented a major life disruption. Then she did not make the progress in rehabilitation she needed to remain in rehabilitation. To discuss the next steps, a team and family meeting was scheduled. There the doctors told her that she would likely never walk again. This news totally devastated her. I could see it impact her physically as I watched her expel all the air out of her lungs, curl into herself, and cast her eyes down fighting not to cry. I could hear it in her trembling question as she choked back her tears, "Do you mean I'll always have to use a wheelchair?"

And that was the moment she gave up her will to live. I could not only see and hear it, but I could also feel it. And it tore my heart right out of my chest.

Mom's appetite decreased. She stopped reading and showed no interest in talking with any of the other nursing home residents. She enjoyed the visit from Marty, the therapy dog, and liked to attend the events when volunteer choral groups came in. But her world was becoming smaller and smaller, with nothing to share in a conversation. She retreated first into the past and then into silence, broken only by moans of pain, utterances of *awful . . . awful*, and the occasional angry or hostile statement. She was depressed but unaware of her cognitive decline, so her dementia was indeed advancing.

But let us return to the mortality predictors. Male gender? No points here. Neither did she have a history of cancer or congestive heart failure. However, she did have COPD.

After her hospitalization for pneumonia, her diet was changed to soft foods and liquids, which she said were tasteless so she consumed less of them, too. Now she was eating "No more than 25% of food at most meals." So we check that one on the list.

The less you do, the less you *can* do. This was certainly true in my mother's case. The downward spiral was well underway and then the last four applied to a more or less extent:

- Unstable overall condition
- Bowel incontinence (not really—she just stopped bothering to call for the bed pan)

- Bedfast (not until the last week of her life did the nurses stop getting her up and into her wheelchair)
- Sleeping most of the day (only the last week of her life)

Although these criteria applied to varying degrees for my mother, as with all such guidelines, they will apply differently from one person to another. That is why it is so important to use such guidelines with a healthy dose of reservation. As the history of science and medicine has taught us over and over, there are precious few absolute, without-a-doubt certainties when it comes to dealing with the individualistic and idiosyncratic nature of human beings.

To see someone die of dementia is very much like watching a snowman melt. A typical snowman has three round sections from the head (the smallest) to upper and then lower torso (the largest). The snowman may have milk bottle cap eyes and a smile made of pebble teeth pushed into its face like a string of pearls in the form of a smile. Fallen sticks picked up off the ground make good arms. When the temperature warms, first the bottle cap eyes droop and fall, and then the teeth start dropping out. The head gradually gets smaller and smaller, and then the torso and the lower body get thinner and thinner. Finally, the snowman is just an indistinct pool of water that is absorbed by the earth.

Death certificates may list immediate, secondary, and underlying causes of death. The immediate cause is typically heart or respiratory failure. According to the American College of Physicians (1998)

> The cause-of-death section of the certificate has three main parts: the chain of causation from immediate to underlying causes, the interval between onset of each of these conditions and death, and other contributing conditions unrelated to the underlying cause. . . . The underlying cause, which usually provides the most important epidemiologic information, may predate the immediate cause by several years. For example, acute myocardial infarction (the immediate cause) is produced by arteriosclerotic heart disease (the underlying cause). (p. 172)

The underlying cause of death is the one reported in the New York State vital statistics database. It is classified by medical code from the World Health Organization's International Classification of Diseases (ICD, 10th Revision). Here is what is listed on my mother's death certificate:

Immediate cause: Respiratory failure/multiorgan failure
Due to or as a consequence of: advanced dementia
Due to or as a consequence of: hyperkalemia (excessive potassium in the blood), hypernatremia (excessive sodium).

Is this right? The American College of Physicians has found that "death certificates are often inaccurate" and that a significant error rate exists in how underlying causes are reported. As I read it, I thought to myself, "For the underlying cause, why not write just plain *old age*? Or how about *sick and tired of pain, complete lifestyle disruption, loss of independence and freedom, and the will to live*"?

Dementia is a deterioration of brain function and cognition, and as we've seen, it can be fatal in and of itself. There are many other forms of damage and injury to the brain; however, they are not all progressive and certainly not fatal. In fact, many stroke survivors (like my mother) and individuals with traumatic brain injuries recover to lead, if not their complete preinjury lives, at least satisfying and productive ones. In the next chapter, we will meet two very interesting women who were born with their particular forms of brain impairment.

2

The Brain Born With a Disability—When The Mind Grows

And the day came when the risk to remain tight in a bud was more painful than the risk it took to blossom.
—Anaïs Nin

*T*heresa and Maggie were both born with a *developmental disability*, although with quite different ones. Theresa has good, even strong, physical capabilities, whereas Maggie, with a degree in English, relied on her intelligence and mental acuity. Together they made a successful team as each did for the other what neither one could do alone.

I first met them in 1985 when I was interviewing Maggie for my PhD dissertation research. At the time, Maggie was 42 years old and Theresa was 34 years old, and they had come to Chicago for Maggie's speech device training. It was an AAC device, which stands for *augmentative and alternative communication* device. It would give her intelligible speech and allow her to communicate actual words and sentences by having a synthetic voice speak the words she typed in. Up to this point, she used a board with the letters of the alphabet and numbers 0–9. She would point to each letter to form a word and would rely on the memory of the listener to put the words together in the form of a series of sentences.

This first meeting with her and Theresa as well as subsequent meetings with them over the years was described in the book, *Living in the State of Stuck* (2005b). During a 25-year span, I followed them from their apartment outside of Chicago to owning their own home in Springfield, Illinois; from Maggie being employed to being out of a job; to both of their physical declines and, ultimately, to Maggie's death in September 2009.

ONE PLUS ONE IS MORE THAN TWO

Maggie was born with severe (athetoid) cerebral palsy and never developed discernible unaided speech. Theresa was born with Down syndrome. They met in 1970 when they both attended the same sheltered workshop (a supervised workplace to acquire job skills and vocational experience). Theresa was very helpful to Maggie, and when they were faced with living in a nursing home, they decided that together they could live on their own.

As Maggie's personal assistant, Theresa did all of the driving, shopping and cooking, housekeeping, and care of Maggie. They led fulfilled lives as they served on the boards of disability organizations, advocated for disability rights, participated in their church, and traveled, including frequent trips to Washington, DC.

But then in 1991, I got a phone call from Theresa telling me that Maggie had been in and out of hospitals and rehabilitation facilities for most of the past year. It started with the loss of function in her left arm and hand and then the loss of function of her legs. She had surgery on her neck and that left her paralyzed from the neck down. As a result, she needed a new power wheelchair, which Maggie later described.

> The chair itself is the optimum in high-tech. It is all controlled by using a joystick that I hold in my mouth. This enables me to be in the recliner mode, the drive mode, and the Light Talker mode, meaning I can use my communication device in this mode. I change modes by pushing a button at the side of my head. People have said it looks like a rocket, especially when I'm tilted all the way back. (Scherer, 2005b, p. 93)

Maggie and Theresa moved back to Maggie's hometown "to be close to family and friends." Maggie reported that

> Theresa is doing extremely well considering all she has been through with me, especially the move that she was not too happy about. She had spent almost every night with me in the hospitals and . . . just wanted things to be normal again. I, on the other hand, became extremely depressed because the only activity I could engage in was to think of all of what I used to do. There are times now, though, when I think she has accepted my new disability better than I have—or did until the past few months. Before I got my new wheelchair she would say, "Things will get better when your wheelchair comes" and "We will just have to struggle through it like I said before your surgery." (Scherer, 2005b, p. 93)

In the late 1990s, Maggie bought a lot and built a single-floor home designed around their needs. Then, in July 2003, I got a surprise one day when the phone rang and it was Theresa saying that they were driving to Pittsburgh in a couple of weeks for a conference sponsored by Prentke-Romich on their *Pathfinder* (Maggie's new AAC device). They wanted a vacation after that and said that they would like to drive to Rochester to visit.

They arrived in a 6-year-old Ford van that they bought used and now had about 124,000 miles on it. Theresa operated the lift in the back of the van for Maggie and her wheelchair to get in and out. The passenger seat was removed so that Maggie "can sit up close" while Theresa drives.

Theresa wore a neatly pressed short sleeve top, sandals, and shorts with an elasticized waist and large leg openings so that they hung on her like a drawstring sack. She had dressed Maggie in sandals and stockings, yellow slacks, and a white top that appeared brand new. Earrings completed Maggie's attire. Her light red hair was thinning and it was flattened in the back from the neck rest on her wheelchair. She had become very thin.

Soon after they arrived in Rochester, we had to call tech support at Prentke-Romich because Maggie's *Pathfinder* had locked up. Tech support was very helpful and patient and led Theresa and I through the diagnostic process step-by-step. Theresa, even though quite proficient, had to have the instructions over the phone repeated frequently and it took trials with different strategies to get it going again. We had to check the battery, turn it on and off, and so on. I was concerned because the purpose of the trip was to visit, and Maggie completely relied on sophisticated AAC technology to communicate—and had for many years. If we couldn't get it working, we would not be able to communicate very well. In 1986, she got Prentke-Romich's *Express* communication system, then the *Light Talker*, moved to the *Liberator*, and finally in 2003, to the *Pathfinder*. As Maggie laughingly put it, she made a good "poster child for AAC." So I was taken aback when Theresa told me that Maggie rarely used her *Pathfinder*! Come to find out, and even though using a manual board was no longer an option for her because of her paralysis, her preference was to have Theresa speak for her. She only used her *Pathfinder* for presentations and with strangers. Theresa said, "It's just easier to use her own voice."

Maggie bought her *Pathfinder* herself for $8,000; to have Medicare pay, she would have had to wait for her *Liberator* to wear out and she didn't want to wait. Her *Pathfinder* had a touch screen and she could also use the keyboard with a joystick. Although Maggie complained that the speed of the joystick was too fast, it seemed the real reason for her nonuse was her inability to participate in a true back-and-forth conversation or exchange. She also reported that the device had become very fatiguing for her to use. Thus, her high-tech AAC device brought some frustrations

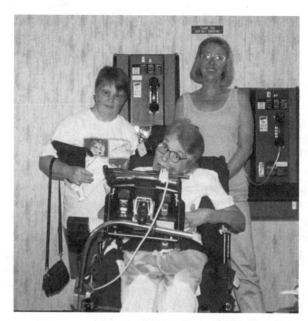

Theresa on the left, Maggie in the center, and me after talking with Prentke-Romich's Tech Support. August 2003.

with it—especially for someone like Maggie, who could be impatient. To illustrate, Maggie sat quite high in her power wheelchair because of the size of the battery underneath. She liked speed but had unreliable control of her wheelchair. She kept running into things—planters, wastebaskets, and she even knocked the filter off their motel room's heating unit. I thought that this must be because, at least in part, of the fact that she sat so high with her feet extended out that she couldn't see the low-level obstacles in her way. But I also knew of her cantankerous/impatient streak (which she openly acknowledged, characterizing herself as being "stubborn as well as determined"). Her humor about it showed through on her choice of an e-mail screen name: bytchee.

Theresa and I were talking while walking back into the motel, and Maggie "hit the accelerator" and moved in front of us. Suddenly, I heard Theresa yell, quite sternly, I thought, "Maggie, be careful!"

This startled me and I drew my eyes up and over to where Maggie had powered herself way ahead of us.

"Maggie, oh, watch out . . ." and Theresa covered her eyes.

Then I saw Maggie run into and topple over a trash bin. Maggie was fine, and so was the trash bin for that matter, so she just kept right on going.

"Maggie, I told you to be careful," and now Theresa broke out into laughter and said, "Ah, well, what are you gonna do?"

Theresa has what might be called "a practical good nature." She's no pushover, by any means, but she is a person who likes things calm and steady. When Maggie was in the hospital, she had said, "We will just have to struggle through it. . . ." And right after Maggie's death, she said, "I will keep going on and advocating for people's rights."

Maggie knew she would predecease Theresa, so her will stipulated that Theresa would be able to stay in the house and provided a trust to help cover her living expenses.

Theresa mourns the loss of Maggie, and she is very grateful to her for the life she was able to lead in a house and not in a nursing home, and for an independent lifestyle filled with travel and good times. Maggie was very grateful for Theresa's help, loyalty, and care. For both, their mutually supportive relationship resulted in a high quality of life neither would have been able to achieve on her own.

TWO MINUS ONE REMAINS A BETTER ONE

Theresa was one of nine children in a poor farming family with parents who both abused her. Until she met Maggie, she had been institutionalized for most of her life.

Theresa was born with an *intellectual disability* (formerly called *mental retardation*) because of Down syndrome. She walks somewhat stiffly as if her feet are on wood blocks instead of in shoes. This makes her kind of plop along. She has the "characteristic look" of someone with Down syndrome: upward and outward slanting eyes that can make it seem at times as if she is squinting. She has a small mouth and nose and her nose is somewhat flattish. When she talks, it's with a rather thick tongue and one has to listen closely to discern the words. She has short fingers and small hands that look chunky. Her neck is short and her overall height is about 5 feet. Now 58 years old, she has a disorder of the temporomandibular joints that cause her jaw pain and resulted in her now having missing teeth in the back of her mouth. She has carpal tunnel syndrome (nerve damage within the carpal tunnel, a bony canal in the palm side of the wrist, usually caused by trauma from repetitive overuse) and had surgery on one hand; the other will follow. She has two hearing aids, but one doesn't work, and when we met in Rochester, she took out the other one because it hurt her ear. She can act intelligent and mature one minute, and then the next get as excited as a child about going to a restaurant or to someplace like the zoo or botanical garden. She loves gardening and has her own garden at home, which she enjoys tending very much.

In 2005, Theresa and Maggie were each presented with the Illinois Governor's Human Rights Award. They were the first people with disabilities to receive this honor. They were awarded the Justin Dart Award from the Coalition of Citizens with Disability in Illinois and the Illinois Network for Centers for Independent Living in 2008. In 2007, a film about their life was released entitled, *Body and Soul*. The film has been shown on Public Broadcasting Service (PBS) stations throughout the United States.

Today, Theresa travels throughout the country giving major presentations on self-advocacy to members of various developmental disability organizations. In 2010, without the need to drive her friend Maggie anymore, she flew for the first time to attend a disability policy seminar in Washington, DC. In the spring of 2011, she travelled to the Republic of Uzbekistan with her film producer to promote her film and show how a person with Down syndrome can be a fully integrated and contributing member of the world community.

CAUSES OF BRAIN INJURY IN INFANTS AND CHILDREN

As with older adults, cognitive disability and brain injury in those who are very young come from various causes and manifest themselves in widely varying ways. Brain injuries can arise from causes ranging across chromosomal and genetic, endocrine/metabolic, and traumatic events. Infants can have strokes as well as adults, and prematurity as well as trauma (e.g., shaken baby syndrome, birth injury and hypoxia, accidental injury) can leave them with lifelong cognitive disability. When a child is born with a disability or acquires a disability before age 22, it is called a *developmental disability*. As already noted, both Theresa and Maggie had developmental disabilities, but from different causes.

What Is a Developmental Disability?

Down syndrome and cerebral palsy are developmental disabilities. According to the U.S. Developmental Disabilities Act, section 102(8), "the term 'developmental disability' means a severe, chronic disability of an individual 5 years of age or older that:

1. Is attributable to a mental or physical impairment or combination of mental and physical impairments;
2. Is manifested before the individual attains age 22;
3. Is likely to continue indefinitely;
4. Results in substantial functional limitations in three or more of the following areas of major life activity;
   (*i*)   Self-care;
   (*ii*) Receptive and expressive language;

(iii) Learning;

(iv) Mobility;

(v) Self-direction;

(vi) Capacity for independent living; and

(vii) Economic self-sufficiency.

5. Reflects the individual's need for a combination and sequence of special, interdisciplinary, or generic services, supports, or other assistance that is of lifelong or of extended duration and is individually planned and coordinated, except that such term, when applied to infants and young children means individuals from birth to age 5, inclusive, who have substantial developmental delay or specific congenital or acquired conditions with a high probability of resulting in developmental disabilities if services are not provided." (Maryland Developmental Disabilities Council, 2010)

Because developmental disabilities affect children, and all U.S. children (with or without disabilities) are entitled to a free appropriate public education (FAPE), disability is defined in special education legislation. The reauthorized Individuals with Disabilities Education Act (IDEA), signed into law in 2004, states

> Child with a disability means a child evaluated in accordance with Sec. 300.304 through 300.311 as having mental retardation, a hearing impairment (including deafness), a speech or language impairment, a visual impairment (including blindness), a serious emotional disturbance (referred to in this part as "emotional disturbance"), an orthopedic impairment, autism, traumatic brain injury, another health impairment, a specific learning disability, deaf-blindness, or multiple disabilities, and who, by reason thereof, needs special education and related services. (Regulations: Part 300 / A / Sec. 300.8 Child with a disability)

As might be expected, medical definitions of developmental disability read somewhat differently from what is used in the educational system. The Centers for Disease Control and Prevention (CDC, 2011) define developmental disabilities as:

> A diverse group of severe chronic conditions that are due to mental and/or physical impairments. People with developmental disabilities have problems with major life activities such as language, mobility, learning, self-help, and independent living. Developmental disabilities begin anytime during development up to 22 years of age and usually last throughout a person's lifetime. (http://www.cdc.gov/ncbddd/dd/dd1.htm)

The CDC lists the following five developmental disabilities, in order of prevalence:

Intellectual disability (this includes Down syndrome)
Autism spectrum disorders
Cerebral palsy
Vision impairment
Hearing loss

The Eunice Kennedy Shriver National Institute of Child Health and Human Development (NICHD) at the National Institutes of Health has yet another definition of developmental disability: "Developmental disabilities are birth defects related to a problem with how a body part or body system works. They may also be known as *functional* birth defects. Many of these conditions affect multiple body parts or systems" (http://www.nichd.nih.gov/health/topics/developmental_disabilities.cfm).

NICHD lists the following types of developmental disabilities:

Nervous System Disabilities
These are birth defects that affect the functioning of the brain, spinal cord, and nervous system, which can impact intelligence and learning. These conditions can also cause problems such as behavioral disorders, speech or language difficulties, convulsions, and movement disorders. Down syndrome and cerebral palsy are included here.

Sensory-Related Disabilities
Include visual impairment and hearing loss. Sensory-related problems are often a key part of complex birth defect patterns.

Metabolic Disorders
This group of functional birth defects affects a person's metabolism, which is the way the body builds up, breaks down, and otherwise processes the materials it needs to function. For example, how your body breaks down sugar to create energy is a metabolic process. An example of a metabolic disorder is hypothyroidism. Unfortunately, there are some metabolic disorders that are not so easily identified or treated, which can lead to lifelong physical, cognitive, and behavioral challenges.

Degenerative Disorders
Some infants born with degenerative disorders appear normal at birth, but then lose abilities or functions and the defect is not detected until an older

age, when the child or person starts to show signs of loss of function. Some degenerative disorders are the result of metabolic disorders. Rett syndrome is an example of a degenerative disorder.

Although there are similarities, there are also significant differences in the aforementioned definitions, which can make accessing and transitioning to new or additional services difficult. If we added those used by those organizations who advocate on behalf and serve the needs of individuals with developmental disabilities and their families (e.g., United Cerebral Palsy, Easter Seals, The Arc, National Down Syndrome Society), then even more distinctions would become apparent. But since we are talking about two developmental disabilities in particular, Down syndrome and cerebral palsy, let's now focus on these in more detail.

What Is Down Syndrome?

One example of a chromosomal cause of cognitive disability is what Theresa has, Down syndrome, named after Dr. Langdon Down who first described this condition in 1866. Whereas some say, "Down's syndrome" particularly in the United Kingdom, the U.S. National Institutes of Health standardized the nomenclature in 1975 to Down syndrome.

Normally, a fertilized egg has 23 pairs of chromosomes. However, it can occur that there is an extra copy of chromosome 21 (also called *trisomy 21* because there are three copies of this chromosome instead of two). According to information from the Eunice Kennedy Shriver NICHD at the National Institutes of Health (1997), 95% of the cases of Down syndrome result from trisomy 21. But not all trisomies are compatible with postnatal life and most trisomic fetuses do not survive to birth. With the widespread availability today of immunization programs to protect against bacterial and viral infections, antimicrobial agents to treat infectious diseases, better nutrition, and surgical correction of congenital abnormalities, many of those born with genetic disorders such as Down syndrome are able to survive and lead longer lives.

Most of the time, the occurrence of Down syndrome is caused by a random event, although maternal age at conception increases the risk of having a baby born with Down syndrome. Otherwise, there are no known behavioral activities of the parents or environmental factors that are associated with the occurrence of Down syndrome. A blood test is done to confirm the diagnosis by analyzing the chromosomes to determine the presence of an extra chromosome 21.

Signs and Symptoms of Down Syndrome

The characteristic features of Down syndrome result from the extra copy of chromosome 21 in every cell in the body, which changes the body's and brain's normal development. To best present the typical signs and symptoms, let us bring back the Vitruvian Man to illustrate what having Down syndrome can be like for individuals like Theresa. Going from head to toe, the following body functions and structures can be involved:

Around the Head
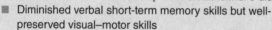
- Diminished frontal and temporal regions of the brain
- Intellectual disability (mental retardation) primarily within the mild to moderate range (IQ score 70–75), with an increased risk for the development of Alzheimer's disease
- Diminished verbal short-term memory skills but well-preserved visual–motor skills
- White spots on the iris of the eye
- Eye problems, such as cataracts, crossed eyes, nearsightedness or farsightedness.
- Flat face with an upward slant to the eye, short neck, and small ears that may fold over slightly at the top
- Hearing loss
- Small nose with a flattened nasal bridge
- Small mouth and problems with articulate speech
- Thyroid dysfunctions
- Predisposition to developing leukemia

Trunk, Arms, and Hands
- Congenital heart disease
- Congenital digestive disorders such as duodenal stenosis or atresia
- Intestinal problems such as blocked small bowel or esophagus
- Celiac disease (gluten intolerance)
- Reproductive sterility in males
- Small hands with deep crease in the palm of the hand and small fingers

Legs and Feet
- Small feet

There can additionally be skeletal problems, poor muscle tone, and loose ligaments throughout the individual's body. The person may be more susceptible to repeated infections, colds and bouts of bronchitis, and pneumonia. But these physical features and conditions do not predict mental development. Each person with Down syndrome will have a unique set of physical attributes that vary in severity, a distinctive personality, and particular behavioral and intellectual characteristics and capabilities. Who they become as adults is primarily determined by the resources, opportunities, and support they receive.

The life expectancy for people with Down syndrome has increased dramatically from age 25 in 1983 to age 56 today. Theresa, now 60 years old, has beat the average in a lot of different ways, and this is likely because of the lifestyle she has been able to achieve. There are many individuals with Down syndrome who, like Theresa, can lead into productive and fulfilling lives. They may learn tasks or progress through developmental stages slower than most, but many can read and write and participate in diverse activities and hold regular jobs.

What Is Cerebral Palsy?

The United Cerebral Palsy (UCP) Foundation estimates that nearly 800,000 children and adults in the United States are living with one or more of the symptoms of cerebral palsy, and the CDC estimate the incidence (number of new cases diagnosed in a year) to be about 10,000 in the United States.

The term *cerebral* refers to the two halves or hemispheres of the brain, in this case, to the motor area of the brain's outer layer (called the cerebral cortex), the part of the brain that directs muscle movement; *palsy* refers to the loss or impairment of motor function. Cerebral palsy originates in the brain, and results in disability of muscles and nerves, body movement, and muscle coordination. Although not a progressive disability, as the person matures and muscles become weaker, additional complications can arise—just as they did for Maggie.

Not very long ago, the predominant view was that cerebral palsy was chiefly caused by complications during birth and labor. In the 1980s, however, scientists funded by the National Institute of Neurological Disorders and Stroke (NINDS) analyzed extensive data from more than 35,000 newborns and their mothers, and discovered that complications during birth and labor accounted for only a fraction of the infants born with cerebral palsy—probably less than 10%. In most cases, they could not find a single, obvious cause. In some cases of cerebral palsy, the cerebral motor cortex hasn't developed normally during fetal growth. In others, the damage is a result of injury to the brain either before, during, or after birth. In either case, the damage is not repairable and the disabilities that result are permanent (NINDS, National Institutes of Health [2010a]).

NINDS researchers are investigating the roles of mishaps early in brain development, including genetic defects, which are sometimes responsible for the brain malformations and abnormalities that result in cerebral palsy. Scientists are also looking for causes from traumatic events in newborn babies' brains, such as bleeding, epileptic seizures, and breathing and circulation problems, which can cause the abnormal release of chemicals that trigger the kind of damage that causes cerebral palsy. According to NINDS, *acquired cerebral palsy* (which begins after birth) can be an outcome of brain infections such as bacterial meningitis or viral encephalitis, or head injury from a motor vehicle accident, fall, or child abuse. There is some evidence that there is a higher incidence of pediatric strokes in the United States than previously thought (Agrawal, Johnston, Wu, Sidney, & Fullerton, 2009) and that there is also a higher incidence of cerebral palsy as the result of prematurity and low birth weight, but there is lack of agreement on this in the research literature (e.g., Groenendaal, Termote, van der Heide-Jalving, van Haastert, & de Vries, 2010; Surman et al, 2009).

Signs and Symptoms of Cerebral Palsy

According to NINDS, individuals with cerebral palsy exhibit various symptoms, including a lack of muscle coordination when performing voluntary movements (*ataxia*), stiff or tight muscles and exaggerated reflexes (*spasticity*), variations in muscle tone (either too stiff or too floppy), and shaking (*tremor*) or random involuntary movements. Let us bring back the Vitruvian Man to illustrate what can additionally be involved when going from head to toe:

Around the Head
- Cerebral motor cortex of the brain is affected resulting in movement impairments
- Intellectual disability (mental retardation) can occur in some cases
- Excessive drooling or difficulties swallowing or speaking
- Impaired vision
- Impaired hearing

Trunk, Arms, and Hands
- Difficulty with precise motions such as writing or buttoning a shirt

Legs and Feet
- Walking with one foot or leg dragging
- Walking on the toes, a crouched gait, or a "scissored" gait

Similar to those with stroke, dementia, or Down syndrome, the person with cerebral palsy will have a unique physical profile, intellectual functioning level, and personality. Not only do the cited characteristics of cerebral palsy differ in type and severity from one person to the next, but they may change in an individual over time.

Cerebral palsy doesn't always cause profound disabilities, just as Down syndrome doesn't. Whereas one child with severe cerebral palsy might be unable to walk and requires extensive care, another with mild cerebral palsy might not require any special assistance. Like Theresa and Maggie, individuals with Down syndrome or cerebral palsy can lead productive lives filled with friendships, travel, and community involvement and participation in a wide range of life situations—especially when the right blend of support from technology and other people are available. But before we can select the most appropriate form of support for anyone with a cognitive disability, we need to first learn more about their needs and the kinds of things they want support to do for them.

3

How the Brain Works

The brain is a monstrous, beautiful mess. Its billions of nerve cells—
called neurons—lie in a tangled web that displays cognitive powers far
exceeding any of the silicon machines we have built to mimic it.
—William F. Allman (from *Apprentices of Wonder:*
Inside the Neural Network Revolution, 1989)

The human brain, then, is the most complicated organization of matter
that we know.
—Isaac Asimov (from the foreword of *The Three-Pound Universe*
by J. Hooper and D. Teresi, 1986)

*A*s we have read, older adults, like Marjorie, may have dementia (including Alzheimer's disease) and a history of brain attack or stroke. Children may have a developmental disability, such as Theresa with Down syndrome or Maggie with cerebral palsy. The outcomes of each of these diagnoses may be classified as *cognitive disability*, and they will range in type and severity. There are certainly more causes of cognitive disability than what we have discussed up to this point and these are reviewed now.

ACQUIRED BRAIN INJURY

The position of both the Brain Injury Association of America (BIAA) and the Brain Injury Network (BIN), advocacy organizations by and for people with brain injury, is that *acquired brain injury* includes traumatic brain injuries (TBIs), strokes, brain illness, and any other kind of brain injury acquired after birth. However, ABI does not include what are classified as degenerative brain conditions such as Alzheimer's disease or Parkinson's disease. BIN's official definition of ABI is

> an injury to the brain that has occurred after birth, but is not related to congenital defect or degenerative disease. Causes of ABI include (but are not limited to) hypoxia, illness, infection, stroke, substance abuse, toxic exposure, trauma, and tumor.

ABI may cause temporary or permanent impairment in such areas as cognitive, emotional, metabolic, motor, perceptual motor, and/or sensory brain function. (BIN, 2011, para. 32)

Thus, the causes of ABI include a wide range of illnesses and injuries such as high fever, diseases like meningitis and AIDS, and exposure to electrical shock. Brain attack or stroke is also an ABI.

Traumatic Brain Injury (TBI)

Individuals of any age can receive a TBI, a form of acquired brain injury. A concise definition has been developed by the Demographics and Clinical Assessment Working Group of the International and Interagency Initiative Toward Common Data Elements for Research on Traumatic Brain Injury and Psychological Health: "TBI is defined as an alteration in brain function, or other evidence of brain pathology caused by an external force" (Menon, Schwab, Wright, & Maas, 2010, p. 1637).

Explanatory notes provide additional specificity for defining the components in the previous definition. The Brain Injury Association of America has a similar definition, albeit not as concise:

Traumatic brain injury is an insult to the brain, not of a degenerative or congenital nature but caused by an external physical force, that may produce a diminished or altered state of consciousness, which results in an impairment of cognitive abilities or physical functioning. It can also result in the disturbance of behavioral or emotional functioning. These impairments may be either temporary or permanent and cause partial or total functional disability or psychosocial maladjustment. (Brain Injury Association of America Board of Directors, 1986, para. 5)

Another definition is provided by the Traumatic Brain Injury Model Systems National Data and Statistical Center (TBINDSC; 2011):

A TBI is defined as damage to the brain caused by an external force as evidenced by altered consciousness and impairment of brain functioning. After the initial medical crisis, TBI presents significant challenges to the individual, family, and society. An injured person may experience a wide range of physical, cognitive, emotional and behavioral changes that affect their ability to function. Financial hardship, substance abuse, anxiety and depression are some of the common problems experienced by individuals following a TBI. (National Institute on Disability and Rehabilitation, 2010)

A TBI, which includes concussion, may be caused by blunt force trauma such as a sports injury, assault, fall, or motor vehicle accident. According to the American Association of Neurological Surgeons (AANS) in 2010, there were an estimated 446,788 sports-related head injuries treated at U.S. hospital emergency rooms in 2009, representing an increase of about 95,000 from the prior year. The sports that yielded the most head injuries in 2009 were cycling (85,389), football (46,948), baseball and softball (38,394), basketball (34,692), and water sports (21,184). Cumulative injuries to the brain can lead to a progressive disease known as *chronic traumatic encephalopathy* (CTE). Many former boxers and football players have been diagnosed postmortem with CTE. McKee et al. (2009) reviewed 48 cases of CTE in the literature with detailed focus on one football player and two boxers. They state that CTE is characterized by particular neuropathological and microscopic changes and clinically with memory disturbances, behavioral and personality changes, parkinsonism, and speech and gait abnormalities. Unfortunately, many individuals who receive repeated concussions and trauma to the head and neck do not present themselves for treatment and therefore are not diagnosed. More unfortunate is when they have an early death.

A TBI may also occur from penetrating trauma such as from a gunshot wound. The brain being shaken is yet another cause of TBI. Many returning service members from Iraq and Afghanistan have received a TBI from the earlier mentioned causes as well as blast injuries and rapid deceleration or acceleration (e.g., vehicular accident).

The individual in our study, Delmar, received a TBI as a young man from a motorcycle accident. His real life story is told in the words of two vocational rehabilitation counselors who worked with Delmar,[4] and we will follow his story through the subsequent chapters of this book.

Delmar

Delmar was a 39-year-old male auto mechanic when he received a traumatic brain injury (TBI) in June 2005. A jeep pulled out in front of his motorcycle and he was thrown through a side window of the jeep. Delmar lost consciousness and has no memory of the day or the events right after. According to medical records, Delmar suffered an "intracranial hemorrhage in the left basal ganglia, as well as sheer hemorrhages in the corpus callosum." There was a small amount of subarachnoid hemorrhage and subdural hematoma. He did not require neurosurgery. He had a left mandible fracture, which was followed by oromaxillofacial surgery. His right arm was fractured in several places along with crush-type injuries to his wrist and hand. This has resulted in limited range of motion in the right hand and wrist resulting in very little gripping strength and poor hand control. Delmar also suffers right-sided weakness caused by the TBI and physical injuries and has problems with tiring easily.

During our first meeting with Delmar, he had a rather flat affect and was highly distractible. He would stay on track in the conversation, but it was very apparent that he was processing all the questions very slowly and would depend on his wife to fill in where he couldn't remember. Delmar also had many memory gaps, problems with being easily fatigued, and delayed reactions. Delmar is able to ambulate without assistance and dress and feed himself and shower without assistance. Delmar is right-hand dominant, so learning to become left-handed has taken a lot of work.

Delmar has been very motivated to regain his life and he has not been afraid to make changes. He is very compliant in all aspects of his therapies and willing to do almost anything to see some kind of improvement. He had the self-awareness to report that no matter what, he still gets very frustrated and agitated and tends to take it out on his family. His wife reports that this has gotten better as Delmar makes progress toward his goals. He has a past history of being a very stable, hardworking family man who was very supportive to his wife and kids and grandmother who lives in a house on his property. He has no history of mental health issues or legal problems or problems with drugs or alcohol. This is a very traditional family in which Delmar worked full time; wife is a stay-at-home mom who cleaned a few houses to make extra money. The family is also active in their local church, which has been very supportive. Delmar has a big workshop out back where he has a side business of creating and making custom gunstocks and grips.

Right-sided weakness is the primary physical outcome of Delmar's accident. But his TBI has left him agitated, fatigued, and with memory difficulties. He has difficulty with holding and stabilizing objects in his right hand.

As we proceed through the chapters, we will see how Delmar progresses and with what types of supports.

Because the consequences of brain injuries often involve multiple systems (cognitive, emotional, behavioral, social), they are often referred to as neurobehavioral disability (e.g., Kreutzer, 1996). If there is diffuse axonal injury, this can result in inefficient information processing and can impact the brain's neurotransmitters. Neurotransmitters include dopamine, norepinephrine, serotonin, acetylcholine, and g-aminobutyric acid (GABA). They ensure smooth regulation of cognition, emotion, behavior, and psychomotor functioning.

NEUROLOGICAL AND MENTAL CONDITIONS ASSOCIATED PRIMARILY WITH BEHAVIORAL PATTERNS

Individuals of any age can exhibit behaviors that others view as *odd* or *different*. This can be accompanied by alterations in thinking, learning, and social participation. In addition to TBI, we will discuss three in this chapter: those with (a) learning disability or (b) autism spectrum disorder (ASD), which typically becomes apparent in childhood, and those with particular (c) psychiatric diagnoses that are usually manifest during or after adolescence.

Learning Disability

LD OnLine is an educational service of public television station WETA in Washington, DC and works in association with the National Joint Committee on Learning Disabilities. They define learning disability as follows:

> A learning disability is a neurological disorder. In simple terms, a learning disability results from a difference in the way a person's brain is "wired." Children with learning disabilities are as smart or smarter than their peers. But they may have difficulty reading [dyslexia], writing [dysgraphia], spelling, reasoning, recalling and/or organizing information if left to figure things out by themselves or if taught in conventional ways. (LD OnLine, 2010, para. 1)

Students with learning disability comprise most students in U.S. schools who are in special education programs. According to the National Institute of Neurological Disorders and Stroke, National Institutes of Health (2010b), 8%–10% of American children younger than 18 years of age have some type of learning disability. Although sharing some characteristics in common, learning disability is different from such disabilities as attention deficit/hyperactivity disorder (ADHD), ASD, and behavioral and mental disorders.

Autism Spectrum Disorder

Children and adults with ASD often exhibit behaviors that others can find puzzling and disconcerting. According to the Centers for Disease Control and Prevention (CDC), the incidence of ASD was 1 in 150 in 2007 (CDC, 2007). *ASD* is a complex neurobiological disorder, and although there are some common characteristics shared among those with ASD, manifestations will be unique to each individual. There are no biological or physiological markers of ASD. However, newer research is beginning to shed light on how the brain may develop differently in these individuals.

Diagnosis is done largely by behavioral observation (Dew & Alan, 2007). The fourth edition with a text revision of the *Diagnostic and Statistical Manual (DSM-IV-TR)*, published by the American Psychiatric Association (2000), separately discusses autism and Asperger syndrome[5] as ASDs under the heading Pervasive Developmental Disability and lists behavioral characteristics that include the following:

Social Skills

Individuals with ASD often do not reveal a full complement of emotions and do not understand them in others. Additionally, they have difficulty comprehending the social, verbal, and nonverbal behavior of others when in social situations. Behaviors of those with ASD may include the following:

■ Misreading or not perceiving the facial expressions of others
■ Inability in understanding sarcasm and take things literally and concretely; for example, a joke may be taken seriously. When someone says "I could eat a horse," the individual looks for a horse and wonders how the person could possibly eat such a large animal (Dew & Alan, 2007).
■ Inability to perceive the "gray areas" in social situations
■ Resistance to changing or altering a routine
■ Fear of new and unfamiliar experiences
■ As discussed in Chapter 1, proprioceptive feedback helps us position our bodies and move through the environment. Individuals with ASD may need to keep their eyes open to know how their own body is moving. Some cannot regulate how much pressure to exert when grasping, for example, that may hurt the hand of someone during a handshake.

Such social difficulties underlie challenges in forming friendships, having a peer group at school, and being viewed as a team player in employment situations. When social engagement does occur, it is typically awkward for all involved.

To better understand ASD, we will explore the challenges that a teenager named Ryan with Asperger syndrome faces. Ryan is 15 years old and attends a special school for children who need extra attention in the classroom. He excels in mechanical and engineering tasks but has a great deal of difficulty relating to other people.

His family's favorite photo of Ryan, taken when he was about 9 years old

Although Ryan has several friends at school, he mostly plays at home with children who are half his age. The level of their social interaction tends to remain simple. Additionally, Ryan functions best at school when there are specific expectations and a set routine. School breaks and summers off present a challenge in the amount of unstructured time. After school is over for the afternoon, homework becomes a secondary option. Ryan views his assignments as a punishment and often "forgets" to do them. To avoid being idle, Ryan often gets into trouble by getting out movies and equipment and leaving them around his house. However, Ryan can also be very thoughtful and perceptive. For example, when his sister came home for a holiday break, he got up and made her tea several mornings during her stay.

Difficulties With Communication

Persons with ASD may have a limited repertoire of gestures and conversational topics as well as difficulty in initiating, maintaining, and terminating conversations. They can evidence awkward body language through posture and movements and say blunt and honest statements to others that are viewed as inappropriate for the situation. Some behaviors may include the following:

- Asking incessant questions
- Using odd word choices such as "ear muffs" to mean headphones (Dew & Alan, 2007)

Some individuals with ASD may need to use sign language and/or augmentative communication devices. The use of visual prompts to augment verbal requests is often very helpful. In his therapy sessions, Ryan often responds best when his counselor uses objects or cards to ask questions. Otherwise, Ryan becomes distracted and begins to ask irrelevant questions such as "Why do you have this poster in your office?"

Restricted Repertoire of Activities or Interests

Individuals with ASD may have a narrow range of interests and focus on one area so much that they become a sort of "walking encyclopedia" on that topic (Dew & Lynch, 2007) because talking about the familiar brings comfort and a sense of control and security. For this reason, too, they prefer order and routine and may exhibit repetitive behaviors such as organizing the papers on their desk in a certain way.

Like many teenage boys, Ryan has found great entertainment in technology, especially the Wii and iPod. Not only is he able to use these gadgets with great skill, but he can also teach others how to use and enjoy them.

While the Wii and iPod are strengths and can be used to bridge social connections, they can also be detrimental when he is obsessed with them and uses them to withdraw from his immediate environment. In other words, what may be viewed as typical teenage technology absorption can be an over immersion for Ryan.

Problematic Behavior

This includes ritualistic or compulsive mannerisms and self-stimulatory behavior such as hand-wringing or singing to oneself. It includes socially inappropriate behaviors such as staring, or conversely, avoiding eye contact, fidgeting, and performing repeated behaviors.

Unfortunately, Ryan has trouble with impulsivity. He has often been caught stealing small, insignificant items from his family members and classmates. Punishment is often futile and the behavior continues to be a challenge for him and his family. Additionally, Ryan has recently grown his hair long enough so that his eyes are covered and can, thus, easily avoid eye contact with others. However, when Ryan is around people that he feels comfortable with, he pulls his hair back out of his eyes.

Sensory Dysfunction

Many individuals with ASD react poorly to being touched. If they are given a hug, it can be as if they were struck. However, others may need deep pressure contact through a firm touch or sleeping between two mattresses (Dew & Lynch, 2007). For many, common noises (traffic, ticking clocks, the humming of a refrigerator) cannot be blocked out, seem very loud, and are distracting. This can also occur with visual stimuli such as ceiling chandeliers and olfactory stimuli, or smells, from food or perfumes.

While Ryan has not acknowledged any sensitivity to stimuli, in fact, he requires the "deep contact" discussed previously. He often asks for big hugs or someone to firmly hold his hand. This seems to establish a sense of comfort and security.

Difficulties With Executive Function

Individuals with ASD usually perform best doing a single activity at a time and find multitasking and organization difficult and stressful. They can have the same types of executive function markers as those with TBI.

Channeling Ryan's efforts and energy can often be a frustrating process. For example, when it comes to weekly chores, only one chore can be given at a time, or Ryan becomes quickly overwhelmed. For the task to be completed, he needs to be reminded and even supervised. However, when he is encouraged properly, he often does an excellent and thorough job. As his mom says, "When he's on to something, he'll make it spotless."

In summary, ASD is a significant behavioral disability that affects the person's assumption of many social roles, connection to others, sense of belonging, and participation in various life situations. Most assessment tests are normed for individuals up to age 21 years, leaving adults with undiagnosed ASD with unmet needs. Adolescents transitioning to adulthood and independent living also face challenges. To identify that a child or adolescent has ASD, there are specific assessment measures that can be used, including the Autism Diagnostic Interview–Revised (ADI-R), the Autism Diagnostic Observation Schedule (ADOS), the Gilliam Autism Rating Scale (GARS), the Asperger Syndrome Diagnostic Scale (ASDS), the Childhood Autism Rating Scale (CARS), and tests of cognitive ability such as the Test of Nonverbal Intelligence (TONI-3) or the Leiter-R (Dew & Lynch, 2007). Once identified, a program of intervention can be derived that is best tailored to that young person's needs as well as strengths. However, that isn't a guarantee.

At Ryan's first middle school, teachers often neglected Ryan as a behavioral disturbance. This ultimately increased Ryan's apathy toward school and slowed his academic progress. Without the proper encouragement and structure, Ryan's social connections also suffered. When he started in a new high school where teachers were used to helping students with different kinds of needs, Ryan thrived. His grades improved; he began to involve himself in community service activities and wants to be a social studies teacher when he gets older.

Mental, Emotional, and Behavioral Disabilities

Clinical depression, anxiety disorders, schizophrenia, and bipolar disorder are examples of diagnoses that may involve particular patterns of neuropsychological functioning and difficulties with thinking, remembering, and learning. These disorders may be treated by psychotherapy, psychiatric medication, social intervention, or any combination of these.

The *Diagnostic and Statistical Manual of Mental Disorders*, now in its fourth edition with a text revision (*DSM-IV-TR*), was developed by the American Psychiatric Association (2000) to be the standard classification used by psychiatrists, psychologists, and other mental health professionals to classify *mental, emotional, and behavioral disabilities*. It is a system divided into five sections or axes with Axes I–IV having three major components: diagnostic classification, diagnostic criteria sets, and descriptive text. Here are the major sections in Axes I–IV:

- **Axis I:** Clinical disorders. Many included here affect rational thinking and judgment. Hallucinations (sensing things that are not there) and delusions (distorted thoughts related to facts and reality) are also included among symptoms linked to various disorders. Examples are:

- Adjustment disorders
- Anxiety disorders (includes phobias)
- Cognitive disorders (delirium, dementia, and amnestic)
- Impulse-control disorders (not classified elsewhere)
- Mood disorders
- **Axis II:** Personality disorders and mental retardation
- **Axis III:** General medical conditions such as diseases of the nervous system and sense organs
- **Axis IV:** Psychosocial and environmental problems such as:
  - Problems with primary support group
  - Problems related to the social environment
  - Educational problems
  - Occupational problems
- **Axis V:** Global assessment of functioning scale

Axis V rates an individual's Global Assessment of Functioning Scale on a continuum from 0–100 and it addresses overall psychological, social, and occupational functioning. The description for the top 20 percent emphasizes positive and effective functioning and the absence or minimization of symptoms whereas the description for the bottom 20 percent includes some or persistent danger of hurting the self or others and failure in personal care and communication.

Persons with mental, emotional, and behavioral disabilities can have many of the same difficulties in thinking, remembering, and learning as those with cerebral palsy; or those who have survived a brain attack or stroke; or have dementia or ASD. Although the differences among these diagnoses are large, and every person is unique with a particularized pattern of characteristics and needs, there is a good deal of similarities. That is why an umbrella term is frequently used to describe the everyday capabilities and functioning of people with brain disorders when referring to them as a group. That term is *people with cognitive disability*.

"COGNITIVE DISABILITY" AS THE OUTCOME OF ANY BRAIN ILLNESS, INJURY, OR CONDITION

The term *cognitive disability* is applied when there are alterations in what we think of as standard and predictable thinking, remembering, learning, and behaving. As we have been discussing, people who have diagnoses associated with the brain may have them as a result of disease/illness, injury, biochemical imbalance, genetics, or aging. They can occur anytime in the life span and vary in severity. Table 3.1 summarizes much of the discussion

TABLE 3.1
Examples of Diagnoses Associated With the Brain and the Ages When Cognitive Disability Is Typically Manifest

INFANCY	CHILDHOOD	OLDER AGE	ANY AGE
Intellectual disability, including Down syndrome *Theresa* *(Chapter 2)*	Learning disability *Louisa* *(Chapter 6)*	Dementia, including Alzheimer's disease *Marjorie* *(Chapter 1)* *James* *(Chapter 6)*	Traumatic and acquired brain injury *Delmar* *(Chapter 3)*
Cerebral palsy *Maggie* *(Chapter 2)*	Asperger syndrome *Ryan* *(Chapter 3)*	Stroke *Marjorie* *(Chapter 1)*	Mental, emotional, and behavioral disability *Louisa* *(Chapter 6)*

Source: Institute for Matching Person & Technology, Inc., 2011

up to this point according to when the manifestations of cognitive disability typically become apparent.

This book is primarily concerned with cognitive and neurobehavioral disabilities, regardless of the cause or reason for it or when it was identified. According to the Coleman Institute at the University of Colorado System,

> When we refer to "cognitive disabilities". . . we are primarily referring to mental retardation and developmental disabilities, acquired brain injury, Alzheimer's disease, and severe and persistent mental illness. These conditions affect over 20 million American citizens—seven percent of the U.S. population. Prevalence rates for cognitive disability will grow rapidly as our nation ages and as advances in the medical and rehabilitative sciences extend the longevity of persons with disabilities. (Braddock, n.d., para. 3)

Cognitive disability stems from a substantial limitation in one's capacity to think, including conceptualizing, planning and sequencing thoughts and actions, remembering, and interpreting the meaning of social and emotional cues, and of numbers and symbols. (Coleman Institute, University of Colorado System, 2010, para. 3–4)

In a 2006 presentation on *Technology for Improving Cognitive Function* for the Interagency Committee on Disability Research, a consortium of U.S. federal government agencies devoted to disability and rehabilitation, Dr. David Braddock, executive director of the Coleman Institute, provided the following figure on the prevalence of cognitive disability in the United States according to type of disability (Figure 3.1).

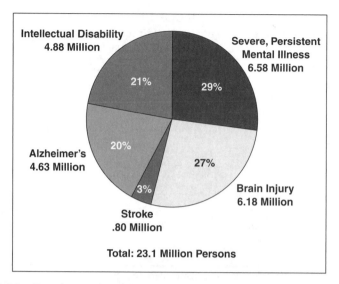

FIGURE 3.1   Prevalence of cognitive disability in the United States, 2010.
Source: Braddock, D. (2010). Boulder, CO: University of Colorado, Coleman Institute for Cognitive Disabilities.

Prevalence figures provide the total number of individuals within a certain geographic area (in this case, the entire United States) within a defined time (typically a year), which have a certain condition. *Incidence* figures employ the same parameters, but indicate the number of new cases identified in, say, the United States in the year 2006. When incidence increases, this will raise the prevalence rate. Increased survival rates and longer life spans make the prevalence go up. As has been discussed earlier, we have increased the survival rates of infants born prematurely and with significant disability, thus we are seeing more cases of cerebral palsy and severe intellectual disability. Trauma care advances have allowed more persons with TBI and stroke to survive. We have also extended the lives of persons with degenerative diseases such as dementia, including Alzheimer's disease.

Figure 3.2 is one I created from the incidence data provided up to now in this text. As indicated in the figure, each year in the United States, at least 4.6 million new cases of dementia are diagnosed, 3 million individuals have a stroke or brain attack, and 1.4 million people sustain a TBI.[6] Regarding infants and children, approximately 11,500 are diagnosed with cerebral palsy and 340,000 with Down syndrome.

Focusing on one type of brain impairment, the Traumatic Brain Injury Model Systems National Data and Statistical Center (TBINDSC) includes longitudinal information (up to 20 years post injury) on persons with TBI from throughout the United States. In December 2010, the database included 10,263 individuals (TBINDSC, 2011); and as of that date, the average age

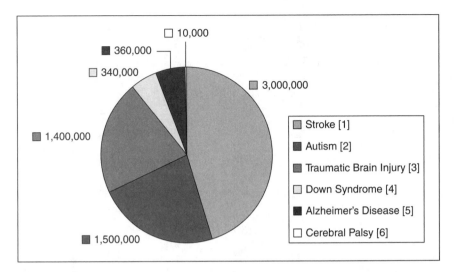

FIGURE 3.2 Incidence of various types of brain disorders in the United States.
[1] Prevalence of Stroke—United States, 2005. Morbidity and Mortality Weekly Report. May 18, 2007 / 56(19);469–474 http://www.cdc.gov/mmwr/preview/mmwrhtml/mm5619a2.htm; http://www.strokecenter.org/patients/stats.htm
[2] U.K. Autism Study Finds Prevalence One in 64: Autism Society Welcomes New Study and Calls for Continued Focus on Supporting People with Autism in America. 2009. http://support.autism-society.org/site/News2?page=NewsArticle&id=13963
[3] Traumatic Brain Injury in the United States: Emergency Department Visits, Hospitalizations, and Deaths. http://www.cdc.gov/ncipc/pub-res/tbi_in_us_04/tbi_ed.htm
[4] Down Syndrome. http://www.nichd.nih.gov/publications/pubs/downsyndrome.cfm
[5] Brookmeyer, R., Gray, S., & Kawas, C. (1998). Projections of Alzheimer's disease in the United States and the public health impact of delaying disease onset. *American Journal of Public Health, 88*(9), 1337–1342.
[6] United Cerebral Palsy. Cerebral Palsy Fact Sheet. http://affnet.ucp.org/uploads/cp_fact_sheet.pdf

at injury was 40 years of age. The primary cause of injury is vehicular accidents (53%), followed by falls (23%) and violence (13%). Most individuals in the database are male (74%).

Internationally, data were collected from a range of settings (research, primary care, rehabilitation) in the Czech Republic, Germany, Italy, Slovenia, and Spain in 1,200 individuals with the variety of diagnoses shown in Figure 3.3 including TBI. Interviewers rated each person's health and functioning with higher scores representing greater difficulties; data are shown in Figure 3.3. *Capacity* is defined as what a person *can* do in a standardized environment, often a clinical setting, without the barriers or facilitators of the person's usual environment. *Performance* indicates what a person actually *does* in the current or usual environment, with all barriers and facilitators in place. When performance exceeds capacity, then the individual is likely experiencing an accommodating environment with needed supports in place. However, when capacity is higher than performance, it indicates

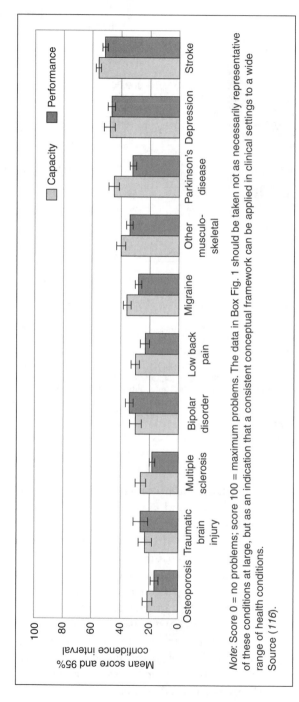

FIGURE 3.3 Mean and 95% confidence interval of the overall scores of capacity and performance in selected health conditions.

Source: World Health Organization. (2011). *World report on disability.* Geneva, Switzerland: Author. Retrieved from http://whqlibdoc.who.int/publications/2011/9789240685215_eng.pdf

that the person is experiencing barriers and lack of needed supports. The results in Table 3.1 indicate that

> capacity scores were worst in people with stroke, depression, and Parkinson disease, while individuals with osteoporosis had the fewest limitations. Performance scores tended to be better than capacity scores, except for individuals with bipolar disorder or traumatic brain injury. This suggests that most individuals had supportive environments that promoted their functioning at or above the level of their intrinsic ability—something that applied particularly for multiple sclerosis and Parkinson disease. For people with conditions such as bipolar disorder and traumatic brain injury, the environmental factors hindered optimal performance. The data suggest that it is possible in clinical settings to disentangle aspects of disability that are particular to the individual (the capacity score) from the effects of a person's physical environment (the difference between capacity and performance). (World Health Organization, 2011, p. 38)

What is missing in all the presented figures and data is the category of dementia, even though Alzheimer's disease is included in some. A longitudinal study conducted from 2001 to 2005 found an estimated 5.4 million people in the United States aged 71 years or older having cognitive impairment without dementia in 2002 and that 11.7% of this group subsequently progressed to dementia each year (Plassman et al., 2008). The authors further found an annual death rate of 8% among those with cognitive impairment without dementia and almost 15% among those with cognitive impairment caused by medical conditions. They concluded that cognitive impairment without dementia is more prevalent in the United States than dementia, and its subtypes vary in prevalence and outcomes.

Until now, the emphasis has been to illustrate general categories of cognitive disability with specific cases not only to illustrate that each person is unique, but also to illustrate general characteristics and commonalities. To understand cognitive disability requires an understanding of the complexity of thinking, remembering, and learning—in other words, the complexity of the brain.

THE INNER WORKINGS OF THE BRAIN

The brain has been considered the last great unknown frontier; however, so has outer space and the Earth's oceans. It all depends on who you ask—a neuroscientist, an astrophysicist, or an oceanographer. As for us, we are now going to explore the structure and functions of the brain and see just how much is known. The subsequent information has been synthesized from several sources

(Armstrong & Morrow, 2010; Braddom, 2006; Holtz, 2010; Kreutzer, DeLuca, & Caplan, 2010; Stuss, Winocur & Robertson, 2010; Tonkonogy & Puente, 2009).

The image below shows the head of our friend, the Vitruvian Man. To get inside his head, we must first pass through the bones protecting his brain known as the *cranium* or *skull*.

Head of Vitruvian Man

Once we have removed the skull and look at that "monstrous, beautiful mess" of gray matter we call the cerebrum, we can see that it "sits" above a brain stem that literally "stems" or connects the brain to the spinal cord (Figure 3.4). The *brain stem* is the part of the brain that controls our

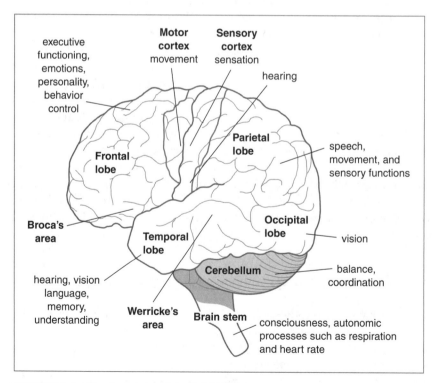

FIGURE 3.4   Key functions of the left hemisphere of the brain.

consciousness and such autonomic functions as respiration and the beating of our hearts. Under and behind the cerebrum is the cerebellum, which is largely responsible for our balance and muscle coordination. It has also been found to be instrumental in other cognitive functions and acts almost like a "mini-brain" (Figure 3.4).

Returning to the cerebrum, we note that it is the largest area of the brain. It controls all higher mental functions, including thinking, remembering, and learning. We can see that it is divided into two halves or hemispheres. While they cover the Vitruvian Man's face, think of them being pulled up and over so that they sit on top of his head (see below).

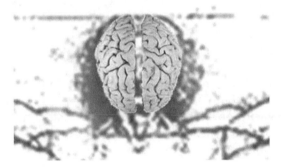

Brain Hemispheres of the Vitruvian Man

We have already briefly discussed the two hemispheres in Chapter 1 regarding the effects of stroke or brain attack in which it was noted that a stroke on the left side or hemisphere of the brain affects the opposite or right side of the body. For example, the right hand is controlled from the left hemisphere's motor area and the left hand from the right hemisphere. This is known as *contralateralization of brain function*.

The two hemispheres look similar and are functionally symmetrical but are not two independent parts of a whole. They are connected and closely coordinated by a large group of nerves called the *corpus callosum* (as well as smaller connections). And although the hemispheres perform many of the same coordinated functions, there are differences. As one example, most people are dominant for language in their left hemisphere so that a stroke or brain attack in that area may leave them with affected language skills. And there is evidence that there are other differences between the two hemispheres, namely, in ways of thinking and learning. Table 3.2 lists some of these left- and right-brain differences, which are likely familiar because they have appeared frequently in the popular literature.

TABLE 3.2
Differences in Right Brain versus Left Brain Thinking

RIGHT BRAIN	LEFT BRAIN
Intuitive	Logical
Creative	Analytical
Spontaneous	Rational
Synthesizing	Sequential
Subjective	Objective
Global thinker	Looks at parts

Research indicates that there are many additional explanations for individual differences in cognitive performance. For example, Prat and Just (2008) propose a set of at least three cortical network-level attributes underlying individual differences in cognitive performance:

1. **Neural Efficiency.** Individuals with higher skill levels tend to use fewer neural resources.
2. **Neural Synchronization.** Higher skill level is associated with higher levels of cortical synchronization and coordination, in other words, more coordination among the various areas and across hemispheres of the brain.
3. **Neural Adaptability.** An effective cortical system must be able to adapt to meet changing cognitive demands. Specifically, skilled readers activated the left hemisphere language regions more when reading sentences with low-frequency words (those not used often) than they did when reading sentences with high-frequency words, showing more adaptive modulation of neural resources in the face of changing lexical demands compared with less-skilled readers.

Regarding brain and behavior links, the authors believe that individual differences in brain attributes may be related to individual differences in speed of processing information and fluid intelligence. Although tests of fluid intelligence primarily measure frontal lobe function, intelligence is just as apt to be related to the quality of the communication between the frontal lobes and other important brain regions.

Within each hemisphere of the brain are four lobes: frontal, parietal, temporal, and occipital lobes. Figure 3.4 shows the location of these lobes in the left hemisphere (they are also in the right hemisphere) and identifies the major functions associated with each lobe.

When we know the area of the brain affected by an injury or illness, then we can usually accurately identify what activities will be involved.

Conversely, when we see particular patterns of characteristics and behavior, we can tell fairly accurately what part of the brain was involved. Uncertainty arises because while most individuals' brains are organized very similarly, there are differences. For example, roughly 95% of individuals have language function localized in the left hemisphere. However, the other 5% are localized in the right hemisphere; and we don't know for certain who is who unless or until there's a problem. If in Broca's area, shown in Figure 3.4, this will affect the ability to process grammar and to communicate fluently. If in Wernicke's area, speech comprehension is affected. There is difficulty recalling the names of objects, and the person will often say similar-sounding or related words. The following are some additional disabilities and the corresponding section of the brain affected:

blindness = occipital lobes
seizure, time distortion = temporal lobes
ataxia = cerebellum
loss of consciousness, paresis, and paresthesias = brain stem

The frontal and temporal lobes of the brain are the ones most often affected by TBI. Thus, we would expect to see someone with a TBI to have difficulties with attention, problem solving, and memory, among other things. And, if a friend of ours has suddenly developed forgetfulness, confusion, and disorientation, we might suspect he or she recently received a concussion or blow to the head (i.e., mild TBI).

The major functions of each of the four lobes can be summarized as follows:

The *occipital lobe* controls our vision, what we see and how we process visual images. This is where the visual cortex is located.

The *temporal lobe* controls our hearing, what we hear and how we process sounds. This is where the auditory cortex is located. In the left hemisphere's temporal lobe is Wernicke's area, which is where we recognize language. Although not its primary function, the temporal lobe is involved in memory and our feelings and emotions and works with the primary controller of these functions: the limbic system (*hippocampus, thalamus, and hypothalamus*). The hippocampus creates connections from throughout the brain, and it is where our vivid three-dimensional memories are formed. For example, we can all conjure vivid memories of certain past experiences and recall the sounds, colors, and smells of that moment, as well as our emotions during it. It is the hippocampus that takes all these different aspects stored in separate areas of the brain and unites them into the full-recalled memory.

The *parietal lobe* processes pain and touch and is involved in cognitive functions such as spatial relations and visuospatial processing (calculating the location and movement of objects, orientation in space and place). Damage to the right parietal lobe is associated with spatial neglect of the left side of the body, and damage to the left lobe is associated with deficits in mathematics and writing.

The *frontal lobe* is the brain's central command center. This is where our higher level cognitive processing and emotion occur, as well as memory and motor control. It is the region of the brain last to develop as we mature, and it isn't until our early 20s that truly advanced cognition occurs. This is also the area of "executive functioning" that encompasses problem solving, decision making, impulse control, reasoning and judgment, as well as empathy for others. Executive functioning problems include difficulties in such areas as

- multitasking
- remembering
- planning and organizing ways to accomplish a task or project
- strategizing about the best and most efficient means of achieving a goal
- paying attention to details and then remembering what they are and organizing them in a meaningful way
- building on past experiences to form current strategies
- critically evaluating what one reads or hears
- controlling impulsive behaviors
- evaluating a chosen path and making a correction
- regulating emotions

Problems with executive function are particularly frustrating for the individual and all involved because these behaviors underlie appropriate interpersonal and social behaviors and make us an attractive social partner.

We are still learning a lot about the brain and how it functions, and there is much more to learn. For example, the brain's "gray matter" is responsible for memory storage. "White matter" also exists in the brain and has been viewed as the transport system for conveying messages from one brain region to the other; however, its importance in other areas is still being uncovered. Recent research has discovered and attached more control to white matter over memory (Pohjasvaara et al., 2007), psychosis (Ziermans et al., 2010), and depression (Olesen et al., 2010; Tham, Woon, Sum, Lee, & Sim, 2011) than was previously hypothesized. It is also possible to image and detect white matter remodeling after brain injury (Jiang, Zhang, & Chopp, 2010) and monitor changes in measures of white matter as it may be that these changes parallel the phases of bipolar depression (Benedetti et al., 2011).

We know that the brain continues to mature into adulthood and to adapt and develop connections even after injury and disease. This is called *neuroplasticity* and it means new neural pathways can be established to make possible or restore a certain type of brain function. Exciting findings like these have meant that functional recovery can continue long after the assault to the brain.

This chapter has focused necessarily on the functions and structure of the brain. We now understand the earlier apparent contradiction about people with quite different disorders received at very different ages exhibiting similar characteristics, yet each person with a cognitive disability being a unique individual. We see that there is no contradiction at all. For different reasons, whether disease or trauma, people who have the same areas of the brain affected will exhibit similar behaviors. Thus, we can consider some common ways to optimize their functional performance and life quality and support their life pursuits. In the next chapter interventions for people with cognitive disability are discussed.

4

Treatment and Rehabilitation Practices: Intervening in Cognitive Disability

Man can alter his life by altering his thinking.
—William James

*H*ow brain injuries are diagnosed and treated differs according to age at onset and type of injury. Developmental cognitive disability, which occurs in infancy and childhood (e.g., Theresa born with Down syndrome, Maggie with cerebral palsy, and Ryan with Asperger syndrome), is typically diagnosed after behavioral and maturational anomalies are observed and are then confirmed by blood and other medical tests. Acquired brain injury (ABI), including traumatic brain injury (TBI), can occur at anytime in the life span (Marjorie's stroke and Delmar's TBI), and treatment is often initiated by paramedics and then continued in a hospital emergency room, and sometimes followed by critical care, inpatient hospitalization, inpatient rehabilitation, outpatient rehabilitation, or other supports. Care may involve physiatrists, neurologists, psychiatrists, primary care physicians, rehabilitation professionals, and most importantly, family members. Then there are cognitive and neurobehavioral disabilities associated with a degenerative condition, typically associated with advanced age (Marjorie's dementia) and which are managed by primary care physicians, neurologists, gerontologists, and family members. Additionally, it is important to note that diagnoses can differ between regions and practitioners. Especially with disabilities that require qualitative assessment, appropriate diagnosis can be difficult and subject to the health care professional's experience and expertise.

TREATING DEVELOPMENTAL DISABILITY

As discussed in Chapter 2, nothing can be done to "cure" developmental disabilities such as Down syndrome, cerebral palsy, or Asperger syndrome, but interventions applied as early as possible can make a great deal of difference in current and future functioning. Orthopedic and neurological impairments can often be surgically corrected or medically managed. Even though the outcomes may improve functioning and reduce pain, the individual still may not be able to walk without a brace or other orthotic device, and perhaps not at all. In this situation, a wheelchair is usually prescribed. Often, children with developmental disability undergo many surgeries and treatments during their initial development with the goal of strengthening or extending the use of existing capabilities (Scherer, 2005b). Sensory disability can be greatly helped with advances in technology, and the means to communicate can be made possible through alternative and augmented communication devices.

Although specialized institutions and agencies were historically established to care for individuals with cognitive disabilities, today, community programs designed solely to educate children with disabilities are typically serving only the most severely affected. Thus, had Theresa and Maggie been born in the late 1980s, they would not have been sent to an institution, nor in all likelihood, a sheltered workshop. They would have received their medical care and rehabilitation in the community and local public school.

Before the 1970s when the United States Congress funded significant supports and services for children with intellectual disability, cerebral palsy, epilepsy, and Down syndrome, families had two choices: Keep the child with a disability at home with little or no services or put him or her in a state institution. The goal today is to help children with developmental disabilities participate in life by playing with other children, attending school, and being a valued member of the family and community. Through a series of legislative mandates passed over the past 30 years or more, most children with disability are educated in the same settings as their peers without disability. As in Ryan's situation, this does not mean that every school is capable of meeting the needs of all children with disability. However, the availability of programs where students like Ryan can function and grow has been steadily increasing.

Reauthorized "special education" legislation, the *Individuals with Disabilities Education Improvement Act (IDEA) of 2004*, along with *No Child Left Behind (NCLB)* legislation, mandates a free and appropriate education for children with disability, including the supports to succeed in meeting their Individualized Educational Program (IEP; U.S. Department of Education, 2007). IEPs organize goals for a student and the incremental means for achieving those goals. The purpose of these plans is to ensure that the right blend of technologies, supports, and accommodations are provided in light of the student's needs and strengths (Scherer, 2004). In-school interventions may include physical and occupational therapy, speech therapy, and the administration of medications that control seizures, relax muscle spasms, and alleviate pain. Because the recent IDEA amendments state that all IEPs must consider whether the child requires assistive technology devices and services to receive a Free and Appropriate Education (FAPE), this may also include braces and other orthotic devices, communication aids such as computers with voice output, and various additional products designed to minimize functional limitations and allow the achievement of academic goals and participation in the full academic curriculum. At Ryan's current school, SMART Boards are used to involve children in their learning in a very visual and participatory fashion. Ryan has also benefited from using computers in his classroom and programming an agenda on his iPod to remind him of assignments and medication times. We will discuss more of these technologies in Chapter 6.

The federal government lists 11 categories in IDEA based on what is sometimes referred to as "educational diagnosis" as opposed to a "medical diagnosis." This means that the criteria for special education may be different from diagnostic criteria used by the medical or mental health profession. This is often confusing to parents, doctors, psychologists, and others not familiar with the criteria necessary for special education. For example, Ryan has a recognized disability by doctors and his therapist but not by his previous school. As Ryan's family has learned, the written mandate and the actual outcomes or products can be quite different.

The 11 categories of children identified as meeting the requirements for special education services are as follows:

1. Intellectual disability (legislation passed in October 2010 [P.L. 111–256, Rosa's Law], amends the language in all federal health, education, and labor laws from "mental retardation" to "intellectual disability")
2. Hearing impairments (including deafness)
3. Speech or language impairments
4. Visual impairments (including blindness)
5. Serious emotional disturbance
6. Autism
7. TBI
8. Orthopedic impairments (physical impairments)
9. Other health impairments (includes health issues that significantly impact student functioning such as attention-deficit hyperactivity disorder [ADHD], swallowing difficulties, use of respirator or other medical equipment, etc.)
10. Specific learning disabilities (SLD) that include seven areas of learning challenges: basic reading, reading comprehension, math calculation,

math reasoning, written expression, oral expression, and listening comprehension

11. Developmental delay

Section 504 of the Rehabilitation Act of 1973

This legislation prohibits discrimination against persons with disability in all programs and activities conducted by recipients of federal financial assistance. It applies to students in elementary, middle, and high school as well as students with disability in postsecondary education.

Section 504 guarantees an appropriate special education as well as accessibility to regular education programs. It requires that all children with disability be provided a free, appropriate public education in the least restrictive environment. A person with a disability under Section 504 is any person who

1. has a physical or mental impairment, which substantially limits one or more major life activities,
2. has a record of such an impairment, or
3. is regarded as having such an impairment.

This definition differs from that found in the IDEA, which places specific disability in the 11 categories listed previously.

Section 504 states that educational programs for students with disability must be equal to those provided to students without disability. Thus, individuals who are not qualified for special education under IDEA may be qualified for special services and accommodations under Section 504.

Regardless if the child with a developmental disability is in a special education program mandated by IDEA or is a "504 student," the number of students with disability has increased substantially over the past 15 years. National statistics indicate the number of students with disability rose approximately 30.3% over this period (U.S. Department of Education Office of Special Education and Rehabilitative Services, 2003). Students with special education needs account for at least 13.5% (National Education Association [NEA], 2007) of the educational population and with rising incidence. For example, according to statistics from IDEA, the growth of autism in students aged 3–22 years (such as Ryan with Asperger syndrome) has increased by 805% in the past 10 years. In 1993, there were 15,580 cases reported, and in 2003, there were 163,773 cases reported. The percentage of children identified as having a disability is expected to increase because of improved and expanded diagnostics, an increase in number of students with autism, and improved medical response to premature births and severe traumas such as TBI.

Just as autism is a *spectrum disorder*, so too are other developmental disabilities as well as the services needed. Although students with developmental disability have educational and physical challenges, their potential is as unlimited as anyone without an identified disability. The key is to identify abilities and strengths, then leverage strengths while managing limitations. This requires matching students with the opportunities and supports necessary to achieve lives of productivity and quality. For Ryan, he will need to find a college where the faculty monitor and encourage students. Because Ryan benefits from structure, a community where regulations and expectations are clear will be essential. Twenty years ago, such a facility would have been rare. Now, Ryan will be able to go in higher education with a choice in colleges that offer the programs he needs.

TREATING DEGENERATIVE DISABILITY

The situation is somewhat different at the other end of the life span for those individuals who have a degenerative cause of cognitive disability (e.g., Lichtenberg & Schneider, 2010). Until recently, when an aging person was observed putting things in the wrong places and then forgetting where they put them, not performing personal care activities, and saying and doing inappropriate things, then that individual likely moved in with adult children or other relatives to be cared for and monitored. That still occurs today, but just as frequently, the individual's primary care physician may recommend the family consider assisted living or a nursing home with a unit designed for those with moderate-to-severe dementia.

In some ways, we have situations the reverse of what they were traditionally. The families of infants and children with developmental disability now assume a major portion of caregiving because placing their child in an institution would be seen by today's society as acting irresponsibly. At the same time, options for caregivers of aging persons with dementia increasingly include placement in specialized facilities which, in spite of efforts to lower the staff–patient ratio and create an attractive and homey atmosphere, are institutions for all practical purposes.

TREATING ACQUIRED BRAIN INJURY

A severe brain injury that occurs as a result of trauma or through changes at the cellular level from such causes as high fever, oxygen deprivation, or stroke is typically of rapid onset with immediately recognizable signs and symptoms of injury to the brain. Paramedics and emergency room personnel are usually the first to see the newly injured person. According to the Centers for Disease Control and Prevention (Faul, Xu, Wald, & Coronado, 2010), TBI-related emergency department visits increased by 14.4% and hospitalizations by almost 20% from 2002 to 2006. This was caused, in large part, by the increased number of cases presenting with injuries because of falls (62% increase in children 14 years and younger, 46% increase in adults 65 years and older) over this time span. As large as these numbers appear, it is important to note that these data do not include the number of visits caused by nontraumatic causes such as stroke.

Once in the emergency room, the individual may be treated by a neurosurgeon, neurologist, psychiatrist, or a combination of these specialists. After a physical exam, laboratory (Manley et al., 2010) and neuroimaging tests are ordered to identify the location and extent of the injury (Malia et al., 2004). Although not all effects of brain injury can be observed with today's technology, imaging is important for seeing brain activity and detecting blockages (Bigler, 2010; Duhaime et al., 2010; Haacke et al., 2010). An electroencephalogram (EEG) is usually the first test because it records electrical activity within the cortex (*clinical death* is defined as the absence of brain activity as detected by an EEG)*. Additionally, the following may be done:

1. A computed tomography (CT) scan records X-ray images on film and provides cross-sectional views of the brain and its structure.
2. Magnetic resonance imaging (MRI) will produce computer-generated images of the brain's structures as well as differentiate types of soft tissues. It provides an anatomical view of the brain.
3. Functional magnetic resonance imaging (fMRI) indicates blood flow through the brain and, as implied in the name, gives a functional view of the brain.

Advances in imaging have led to improved detection of TBI and ABI and, some believe, the prediction of outcome (Kou et al., 2010). The images obtained are used to help diagnose the extent and severity of the brain injury and guide an initial treatment course.

Diagnosing the extent of the injury is not easy because of diffuse symptoms and preinjury factors (e.g., history of substance abuse and such co-occurring conditions as additional injuries and medical conditions such as diabetes). Developmental differences among children can complicate diagnoses in this population (Farmer, Kanne, Grisso, & Kemp, 2010). A World Health Organization (WHO)-sponsored systematic review of the mild TBI literature (Holm, Cassidy, Carroll, & Borg, 2005) notes that although mild, TBI accounts for approximately 80% of cases of reported TBI; there is not a universally agreed-upon definition of what constitutes a mild TBI (see also

---

*For suspected stroke and TBI, the first and most important is a CT scan to see if there are signs of blood as that determines emergency treatment. For stroke, if there is blockage instead of blood (ischemic vs hemorrhagic), "clot buster" drugs are administered. If its hemorrhagic, or a TBI is hemorrhaging, there may be a craniotomy to stop the bleeding and relieve pressure from swelling tissue.

Menon, Schwab, Wright, & Maas, 2010). Terminologies such as mild TBI, concussion, and minor head injury have been used interchangeably over the years, creating confusion (e.g., Brain Injury Association of America, 2011; Wilk et al., 2010). Yet, there have been efforts to develop diagnostic criteria. For example, the Mild Traumatic Brain Injury Committee of the Brain (BI-ISIG) Injury Interdisciplinary Special Interest Group of the American Congress of Rehabilitation Medicine (ACRM, 1993) defines mild TBI based on signs and symptoms, alone or in combination, in three categories:

1. *Physical symptoms* of brain injury (e.g., nausea, vomiting, dizziness, headache, blurred vision, sleep disturbance, quickness to fatigue, lethargy, or other sensory loss) that cannot be accounted for by peripheral injury or other causes;
2. *Cognitive deficits* (e.g., involving attention, concentration, perception, memory, speech/language, or executive functions) that cannot be completely accounted for by emotional state or other causes; and
3. *Behavioral change(s) and/or alterations in degree of emotional responsivity* (e.g., irritability, quickness to anger, disinhibition, or emotional lability) that cannot be accounted for by a psychological reaction to physical or emotional stress or other causes (ACRM, 1993, p. 87).

Most professional groups generally define mild TBI as having a disruption of or loss of consciousness of less than 30 minutes, moderate TBI with loss of consciousness more than 30 minutes up to 24 hours, and severe TBI as loss of consciousness more than 24 hours.

Most individuals with mild TBI (e.g., caused by a concussion from a sports injury) are sent home with follow-up instructions for aftercare. Others with mild TBI and many with moderate and severe TBI are admitted to the hospital for medical stabilization and treatment.[7] Treatment may result in a transition to an inpatient rehabilitation setting or to a long-term acute care hospital where various professionals are involved in providing treatment. Medical specialists from physiatry, rehabilitation neuropsychology, and nursing along with various allied health providers representing case management, occupational, physical, recreational, and speech therapy may be involved with a particular individual's care. This care should be delivered through an interdisciplinary or transdisciplinary team model centered on the person with TBI and their unique needs (Butt & Caplan, 2010).[8]

The injury itself is treated, along with co-occurring disorders or diseases (such as mood, anxiety, stress, or substance use disorders). Psychosocial issues (financial, family, housing, or school/work) are viewed with the objective of returning the individual to prior roles and community participation (U.S. Department of Veterans Affairs & U.S. Department of Defense, 2009).

According to Im, Scherer, Gaeta, and Elias (2010); Im, Trudel, Scherer, and Gaeta (2010); and Trudel, Scherer, and Elias (2009), inpatient care is necessary for individuals with a TBI who have significant medical issues and/ or cognitive, behavioral, or physical impairments that make returning home unsafe. Problems in any of these areas can result in decreased independence and safety. These authors note that after the patient is medically stabilized in the acute care setting, inpatient rehabilitation usually begins. TBI rehabilitation units can be embedded within a larger medical center or in a freestanding rehabilitation facility. In general, TBI inpatient rehabilitation programs are divided into two categories: acute and subacute, the latter being for individuals who do not yet have the energy and strength to participate in rigorous daily rehabilitation sessions. *Acute inpatient rehabilitation* refers to a more intensive rehabilitation program and management, and those who specialize in TBI rehabilitation offer medical, psychosocial, physical, and cognitive rehabilitation services specific to the needs of those recovering from a TBI. The rehabilitation treatment program in an inpatient rehabilitation unit encompasses not only the therapy provided but also everything else that occurs on the unit, including nursing care, monitoring of behavior, nutritional assessment and planning, and nonpharmacological strategies and techniques employed to foster the optimal environment for recovery. As a result, therapy for the patient occurs 24 hours per day on the unit and provides the opportunity to carry over treatment, strategies, and training all day long and observe the recovery process more closely to adjust to a patient's needs more effectively. Even the physical structure and environment of the unit itself is often used to facilitate management of the patients. For instance, limiting the points of access on and off the unit often deters patients from wandering into unsafe areas. Additionally, low stimulation settings help decrease agitation and irritability. All of these aspects of management facilitate recovery and help minimize the use of medications and their side effects.

However, variability even among specialized TBI rehabilitation programs makes it important to ensure that a patient is sent to a facility that is equipped to effectively manage the unique combination of difficulties experienced by that particular person. Unfortunately, this does not always occur, nor is funding an acute inpatient rehabilitation stay easy to manage. Im, Scherer et al. (2010) state,

> In order to be eligible for acute inpatient rehabilitation of any kind (which implies close physician, nursing, and therapy staff attention with supervision and management by a rehabilitation medicine specialist), most medical insurance companies require that the patient must be able to engage in and benefit from three hours of a combination of physical, occupational, and speech/ language/swallow therapy daily. The length of stay in acute

rehabilitation tends to be limited by medical insurance coverage to a few weeks. Unfortunately the benefits TBI acute inpatient rehabilitation offers in addressing medical complications of TBI, stimulating more severely injured TBI patients with altered levels of consciousness, and managing behavioral difficulties that may develop in the confused or agitated TBI patient to provide a safe environment for recovery are often overlooked by insurance companies who are more concerned about measurable functional improvement. This results in less than optimal time spent in acute inpatient rehabilitation for some TBI patients before they are sent to a less monitored and intensive rehabilitation setting. (p. 44)

If insurance coverage is inadequate or the insurer denies coverage, the person may not get optimal benefit from the inpatient stay or may struggle more than is necessary. Follow-up care becomes all the more important, especially when impaired problem solving skills, irritability, poor ability to relate to others, and poor attention or concentration become apparent only after resumption of daily activities and encounters with stressful situations.

COGNITIVE, EMOTIONAL/BEHAVIORAL, AND PSYCHOSOCIAL REHABILITATION FOR BRAIN IMPAIRMENT

Clinical information, the results of laboratory testing, as well as brain scanning and imaging all aid in the determination of cognitive disability. The results of neuropsychological assessment are equally important.

Brain injury programs use information from various standardized assessments and tests to help determine and guide treatment planning from acute care to community (re)integration. Table 4.1 lists neuropsychological measures commonly used throughout the treatment and rehabilitation process, although the particular measures used for any given individual and preferred by a particular professional varies widely. Table 4.2 is one measure in its entirety, the *Rancho Los Amigos Cognitive Scale–Revised*. It has been selected because it applies throughout the rehabilitation continuum and addresses cognitive, emotional/behavioral, and psychosocial functioning.

There is no consensus which test or set of tests yields the most useful information. Additionally, it is common for an abbreviated battery of tests to be used early in treatment with more extensive testing being done in outpatient settings. For example, in acute care, testing might concentrate on lower level of awareness, consciousness, posttraumatic amnesia, and agitation, whereas higher level cognitive assessment tools, vocational/occupational interests, family functioning measures, and so on are usually reserved for the outpatient setting.

TABLE 4.1
A List of Commonly Used Measures

COGNITION

Automated Neuropsychological Assessment Metrics (ANAM; http://www.army medicine.army.mil/prr/anam.html) is a brief computer-based cognitive screening tool that takes about 20 minutes to complete. It was developed by the U.S. Army to collect baseline information predeployment on performance that can be used if a service member has an injury that may affect attention, memory, and thinking ability.

Awareness Questionnaire (AQ; http://www.tbims.org/combi/aq/index.html) An 18-item measure of self-awareness. Can be self-rated or rated by a clinician or significant other. The abilities of the person with traumatic brain injury (TBI) to perform various tasks after the injury is compared with before the injury and rated on a 5–point scale ranging from *much worse* to *much better*. The AQ takes about 10 minutes to administer.

Cognitive Abilities Screening Instrument-Short Form (CASI-S; http://online library.wiley.com/doi/10.1002/(SICI)1099-1166(199910)14:10%3C882::AID-GPS42%3E3.0.CO;2-D/abstract) is a brief bedside cognitive assessment that does not require motor responses.

Cognitive Log (Cog-Log; http://www.tbims.org/combi/coglog/index.html) A 10-item brief measure intended to be used at bedside. Used for serial measurement of cognition by clinician raters.

Coma/Near Coma Scale (CNC; http://www.tbims.org/combi/cnc/index.html) An 11-item instrument used by clinicians to assess low-level, brain-injured patients.

Coma Recovery Scale-Revised (CRS-R; http://www.tbims.org/combi/crs/index.html) A 23-item instrument used to assist with differential diagnosis, prognostic assessment, and treatment planning with patients with disorders of consciousness.

Confusion Assessment Protocol (CAP; http://www.tbims.org/combi/cap/index.html) A 58-item instrument used by clinicians to measure confusion.

Functional Assessment Measure (FAM; http://www.tbims.org/combi/FAM/index.html) A 12-item adjunct or addition to the Functional Independence Measure (FIM; http://www.tbims.org/combi/FIM/index.html; TM).
FIM (TM) adding more brain injury/stroke related items. Rated by clinicians.

Glasgow Outcome Scale (GOS; http://www.tbims.org/combi/gos/index.html) A one-item instrument used by clinicians to measure disability typically in the trauma setting. The GOS-E extends the original five GOS categories to eight. The eight categories are dead, vegetative state, lower severe disability, upper severe disability, lower moderate disability, upper moderate disability, lower good recovery, and upper good recovery.

Extended Glasgow Outcome Scale (GOS-E; http://www.tbims.org/combi/gose/index.html)
A one-item instrument used by clinicians to measure disability. An extension of the GOS that has eight categories rather than five.

TABLE 4.1
A List of Commonly Used Measures (*Continued*)

High Level Mobility Assessment Tool (*HiMAT*; http://www.tbims.org/combi/himat/index.html)
A 13-item measure used to quantify high-level mobility outcomes following TBI.

JFK Coma Recovery Scale-Revised (*CRS-R*; http://www.tbims.org/combi/crs/index.html) 23 items in six subscales addressing auditory, visual, motor, oromotor, communication, and arousal functions and in hierarchically arranged items associated with brain stem, subcortical, and cortical processes.

Rancho Los Amigos Cognitive Scale Revised (see Table 4.2)
A commonly used broad measure of cognitive functioning focusing on psychosocial behavior.

Mayo-Portland Adaptability Inventory (*MPAI*; http://www.tbims.org/combi/mpai/index.html)
A 35-item instrument designed to (a) assist in the clinical evaluation of people during the postacute (posthospital) period following acquired brain injury (ABI), and (b) assist in the evaluation of rehabilitation programs designed to serve these people. Can be self-rated or rated by a clinician or significant other.

Mississippi Aphasia Screening Test (*MAST*; http://www.tbims.org/combi/mast/index.html)
A 46-item instrument used by clinicians to measure communication and language skills.

Moss Attention Rating Scale (*MARS*; http://www.tbims.org/combi/mars/index.html)
A 22-item instrument designed to be completed by clinicians based on their everyday, routine interaction with the patient. Attention-related behaviors include Restlessness/Distractibility, Initiation, and Sustained/Consistent Attention (Hart et al., 2006).

Neurobehavioral Functioning Inventory (*NFI*; http://www.tbims.org/combi/nfi/index.html)
A 76-item instrument used to measure symptoms and behaviors after brain injury. Proprietary.

The Orientation Log (*O-Log*; http://www.tbims.org/combi/olog/index.html)
A 10-item measure used by clinicians to measure orientation to time, place, and circumstance in a rehabilitation population. The O-Log can be used for serial assessment of orientation to document changes over time. The O-Log has been used with people experiencing TBI, cerebrovascular accident (CVA), tumor, infectious disease, and degenerative disorders.

The Patient Competency Rating Scale (*PCRS*; http://www.tbims.org/combi/pcrs/index.html)
The PCRS is a 30-item self-report instrument of self-awareness that asks the subject to use a 5-point Likert scale to rate his or her degree of difficulty in various tasks and functions. Can be self-rated or rated by a clinician or significant other.

(Continued)

TABLE 4.1
A List of Commonly Used Measures (*Continued*)

Repeatable Battery for the Assessment of Neuropsychological Status (*RBANS*; Randolph, 2010).
A screening measure primarily for older persons with memory, language, and visual–perceptual subtests.

Wisconsin Card Sorting Test (*WCST*) is a measure of the following aspects of executive functioning: strategic planning, organized searching, utilizing environmental feedback to shift cognitive sets, directing behavior toward achieving a goal, and modulating impulsive responding. The test can be administered to those 6.5 years to 89 years of age and requires 12–20 minutes to complete.

EMOTIONAL AND BEHAVIORAL

Adult Asperger Assessment (*AAA*; http://www.autismresearchcentre.com/tests/aaa_test.asp)
A new tool, still a research measure, for clarifying the clinical presentation of adults thought to have Asperger syndrome. Research version is free.

Agitated Behavior Scale (*ABS*; http://www.tbims.org/combi/abs/index.html)
A 14-item instrument used for serial assessment of agitation by clinician raters.

Apathy Evaluation Scale (*AES*; http://www.tbims.org/combi/aes/index.html)
An 18-item instrument used for evaluation of apathy. Can be self-rated or rated by a clinician or significant other.

DEPRESSION AND ANXIETY

Beck Depression Inventory Second Edition, Beck Anxiety Inventory, Geriatric Depression Scale, Center for Epidemiological Studies Depression Scale

NIH Toolbox for the Assessment of Neurological and Behavioral Function (*NIH Toolbox*; http://www.nihtoolbox.org/) to consist of a standard set of concise, well-validated measures of cognition (such as executive function, episodic memory, working memory, processing speed, language, attention), emotion (negative affect, positive affect, stress and coping, social relationships), motor functioning (locomotion, strength, nonvestibular balance, endurance, dexterity), and sensation (vision, audition, vestibular balance, somatosensation, taste, olfaction). These measures will be available in English and Spanish for people aged 3–85 years.

Satisfaction With Life Scale (*SWLS*; http://www.tbims.org/combi/swls/index.html)
A five-item instrument used to measure life satisfaction. Self-rated.

(Problematic) Substance Use Identified in the TBI Model Sytems National Dataset (http://www.tbims.org/combi/subst/index.html)
A report on research involving substance use and traumatic brain injury, and how to measure substance use. There is also the Michigan Alcohol Screening Test.

TABLE 4.1
A List of Commonly Used Measures (*Continued*)

PSYCHOSOCIAL

Community Integration Questionnaire (*CIQ*; http://www.tbims.org/combi/ciq/index.html)
The CIQ consists of 15 items relevant to living, loving and working, or more formally home integration (H), social integration (S), and productive activities (P). It is scored to provide subtotals for each of these, as well as for community integration overall. Can be self-rated or rated by a clinician or significant other.

The Craig Handicap Assessment and Reporting Technique (*CHART*; http://www.tbims.org/combi/chart/index.html)
A 32-item instrument in six domains used to measure participation. Can be self-rated or rated by or significant other. There is a 19-item short form (http://www.tbims.org/combi/chartsf/index.html). Can be self-rated or rated by or significant other.

Disability Rating Scale (*DRS*; http://www.tbims.org/combi/drs/index.html)
An eight-item instrument used by clinicians to measure disability. One advantage of the DRS is its ability to track an individual from coma to community.

The Family Needs Questionnaire (*FNQ*; http://www.tbims.org/combi/fnq/index.html)
A 40-item instrument used to measure family needs as rated by a significant other. Proprietary.

Participation Objective, Participation Subjective (http://www.tbims.org/combi/pops/index.html)
This instrument, known as POPS, asks questions regarding 26 activities or elements of participation sorted into five categories: Domestic Life; Major Life Activities; Transportation; Interpersonal Interactions and Relationships; and Community, Recreational, and Civic Life. Objective questions relate to the frequency of an activity; subjective questions relate to the importance of an activity and the satisfaction with their current participation in an activity.

Services Obstacles Scale (*SOS*; http://www.tbims.org/combi/sos/index.html)
A six-item instrument that measures perceptions regarding brain injury-related services. Can be self-rated or rated by a significant other.

Supervision Rating Scale (*SRS*; http://www.tbims.org/combi/srs/index.html)
A one-item instrument used by clinicians to measure amount of received supervision.

PREDISPOSITION TO TECHNOLOGY USE

Cognitive Support Technology Predisposition Assessment (CST PA) and *Assistive Technology Device Predisposition Assessment (ATD PA)* are measures developed by the author to identify influences affecting a person's predisposition to use and subsequently gain benefit from technology use. Each measure addresses subjecting ratings of capabilities, well-being, personal and psychosocial characteristics, and expectations of (baseline) and gain from (follow-up) technology use. These measures will be discussed in detail in this book.

Source: Adapted from The Center for Outcome Measurement in Brain Injury. (2011). *COMBI: Featured scales*. Retrieved from http://www.tbims.org/combi/list.html

TABLE 4.2
Rancho Los Amigos Cognitive Scale Revised
(http://www.rancho.org/research/cognitive_levels.pdf)

This multilevel scale of cognitive recovery ranges from 1 (*no response / total assistance*) to 10 (*purposeful and appropriate/modified independent*) and is used

- for assessment of recovery,
- for communication between health care professionals and facilities, and
- in research.

It is a very broad measure of cognitive functioning and uses psychosocial behavior as its criteria. It can be used to measure the effectiveness of various treatments. Doctors and insurance companies often use the scale to evaluate a patient's potential for rehabilitation. The scale can be an effective tool for making, planning, and placement decisions. It generally can distinguish those patients who will be able to return to competitive employment from those who will be able to handle only supported work.

LEVELS OF COGNITIVE FUNCTIONING

Level I - No Response: Total Assistance

- Complete absence of observable change in behavior when presented visual, auditory, tactile, proprioceptive, vestibular or painful stimuli.

Level II - Generalized Response: Total Assistance

- Demonstrates generalized reflex response to painful stimuli.
- Responds to repeated auditory stimuli with increased or decreased activity.
- Responds to external stimuli with physiological changes generalized, gross body movement and/or not purposeful vocalization.
- Responses noted above may be same regardless of type and location of stimulation.
- Responses may be significantly delayed.

Level III - Localized Response: Total Assistance

- Demonstrates withdrawal or vocalization to painful stimuli.
- Turns toward or away from auditory stimuli.
- Blinks when strong light crosses visual field.
- Follows moving object passed within visual field.
- Responds to discomfort by pulling tubes or restraints.
- Responds inconsistently to simple commands.
- Responses directly related to type of stimulus.
- May respond to some persons (especially family and friends) but not to others.

TABLE 4.2
Rancho Los Amigos Cognitive Scale Revised (*Continued*)

Level IV - Confused/Agitated: Maximal Assistance

- Alert and in heightened state of activity.
- Purposeful attempts to remove restraints or tubes or crawl out of bed.
- May perform motor activities such as sitting, reaching and walking but without any apparent purpose or upon another's request.
- Very brief and usually non-purposeful moments of sustained alternatives and divided attention.
- Absent short-term memory.
- May cry out or scream out of proportion to stimulus even after its removal.
- May exhibit aggressive or flight behavior.
- Mood may swing from euphoric to hostile with no apparent relationship to environmental events.
- Unable to cooperate with treatment efforts.
- Verbalizations are frequently incoherent and/or inappropriate to activity or environment.

Level V - Confused, Inappropriate Non-Agitated: Maximal Assistance

- Alert, not agitated but may wander randomly or with a vague intention of going home.
- May become agitated in response to external stimulation, and/or lack of environmental structure.
- Not oriented to person, place or time.
- Frequent brief periods, non-purposeful sustained attention.
- Severely impaired recent memory, with confusion of past and present in reaction to ongoing activity.
- Absent goal directed, problem solving, self-monitoring behavior.
- Often demonstrates inappropriate use of objects without external direction.
- May be able to perform previously learned tasks when structured and cues provided.
- Unable to learn new information.
- Able to respond appropriately to simple commands fairly consistently with external structures and cues.
- Responses to simple commands without external structure are random and non-purposeful in relation to command.
- Able to converse on a social, automatic level for brief periods of time when provided external structure and cues.
- Verbalizations about present events become inappropriate and confabulatory when external structure and cues are not provided.

(Continued)

TABLE 4.2
Rancho Los Amigos Cognitive Scale Revised (*Continued*)

Level VI - Confused, Appropriate: Moderate Assistance

- Inconsistently oriented to person, time and place.
- Able to attend to highly familiar tasks in non-distracting environment for 30 minutes with moderate redirection.
- Remote memory has more depth and detail than recent memory.
- Vague recognition of some staff.
- Able to use assistive memory aide with maximum assistance.
- Emerging awareness of appropriate response to self, family and basic needs.
- Moderate assist to problem solve barriers to task completion.
- Supervised for old learning (e.g., self care).
- Shows carry over for relearned familiar tasks (e.g., self care).
- Maximum assistance for new learning with little or nor carry over.
- Unaware of impairments, disabilities and safety risks.
- Consistently follows simple directions.
- Verbal expressions are appropriate in highly familiar and structured situations.

Rancho Level VI is characterized by continuing confusion but the emergence of appropriate behavior. Persons often require frequent repetition. During this stage, the person is likely still in post-acute rehabilitation and the selection of cognitive support technologies and features should begin.

Level VII - Automatic, Appropriate Behavior: Minimal Assistance for Daily Living Skills

- Consistently oriented to person and place, within highly familiar environments. Moderate assistance for orientation to time.
- Able to attend to highly familiar tasks in a non-distraction environment for at least 30 minutes with minimal assist to complete tasks.
- Minimal supervision for new learning.
- Demonstrates carry over of new learning.
- Initiates and carries out steps to complete familiar personal and household routine but has shallow recall of what he/she has been doing.
- Able to monitor accuracy and completeness of each step in routine personal and household ADLs and modify plan with minimal assistance.
- Superficial awareness of his/her condition but unaware of specific impairments and disabilities and the limits they place on his/her ability to safely, accurately and completely carry out his/her household, community, work and leisure ADLs.
- Minimal supervision for safety in routine home and community activities.
- Unrealistic planning for the future.
- Unable to think about consequences of a decision or action.
- Overestimates abilities.
- Unaware of others' needs and feelings.
- Oppositional/uncooperative.
- Unable to recognize inappropriate social interaction behavior.

TABLE 4.2
Rancho Los Amigos Cognitive Scale Revised (*Continued*)

Most persons at this level are at home, and are returning to school and possibly work environments. Deficits in memory, information processing, fatigue, behavioral control, and social interactions may hamper performance in these settings, and may be perceived as intentional. Intervention at this level should involve persons involved at the school, community, or work environments. Family members should know that judgment may still be impaired and close supervision may be necessary. Because of the transitional nature of this level of recovery, support for families as well as the individual can be particularly helpful.

Level VIII - Purposeful, Appropriate: Stand-By Assistance

- Consistently oriented to person, place and time.
- Independently attends to and completes familiar tasks for 1 hour in distracting environments.
- Able to recall and integrate past and recent events.
- Uses assistive memory devices to recall daily schedule, "to do" lists and record critical information for later use with stand-by assistance.
- Initiates and carries out steps to complete familiar personal, household, community, work and leisure routines with stand-by assistance and can modify the plan when needed with minimal assistance.
- Requires no assistance once new tasks/activities are learned.
- Aware of and acknowledges impairments and disabilities when they interfere with task completion but requires stand-by assistance to take appropriate corrective action.
- Thinks about consequences of a decision or action with minimal assistance.
- Overestimates or underestimates abilities.
- Acknowledges others' needs and feelings and responds appropriately with minimal assistance.
- Depressed.
- Irritable.
- Low frustration tolerance/easily angered.
- Argumentative.
- Self-centered.
- Uncharacteristically dependent/independent.
- Able to recognize and acknowledge inappropriate social interaction behavior while it is occurring and takes corrective action with minimal assistance.

Level IX - Purposeful, Appropriate: Stand-By Assistance on Request

- Independently shifts back and forth between tasks and completes them accurately for at least two consecutive hours.
- Uses assistive memory devices to recall daily schedule, "to do" lists and record critical information for later use with assistance when requested.

(Continued)

TABLE 4.2

Rancho Los Amigos Cognitive Scale Revised (*Continued*)

- Initiates and carries out steps to complete familiar personal, household, work and leisure tasks independently and unfamiliar personal, household, work and leisure tasks with assistance when requested.
- Aware of and acknowledges impairments and disabilities when they interfere with task completion and takes appropriate corrective action but requires stand-by assist to anticipate a problem before it occurs and take action to avoid it.
- Able to think about consequences of decisions or actions with assistance when requested.
- Accurately estimates abilities but requires stand-by assistance to adjust to task demands.
- Acknowledges others' needs and feelings and responds appropriately with stand-by assistance.
- Depression may continue.
- May be easily irritable.
- May have low frustration tolerance.
- Able to self monitor appropriateness of social interaction with stand-by assistance.

Level X - Purposeful, Appropriate: Modified Independent

- Able to handle multiple tasks simultaneously in all environments but may require periodic breaks.
- Able to independently procure, create and maintain own assistive memory devices.
- Independently initiates and carries out steps to complete familiar and unfamiliar personal, household, community, work and leisure tasks but may require more than usual amount of time and/or compensatory strategies to complete them.
- Anticipates impact of impairments and disabilities on ability to complete daily living tasks and takes action to avoid problems before they occur but may require more than usual amount of time and/or compensatory strategies.
- Able to independently think about consequences of decisions or actions but may require more than usual amount of time and/or compensatory strategies to select the appropriate decision or action.
- Accurately estimates abilities and independently adjusts to task demands.
- Able to recognize the needs and feelings of others and automatically respond in appropriate manner.
- Periodic periods of depression may occur.
- Irritability and low frustration tolerance when sick, fatigued and/or under emotional stress.
- Social interaction behavior is consistently appropriate.

Original Rancho Los Amigos Cognitive Scale co-authored by Chris Hagen, Ph.D., Danese Malkmus, M.A., Patricia Durham, M.A., Rancho Los Amigos Hospital, 1972. Revised 11/15/74 by Danese Malkmus, M.A., and Kathryn Stenderup, O.T.R.

Source: Hagen, C. (1998). *The Rancho levels of cognitive functioning: The revised levels* (3rd ed.). Downey, CA: Rancho Los Amigos Medical Center.
Note. ADLs = activities of daily living.

Outcome measures used to determine the effectiveness of interventions and rehabilitation for brain impairment continue to focus heavily on changes over time in body functions and structures, and when quality of life is addressed, it is apt to be limited to health-related quality of life (e.g., Maas et al., 2010). A recent study reported, however, that health-related quality-of-life measures are predominantly measures of function, which results "in a bias against people with long-standing functional limitations not related to current health" (Hall, Krahn, Horner-Johnson, & Lamb, 2011, p. 98). The authors further note that self-reported health, health-related quality of life, quality of life, and function are different constructs requiring that researchers and clinicians "be mindful about what they intend to measure and select their scales accordingly" (p. 98).

As stated by B. A. Wilson (2006a,b), improved ways of evaluating rehabilitation are needed that relinquish the dependence on traditional outcome measures that frequently fail to apprehend the real needs of patients and families. In fact, some recent efforts have begun to expand the scope of focus (e.g., Wilde et al., 2010). It remains the case, however, that too little attention is given to

- the preferences and goals of individuals with brain injuries and their family members,
- a person's predisposition to benefit from some interventions over others,
- the match of expectations of benefit with realization of benefit from the chosen interventions, and
- social and environmental factors impacting benefit.

It is certainly true that the failure to accurately detect a brain impairment can lead to misdiagnosis and selection of an inappropriate or ineffective intervention. After diagnosis and initial treatment and stabilization, the challenge is to determine the most appropriate rehabilitation course for that unique individual and assist the individual to achieve full community participation. This is the case regardless if the person has dementia, a developmental cognitive disability, a psychiatric diagnosis, or ABI.

Neurobehavioral programs have historically focused on treatment of mood, behavior, and executive function while ensuring supervision and safety in a residential, nonhospital setting (e.g., Novack, Sherer, & Penna, 2010). Such programs focus on psychosocial outcomes with an emphasis on the application of behavioral principles and the development of functional skills. Neurobehavioral programs typically have treatment teams, use direct support personnel as needed, and are often led by neuropsychologists or behavior analysts.

True to a *biopsychosocial approach*, neurobehavioral rehabilitation begins with an understanding of the current cognitive, emotional/behavioral, and psychosocial functioning of the individual. The *biopsychosocial approach* or model was first articulated by George L. Engel (1977), a psychiatrist at the University of Rochester Medical Center in Rochester, New York.[9] He stated that treating body functions and structures, that is a pathophysiological view of illness and disability, is insufficient for understanding the patient's illness, and he put forth a systems perspective of treatment that considers the parts, the whole, and the dynamic interaction of biological, psychological (emotional/behavioral), and social factors impacting the individual. The biopsychosocial approach is used to guide patient treatment and medical education at the University of Rochester Medical Center, as well as many other programs around the world, and is the foundation for the WHO's (2001) *International Classification of Functioning, Disability, and Health (ICF)*.

The *ICF* is a component of the WHO's Family of International Classifications (WHO-FIC) designed to provide a common worldwide language of disease and disability (http://www.who.int/classifications/). WHO-FIC consists of the following:

- *International Classification of Diseases* (ICD), which, as the name implies, classifies diseases and other health problems
- *ICF*, which measures health and disability at both individual and population levels
- International Classification of Health Interventions (ICHI), which is a common tool for reporting and analyzing the distribution and evolution of health interventions

The way disability is defined and understood has changed significantly over the past few decades (Bickenbach, 2009; Cerniauskaite et al., 2011). Rather than viewing disability as a medical condition, the *ICF* emphasizes functional status over diagnosis. The *ICF* also calls for the elimination of distinctions, explicitly or implicitly, between health conditions that are "mental" and "physical." As stated by the United Nations (UN) Economic and Social Commission for Asia and the Pacific (ESCAP), Statistics Division:

> Similarly, the model of the ICF ignores etiology of health conditions since there is no *a priori* link between a health condition and disability as it is experienced. Research into the precise determinants of disability is of course of great importance, but unwarranted assumptions about what a person with a certain disease can or cannot do in life are detrimental to good science. (ESCAP, 2010, para. 45)

Additionally, the *ICF* applies to all people worldwide regardless of age, gender, ethnicity or race, and health condition. This universality means

TABLE 4.3
ICF Body Functions and Structures

DIMENSIONS OF FUNCTIONING	DIMENSIONS OF DISABILITY
Body Functions and Body Structures	Impairments
Activities	Activity limitations
Participation	Participation restrictions

Note. Notice that the term "disability" in the ICF refers to **all three** dimensions taken together. ICF = *International Classification of Functioning, Disability, and Health.*
Source: United Nations Economic and Social Commission for Asia and the Pacific (ESCAP), Statistics Division. (2008). *Training manual on disability statistics*. Retrieved from http://www.unescap.org/stat/disability/manual/Chapter2-Disability-Statistics.asp

health is a continuum within dimensions of functioning, and each person has a particular pattern of functioning. Thus, disability viewed from this viewpoint is universal.

Yet, the need to address the individual's unique and individualized pattern of functioning is well recognized.

People with the same impairments experience different kinds and degrees of incapacity and vastly different restrictions on what actually happens in their lives. Impairments are not proxies for disability; they give only one particular perspective on disability. *Disability* is the complete lived experience of nonfatal health outcomes, not merely body level decrements in functioning.

> The converse is also true: people can experience the same restrictions in what they can do in their day-to-day lives even though they have different impairments. At the level of actual performance, the contrast is even greater. Impairments as diverse as missing limbs and anxiety can both attract stigma and discrimination that may limit a person's participation in work . . . . (ESCAP, 2010, para. 21)

The *ICF* classification has been found to be effective for describing the characteristics and severity of cognitive disability and addressing the impact of treatment on functioning and participation over time (e.g., Arthanat, Nochajski, & Stone, 2004; Svestkova, Angerova, Sladkova, Bickenbach, & Raggi, 2010). The *ICF* framework conceptualizes disability, not solely as a problem that resides in the individual, but as a health experience that occurs in a context. Thus, the *ICF* framework has two major parts, each having two components:

1. Functioning and disability
   a. Body functions and structures
   b. Activities and participation that exist within

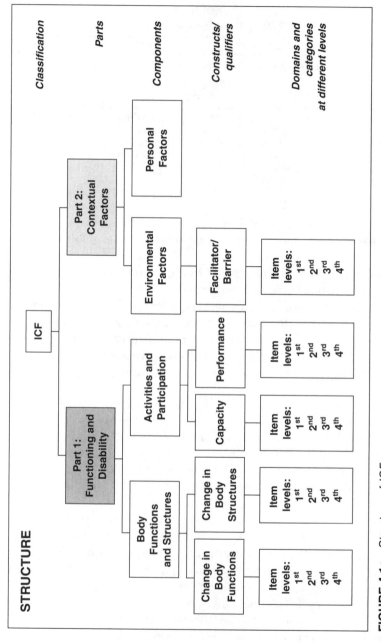

FIGURE 4.1a   Structure of *ICF*
Source: World Health Organization, 2001, p. 215

Body	
FUNCTION:	STRUCTURE:

Mental Functions
Sensory Functions and Pain
Voice and Speech Functions
Functions of the Cardiovascular,
  Haematological, Immunological and
  Respiratory Systems
Functions of the Digestive, Metabolic,
  and Endocrine Systems
Genitourinary and Reproductive
  Functions
Neuromusculoskeletal and Movement-
  Related Functions
Functions of the Skin and Related
  Structures
	Structure of the Nervous System
	The Eye, Ear and Related Structures
	Structures Involved in Voice and
	  Speech
	Structure of the Cardiovascular, Immu-
	  nological and Respiratory Systems
	Structures Related to the Digestive,
	  Metabolic and Endocrine Systems
	Structure Related to Genitourinary and
	  Reproductive Systems
	Structure Related to Movement
	Skin and Related Structures

Activities and Participation	
Learning and Applying Knowledge General Tasks and Demands Communication Mobility Self-Care Domestic Life Interpersonal Interactions and Relationships Major Life Areas Community, Social and Civic Life	
Environmental Factors	
Products and Technology Natural Environment and Human-Made Changes to Environment Support and Relationships Attitudes Services, Systems and Policies	

FIGURE 4.1b Complete list of chapters in the *International Classification of Functioning, Disability, and Health.*
Source: WHO, 2001

2. Contextual factors
   a. Environmental factors
   b. Personal factors

Further delineations include domains, which are classified from body, individual, and societal perspectives. Figure 4.1 provides a diagram of the *ICF* framework and hierarchy.

Body Functions are the physiological functions of body systems, including psychological functions. *Body* refers to the human organism as a whole, and thus, includes the brain. Hence, mental (or psychological) functions are subsumed under body functions. *Body Structures*, on the other hand, are the structural or anatomical parts of the body such as organs, limbs, and their components. In our case, we are primarily interested in *ICF*'s Body Structure Chapter 1, "Structures of the Nervous System," s110 Structure of the Brain, which is organized as shown in the chart that follows. They consist of such elements as consciousness, orientation to time, place and person (see Table 4.2).

Body Structures (s)

Chapter 1 Structures of the Nervous System (s1)
- s110 Structure of brain
  - s1100 Structure of cortical lobes (frontal, temporal, parietal, occipital)
  - s1101 Structure of midbrain
  - s1102 Structure of diencephalon (thalamus and hypothalamus)
  - s1103 Basal ganglia and related structures
  - s1104 Structure of cerebellum
  - s1105 Structure of brain stem (medulla oblongata, pons)
  - s1106 Structure of cranial nerves
  - s1108 Structure of brain, other specified
  - s1109 Structure of brain, unspecified
- s120 Spinal cord and related structures
- s130 Structure of meninges
- s140 Structure of sympathetic nervous system
- s150 Structure of parasympathetic nervous system
- s198 Structure of the nervous system, other specified
- s199 Structure of the nervous system, unspecified

Chapter 2 The Eye, Ear, and Related Structures (s2)
Chapter 3 Structures Involved in Voice and Speech (s3)
Chapter 4 Structures of the Cardiovascular, Immunological, and Respiratory Systems (s4)
Chapter 5 Structures Related to the Digestive, Metabolic, and Endocrine Systems (s5)
Chapter 6 Structures Related to the Genitourinary and Reproductive Systems (s6)
Chapter 7 Structures Related to Movement (s7)
Chapter 8 Skin and Related Structures (s8)

Because the emphasis in this book is on thinking, remembering, and learning, that places our primary interest on functioning and its enhancement. Thus, we will focus primarily on body functions rather than structure, which are divided into eight chapters or domains as follows:

Body Functions (b)

Chapter 1 Mental Functions (b1)
Chapter 2 Sensory Functions and Pain (b2)
Chapter 3 Voice and Speech Functions (b3)
Chapter 4 Functions of the Cardiovascular, Haematological, Immunological, and Respiratory Systems (b4)
Chapter 5 Functions of the Digestive, Metabolic, and Endocrine Systems (b5)
Chapter 6 Genitourinary and Reproductive Functions (b6)
Chapter 7 Neuromusculoskeletal and Movement-Related Functions (b7)
Chapter 8 Functions of the Skin and Related Structures (b8)

In *ICF*'s Body Functions, Chapter 1, "Mental Functions," is further subdivided into *Global Mental Functions* (8 categories) and *Specific Mental Functions* (14 categories). The *ICF* consists of 30 chapter codes (excluding Personal Factors) and, at more detailed levels, the number of codes can reach 1,424 items. This degree of complexity has led research groups to develop *core sets* of *ICF* codes for specific health conditions and disabilities. An *ICF* core set typically includes the least number of domains to be practical, but as many as required to sufficiently characterize a specific condition.

The *ICF* focuses on analyzing the relationship between capacity (what the person *can* do) and performance (what the person *does* do). If capacity is greater than performance, then that gap should be addressed by both removing barriers and identifying facilitators. The WHO sees disability as existing within a context, as being dynamic over time, and in relation to circumstances. A *disability* is the outcome of the interaction between the individual and his or her personal, community, institutional, and social environments.

To better understand the *ICF* hierarchy, think of an evergreen forest consisting of many trees. In the *ICF*, the universe of health and disability is what is being classified (this is the entire forest). Within this forest, we classify the dimensions of impairments, say Activities and Participation (the trees). In the Activities and Participation dimension, we have several chapters or domains ranging from simple to complex activities—from sensing and recognizing to interpersonal behaviors (the trunks). For example, the chapter on Interpersonal Interactions and Relationships includes activities such as general interactive skills (the branch) and included in that broad category are behaviors such as initiating social contact, responding to cues, and so on (the evergreen needles). So that one "sees the forest for the trees," the *ICF* framework is to be viewed as providing both a detailed description of an individual and a holistic view of that person.

With the biopsychosocial approach and the *ICF* framework as a foundation, the totality of cognitive, emotional/behavioral, and psychosocial functioning of the individual is considered when planning interventions. Testing and measurement are imperative to obtaining this understanding. We have mentioned laboratory tests, imaging, and neuropsychological assessment and testing earlier. An important aspect of neuropsychological testing is not only cognitive but also emotional/behavioral and social assessment. One might wonder if the WHO has developed its own measure of functioning and disability based on its *ICF* framework. In fact, there is the *ICF* checklist; however, in a study of 55 patients with TBI, it was found to be inadequate (Koskinen, Hokkinen, Sarajuuri, & Alaranta, 2007). There is a need, therefore, for a measure specific to individuals with cognitive and neurobehavioral disability and the limitations or restrictions they face. As an illustration of the need to delineate characteristics of specific forms of cognitive disability, Table 4.4 presents an *ICF* core set addressed to older adults with dementia and Table 4.5 (Scherer et al., 2010) presents measures appropriate for a comprehensive biopsychosocial assessment of relevant domains considering the relevant *ICF* components.

Cognitive Rehabilitation Needs

Cognitive rehabilitation, which focuses on individuals with brain injuries, consists of function-oriented approaches and interventions that are practiced by professionals who represent diverse areas of specialty, including neuropsychology, rehabilitation psychology, psychiatry, occupational therapy, speech–language pathology, social work, and vocational rehabilitation counseling. The organizing principle of cognitive rehabilitation is to help the person relearn lost abilities and develop specific strategies to compensate for injury-related limitations and restrictions. It has been shown that comprehensive rehabilitation that integrates interventions for cognitive, interpersonal, and functional skills yields greater improvements in self-regulation of cognitive and emotional processes, community integration, employment, and quality of life compared with standard discipline-specific neurorehabilitation treatment (Hart, 2010; High, Sander, Struchen, & Hart, 2005), and it has been shown to be effective (Altman, Swick, Parrot, & Malec, 2010; Cicerone et al., 2000; Cicerone et al., 2005; Cicerone et al., 2011; Cicerone, Mott, Azulay, & Friel, 2004; H. Kim & Colantonio, 2010; Tsaousides & Gordon, 2009). The goal of cognitive rehabilitation is to increase the individual's functioning, adaptation, and quality of life by reinforcing, strengthening, or reestablishing previous learned patterns of behavior and establishing new patterns through compensatory mechanisms.

The frontal and temporal lobes of the brain are often damaged in TBI. As discussed in Chapter 3, these areas of the brain control intellectual abilities,

TABLE 4.4
ICF Core Set for Dementia

ICF CODE	CATEGORY DESCRIPTION
	BODY FUNCTIONS
	Chapter 1: Mental Functions
b110	Consciousness functions
b114	Orientation functions
b117	Intellectual functions
b130	Energy and drive functions
b140	Attention functions
b144	Memory functions
b147	Psychomotor functions
b152	Emotional functions
b156	Perceptual functions
b160	Thought functions
b164	Higher-level cognitive functions
b167	Mental functions of language
b172	Calculation functions
b176	Mental function of sequencing complex movements
b180	Experience of self and time functions
	Chapter 2: Sensory Functions and Pain
b210	Seeing functions
b215	Functions of structures adjoining the eye
b230	Hearing functions
b235	Vestibular functions
b240	Sensations associated with hearing and vestibular function
b260	Proprioceptive function
b265	Touch function
	Chapter 3: Voice and Speech Functions
b320	Articulation functions
b330	Fluency and rhythm of speech functions
	Chapter 4: Functions of Cardiovascular, Haematological, Immunological, and Respiratory Systems
b410	Heart functions
b415	Blood vessel functions
b420	Blood pressure functions
b430	Haematological system functions
b435	Immunological system functions
b440	Respiration functions

(Continued)

TABLE 4.4
***ICF* Core Set for Dementia (*Continued*)**

ICF CODE	CATEGORY DESCRIPTION
	Chapter 5: Functions of Digestive, Metabolic and Endocrine Systems
b525	Defecation functions
b540	General metabolic functions
b545	Water, mineral and electrolyte balance functions
b555	Endocrine gland functions
	Chapter 6: Genitourinary and Reproductive Functions
b620	Urination functions
	Chapter 7: Neuromusculoskeletal and Movement-Related Functions
b735	Muscle tone functions
b740	Muscle endurance functions
b750	Motor reflex functions
b755	Involuntary movement reaction functions
b760	Control of voluntary movement functions
b765	Involuntary movement functions
b770	Gait pattern functions
b780	Sensations related to muscles and movement functions
	BODY STRUCTURES
	Chapter 1: Structures of the Nervous System
s110	Structure of brain
	Chapter 4: Structures of the Cardiovascular, Immunological and Respiratory Systems
s410	Structure of cardiovascular system
	ACTIVITIES AND PARTICIPATION
	Chapter 1: Learning and Applying Knowledge
d130	Copying
d135	Rehearsing
d160	Focusing attention
d163	Thinking
d166	Reading
d170	Writing
d172	Calculating
d175	Solving problems
d177	Making decisions
	Chapter 2: General Tasks and Demands
d210	Undertaking a single task
d220	Undertaking multiple task
d230	Carrying out daily routine

TABLE 4.4
ICF Core Set for Dementia (Continued)

ICF CODE	CATEGORY DESCRIPTION
	Chapter 3: Communication
d310	Communicating with – receiving – spoken messages
d315	Communicating with – receiving – nonverbal messages
d325	Communicating with – receiving – written messages
d330	Speaking
d335	Producing nonverbal messages
d345	Writing message
d350	Conversation
d360	Using communication devices and techniques
	Chapter 4: Mobility
d410	Changing basic body position
d415	Maintaining a body position
d440	Fine hand use (picking up, grasping)
d450	Walking
d460	Moving around in different locations
d475	Driving
	Chapter 5: Self-Care
d510	Washing oneself
d520	Caring for body parts
d530	Toileting
d540	Dressing
d550	Eating
d560	Drinking
	Chapter 6: Domestic Life
d620	Acquisition of goods and services
d630	Preparing meals
d640	Doing housework
d650	Caring for household objects
d660	Assisting others
	Chapter 7: Interpersonal Interactions and Relationships
d710	Basic interpersonal interactions
d720	Complex interpersonal interactions
d750	Informal social relationships
d760	Family relationships
d770	Intimate relationships

(Continued)

TABLE 4.4
ICF Core Set for Dementia *(Continued)*

ICF CODE	CATEGORY DESCRIPTION
	Chapter 9: Community, Social and Civic Life
d910	Community life
d920	Recreation and leisure
	ENVIRONMENTAL FACTORS
	Chapter 1: Products and Technology
e110	Products or substances for personal consumption
e115	Products and technology for personal use in daily living
e120	Products and technology for personal indoor and outdoor mobility and transportation
e125	Products and technology for communication
e165	Assets
	Chapter 2: Natural Environment and Human Made Changes to Environment
e225	Climate
e240	Light
e245	Time-related changes
	Chapter 3: Support and Relationships
e310	Immediate family
e315	Extended family
e320	Friends
e325	Acquaintances, peers, colleagues, neighbours and community members
e330	People in positions of authority
e340	Personal care providers and personal assistants
e355	Health professionals
	Chapter 4: Attitudes
e410	Individual attitudes of immediate family members
e420	Individual attitudes of friends
e425	Individual attitudes of acquaintances, peers, colleagues, neighbours and community members
e440	Individual attitudes of personal care providers and personal assistants
e450	Individual attitudes of health professionals
e460	Societal attitudes

Note. Categories selected and the chapter of the *ICF* to which a category belongs. *ICF* = *International Classification of Functioning, Disability and Health.*
Source: Scherer, M. J., Federici, S., Tiberio, L., Pigliautile, M., Corradi, F., & Meloni, F. (2010). ICF core set for matching older adults with dementia and technology. *Ageing International.* doi: 10.1007/s12126-010-9093-9

TABLE 4.5
Geriatric Assessment and *ICF* Codes

GERIATRIC ASSESSMENT		Examples of tests and assessment techniques	ICF CODE
Mental health	Neuropsychological as-sessment	Cognitive function		
		Orientation and Attention		
		Digit Span*	b140, d135, d160
		Trial making test A and B (TMT)*	b140, d160
		Stroop tests*	b140, d160, d220
		Corsi's Block-tapping test*	b140, d135, d160
		Perception		
		Letter cancellation tests and variants*	b140, b156, d160, d210
		Memory		
		Benton Visual Retention Test (BVRT)*	b144
		Auditory Verbal Learning Test (AVLT)*	b144
		Babcock Story Recall Test (BSRT)*	b144, d325, d330
		Complex Figure Test (CFT): Recall administration*	b144
		Verbal Functions and Language		
		Controlled Oral Word Association (COWA - sometimes labelled FAS)*	b167, d210

(Continued)

TABLE 4.5
Geriatric Assessment and *ICF* Codes (*Continued*)

GERIATRIC ASSESSMENT		*ICF* CODE
	Boston Naming Test (BNT)*	b167
	Category fluency*	b167, d210
	Token Test*	b167, d310
	Boston Diagnostic Aphasia Examination (BDAE)*	b167, d130, d166, d310, d315, d330, d345, d355
Construction	Coping Drawings*	d176, d130, d440
	Complex Figure Test (CFT): copy administration*	d164, b176, d130, d440
	Clock face*	b176, d130, d440
Concept formation and Reasoning	Raven's Coloured Progressive Matrices; RCPM)*	b164, d163
	Proverbs and Similarities*	b164, d163, d310
	Wisconsin Card Sorting Test (WCST)*	b164, d220
Executive Functions and Motor Performance	Tower of London*	b164, d163, d175, d220, d440
	Frontal Assessment Battery (FAB)*	b164, d163, d220
	Examining for apraxia*	b176, d130, d440

Functional status	*Observational Methods, Rating Scale, and Inventories*	Mini-Mental State Examination (MMSE)*	b114, b117, b140, b144, b167, b172, b176, d130, d135, d160, d166, d170, d172, d310, d345, d440

Functional status	*Observational Methods, Rating Scale, and Inventories*	Mini-Mental State Examination (MMSE)*	b114, b117, b140, b144, b167, b172, b176, d130, d135, d160, d166, d170, d172, d310, d345, d440
		Addenbrooke's Cognitive Examination Revised (ACE-R) – (Mioshi et al., 2006)	b114, b117, b140, b144, b156, b167, b172, b176, d130, d135, d160, d166, d170, d172, d310, d345
		Neuropsychiatric Inventory (NPI)*	b110, b130, b147, b152, d710, d720, d750
		Clinical Dementia Rating Scale (CDR)*	d130, d163, d175, d177, d210, d220, d230, d510, d520, d530, d540, d550, d560, d620, d630, d640, d710, d720, d750, d910, e165, b114, b117, b144, b164, b167, b176, b620
	Tests of Personal Adjustment and Emotional Functioning	Geriatric Depression Scale (GDS)*	b152
Functional assessment		Activity of Daily Living (ADL)- (Katz et al., 1963)	b176, b525, b620, d410, d440, d450, d460, d510, d520, d530, d540, d550, d560

(Continued)

TABLE 4.5
Geriatric Assessment and *ICF* Codes (Continued)

GERIATRIC ASSESSMENT		ICF CODE
Physical health, social and economical conditions	Instrumental Activity of Daily Living (IADL) – (Lawton et al., 1969)	b176, d177, d230, d360, d440, d450, d460, d475, d620, d630, d640, e110, e115, e120, e125, e165
Caregiver Stress Assessment	Caregiver Burden Inventory - (Novak & Guest, 1989)	e410, e440
Clinical assessment	Brief Symptom Inventory*	e140
		b160, b320, b330, b410, b415, b420, b440, d330, d355, d360, d475, d650, d660, d710, d720, d760, d770, d910, d920, e110, e115, e120, e125, e165, e225, e240, e245, e310, e315, e320, e325, e330, e340, e355, e410, e420, e425, e440, e450, e460
	Hachinski Scale (Hachinski et al., 1975)	b152, b210, b215, b235, b240, b410, b415, b420
	Tinetti Balance Scale (Tinetti, 1986)	b415, b450, b460, b740, b770
Anamnestic analysis		b117, b152, b180, b210, b215, b230, b235, b240, b260, b265

Neurological assessment	b110, b114, b130, b147, b152, b176, b180, b210, b235, b240, b260, b265, b320, b330, b735, b740, b750, b755, b760, b765, b770, b780, d130, d410, d415, d450, d460, d710, d720, e115, e120
Clinical exams	b415, b430, b435, b540, b545, b555, s410
Neuroimaging technique	s110

Note. The geriatric assessment procedure is a multidimensional assessment that explores five categories: mental health, functional status, physical health, social and economical conditions (first column). These categories are evaluated by the means of neuropsychological assessment, functional assessment, caregiver stress assessment, clinical assessment, anamnestic analysis, neurological assessment, clinical exams and neuroimaging technique (second column). The cognitive functions explored in the neuropsychological assessment are reported in the third column. Clinicians use different types of tests and assessment techniques and some of them are reported in the fourth column. The last column lists the *ICF* categories relevant to dementia and which have involved a geriatric assessment tool (clinical interview, neurological examination, test, and rating scales). The resulting *ICF* core set for dementia includes a total of 110 second-level categories. *ICF = International Classification of Functioning, Disability and Health.*

Source: Scherer, M. J., Federici, S., Tiberio, L., Pigliautile, M., Corradi, F., & Meloni, F. (2010). ICF core set for matching older adults with dementia and technology. *Ageing International.* doi: 10.1007/s12126-010-9093-9

*Lezak, M. D., Howieson, D. B., Loring, D. W., Hannay, H. J., & Fischer, J. S. (2004). *Neuropsychological assessment* (4th ed.). New York: Oxford University Press.

executive functions, personality, behavior, and emotion. Individuals with other forms of brain impairment may experience similar challenges.

Problems with memory, conceptualizing, planning and sequencing thoughts and actions, lack of concentration, increased anxiety and irritability, difficulty interpreting subtle social cues, and understanding numbers and symbols are common, as are visual, auditory and/or vestibular deficits, balance problems, and loss of coordination. Thus, cognitive rehabilitation addresses memory retraining and problem solving as well as enhanced self-awareness; compensation and coping; social skills; emotional self-regulation; participation in social, work, and leisure activities; health maintenance; and personal care. Personal assistance and support from technologies, as well as environmental restructuring and the use of cognitive and behavioral strategies, are all important resources.

Figure 4.2a depicts the *ICF*'s hierarchy within Body Functions, Chapter 1, "Mental Functions," Global Mental Functions. Figure 4.2b depicts the hierarchy within *ICF*'s Body Functions, Chapter 1, "Mental Functions," Specific Mental Functions. Table 4.6 lists the Specific Mental Function with examples of difficulties experienced by Marjorie, Theresa, and Delmar and examples of strategies found to be useful for the various types of cognitive deficits listed. As an exercise for the reader, fill in the relevant cells with the characteristics of Ryan along with ideas for useful strategies to support his needs and goals.

An important aspect of cognitive rehabilitation is returning the individual to a life of quality, ideally in the community and with family. Other discharge destinations include a supported apartment, group home, or adult foster care, and/or with enrollment in a comprehensive day treatment program or outpatient services.

Behavior/Emotional Symptoms

Emotional Functions are one of the 14 categories of Specific Mental Functions in the *ICF* framework. Emotional Functions (b152) relate to the feeling and affective components of the processes of the mind and include functions of appropriateness of emotion; regulation, and range of emotion; affect; sadness, happiness, love, fear, anger, hate, tension, anxiety, joy, sorrow; lability of emotion; and flattening of affect. Excluded are temperament and personality functions (b126) and energy and drive functions (b130) because they are part of Global Mental Functions.

Depending on diagnostic criteria, *International Classification of Diseases, Ninth Revision* (*ICD–9*) versus the American Psychiatric Association's *Diagnostic and Statistical Manual of Mental Disorders, Text Revision of the Fourth Edition* or *DSM-IV-TR*, the following behavioral or personality changes, which correlate both with aspects of emotional functions and global mental functions in the *ICF*, may be considered part of

Figure 4.2a. *ICF* Hierarchy Within Body Functions, Chapter 1, "Mental Functions," Global Mental Functions. *(Continued)*
Source: World Health Organization, 2001.

International Classification of Functioning, Disability and Health

b BODY FUNCTIONS

CHAPTER 1 (b1)	CHAPTER 2 (b2)	CHAPTER 3 (b3)	CHAPTER 4 (b4)	CHAPTER 5 (b5)	CHAPTER 6 (b6)	CHAPTER 7 (b7)	CHAPTER 8 (b8)
MENTAL FUNCTIONS	SENSORY FUNCTIONS AND PAIN	VOICE AND SPEECH FUNCTIONS	FUNCTIONS OF THE CARDIO-VASCULAR, HAEMATOLOGI-CAL, IMMUNO-LOGICAL AND RESPIRATORY SYSTEMS	FUNCTIONS OF THE DIGES-TIVE, META-BOLIC AND ENDOCRINE SYSTEMS	GENITO-URINARY AND REPRODUCTIVE FUNCTIONS	NEURO-MUSCULO-SKELETAL AND MOVEMENT-RELATED FUNCTIONS	FUNCTIONS OF THE SKIN AND RELATED STRUCTURES

b110–b139	b140–b189
global mental functions	specific mental functions

b110	b114	b117	b122	b126	b130	b134	b139
Consciousness functions	Orientation functions	Intellectual functions	Global psycho-social functions	Temperament and personality functions	Energy and drive functions	Sleep functions	Global mental functions, other specified and unspecified
General mental functions of the state of awareness and alertness, including the clarity and continuity of the wakeful state.	General mental functions of knowing and ascertaining one's relation to self, to others, to time and to one's surroundings.	General mental functions, required to understand and constructively integrate the various mental functions, including all cognitive functions and their development over the life span.	General mental functions, as they develop over the life span, required to understand and constructively integrate the mental functions that lead to the formation of the interpersonal skills needed to establish reciprocal social interactions, in terms of both meaning and purpose.	General mental functions of constitutional disposition of the individual to react in a particular way to situations, including the set of mental characteristics that makes the individual distinct from others.	General mental functions of physiological and psychological mechanisms that cause the individual to move towards satisfying specific needs and general goals in a persistent manner.	General mental functions of periodic, reversible and selective physical and mental disengagement from one's immediate environment accompanied by characteristic physiological changes.	

Figure 4.2a. *Continued*

International Classification of Functioning, Disability and Health

b Body Functions

CHAPTER 1 (b1)	CHAPTER 2 (b2)	CHAPTER 3 (b3)	CHAPTER 4 (b4)	CHAPTER 5 (b5)	CHAPTER 6 (b6)	CHAPTER 7 (b7)	CHAPTER 8 (b8)
MENTAL FUNCTIONS	SENSORY FUNCTIONS AND PAIN	VOICE AND SPEECH FUNCTIONS	FUNCTIONS OF THE CARDIOVASCULAR, HAEMATOLOGICAL, IMMUNOLOGICAL AND RESPIRATORY SYSTEMS	FUNCTIONS OF THE DIGESTIVE, METABOLIC AND ENDOCRINE SYSTEMS	GENITO-URINARY AND REPRODUCTIVE FUNCTIONS	NEUROMUSCULOSKELETAL AND MOVEMENT-RELATED FUNCTIONS	FUNCTIONS OF THE SKIN AND RELATED STRUCTURES

b110–b139	b140–b189
global mental functions	specific mental functions

b140	b144	b147	b152	b156	b160
Attention functions	Memory functions	Psychomotor functions	Emotional functions	Perceptual functions	Thought functions
Specific mental functions of focusing on an external stimulus or internal experience for the required period of time.	Specific mental functions of registering and storing information and retrieving it as needed.	Specific mental functions of control over both motor and psychological events at the body level.	Specific mental functions related to the feeling and affective components of the processes of the mind.	Specific mental functions of recognizing and interpreting sensory stimuli.	Specific mental functions related to the ideational component of the mind.

Figure 4.2b. *ICF* Hierarchy of Body Functions, Chapter 1, "Mental Functions," Specific Mental Functions. *(Continued)*
Source: World Health Organization, 2001

b164	b167	b172	b176	b180	b189
Higher-level cognitive functions	Mental functions of language	Calculation functions	Mental function of sequencing complex movements	Experience of self and time functions	Specific mental functions, other specified and unspecified
Specific mental functions especially dependent on the frontal lobes of the brain, including complex goal-directed behaviors such as decision-making, abstract thinking, planning and carrying out plans, mental flexibility, and deciding which behaviors are appropriate under what circumstances; often called executive functions.	Specific mental functions of recognizing and using signs, symbols and other components of a language.	Specific mental functions of determination, approximation and manipulation of mathematical symbols and processes.	Specific mental functions of sequencing and coordinating complex, purposeful movements.	Specific mental functions related to the awareness of one's identity, one's body, one's position in the reality of one's environment and of time.	

b164 Higher-level cognitive functions

Inclusions

Functions of abstraction and organization of ideas; time management, insight and judgment; concept formation, categorization and cognitive flexibility

Exclusions

Memory functions (b144); thought functions (b160); mental functions of language (b167); calculation functions (b172)

b1640	b1641	b1642	b1643	b1644
Abstraction	Organization and planning	Time management	Cognitive flexibility	Insight
Mental functions of creating general ideas, qualities or characteristics out of, and distinct from, concrete realities, specific objects or actual instances.	Mental functions of coordinating parts into a whole, of systematizing; the mental function involved in developing a method of proceeding or acting.	Mental functions of ordering events in chronological sequence, allocating amounts of time to events and activities.	Mental functions of changing strategies, or shifting mental sets, especially as involved in problem-solving.	Mental functions of awareness and understanding of oneself and one's behavior.

Figure 4.2b.   *Continued*

b1645	b1646	b1648	b1649
Judgment	Problem-solving	Higher-level cognitive functions, other specified	Higher-level cognitive functions, unspecified
Mental functions involved in discriminating between and evaluating different options, such as those involved in forming an opinion.	Mental functions of identifying, analyzing and integrating incongruent or conflicting information into a solution.		

Figure 4.2b. *Continued*

TABLE 4.6

ICF Body Functions and Structures Domains and Categories With Examples of Behaviors and Strategies

ICF BODY FUNCTIONS AND STRUCTURES DOMAINS	CATEGORIES	EXAMPLES OF BEHAVIORAL OBSERVATIONS	MAY HAVE DIFFICULTY DOING	THERESA (INTELLECTUAL DISABILITY)	DELMAR (TBI)[A]	MARJORIE (DEMENTIA)	EXAMPLES OF USEFUL STRATEGIES
Chapter 1: Mental functions—Specific	**Attention (b140)** Specific mental functions of focusing on an external stimulus or internal experience for the required period of time.	Will not focus or concentrate, distractible, cannot easily shift attention, or continually shifts attention	Organizing step-by-step, performing a task to completion	No significant problems	*Could stay on track in a conversation but with difficulty processing*	Could not focus and concentrate to read or participate in a give-and-take conversation	Cueing, use of color and imagery, sound signals, step-by-step order of presentation, eliminate distractions and extraneous stimuli; lights, and sounds
	Memory (b144) Specific mental functions of registering and storing information and retrieving it as needed.	Misses appointments, cannot locate items	Remembering things presented visually (right hemisphere injury) or verbally (left hemisphere injury)	Has learned strategies for remembering appointments, key dates, etc.	*Many memory gaps*	Short-term memory loss and memory retrieval that she would try to conceal	Advanced organizers, rehearsal and practice, pair visual with auditory, provide context familiarity, cueing, post highly visible notes, provide scripts that describe steps for what needs to be done, send e-mail reminders to oneself

(Continued)

TABLE 4.6

ICF Body Functions and Structures Domains and Categories With Examples of Behaviors and Strategies *(Continued)*

ICF BODY FUNCTIONS AND STRUCTURES DOMAINS	CATEGORIES	EXAMPLES OF BEHAVIORAL OBSERVATIONS	MAY HAVE DIFFICULTY DOING	THERESA (INTELLECTUAL DISABILITY)	DELMAR (TBI)^	MARJORIE (DEMENTIA)	EXAMPLES OF USEFUL STRATEGIES
	Psychomotor (b147) Specific mental functions of control over both motor and psychological events at the body level.	Agitation and restlessness, poor eye and hand coordination, slow speech, frequent and/or inappropriate gestures such as hand-wringing	Participating in social situations and conversations.	Nothing significant	*Delayed reactions, fatigue*	End of life dyskinesia	Behavioral techniques to extinguish undesirable actions, operant conditioning to shape desired actions, habit reversal (awareness training—use of mirrors: self-monitoring, relaxation, response training)
	Emotional (b152) Specific mental functions related to the feeling and affective components of the processes of the mind.	Mood swings, temper outbursts, anxiety attacks, has "meltdowns"	Socially expected and appropriate behaviors, has "meltdowns"	Socially acceptable and appropriate	*Flat affect, frustration, anger*	Flattened affect, irritability	Identify triggers and then control their occurrence, maintain calm demeanor and focus on the present and the individual, avoid spontaneous social interactions.

Perceptual (b156) Specific mental functions of recognizing and interpreting sensory stimuli.	Inability to discriminate sounds, colors, shapes, smells, tastes, textures	Enjoying foods and achieving an adequate dietary intake, operating devices and machinery	No known difficulties	Not mentioned	Poor gustatory perception and taste discrimination	Experiment with spices to amplify taste, use of bright colors, pairing sounds with other stimuli
Thought (b160) Specific mental functions related to the ideational component of the mind.	Incoherent thoughts and delusions, illogical thinking	A sequence of tasks that require logic and planning, following through with a plan.	No known difficulties	*Processing all the questions very slowly; can make custom gun grips and stocks*	Rumination and ideational perseveration (not letting go of a thought), processing speed slowed	Interrupt inappropriate thoughts, cognitive behavioral therapy, provide a "bin" of the needed ingredients with step-by-step instructions.

(Continued)

TABLE 4.6

ICF Body Functions and Structures Domains and Categories With Examples of Behaviors and Strategies (Continued)

ICF BODY FUNCTIONS AND STRUCTURES DOMAINS	CATEGORIES	EXAMPLES OF BEHAVIORAL OBSERVATIONS	MAY HAVE DIFFICULTY DOING	THERESA (INTELLECTUAL DISABILITY)	DELMAR (TBI)[A]	MARJORIE (DEMENTIA)	EXAMPLES OF USEFUL STRATEGIES
	Higher-level cognitive functions (b164) Specific mental functions especially dependent on the frontal lobes of the brain, including complex goal-directed behaviors such as decision-making, abstract thinking, planning and carrying out plans, mental flexibility, and deciding which behaviors are appropriate under what circumstances; often called executive functions.	Poor decision-making, stubbornness and fixation on an idea, poor insight into one's behavior, difficulty with novel situations, slow processing speed, rigid thinking, concrete interpretation, perfectionism, focus on the wrong details, difficulty with "if . . . then" thinking, overloaded easily	Time management, insight and judgment, cognitive flexibility, conceptual and abstract thinking	Ability to abstract limited, as is cognitive flexibility, needs supports for problem-solving	*Processing all the questions very slowly; had the self-awareness to self-report that no matter what he still gets very frustrated and agitated and tends to take it out on his family.*	Ability to abstract limited, little cognitive flexibility or insight into herself and her behavior, little problem-solving ability	Organize the work space, eliminate distractions, create a schedule, break long assignments into chunks and assign short time frames for completing each chunk, use visual organizational aids, pace the presentation of new information, provide written summaries, provide models of completed tasks, use checklists

Language (b167) Specific mental functions of recognizing and using signs, symbols and other components of a language.	Expression and word finding, comprehension of written or spoken language, repetitive or perseverative in conversations, gives odd verbal responses	Producing meaning messages and communications, correctly interpreting what others are saying	Few difficulties when concrete	Apparently no difficulties except with *speed of processing and memory gaps.*	Produced meaningful messages and communications, correctly interpreted what others were saying	Ask specific and clear questions, allow time Present information in chunks and slowly, use short sentences, use large text and simple formats, use repetition, pair visual with auditory, provide a reader
Calculation (b172) Specific mental functions of determination, approximation and manipulation of mathematical symbols and processes.	Overdraws checking account, difficulty at checkout and counting money	Correct payment of bills, managing a checking account		Not discussed	Stopped payment of bills, could no longer write checks and manage her checking account	Portable calculators, presorted coins and bills.

(Continued)

TABLE 4.6
ICF Body Functions and Structures Domains and Categories With Examples of Behaviors and Strategies *(Continued)*

ICF BODY FUNCTIONS AND STRUCTURES DOMAINS	CATEGORIES	EXAMPLES OF BEHAVIORAL OBSERVATIONS	MAY HAVE DIFFICULTY DOING	THERESA (INTELLECTUAL DISABILITY)	DELMAR (TBI)[a]	MARJORIE (DEMENTIA)	EXAMPLES OF USEFUL STRATEGIES
	Sequencing complex movements (b176) Specific mental functions of sequencing and coordinating complex, purposeful movements.	Cannot prepare a meal correctly or organize one's grooming and dressing.	Doing things in the right order and completely	No significant limitations and is able to live independently	*Can make custom gun grips and stocks*	Stopped performing some components and then relied completely on assistance	Create checklists and "to do" lists as well as time organizers, watches with alarms, visual calendars and/or time management software such as the Franklin Day Planner, Palm Pilot, or Lotus Organizer
	Experience of self and time (b180) Specific mental functions related to the awareness of one's identity, one's body, one's position in the reality of one's environment and of time.	Altered view of one's size and weight, sense of place (being there before when not the case or déjà vu) sense of never being there before when not the case (jamais vu), phantom limb sensation.	Presenting the self accurately and in a socially acceptable manner.	No difficulties	Not discussed	Some difficulties with time orientation, passage of time.	With proprioceptive loss, small weights on the arm to increase muscle and joint feedback.

Note. ICF = International Classification of Functioning, Disability and Health.
[a]As quoted from the case report.

postconcussion syndrome—and brain impairment in general (e.g., Fann, Hart, & Schomer, 2009): irritability, depression, anxiety, emotional lability and pseudobulbar affect (involuntary and uncontrollable crying and/or laughing or other emotional displays), fatigue, insomnia, reduced alcohol tolerance, personality changes such as increases in socially inappropriate behaviors, apathy, lack of spontaneity, or impaired ability to initiate activity. Table 4.7 cited below shows the connection, not only within the WHO's family of classifications (in this chapter, the *ICD–9* and *ICD–10*,

TABLE 4.7
Alignment of the *DSM-IV-TR*, *ICD–9*, and *ICD–10*, and the *ICF* Classifications

EXAMPLES OF *DSM-IV-TR* DIAGNOSES AND CODES ALIGNED WITH *ICD–9–CM*	SPECULATIVE CROSSWALK WITH WHO'S *ICD–10* CHAPTER V MENTAL DISORDERS AND CODES	SAMPLE CROSSWALK WITH WHO'S *ICF* SPECIFIC MENTAL FUNCTIONS CATEGORIES
Diseases of the Nervous System and Sense Organs (320–389)	Organic, including symptomatic, mental disorders (F00–F09)	Intellectual (b117), Memory (b144), Attention (b140), Higher-level cognitive (b164), Thought (b160), Emotional (b152), Psychosocial (b122)
Nondependent alcohol abuse (305.0), substance induced delusions (292.11), hallucinations (292.12), delirium (292.81), mood disorders (292.84)	Mental and behavioral disorders due to psychoactive substance abuse (F10–F19).	Memory (b144), Attention (b140), Higher-level cognitive (b164), Thought (b160), Emotional (b152), Psychosocial (b122)
Schizophrenia (295.1–9), Schizotypal Personality Disorder (301.22), Delusional Disorder (297.1)	Schizophrenia, schizotypal and delusional disorders (F20–F29)	Memory (b144), Attention (b140), Higher-level cognitive (b164), Thought (b160), Emotional (b152), Psychosocial (b122)
Bipolar I Disorder, Most Recent Episode Manic, Severe With Psychotic Features (296.44)	Mood (affective) disorders (F30–F39)	Memory (b144), Attention (b140), Higher-level cognitive (b164), Thought (b160), Emotional (b152), Psychosocial (b122)
Posttraumatic Stress Disorder (309.81)	Neurotic, stress-related and somatoform disorders (F40–F48)	Attention (b140), Higher-level cognitive (b164), Thought (b160), Psychosocial (b122)

(Continued)

TABLE 4.7

Alignment of the *DSM-IV-TR, ICD–9*, and *ICD–10*, and the *ICF*

Classifications (*Continued*)

EXAMPLES OF *DSM-IV-TR* DIAGNOSES AND CODES ALIGNED WITH *ICD–9–CM*	SPECULATIVE CROSSWALK WITH WHO'S *ICD–10* CHAPTER V MENTAL DISORDERS AND CODES	SAMPLE CROSSWALK WITH WHO'S *ICF* SPECIFIC MENTAL FUNCTIONS CATEGORIES
Axis III medical conditions related to the development or worsening of the mental disorder	Behavioral syndromes associated with physiological disturbances and physical factors (F50–F59)	Memory (b144), Attention (b140), Higher-level cognitive (b164), Emotional (b152), Psychosocial (b122)
All Axis II Personality Disorders ■ Paranoid ■ Antisocial ■ Avoidant ■ Borderline ■ Dependent ■ Histrionic ■ Narcissistic ■ Obsessive–Compulsive ■ Schizoid ■ Schizotypal	Disorders of adult personality and behavior (F60–F69)	Memory (b144), Attention (b140), Higher-level cognitive (b164), Emotional (b152), Psychosocial (b122)
Intellectual disability that is Mild (317), Moderate (318.0), Severe (318.1), Profound (318.2)	(Intellectual Disability)/Mental retardation (F70–F79)	Intellectual (b117), Memory (b144), Attention (b140), Higher-level cognitive (b164), Thought (b160), Psychosocial (b122)
Child or Adolescent Antisocial Behavior (V71.02), Childhood Disintegrative Disorder (299.1) Disorder of Infancy, Childhood, or Adolescence NOS (313.9)	Disorders of psychological development (F80–F89)	Attention (b140), Emotional (b152), Psychosocial (b122)
Autistic Disorder (299)	Behavioral emotional disorders with onset usually occurring in childhood or adolescence (F90–F98)	Emotional (b152), Psychosocial (b122)

Note. WHO = World Health Organization.
Source: Institute for Matching Person & Technology based on the *Diagnostic and Statistical Manual of Mental Disorders, Fourth Edition, Text Revision (DSM-IV-TR)*, International Classification of Disease, 9th edition, Clinical Modification (ICD–9–CM), and the World Health Organization's *International Classification of Functioning, Disability and Health (ICF)*. See also Peterson, D. B. (2010). *Psychological aspects of functioning, disability, and health.* New York, NY: Springer Publishing.

and the *ICF*), but also with the *DSM-IV-TR* (Peterson, 2010), which was changed to be in line with updates to the *International Classification of Diseases, Ninth Revision, Clinical Modification* (*ICD–9–CM*).[10] As we increasingly work across disciplines to understand the roots and manifestations of cognitive disability, a common language and coding scheme provides a useful means of sharing information.

Although shared coding represents a good step forward in data sharing, problems remain when some codes (e.g., Global Psychosocial Functions [b122]) that cut across all classifications manifest differently for each.

Depression is a common emotional disorder in those with stroke (Caplan, 2010) and TBI (Seel et al., 2003) and, as indicated in Tables 4.5 and 4.6, many symptoms overlap with those associated with cognitive disability (Ricker, 2010). Insomnia, agitation or psychomotor retardation, fatigue, and decreased concentration are typical of both. Table 4.8 lists the most common symptoms of depression.

Psychological theories offer an understanding of the roots of depression but rarely consider physiological bases. For example, Abraham Maslow's theory of needs satisfaction (1954) emphasizes the drive to satisfy needs

TABLE 4.8
Symptoms of Depression

When someone is depressed, that person has several symptoms nearly every day, all day, that last at least 2 weeks. These symptoms include

- Loss of interest in enjoyable activities, including sex*
- Feeling sad, blue, or down in the dumps*
- Feeling slowed down or feeling restless and unable to sit still
- Feeling worthless
- Changes in appetite or weight loss or gain
- Thoughts of death or suicide; suicide attempts
- Problems concentrating, thinking, remembering, or making decisions
- Trouble sleeping or sleeping too much
- Loss of energy or feeling tired all of the time

Other symptoms may include

- Headaches
- Other aches and pains
- Digestive problems
- Sexual problems
- Feelings of pessimism or hopelessness
- Being anxious or worried

Note. If a person has experienced five or more of these symptoms, including at least one of the first two symptoms marked with an asterisk (*) for at least 2 weeks, they should tell their health care provider immediately. The successful treatment of depression today combines new drug treatments with psychotherapy for learning new problem-solving techniques and coping strategies.
Source: Scherer (2005b)

(motivation) and a "psychological readiness" (or satisfaction of lower level needs) before one can be expected to be motivated to move up the hierarchy. Frustrated needs result in anger and/or anxiety, which, if turned inward, may lead to depression. Thus, a disability of any type can significantly interfere with needs satisfaction and lead to depression. Depression occurs commonly and early in persons who sustain a spinal cord injury (SCI) with estimated rates ranging from 11% to 37%. The example of Ken in the book, *Living in the State of Stuck: How Assistive Technology Impacts the Lives of People With Disabilities*, underscores the importance of ongoing assessment and treatment of depression in persons with SCI. As noted by Dryden et al. (2005), both person and injury factors are associated with the development of depression, with too few receiving a diagnosis and adequate treatment. The larger point is that all individuals with a new injury and disability should have a mental health assessment and appropriate services during initial hospitalization and periodically after discharge into the community as depressed persons have been shown to have lower ratings of overall health, life satisfaction and purpose in life (Cushman & Scherer, 1996), and are at high risk for suicide.

Depression may arise from impaired self-awareness that stems from frontal lobe injury and more extensive therapy may be required. In the period of adjustment and acceptance that occurs after the injury, it is critical for rehabilitation to establish new hopes and goals based on an accurate understanding of postinjury strengths and weaknesses.

After a brain injury, pain and fatigue can contribute to behavioral problems. Mood swings, personality changes, anxiety, sleep problems, temper outbursts and irritability, impulsivity, and inflexibility are also common after a brain injury. More severe frontal lobe injuries often lead to *egocentrism*—the excessive focus on one's self and difficulty appreciating the perspective of others.

The role of neurotransmitters in understanding behavior post brain injury is becoming clearer. For example, dopamine affects drive, and norepinephrine impacts energy and interest. Together, they impact motivation. A loss of impulse control caused by serotonin dysfunction together with dopamine can lead to poor impulse control over the sex drive and to inappropriate sexual behaviors. Poor self-monitoring and impulse control, loss of temper along with inflexibility, poor information processing, and problems with shifting attention can lead to violent behaviors. Clearly, this greatly affects the ability to get along with others and return to the community.

Psychosocial Symptoms

Although anger, irritability, and depression may be common reactions after brain injury, psychosocial problems related to emotion and behavior dysregulation are far broader and more complex. This applies to brain impairment in general. As noted earlier, behavioral symptoms are in some instances caused by the brain injury itself, because regions of the brain may be directly damaged or have disruptions in patterns of electrochemical activation. Other times, as noted by Trudel et al. (2009), psychosocial symptoms emerge from the person's reaction to having the injury and the confusion and changes that ensue. Brain injuries may also cause preexisting psychological or substance abuse problems to recur or increase. As noted by B. A. Wilson (2006b), a relatively recent development in neuropsychological rehabilitation is the recognition that cognition, emotion, behavior, and social functioning are interlinked and should all be addressed in the rehabilitation process.

Many individuals return to productive work, social roles, family responsibilities, and their premorbid lifestyle. However, there are those with residual effects of the injury who are at risk for unsatisfactory outcomes and who cannot be expected to resume their typical activities and roles without supports.

COMMUNITY-INTEGRATED REHABILITATION

Community-integrated rehabilitation (CIR) is a broad term encompassing several approaches that provide further rehabilitation after initial acute (inhospital) rehabilitation. As noted by Sander, Clark, and Pappadis (2010), a comprehensive definition of community integration is needed, which includes the viewpoints and preferences of persons with TBI.

According to Im, Trudel et al. (2010), CIR includes neurobehavioral programs, residential programs, comprehensive holistic (day treatment) programs, and more recently, home-based programs. These authors also state that residential CIR programs were initially developed for individuals who required extended comprehensive rehabilitation but needed 24–hour supervision or did not have access to adequate outpatient/day services. The homelike environment and staff support served to facilitate development of skills needed to negotiate everyday life, easing generalization across community environments.

Comprehensive holistic day treatment CIR programs provide a milieu-oriented, multimodal approach with a neuropsychological focus. Interventions target awareness, cognitive functions, social skills, and vocational preparation through individual, group, and family-involved interventions delivered by a treatment team. Home-based CIR involves a highly variable degree of services and supports for the individual able to reside in a home environment. Typically, such individuals do not require 24–hour supports or supervision. Home-based CIR may include the spectrum of outpatient services commonly accessed through individual treatment providers, or clinics, or minimal professional supports. There is usually no identified "treatment team," although collaboration across several health and social service systems may be evident. Behavioral approaches using self-monitoring and cueing are employed, as well as models wherein family members or in-home paraprofessionals are engaged as therapeutic change agents. Additionally, home-based CIR involves participant education and the growing use of assistive technologies and cognitive supports.

For individuals with mild-to-moderate brain injuries who have difficulty across cognitive, behavioral, and emotional domains of functioning but are able to function independently in the community with minimal support from family or friends, home-based CIR can help them resume their former roles as related to work and relationships.

There are a substantial number of persons with TBI who have long-lasting and even lifelong difficulties related to their injury, whether they are cognitive, behavioral, psychosocial, or physical. These individuals may continue using many of the services discussed earlier. Case managers and social workers as well as disability advocacy organizations can help obtain further appropriate services such as transportation, financial management, and housing assistance. Many states have specific Medicaid waivers and assistance programs to help facilitate provision of appropriate services to those with brain injuries. In addition, support groups and recreational/community organizations for persons with brain injuries and their families can fill extremely beneficial social and advisory roles. Other nonspecific sources of aid, such as through local church and community programs, can provide valuable assistance, including volunteer or financial help, and even links to people who can facilitate increased community participation.

The structure, level of intensity, and services available for both inpatient and outpatient rehabilitation programs vary widely from one area to another, whether comparing facilities, cities, states, and countries. Unfortunately, socioeconomic and medical insurance status also can limit the types of services available to a particular person. There is no single proven method or course of cognitive rehabilitation that works for every person; thus, it can be difficult for patients, professionals, and families to determine the best course of action in certain circumstances. For instance, individuals with mild TBI may not require inpatient acute medical or rehabilitation services at all and are able to address their TBI management completely at the outpatient level. Others who make rapid medical recovery or have great family support after their TBI may transition straight from acute inpatient medical care to outpatient TBI rehabilitation programs, skipping inpatient rehabilitation.

Some facilities have transitional living programs, which help patients bridge the gap from the inpatient to the outpatient setting. These programs often have an inpatient component where the patient stays overnight and is required to attend therapy sessions in the facility. However, they also allow the patients to exercise more freedom and usually place fewer restrictions on patients, permitting them to leave the facility during certain times.

Long-Term Care

Considering the various physical, cognitive, behavioral, and psychosocial issues that can develop after a brain injury, and which apply to brain impairment in general, each person benefits most from a rehabilitation program tailored to one's individual needs.

Unfortunately, patients who are medically stable but are no longer making significant progress functionally after an extended time may not meet requirements for ongoing inpatient rehabilitation even though they remain at a low level of function overall. Although many families are able to address significant functional needs at home, the burden of care can be overwhelming both in terms of time and money. The burden on the caregivers for those persons with significant long-term needs who do return home should not be underestimated because it can be a 24-hour-per-day occupation and quite taxing physically, mentally, and emotionally (Chwalisz & Dollinger, 2010). For this reason, some individuals ultimately require long-term placement or services even after initially returning home with family support. As a result, those with significant challenges from a brain injury who have extended needs postinjury may require long-term care in a skilled nursing setting where they will continue to receive nursing and medical care (usually with less intensive medical supervision) but no longer continue on an active rehabilitation program. Some facilities may help keep patients in the home environment by providing respite care, which offers short inpatient stays to allow caregivers some time to take care of their own needs.

Other persons may require long-term supports in the context of living in the community. Levels of support may range from 24-hour supervision to a few hours per week to assist with a challenging activity such as shopping, checking a pill planner, or banking. Again, supporting the unique needs of the individual with a brain impairment is key to optimizing quality of life and success. Clearly, there is also a need for additional programs and services that offer a variety of options for the individual with brain impairment and their caregivers.

PARTICIPATION IN DESIRED LIFE SITUATIONS: LEADING A "GOOD LIFE"

As presented earlier in this chapter, the *ICF* classification or framework has two major parts, each having two components:

1. Functioning and disability
   a. Body functions and structures
   b. Activities and participation, which exist within
2. Contextual factors
   a. Environmental factors and
   b. Personal factors

Figure 4.2b presented the hierarchy of the component Body Functions and the domain of "Mental Functions" (Chapter 1 of *ICF*) with a focus on Specific Mental Functions, particularly Higher-Level Cognitive Functions. Figure 4.3 is similarly structured according to the Activities and Participation component with a focus on the domain of "Domestic Life" (Chapter 6 of *ICF*) and especially the acquisition of goods and services.

As cognitive rehabilitation progresses, attention increasingly turns to Activities and Participation as much as Body Functions. According to the WHO, *activities* are the execution of tasks or actions by an individual, and limitations in activities are difficulties an individual may have in executing them. *Participation* is an individual's involvement in life situations, and *participation restrictions* are problems in such involvement.

Capacity is the generic qualifier that refers to limitations that exist without assistance. It describes an individual's ability to execute a task or perform an action. It indicates the highest probable level of functioning of a person at a given moment in a given situation. For example, a person may have moderate difficulty with bathing the whole body without the use of assistive devices or personal help. *Performance* is a generic qualifier regarding a problem in the person's current environment and their involvement in life and in life situations. The current environment always includes the overall societal context or milieu so that performance also indicates "involvement in a life situation." The current environment also includes assistive devices or personal assistance whenever the individual actually uses them to perform actions or tasks. For example, a person may have mild difficulty with bathing the whole body with the use of assistive devices because they are not available in his or her current environment, such as having a long-handled sponge.

In the case of Delmar, for example, the following table indicates where he is experiencing some activity limitations and participation restrictions in the area of conversation. The current intervention is to have his wife step in and help him, but another strategy might be to join a support group to practice conversation skills.

Health Condition	TBI / ABI *Delmar*
Impairment	Organization and planning (b1641)
Activity limitation	Difficulties ordering his ideas and those of others in a conversation
Participation restriction	Socializing with old friends
Intervention	Wife stepping in; a support group that focuses on conversational skills

Note. TBI = traumatic brain injury; ABI = acquired brain injury.

International Classification of Functioning, Disability and Health

d Activities and Participation

CHAPTER 1 (d1)	CHAPTER 2 (d2)	CHAPTER 3 (d3)	CHAPTER 4 (d4)	CHAPTER 5 (d5)
LEARNING AND APPLYING KNOWLEDGE	GENERAL TASKS AND DEMANDS	COMMUNICATION	MOBILITY	SELF-CARE
Learning, applying the knowledge that is learned, thinking, solving problems, and making decisions	Carrying out single or multiple tasks, organizing routines and handling stress	Communicating by language, signs and symbols, including receiving and producing messages, carrying on conversations, and using communication devices and techniques	Changing body position or location or by transferring from one place to another, by carrying, moving or manipulating objects, by walking, running or climbing, and by using various forms of transportation	Caring for oneself, washing and drying oneself, caring for one's body and body parts, dressing, eating and drinking, and looking after one's health

CHAPTER 6 (d6)	CHAPTER 7 (d7)	CHAPTER 8 (d8)	CHAPTER 9 (d9)
DOMESTIC LIFE	INTERPERSONAL INTERACTIONS AND RELATIONSHIPS	MAJOR LIFE AREAS	COMMUNITY, SOCIAL AND CIVIC LIFE
Acquiring a place to live, food, clothing and other necessities, household cleaning and repairing, caring for personal and other household objects, and assisting others	Basic and complex interactions with people (strangers, friends, relatives, family members and lovers) in a contextually and socially appropriate manner	Tasks and actions required to engage in education, work and employment and to conduct economic transactions	Actions and tasks required to engage in organized social life outside the family, in community, social and civic areas of life

FIGURE 4.3   *ICF* Hierarchy of Activities and Participation, Chapter 6, Domestic Life, Acquisition of Goods and Services. (*Continued*)
Source: World Health Organization.

d610–d629	d630–d649	d650–d669
Acquisition of necessities	Household tasks	Caring for household objects and assisting others

d610	d620
Acquiring a place to live	Acquisition of goods and services
Buying, renting, furnishing and arranging a house, apartment or other dwelling.	Selecting, procuring and transporting all goods and services required for daily living, such as selecting, procuring, transporting and storing food, drink, clothing, cleaning materials, fuel, household items, utensils, cooking ware, domestic appliances and tools; procuring utilities and other household services.

d620 Acquisition of goods and services

Selecting, procuring and transporting all goods and services required for daily living, such as selecting, procuring, transporting and storing food, drink, clothing, cleaning materials, fuel, household items, utensils, cooking ware, domestic appliances and tools; procuring utilities and other household services.

Inclusions

Shopping and gathering daily necessities

Exclusion

Acquiring a place to live (d610)

d6200	d6201	d6208	d6209
Shopping	Gathering daily necessities	Acquisition of goods and services, other specified	Acquisition of goods and services, unspecified
Obtaining, in exchange for money, goods and services required for daily living (including instructing and supervising an intermediary to do the shopping), such as selecting food, drink, cleaning materials, household items or clothing in a shop or market; comparing quality and price of the items required, negotiating and paying for selected goods or services, and transporting goods.	Obtaining, without exchange of money, goods and services required for daily living (including instructing and supervising an intermediate to gather daily necessities), such as by harvesting vegetables and fruits and getting water and fuel.		

FIGURE 4.3 *Continued*

For individuals like Delmar who have physical, sensory, and cognitive disability, there are resources in addition to strategies and helpful others. Assistive technologies can facilitate independence in accomplishing tasks and performing actions (*activities*) such as reading, writing, walking/moving, dressing, and eating. For example, an individual with paralysis of the dominant arm can read a book independently with electronic page-turning devices and write with the assistance of a splint or word processor adapted with modified means of input and data entry. Various adapted aids and utensils are available to promote independence in grooming and eating. Manual and power wheelchairs can provide independence in moving from location to location for a person with paralysis or paresis in the lower extremities. In other words, one may have the capacity to walk, but it may not be functional; thus, the person may require assistive technology or devices to increase functional independence, or the ability to navigate one's environment independently. The capacity to perform various activities enables a person with a disability to *participate* in life situations such as education, employment, and civic life. Assistive technologies enhance participation by providing the means to get around independently (e.g., wheelchairs, adapted vehicles, and ramps), care for oneself (e.g., built-up handles on eating utensils), and interact with others (e.g., voice-controlled computer input, telephone dialing devices). By enabling a person to perform desired tasks, assistive technologies offer the potential to provide a sense of autonomy as well as reconnection to the community. By accommodating a person's weaknesses and supporting his or her strengths, assistive technologies can reduce psychosocial as well as physical stress, thus leading to an enhanced subjective well-being and quality of life (Scherer, 2002a, 2004, 2005b). Furthermore, according to Scherer and Glueckauf (2005):

> The World Health Organization's International Classification of Functioning, Disability, and Health (ICF) emphasizes what people do on a daily basis (i.e., *Performance*), as opposed to what they have the ability to do (i.e., *Capacity*), and this places the onus on rehabilitation practitioners to demonstrate positive outcomes of interventions as a standard of practice, and not the mere enhancement of functional capabilities. In addition, contextual factors are an important component of the ICF model, particularly environmental and psychological resources. These factors are assumed to affect the extent to which the individual participates in community and societal roles and thus, are strongly implicated in the overall success of rehabilitation efforts. (p. 132)

In summary, capacity is what the person can do and assumes a "standardized" environment; for example, a clinic's testing area. *Performance* is what the person *does do* in a "current" or natural environment. The WHO

(2001) says that "The gap between capacity and performance reflects the difference between the impacts of current and uniform environments, and thus provides a useful guide as to what can be done to the environment of the individual to improve performance" (para. 15).

As stated by Magasi, Heinemann, and Whiteneck (2008), people with disability, perhaps most especially those with cognitive disability, experience barriers to participation across many major life domains such as education and employment, a social life outside the family, family role functioning, and access to recreational and leisure activities. This is what gives quality to life and a personal sense of well-being.

Community Acceptance and Resources

For a person with a cognitive disability to achieve full participation in desired life situations, there must be reciprocity. That is, the milieu in which that person resides must have the resources to support the person's participation and the social attitudes that foster inclusion.

When I started my career in the broadly designated "helping profession," it was in the mental health system during a time when individuals with moderate-to-severe psychiatric diagnoses were often sent to institutions for their treatment. Lengths of stay could be long and individuals typically received medications to quiet and calm them, if not alleviate their mental and behavioral symptoms. Often, these medications were so strong that they left individuals lethargic and with such physical sequela as *tardive dyskinesia*, defined by the National Institute of Neurological Disorders and Stroke (2010c) as a neurological syndrome caused by the long-term use of neuroleptic drugs and characterized by repetitive, involuntary, purposeless movements such as grimacing and tongue protrusion, as well as rapid movements of the fingers, arms, legs, and trunk.

But it was also a time when the system was changing from one that emphasized institutionalization to one that placed priority on community services and supporting the individual on his or her own home or neighborhood. Although the intent was humanitarian, the practice was to discharge individuals who had been in institutions into communities who were not prepared or ready to receive them. Community mental health centers, designed to deliver care within defined geographic areas, valiantly tried to fill the needs but services were inadequate. I know because I worked for one. My caseload ranged from individuals with anxiety disorders to those with bipolar disorder and schizophrenia. My colleagues and I, through individual sessions, group therapy, and whatever we thought would work, tried our best to bring order, reason, and good judgment to lives so ill equipped for community living that we felt we were going to lose our own grip with reality. When our "clients" missed a series of appointments, we went to their homes; when they had reactions to psychotropic medications, we carefully monitored them and kept in close contact with the prescribing psychiatrist; when they kept reappearing through that revolving door to seek help and have their cases reopened, we were there waiting—and serve them again, we did.

In my opinion, the most underserved people are those with mental, emotional, cognitive, and behavioral disabilities. It was, and remains, very difficult, frustrating, and heartbreaking for professionals as well as for the individuals and their families to receive adequate care and services.

Just why was it so difficult? It certainly wasn't because of uncaring professionals. Rather, it's because every step forward that was made was too frequently followed by a step or more backward. Here are some reasons why:

1. You can legislate community reentry, but you cannot legislate community reintegration or acceptance. People stigmatize those who do not behave as they do and as society expects. When someone does behave in an unexpected way, when their behavior seems unusual and is not understood, then they are feared, distrusted, and rejected. Such reactions erode self-esteem that has emotional and behavioral ramifications.
2. My clients didn't feel welcomed by their communities and, thus, they didn't feel they belonged. Hence, they didn't seek out opportunities or resources. Indeed, many led isolated and lonely lives. For example, one woman who lived in a one-room, cockroach-filled apartment behind a grocery store obtained her food by foraging at night in the store's dumpster.
3. The kind and amount of services required to achieve true community reintegration just weren't available or being offered.

Environmental and personal factors are the context within which activities and performance operate (as is also true for body functions and structures). Environmental factors (or the settings in which the person is) tend to either support or discourage participation. As shown in Figure 4.4, Environmental

International Classification of Functioning, Disability and Health				

e ENVIRONMENTAL FACTORS

CHAPTER 1 (e1)	CHAPTER 2 (e2)	CHAPTER 3 (e3)	CHAPTER 4 (e4)	CHAPTER 5 (e5)
PRODUCTS AND TECHNOLOGY	NATURAL ENVIRONMENT AND HUMAN-MADE CHANGES TO ENVIRONMENT	SUPPORT AND RELATIONSHIPS	ATTITUDES	SERVICES, SYSTEMS AND POLICIES

FIGURE 4.4 *ICF* Environmental Factors
Source: World Health Organization.

Factors consist of five chapters and it can be seen that supports extend beyond physical access to social and economic resources and support. Attitudinal and cultural factors are environmental influences that comprise a key component of a person's perspective of available resources, support use in general, and degree of confidence and trust in professionals and their recommendations. When there is a dearth of opportunities and resources, this constitutes environmental barriers. Scarcity of trained personnel represents a barrier within the social environment (as do policies that set a low priority on resource allocation for rehabilitation services).

A major barrier to participation is stigma, which largely arises from perceived deviance (Adler & Adler, 2008). We stigmatize those we view as dissimilar to us, and we fear what we don't understand. Thus, the emotional effects of social rejection can be more detrimental than the physical effects of the disability.

We each have a social identity and a personal identity and there is a dynamic, interactive, dialectical relationship between the two. When a brain injury occurs later in life, such as with stroke or TBI, there may be uneasiness around old friends who had a memory of us as different from the person we are now. And the stoke survivor or TBI survivor is very apt to be treated differently by those friends. As the old friends fade away and friendships become no longer satisfying, then there is a social gap. This is a key advantage of peer support groups because they can provide shared understanding with no history of one another prior to the current self, although that doesn't necessarily diminish the sense of loss/grief for the pre-disability self.

In Beatrice Wright's classic text, *Physical Disability: A Psychological Approach* (1960/1983), she presents the concept of *expectation discrepancy* as the difference between what one expects and what one observes. Brain injuries are often a "hidden disability" without obvious physical manifestations, and when one looks like everyone else, one is expected to act like everyone else. If we expect someone to communicate with us normally and that doesn't happen, we can revise our expectations, reject the individual as deviant, or push the person to change and do better, try new strategies, and so forth.

When expectations do not match reality, there is a need to reconcile the two. This can be done cognitively—expectation revision—or by altering reality. Expectation revision needs to be done within society and needs to be viewed as a part of the therapeutic intervention. On the individual and family level, it helps to focus as much on the body functions that are strong as well as weak, what individuals have and not what they don't have; what tasks and actions they can perform, not what they cannot. This strengths-based approach serves to enhance both personal identity and social identity.

The Convention on the Rights of Persons with Disabilities and its Optional Protocol marks an international "paradigm shift" in attitudes and approaches to persons with disability. It views persons with disability as individuals with rights, who are capable of claiming those rights and making decisions for their lives based on their free and informed consent as well as being active members of society. The convention was adopted on December 13, 2006 at the UN Headquarters in New York and had the highest number of signatories in history to a UN convention on its opening day. It is intended as a human rights instrument with an explicit social development dimension. It adopts a broad categorization of persons with disability and reaffirms that all persons with all types of disabilities must enjoy all human rights and fundamental freedoms. It clarifies and qualifies how all categories of rights apply to persons with disability and identifies areas where adaptations have to be made for persons with disability to effectively exercise their rights and areas where their rights have been violated, and where protection of rights must be reinforced. The full text of the convention can be accessed at this URL: http://www.un.org/disabilities/documents/convention/convoptprot-e.pdf.

Although communities have the responsibility to be accessible to persons with disability (e.g., as mandated by the Americans With Disabilities Act of 1990), it is important to recognize that deviance, social stigma, and rejection does not always arise solely from a failure of society to accommodate and accept individuals with differences. Blame needs to be shared with those who put people into the community prematurely or inadvisably and without sufficient and appropriate supports, as I experienced when I was working with the mental health system.

I also recall the time, not too long ago, when I was visiting a crowded museum and out of the clear blue and with no warning, I was physically struck on the back by a tall and heavyset young man. The sound of the loud thump from my back, the fact that he was so much larger than me, caused everyone in the room to stop in their tracks and stare at us. It was winter, and I had worn a wool jacket with a polar bear stitched on the back. When I turned around to address my attacker, it immediately became obvious to me that the young man, accompanied only by his short and medium-framed father, had some form of intellectual or cognitive disability. Something about the polar bear on my jacket had angered him.

The young man was rigid but still flushed with anger and his father's face had turned white. I was afraid he was going to hit me again. With my knowledge, and admittedly through my own anger, I stiffened myself to a height where I was taller than the father and said in a quiet but clear voice something like, "Sir. Without good behavioral controls, people should not be in situations where they can potentially hurt others." The others in the room, who had been completely stationary and silent through all this, now started to move quickly to exit the room with eyes deliberately and completely averted from me, the young man, and his father.

Thus, I concluded then that society is confused at this point in our history regarding the community participation of those with some kinds of disabilities. Although it is generally accepted, society is also skeptical about violations in appropriate public conduct and afraid to deal with them when they do occur. Of necessity, then, it falls back to the intervention team members to be the gatekeepers, or better still, facilitators who can build bridges to full inclusion by providing necessary and appropriate supports.

To summarize, advances in the options for the treatment and rehabilitation of individuals with cognitive disability have made community participation the ultimate outcome. However, society continues to lag in making this achievement a reality. We will return to this point in the subsequent chapters.

5

The Potential of Technology to Assist Individuals With Cognitive Disability

Because we do not understand the brain very well we are constantly
tempted to use the latest technology as a model for trying to
understand it. In my childhood we were always assured that the brain
was a telephone switchboard. . . . At present, obviously, the metaphor
is the digital computer.
—John R. Searle

A current metaphor for the brain may be a digital computer, yet we know the brain is much more complex than that. However, a digital computer can be very useful to a person with a brain impairment, particularly one who has difficulties with attention, memory, calculation, and many higher level cognitive functions.

As we have been discussing, an aspect of cognition refers to a person's thinking and memory skills. Thinking skills include paying attention, being aware of one's surroundings, organizing, planning, following through on decisions, solving problems, judgment, reasoning, and awareness of problems. Memory skills include the ability to remember things before and after the brain injury. Because of the damage caused by a brain injury, some or all of these skills can be altered.

We are now ready to see how the power of technology can be used to support and enhance life quality for people of various ages and who have very different cognitive disability. Let us first recall the foundational points from Chapters 1–4:

■ There is a terrific amount we still need to learn about the complexities of brain function or dysfunction and how to help a person become an active and satisfied participant in all chosen life activities and situations.

■ Each person with a cognitive disability has unique needs as well as goals, characteristics, and preferences. This must drive the choice of support use.

■ There are anatomical and physiological reasons why people with cognitive disability are as they are and behave as they do. They are not being willfully obstinate, difficult, or frustrating—and if they are, that can also be because of their injury. But that doesn't mean their behaviors are easy to take, especially for family members, and they may require additional support to facilitate safe, appropriate community participation.

■ The system of services for helping a person with a cognitive disability is complex, yet more attention needs to be given to cognitive rehabilitation and cognitive supports, particularly those that can be provided economically and reliably through technology.

Although we have noted that treatments and interventions vary among the cognitive disability groups discussed here, many can apply across groups, and this is just as true for technologies. Furthermore, technologies often can be easily adapted to suit individual needs and preferences.

WHAT ARE ASSISTIVE TECHNOLOGIES?

In the United States, an *assistive technology device* or ATD was originally defined in the Technology-Related Assistance for Individuals with Disabilities Act of 1988 (Pub. L. 100–407). This legislation, often called the Tech Act for short, was reauthorized in 1994, 1998, and 2004 as the Assistive Technology Act. The most current version of the Act was reauthorized in 2010. The original Tech Act defined ATD, and this definition has remained the same throughout its reauthorizations: "Any item, piece of equipment, or product system, whether acquired commercially, modified or customized, that is used to increase, maintain, or improve functional capabilities of individuals with disabilities" (Title 29, Chapter 31, § 3002[a][3]).

The term *assistive technology service* is defined in the Act as "any service that directly assists an individual with a disability in the selection, acquisition, or use of an assistive technology device" (Title 29, Chapter 31, § 3002[a]).

In short, an ATD is what the person uses, and the assistive technology (AT) service is how he or she obtains and maintains it. Included within this definition for devices are those for individuals with cognitive disability that vary from simple notepads to sophisticated computerized devices. The law gives the following examples of AT services:

(A)   the evaluation of the assistive technology needs of an individual with a disability, including a functional evaluation of the impact of the provision of appropriate assistive technology and appropriate services to the individual in the customary environment of the individual;

(B)   a service consisting of purchasing, leasing, or otherwise providing for the acquisition of assistive technology devices by individuals with disabilities;

(C)   a service consisting of selecting, designing, fitting, customizing, adapting, applying, maintaining, repairing, replacing, or donating assistive technology devices;

(D)   coordination and use of necessary therapies, interventions, or services with assistive technology devices, such as therapies, interventions, or services associated with education and rehabilitation plans and programs;

(E)   training or technical assistance for an individual with a disability or, where appropriate, the family members, guardians, advocates, or authorized representatives of such an individual;

(F)   training or technical assistance for professionals (including individuals providing education and rehabilitation services and entities that manufacture or sell assistive technology devices), employers, providers of employment and training services, or other individuals who provide services to, employ, or are otherwise substantially involved in the major life functions of individuals with disabilities; and

(G)   a service consisting of expanding the availability of access to technology, including electronic and information technology, to individuals with disabilities. (Title 29 of the US Code, Chapter 31, § 3002. Definitions). [See http://uscode.house.gov/ for explanations about the U.S. Code]

Also under the Tech Act (1988), each U.S. state and territory receives money to fund an Assistive Technology Act Project (ATAP) to provide services to persons with disability for their entire life span, as well as to their families or guardians, service providers, and agencies and other entities that are involved in providing services such as education and employment to persons with disability. The list of ATAPs can be found at http://www.ataporg.org/atap/.

The Tech Act definitions of ATD and AT services have been used in most legislation related to persons with disability (e.g., Individuals with Disabilities Education Act [IDEA] and the Americans with Disabilities Act [ADA]). Other nations, professional groups, and nongovernmental organizations (NGOs) have set forth their own definitions and polices regarding ATDs and AT services. Internationally, the United Nations Convention on the Rights of Persons with Disabilities and its Optional Protocol, adopted in 2006, views the provision of ATDs and AT services as an important component of the human rights of persons with disability worldwide. It states in Article 4, General Obligations, Section 1:

(g) To undertake or promote research and development of, and to promote the availability and use of new technologies, including information and communications technologies, mobility aids, devices and assistive technologies . . .

The Convention also recognizes the need to provide information about assistive technologies and promote the training of professionals and staff to better provide devices and services.

The most recent data regarding ATD use in the United States, as reported by the National Center for Health Statistics, Centers for Disease Control and Prevention (Russell, Hendershot, LeClere, Howie, & Adler, 1997), indicate that the most frequently used devices are those for mobility:

- Approximately 7.4 million Americans used ATDs to accommodate mobility impairments.
- Approximately 4.6 million Americans used ATDs to accommodate orthopedic impairments.
- Approximately 4.5 million Americans used ATDs to accommodate hearing impairments.
- Approximately 500,000 Americans used ATDs to accommodate vision impairments (exclusive of eyeglasses and contact lenses).

The number of users of ATDs and AT services has increased significantly in each of the preceding categories since these data were collected in 1994, as have the number of available products, the styles and sizes they come in, and their features and accessories. To illustrate, AbleData is a U.S.-based website of approximately 40,000 ATDs or AT products in 20 categories, as described in the list opposite. Once the relevant category is selected, then a hot link will go to information about specific devices with further links to manufacturers for technical specifications, availability, cost, and so on. This process is shown step-by-step in Figure 5.1, when I searched for prompting devices. The richness and usefulness of the information provided will be very apparent.

There are additional excellent databases of AT products in the United States such as rehabtool.com and assistivetech.net. The resources page of the website of the Family Center on Technology and Disability (FCTD) is also a rich resource. Internationally, an excellent database is produced by a network of organizations, the European Assistive Technology Information Network (www.eastin.info). It is important to note that any published book naming or discussing specific devices and websites will rapidly go out of date in today's technologically innovative world, so having an easy-to-access resource such as AbleData and the others noted previously will ensure currency. For practicality and simplicity, we will focus on the AbleData site knowing there are others available.

AbleData's Categories of Assistive Technology Products

AbleData classifies products according to each product's intended function or any special features it possesses. The products are classified in 20 areas listed subsequently. The list can be accessed on the AbleData website from this URL: http://www.abledata.com.

From the website, you can click on a topic that will list the major categories within that topic. Then you can click on a specific product type within that category and get a list of products with links to their manufacturers and distributors.

■ **Blind and Low Vision**
Products for people with visual disability
Major Categories: computers, educational aids, health care, information storage, kitchen aids, labeling, magnification, office equipment, orientation and mobility, reading, recreation, sensors, telephones, time, tools, travel, typing, writing (Braille)

■ **Deaf and Hard of Hearing**
Products for people with hearing disability
Major Categories: amplification, driving, hearing aids, recreational electronics, sign language, signal switches, speech training, telephones, time

■ **Deaf Blind**
Products for people who are both deaf and blind

■ **Communication**
Products to help people with disability related to speech, writing, and other methods of communication
Major Categories: augmentative and alternative communication, head wands, mouth sticks, signal systems, telephones, typing, writing

■ **Aids for Daily Living**
Products to aid in activities of daily living
Major Categories: bathing, carrying, child care, clothing, dispenser aids, dressing, drinking, feeding, grooming/hygiene, handle padding, health care, holding, reaching, time, smoking, toileting, transfer

■ **Housekeeping**
Products to assist in cooking, cleaning, and other household activities as well as adapted appliances
Major Categories: food preparation, housekeeping, general cleaning, ironing, laundry, shopping

■ **Computers**
Products to allow people with disability to use desktop and laptop computers and other kinds of information technology
Major Categories: software, hardware, computer accessories

(Continued)

AbleData's Categories of Assistive Technology Products *(Continued)*

■ **Controls**
Products to provide people with disability with the ability to start, stop, or adjust electric or electronic devices
Major Categories: environmental controls, control switches

■ **Orthotics**
Braces and other products to support or supplement joints or limbs
Major Categories: head and neck, lower extremity, torso, upper extremity

■ **Prosthetics**
Products for amputees
Major Categories: lower extremity, upper extremity

■ **Therapeutic Aids**
Products to assist in treatment for health problems and therapy and training for certain disabilities
Major Categories: ambulation training, biofeedback, evaluation, exercise, fine and gross motor skills, perceptual motor, positioning, pressure/massage modality equipment, respiratory aids, rolls, sensory integration, stimulators, therapy furnishings, thermal/water modality equipment, traction

■ **Walking**
Products to aid people with disability who are able to walk or stand with assistance
Major Categories: canes, crutches, standing, walkers

■ **Wheeled Mobility**
Products and accessories to enable people with mobility disability to move freely indoors and outdoors
Major Categories: wheelchairs (manual, sport, and powered), wheelchair alternatives (scooters), wheelchair accessories, carts, transporters, stretchers

■ **Seating**
Products to assist people to sit comfortably and safely
Major Categories: seating systems, cushions, therapeutic seats

■ **Education**
Products to provide people with disability with access to educational materials and instructions in school and in other learning environments
Major Categories: classroom, instructional materials

■ **Workplace**
Products to aid people with disability at work
Major Categories: agricultural equipment, office equipment, tools, vocational assessment, vocational training, work stations

■ **Recreation**
Products to assist people with disability with their leisure and athletic activities
Major Categories: crafts, electronics, gardening, music, photography, sewing, sports, toys

AbleData's Categories of Assistive Technology Products *(Continued)*

■ **Transportation**
Products to enable people with disability to drive or ride in cars, vans, trucks, and buses
Major Categories: mass transit vehicles and facilities, vehicles, vehicle accessories

■ **Environmental Adaptations**
Products to make the built environment more accessible
Major Categories: indoor environment, furniture, outdoor environment, vertical accessibility, houses, specialities, lighting, signs

■ **Safety and Security**
Products to protect health and home
Major Categories: alarm and security systems, child-proof devices, electric cords, lights, locks.

AbleData is maintained for the National Institute on Disability and Rehabilitation Research of the U.S. Department of Education by ICF Macro.

Source: Disability and Rehabilitation Research of the U.S. Department of Education by ICF Macro.

Step 1: Here I used Internet Explorer to go to www.AbleData.com on June 17, 2011. I selected **Products**.

FIGURE 5.1 Accessing the AbleData product descriptions. (*Continued*)

Step 2: This is the main page for assistive technology products where there are 20 categories listed. Here are the first two, *Aids for Daily Living* and *Blind and Low Vision*. I clicked on *Aids for Daily Living*.

Step 3: Within *Aids for Daily Living*, there are many subcategories. I selected *Memory Aids* and, specifically, *Prompter*, where I am told that 15 product descriptions are provided

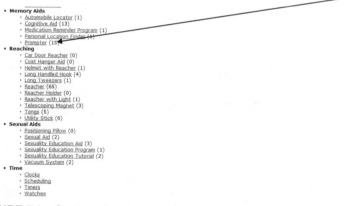

FIGURE 5.1   *Continued*

Step 4: After clicking on *Prompter*, I got a description and photo of the individual products. Here are the first three:

Products are listed alphabetically.

Page 1 of 1

1. B-CALM PRO
   The b-Calm PRO is an audio sensory integration aid and prompter designed for children with sensory disabilities, autism and other neurological or cognitive disabilities that cause a person to be easily distracted by sounds and other sensory stimuli. The b-Calm PRO includes a touch screen MP3 player with a pair of customizable headphones sized for children and a pair of earbud-style headphones. The player is pre-loaded with four AudioSedation tracks that are soothing sounds from nature with acous...[More Information]

2. COMMUNITY INTEGRATION SUITE
   The Community Integration Suite is a prompter and cognitive aid designed for use by individuals with cognitive disabilities. Simplified access to a handheld Pocket PC (not included) provides time-based schedule prompting, as well as personalized task prompting with digital pictures, video, and auditory instructions. Users traveling to work, school, or into the community have access to calendar reminders and support for important vocational and educational tasks. Features enable users to manage ...[More Information]

3. ICOMMUNICATE
   iCommunicate is a symbolic and director selection communicator program and prompter for people with communication or cognitive disabilities. The program allows a person to use their Apple iPad, iPhone or iPod Touch as a communicator and cognitive aid. iCommunicate allows an image (including a picture or a symbol) to be related to a specific word or phrase and to an audio clip. The user selects a picture and the associated audio clip will play. If no audio recording is available, the program has ...[More Information]

Feedback

Has the information on this page helped you find what you need?
test

[Yes] [No]

Quick Product Links

- B-CALM PRO
- COMMUNITY INTEGRATION SUITE
- ICOMMUNICATE
- ISAAC SYSTEM, THE
- JOGGER, THE
- MEDREADY AUTOMATIC MEDICATION DISPENSER
- PHILIPS MEDICATION DISPENSER
- PLANNING AND EXECUTION ASSISTANT TRAINER (PEAT)
- QUARTER HOUR WATCH
- REQALL
- SAFETYNET

Step 5: I wanted more information on each so I clicked on the option for *More Information* at the end of the descriptions. When I clicked on *Community Integration Suite*, this is what I saw. From here, I can get a list of additional AbleLink Technologies products; link directly to their website or contact them for additional information.

COMMUNITY INTEGRATION SUITE

Record 1 of 8
Next Product >>   Return to Search Results

The Community Integration Suite is a prompter and cognitive aid designed for use by individuals with cognitive disabilities. Simplified access to a handheld Pocket PC (not included) provides time-based schedule prompting, as well as personalized task prompting with digital pictures, video, and auditory instructions. Users traveling to work, school, or into the community have access to calendar reminders and support for important vocational and educational tasks. Features enable users to manage calendar events simply, whether the event is recurring or only requires a one-time reminder; set a timer to track time; view past and future events; stay on track with sequential tasks;

FIGURE 5.1   *Continued*

and respond to auditory and visual cueing. OPTIONS: The Community Integration Suite can be upgraded to include Pocket ACE and cell phone hardware.

Notes:

Price: 1099.00.

This product record was updated on November 5, 2010.

This product is available from:

Manufacturer:

AbleLink Technologies, Inc.

618 N. Nevada Ave.
Colorado Springs, Colorado 80903
United States
Telephone: 719-592-0347   719-592-0347   .
Fax: 719-592-0348.
Web: http://www.ablelinktech.com.
Email: info@ablelinktech.com.

Link to more products from AbleLink Technologies, Inc.

FIGURE 5.1 *Continued*

CLASSIFYING ASSISTIVE TECHNOLOGY DEVICES

The World Health Organization's (WHO) *International Classification of Functioning, Disability and Health* (ICF) is in line with the United Nations Convention on the Rights of Persons with Disabilities in recognizing the importance of ATDs for an individual's functioning, performance of activities, and successful participation in desired life roles and situations (Bickenbach, 2009). In fact, rehabilitation services are applied primarily because of limitations in these areas, and we judge the success of rehabilitation according to such outcomes as a person's employment status, educational attainment, and community involvement. This is very much in line with the biopsychosocial perspective we discussed in Chapter 4.

Disability is characterized by the *ICF* as the outcome or result of a complex relationship between an individual's health condition within a context consisting of personal factors as well as external factors that represent the circumstances in which the individual lives. As shown in Figure 5.2, environmental and personal factors are components of Part 2; contextual factors within which functioning and disability occur—that is, factors that impact functioning and disability and include the interaction of body functions and activities and participation. The WHO defines *contextual factors* as the factors that "together constitute the complete context of an individual's life, and in particular the background against which health states are classified in the ICF" (2001, p. 213). The domains included within each

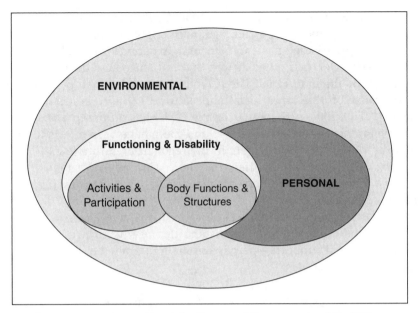

FIGURE 5.2 The Relationship of the Parts and Components of the ICF.

can have either a facilitating (they are "facilitators") or hindering (they are "barriers") impact on the person.

Environmental factors are those in the external or extrinsic world that make up the physical, social, and attitudinal environment in which people live and conduct their lives. It also includes social attitudes, architectural characteristics, legal and social structures, as well as climate and terrain. Environmental factors are addressed on two levels: (a) individual, which is composed of physical, material, and interpersonal features of the environment that an individual comes face to face with (e.g., physical barriers in the workplace as well as attitudes of employers and coworkers); and (b) societal, or those "faceless" systems and structures in the community or society that have an impact on individuals including laws, rules, and regulations. As stated by the WHO:

> Environmental factors are to be coded from the perspective of the person whose situation is being described. For example, curb cuts without textured paving may be coded as a facilitator for a wheelchair user but as a barrier for a blind person. (WHO, 2001, p. 171)

Not only may two individuals experience barriers dissimilarly within a particular environment, but various environments may impact a given individual differently.

This is also impacted by personal factors that are intrinsic to the individual, which include gender, age, coping styles, social background, education, profession, past and current experience, overall behavior pattern, character, and other factors that influence how disability is experienced by the individual. The *ICF* has not yet classified personal factors because of "the large social and cultural variance associated with them" (WHO, 2001, p. 8). However, the WHO has proposed a taxonomical development of personal factors and there have been efforts to identify examples of personal factors in the relevant literature (e.g., Geyh et al., 2010). Personal factors affect the choice and appropriateness of an ATD for a person and the person's realization of benefit from the use of that device will, in turn, impact such personal factors as additional educational attainment, coping, and so forth. This is very likely to result in changed environmental interactions and the desire and need for different or additional supports—perhaps from an upgraded or new device or from new professionals.

As indicated in Figure 5.2, although ATDs and products are located in the Environmental Factors component of the *ICF*, their overall value is ultimately determined by their impact on daily activities and participation in life roles and life situations such as education, work, and community life. It is also crucial that the users of devices realize the benefit from them and that they enhance well-being. What is not conveyed in Figure 5.2 is the yin-yang interconnectedness of Personal and Environmental Factors, as shown in Figure 5.3.

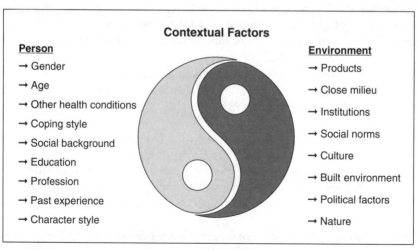

FIGURE 5.3   Yin-Yang of *ICF* Contextual Factors.
Source: World Health Organization

ICF and ISO Classification of Assistive Technology Devices and Services

It is within the Environmental Factors' component that the WHO has placed ATDs and AT services. The following are the five chapters in Environmental Factors (e):

> e1 Chapter 1 Products and Technology
> e2 Chapter 2 Natural Environment and Human-Made Changes to
>   Environment
> e3 Chapter 3 Support and Relationships
> e4 Chapter 4 Attitudes
> e5 Chapter 5 Services, Systems and Policies

Chapter 1, "Products and Technology," is where ATDs are incorporated, whereas AT services are found in Chapter 5, "Services, Systems and Policies" (e580), and assistance from service providers are found in Chapter 3, "Support and Relationships" (e355–e360). Figure 5.4 lists and defines the 12 categories within Chapter 1, "Products and Technology," with a more detailed focus on "Products and Technology for Personal Use in Daily Living" because this is where most products appropriate for persons with cognitive disability are coded. Table 5.1 crosswalks the *ICF* components of both Activities and Participation and Environmental Factors with the 20 AbleData categories of products.

The WHO recognizes that *products and technology for personal use in daily living* does not contain the depth and detail needed by those who specialize in the design, manufacture, distribution, and provision of ATDs. Therefore, in 2003, the ISO 9999 (*assistive products for persons with disability—classification and terminology*) was accepted as a related member of the WHO Family of International Classifications (WHO-FIC). ISO 9999 is a product of the International Organization for Standardization (ISO) and is an international classification of assistive products in which all products that can be used by persons with disability are included. As presented by Heerkens, Bougie, and de Kleijn-de Vrankrijker (2010b), the definition of an assistive product in the 2007 version of ISO 9999 was stated as "any product (including devices, equipment, instruments, technology and software) especially produced or generally available, for preventing, compensating, monitoring, relieving or neutralizing impairments, activity limitations and participation restrictions."

International Classification of Functioning, Disability and Health

e ENVIRONMENTAL FACTORS

CHAPTER 1	CHAPTER 2	CHAPTER 3	CHAPTER 4	CHAPTER 5	
PRODUCTS AND TECHNOLOGY	NATURAL ENVIRONMENT AND HUMAN-MADE CHANGES TO ENVIRONMENT	SUPPORT AND RELATIONSHIPS	ATTITUDES	SERVICES, SYSTEMS AND POLICIES	
e100	e115	e120	e125	e130	e135
Products or substances for personal consumption	Products and technology for personal use in daily living	Products and technology for personal indoor and outdoor mobility and transportation	Products and technology for communication	Products and technology for education	Products and technology for employment
Any natural or human-made object or substance gathered, processed or manufactured for ingestion.	Equipment, products and technologies used by people in daily activities, including those adapted or specially designed, located in, on or near the person using them.	Equipment, products and technologies used by people in activities of moving inside and outside buildings, including those adapted or specially designed, located in, on or near the person using them.	Equipment, products and technologies used by people in activities of sending and receiving information, including those adapted or specially designed, located in, on or near the person using them.	Equipment, products, processes, methods and technology used for acquisition of knowledge, expertise or skill, including those adapted or specially designed.	Equipment, products and technology used for employment to facilitate work activities.

e140	e145	e150	e155	e160	e165
Products and technology for culture, recreation and sport	Products and technology for the practice of religion and spirituality	Design, construction and building products and technology of buildings for public use	Design, construction and building products and technology of buildings for private use	Products and technology of land development	Assets
Equipment, products and technology used for the conduct and enhancement of cultural, recreational and sporting activities, including those adapted or specially designed.	Products and technology, unique or mass-produced, that are given or take on a symbolic meaning in the context of the practice of religion or spirituality, including those adapted or specially designed.	Products and technology that constitute an individual's indoor and outdoor human-made environment that is planned, designed and constructed for public use, including those adapted or specially designed.	Products and technology that constitute an individual's indoor and outdoor human-made environment that is planned, designed and constructed for private use, including those adapted or specially designed.	Products and technology of land areas, as they affect an individual's outdoor environment through the implementation of land use policies, design, planning and development of space, including those adapted or specially designed.	Products or objects of economic exchange such as money, goods, property and other valuables that an individual owns or of which he or she has rights of use.

e198	Products and technology, other specified
e199	Products and technology, unspecified

▶

e115 Products and technology for personal use in daily living

Equipment, products and technologies used by people in daily activities, including those adapted or specially designed, located in, on or near the person using them.

inclusion

general and assistive products and technology for personal use

FIGURE 5.4 ICF Products and Technology. *(Continued)*
Source: World Health Organization

e1150	e1151	e1158	e1159
Products and technology for personal use in daily living	Assistive products and technology for personal use in daily living	Products and technology for personal use in daily living, other specified	Products and technology for personal use in daily living, unspecified
Equipment, products and technologies used by people in daily activities, such as clothes, textiles, furniture, appliances, cleaning products and tools, not adapted or specially designed.	Adapted or specially designed equipment, products and technologies that assist people in daily living, such as prosthetic and orthotic devices, neural prostheses (e.g. functional stimulation devices that control bowels, bladder, breathing and heart rate), and environmental control units aimed at facilitating individuals' control over their indoor setting (scanners, remote control systems, voice-controlled systems, timer switches).		

FIGURE 5.4 *Continued*

TABLE 5.1

Crosswalk of *ICF* d and e Domains and AbleData Categories

ICF DOMAINS	ABLEDATA CATEGORIES
d ACTIVITIES AND PARTICIPATION	
d1 Chapter 1 Learning and Applying Knowledge	Education
	Prosthetics, Orthotics
d2 Chapter 2 General Tasks and Demands	Communication
	Walking, Wheeled
d3 Chapter 3 Communication	Mobility, Seating
d4 Chapter 4 Mobility	Prosthetics, Orthotics
	Transportation
d5 Chapter 5 Self-Care	Therapeutic Aids
d6 Chapter 6 Domestic Life	Housekeeping, Controls
d7 Chapter 7 Interpersonal Interactions and Relationships	Education, Workplace
	Environmental Adaptations
d8 Chapter 8 Major Life Areas	Recreation
d9 Chapter 9 Community, Social and Civic Life	

Cuts Across Domains:
Blind and Low Vision
Deaf and Hard of Hearing
Deaf Blind
Safety and Security
Computers
Transportation
■ On an individual level, it impacts mobility. On a community and societal level, accessible public transportation makes it possible for many to participate in community, social, and civic life.

e1 CHAPTER 1 PRODUCTS AND TECHNOLOGY

e110 Personal consumption (food, drugs)	
e115 Personal use in daily living	Orthotics
	Prosthetics
	Housekeeping
	Aids for Daily Living
	Computers
	Controls
	Blind and Low Vision
	Deaf and Hard of Hearing
	Deaf Blind
	Safety and Security
	Therapeutic Aids

(Continued)

TABLE 5.1
Crosswalk of *ICF* d and e Domains and AbleData Categories (*Continued*)

ICF DOMAINS	ABLEDATA CATEGORIES
e120 Personal indoor and outdoor mobility and transportation	Walking Wheeled Mobility Seating Transportation
e125 Communication	Communication
e130 Education	Education
e135 Employment	Workplace
e140 Culture, recreation and sport	Recreation
e145 Practice of religion and spirituality	
e150 Buildings for public use	Safety and Security Environmental Adaptations
e155 Buildings for private use	Safety and Security Environmental Adaptations
e160 Land development	
e165 Assets	

Source: Institute for Matching Person & Technology, Inc.

The authors further note that this definition was revised in the fifth edition of ISO 9999 to be even more in line with the *ICF*:

> Any product (including devices, equipment, instruments and software), especially produced or generally available, used by or for persons with disability
>
> ■ for participation;
> ■ to protect, support, train, measure or substitute for body functions/structures and activities; or
> ■ to prevent impairments, activity limitations or participation restrictions. (WHO-FIC Collaborating Centre in the Netherlands, 2010, p. 4)

The ISO 9999 contains five different types of assistive products:

1. Products that support a function but are not used as such in the performance of an activity (e.g., nebulizers, oxygen units)
2. Products that are used in the performance of an activity and that support a function or an activity (e.g., walking aids or assistive products for activities of daily living)

3. Products that are a substitute for a function/structure, that protect a function/structure, or that may support a function are not used in the performance of an activity but can be seen as a prerequisite for participation (e.g., a wig or a cap)
4. Products that are primarily used for training
5. Assistive products that are used to measure/monitor a function/structure, the performance of an activity, or an environmental or personal factor

Heerkens et al. (2010b) noted that assistive products used by a person with disability, but which require the assistance of another person for the products' operation, are included in the classification. ISO 9999, however, excludes several products and services from the definition of an assistive product:

■ Items used for the installation of assistive products
■ Solutions obtained by combinations of assistive products that are individually classified in the classification
■ Medicine
■ Assistive products and instruments used exclusively by health care professionals
■ Nontechnical solutions and services, such as personal assistance, guide dogs, or lip reading;
■ Implanted devices
■ Financial support

The list of ISO 9999 2011 codes and their descriptions are provided in Table 5.2 and a more detailed listing of products in Code 05, "Assistive Products for Training in Skills," are given in Appendix D because they are the ones most pertinent to cognitive functioning. Code 05.12 is specific to *assistive products for training in cognitive skill*. This code is defined as "assistive products designed to enhance the abilities that underlie reasoning and logical activities, e.g., memory, attention, concentration, conceptual and applied thinking."

Although some may question the suitability of classifying cognitive support technologies as "products for training," nonetheless, this is where they are included.

The ISO 9999 is used in several national databases of assistive products, including AbleData, which was presented earlier. However, a comparison of the AbleData categories in on pages 125–127 with the ISO 9999 codes in Table 5.2 reveals only moderate overlap (Abledata is addressing this). It is also true that when AbleData categories are cross walked with the *ICF* domains of Activities and Participation and Environmental Factors,

TABLE 5.2
ISO 9999: 2011 Classes

Assistive products for persons with disability—Classification and terminology

ISO 9999:2011 classifies assistive products based on a product's function. At its highest level, ISO 9999 defines 12 functional areas called "classes," each of which is subdivided into "subclasses." Within most subclasses, more specific categories called "divisions" are listed. ISO 9999 is produced by the International Organization for Standardization, an international federation of national standards bodies.

04	ASSISTIVE PRODUCTS FOR PERSONAL MEDICAL TREATMENT
05	ASSISTIVE PRODUCTS FOR TRAINING IN SKILLS
06	ORTHOSES AND PROSTHESES
09	ASSISTIVE PRODUCTS FOR PERSONAL CARE AND PROTECTION
12	ASSISTIVE PRODUCTS FOR PERSONAL MOBILITY
15	ASSISTIVE PRODUCTS FOR HOUSEKEEPING
18	FURNISHINGS AND ADAPTATIONS TO HOMES AND OTHER PREMISES
22	ASSISTIVE PRODUCTS FOR COMMUNICATION AND INFORMATION
24	ASSISTIVE PRODUCTS FOR HANDLING OBJECTS AND DEVICES
27	ASSISTIVE PRODUCTS FOR ENVIRONMENTAL IMPROVEMENT AND ASSESSMENT
28	ASSISTIVE PRODUCTS FOR EMPLOYMENT AND VOCATIONAL TRAINING
30	ASSISTIVE PRODUCTS FOR RECREATION

To see the full text of the classification, contact the International Organization for Standardization at http://www.iso.org.

we do not achieve a one-to-one correspondence, as evidenced in Table 5.2 (Abledata is addressing this as well). Thus, although there has been a recent trend to develop a consistent classification system and a terminology that is usable internationally, it is currently the case that classification systems remain different and that no one classification of ATDs has been uniformly adopted and used (Bauer, Elsaesser, & Arthanat, 2011). Therefore, talking about ATDs and product categories across national boundaries can be confusing. Furthermore, even within a country such as the United States, classifications differ among service delivery systems (e.g., those used by Individualized Education Program (IEP) teams, medical rehabilitation centers, vocational rehabilitation agencies). The confusion is further compounded by the fact that there exists a plethora of terms used to refer to products examples of which are shown in Figure 5.5.

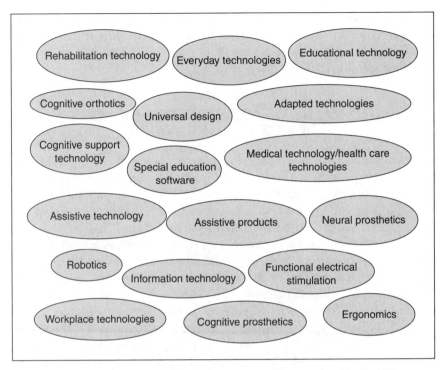

FIGURE 5.5 Terms used to refer to products used by people with disability.

Some outcomes of this lack of consistency and standardization include

- lack of communication as an individual moves from one system to another (e.g., from preschool through elementary and secondary to postsecondary education or vocational rehabilitation);
- confusion in coding for reimbursement under different payers;
- poor international shared language around ATDs; and
- frustration in searching for products in different catalogs and databases.

Cognitive rehabilitation depends on consistency and the ability to generalize across settings, which sometimes actually means retraining the same skills when the setting changes. Thus, when there is a change in AT (e.g., different smartphone or augmentative and alternative communication [AAC] device), the individual's progress can experience a setback. Other consequences are inconsistencies in what is taught and learned in preservice, in-service, and continuing education and training within the relevant disciplines associated with AT services and the selection and provision of devices to the persons who can benefit from them. Collaboration among designers, manufacturers, vendors, providers, consumers, researchers, and policy makers is negatively impacted, which affects how new products are funded, brought to market, and made known to providers and end users. Clearly, the lack of consistency in definition and classification is an issue in need of a solution (Babirad et al., 2010).

THE VALUE OF ASSISTIVE TECHNOLOGY DEVICES AND SERVICES

For individuals with physical, sensory, or cognitive disability, ATDs can facilitate independence in accomplishing activities (i.e., the ability or capacity to execute tasks or actions, such as reading, writing, walking/moving, dressing, and eating). For example, an individual with paralysis in the arms and shoulders caused by a high-level spinal cord injury can read a book independently with electronic page-turning devices and write with the assistance of a splint or word processor adapted with modified means of input and text entry. For those unable to walk because of paralysis, various adapted aids and utensils can promote independence in grooming and eating. The capacity to perform various activities enables a person with a disability to participate in desired life situations. ATDs enhance participation by providing the means to get around independently (e.g., wheelchairs, adapted vehicles, and ramps), care for oneself (e.g., built-up handles on eating utensils), and interact with others (e.g., voice-controlled computer input, telephone dialing devices). By enabling a person to perform desired tasks, assistive technologies offer the potential to provide a sense of autonomy as well as connection to the community. By accommodating a person's weaknesses and supporting his or her strengths, assistive technologies can reduce emotional and psychosocial as well as physical stress (Scherer, 2002a, 2004, 2005b; Scherer, Craddock, & Mackeogh, 2011).

AT is one of many environmental factors that affect the daily functioning of persons with disability, their performance of activities, and their pursuit of vocational, social, and community interests (e.g., Scherer, 2005a,b). Environmental factors encompass supports from one or more persons or organizations (*ICF* Environmental Factors Chapters 3 and 5), service animals (*ICF* Chapter 3), and the removal of barriers to functioning (*ICF* Chapter 2). Also included are the sociocultural environment of the person with a disability; existing accommodations within the built, physical, architectural space; and the nature of the services and resources available to persons with disability. Our focus, however, will continue to be on support from technologies, particularly those useful to individuals with cognitive disability. They include not only cognitive support technologies, but also products for mobility, communication, seeing, hearing, and activities of daily living. They are the topic of the next chapter.

6

Assistive Technologies for Mobility, Communication, Seeing, Hearing, and Activities of Daily Living

A brain is worth little without a tongue.
—French Proverb

*A*s the preceding French proverb indicates, remembering tasks and appointments will be useful only as long as the capabilities and skills exist to perform the task and get to the appointment. Contacting others is one thing, but being able to truly communicate with them is another. Woodworking skills are less efficient when one has little hand control or dexterity. For persons with a cognitive disability, there are often associated losses of function in other areas. Individuals with learning disability and autism, like Ryan, have difficulty processing sensory information. In addition to his right arm and hand weakness, Delmar experiences fatigue. Marjorie had hearing loss in addition to dementia. After her fall and hip replacement, she required a wheelchair and special seating and positioning. Her earlier stroke had also left her with left-handed weakness. As people age, life's emotional and physical bruises add to the toll taken by the mere passage of time, and all body structures become weaker and less efficient. Marjorie was no exception. This is also true for Theresa as she experiences hearing loss, carpal tunnel syndrome, and increasing fatigue. We know that lost visual acuity, fatigue, and weakness bring a higher risk of falling and receiving other injuries. Each of these individuals can benefit from assistive technologies (ATs).

As discussed in previous chapters, Delmar received a traumatic brain injury (TBI) from a motorcycle accident that also resulted in his right arm being fractured in several places along with crush-type injuries to his wrist and hand. In addition to memory problems and fatigue, his limited range of motion in the right hand and wrist gave him poor gripping strength and hand control. However, he is able to craft custom gunstocks and grips made of wood and stone, and his main goal is to be able to continue doing this more efficiently by using one-handed technology.

His rehabilitation team supports his goal and borrowed three types of one-handed keyboards so that Delmar could compare competing products to better choose which works best for him. Delmar was able to keep each one for a few days to give them a fair trial in situations of actual use. The first one he tried was the FrogPad (http://www.frogpad.com), a portable and single-handed keyboard that provides ease of use with handheld computers, personal digital assistants, and wireless phones. However, Delmar's memory problems made this too different for him. He was very uncomfortable with it and felt like it accentuated his problems. The second keyboard he tried was the GlidePoint (which was his rehabilitation team's favorite). It looks more like a regular keyboard, and Delmar could glide his fingers across the GlidePoint surface to click, drag, and highlight by gently tapping on the pad. Delmar did have enough control over his left hand to do this effectively, and he thought with more practice using his left hand, he might be able to use it. The third one that he tried was a panel keyboard that he said was like using a regular keyboard but a lot smaller. Delmar chose the latter.

Other assistive technology devices (ATDs) of interest to Delmar are low-tech, one-handed tools. His rehabilitation team reviewed all the one-handed tools in their technology lab, including pictures of them being used and descriptions of their size, weight, and features. Delmar chose a wrench designed for accessibility with a sleek jaw profile and compact tool length. He also chose needle nose pliers with a comfortable cushioned grip and special design to minimize bending of the wrist. There are foam and rubber grips available that slip over small handles to make them instantly larger, and he wanted several. The AgrAbility Project (http://www.agrability project.org/assistivetech/tips/handtools.cfm) is an excellent resource for educating individuals such as Delmar about available ergonomic and one-handed tools. Other adapted tools are available; a sample of which are as follows:

Hammers:
- Stanley AntiVibe III Hammer
- Stiletto Titanium Hammers
- Lee Valley Tools Nailing Hammer

Pliers:
- Pliers, STORK, Needle Nose, Pistol Grip 912EP
- Stanley MaxGrip Self-Adjusting Pliers

Screwdrivers:
- Stanley Multibit Ratcheting Screwdriver
- Craftsman(r) Professional 12–pc. Grip Driver Set (angled handle for better grip)

Wrenches:
- Craftsman 16–inch Speed Wrench (wrench for confined spaces)
- Craftsman(r) 8–inch Clench Wrench (self-adjusting, ratcheting wrench)

Knives, Scissors, Cutters:
- Cutters, STORK, Diagonal, Light Duty or Medium Duty, Pistol Grip
- North Coast Medical, Inc., cutting utensils
- Fiskars PowerGrip Utility Knife
- Stanley SharpTooth Tool Box Saw—tooth design that cuts in both directions making cutting faster and reducing fatigue

Other:
- Wolfcraft's Quick Jaw clamps—One-Handed Gripper and Clamp
- Anti-Vibration Gloves

When we see the breadth and depth of product lines available to accommodate various needs just within the category of one-handed tools, then we can appreciate just why there are about 40,000 products listed in the AbleData database! Many products (ATDs) come in different sizes, styles, and with options regarding features and accessories. Providing the most appropriate ATD requires a comparison of competing products and time to try them in actual situations of use. Examples of important factors to consider are the need for specialized skills to use effectively, ease of operation, and comfort with use. As in the example of Delmar, professionals who have access to an assortment of basic items for different needs can provide springboards to other ideas, which will allow for creativity and the exercise of personal choice and preference.

Assistive devices range from low-tech aids, such as built-up handles on eating utensils, to high-tech aids—computerized systems. When people speak of high-tech assistive devices, ATs, or rehabilitation technologies, they are usually referring to those with electronic components or those which are operated by a computer. The number of these devices has increased dramatically in recent years.

Devices that consist of nonmechanical, nonelectronic adaptations to existing products (such as Delmar's special grip added to handles and utensils to make it thicker) are called *low-tech* or *simple* devices. Those with simple mechanical operations are considered *medium-tech*. It is important to realize that, by law, all of these devices are ATs and that a low-tech device has as much value as a high-tech one for users who find the device has enhanced their functioning, independence, and quality of life. In general, individuals with the most severe disability require the most customized and computerized technologies to enable their independent functioning. In fact, if the full range of technologies were not available, many individuals with complex needs would not be able to live independently in the community.

FINDING ASSISTIVE TECHNOLOGY DEVICES

A key to appropriate AT selection is knowing what to search for and where to best find it. A good place to begin a search is by identifying the best and most relevant category of products. A crucial point to remember, however, is that a product designed for one primary use and categorized in one category may have other applications of benefit to persons with cognitive disability. For example, a vibrating and talking alarm watch is a good cognitive support technology for memory. It may, however, be listed under products for *deaf and hard of hearing* and *blind and low vision*. Products to amplify and focus sound as well as flashing lights for signaling will also be found in products for *deaf and hard of hearing*.

As noted in Chapter Five, the *International Classification of Functioning, Disability and Health (ICF)* defines assistive products and technology as "any product, instrument, equipment or technology adapted or specially designed for improving the functioning of a disabled person" (WHO, p. 191). The *ICF* does not, however, provide a classification or categorization of products, referring instead to the International Organization for Standardization (ISO) 9999 classification of technical aids (which includes software). In the United States, AbleData will be mapped to ISO 9999. Table 6.1 provides the mapping of the AbleData categories to the *ICF* and ISO 9999. The AbleData categorization is used in this chapter to organize relevant devices helpful to individuals with cognitive disability who also have additional needs. It is important to note, however, that other classifications exist that emphasize products and functional/sensory needs somewhat differently (e.g., online resources such as http://www.rehabtool.com and http://www.fctd.info). In 2003, European experts created a comprehensive information service on AT which includes information on over 66,000 products: The European Assistive Technology

TABLE 6.1
AbleData's Categories of Assistive Technology Products Cross-Walked With the ICF and ISO 9999

ISO 9999—class 22 assistive products for communication and information
ISO 9999—class 12.39 assistive products for orientation
ICF e125—products and technology for communication

■ **Blind and Low Vision**
Products for people with visual disability
Major Categories: computers, educational aids, health care, information storage, kitchen aids, labeling, magnification, office equipment, orientation and mobility, reading, recreation, sensors, telephones, time, tools, travel, typing, writing (Braille)

■ **Deaf and Hard of Hearing**
Products for people with hearing disability
Major Categories: amplification, driving, hearing aids, recreational electronics, sign language, signal switches, speech training, telephones, time

■ **Deaf Blind**
Products for people who are both deaf and blind

ISO 9999—class 22 assistive products for communication and information
ICF e125—products and technology for communication

■ **Communication**
Products to help people with disability related to speech, writing, and other methods of communication
Major Categories: augmentative and alternative communication, headwands, mouthsticks, signal systems, telephones, typing, writing

ISO 9999—class 09 assistive products for personal care and protection
ISO 9999—class 15 assistive products for housekeeping
ICF e115—products and technology for personal use in daily living

■ **Aids for Daily Living**
Products to aid in activities of daily living
Major Categories: bathing, carrying, child care, clothing, dispenser aids, dressing, drinking, feeding, grooming/hygiene, handle padding, health care, holding, reaching, time, smoking, toileting, transfer

■ **Housekeeping**
Products to assist in cooking, cleaning, and other household activities, as well as adapted appliances
Major Categories: food preparation, housekeeping, general cleaning, ironing, laundry, shopping

(Continued)

TABLE 6.1
**AbleData's Categories of Assistive Technology Products Cross-Walked
With the ICF and ISO 9999 (*Continued*)**

- ■ **Computers**
  Products to allow people with disability to use desktop and laptop computers and other kinds of information technology
  Major Categories: software, hardware, computer accessories

- ■ **Controls**
  Products to provide people with disability with the ability to start, stop, or adjust electric or electronic devices
  Major Categories: environmental controls control switches

ISO 9999—class 06 orthoses and prostheses
ICF e115—products and technology for personal use in daily living

- ■ **Orthotics**
  Braces and other products to support or supplement joints or limbs
  Major Categories: head and neck, lower extremity, torso, upper extremity

- ■ **Prosthetics**
  Products for amputees
  Major Categories: lower extremity, upper extremity

ISO 9999—class 04 assistive products for personal medical treatment

- ■ **Therapeutic Aids**
  Products to assist in treatment for health problems and therapy and training for certain disability
  Major Categories: ambulation training, biofeedback, evaluation, exercise, fine and gross motor skills, perceptual motor, positioning, pressure/massage modality equipment, respiratory aids, rolls, sensory integration, stimulators, therapy furnishings, thermal/water modality equipment, traction

---

ICF e120—products and technology for personal indoor and outdoor mobility and transportation
ISO 9999—class 12 assistive products for personal mobility [does not include public transit]

- ■ **Walking**
  Products to aid people with disability who are able to walk or stand with assistance
  Major Categories: canes, crutches, standing, walkers

- ■ **Wheeled Mobility**
  Products and accessories to enable people with mobility disability to move freely indoors and outdoors
  Major Categories: wheelchairs (manual, sport, and powered), wheelchair alternatives (scooters), wheelchair accessories, carts, transporters, stretchers

(Continued)

TABLE 6.1
AbleData's Categories of Assistive Technology Products Cross-Walked With the ICF and ISO 9999 (*Continued*)

■ **Seating**
Products to assist people to sit comfortably and safely
Major Categories: seating systems, cushions, therapeutic seats

■ **Transportation**
Products to enable people with disability to drive or ride in cars, vans, trucks, and buses
Major Categories: mass transit vehicles and facilities, vehicles, vehicle accessories

ISO 9999—class 05 assistive products for training in skills
ICF e130—products and technology for education

■ **Education**
Products to provide people with disability with access to educational materials and instruction in school and in other learning environments
Major Categories: classroom, instructional materials

ISO 9999—class 28 assistive products for employment and vocational training
ICF e135—products and technology for employment

■ **Workplace**
Products to aid people with disability at work
Major Categories: agricultural equipment, office equipment, tools, vocational assessment, vocational training, work stations

ISO 9999—class 30 assistive products for recreation
ICF e140—products and technology for culture, recreation, and sport

■ **Recreation**
Products to assist people with disability with their leisure and athletic activities
Major Categories: crafts, electronics, gardening, music, photography, sewing, sports, toys

ISO 9999—class 18 furnishings and adaptations to homes and other premises
ISO 9999—class 27 assistive products for environmental improvement and assessment
ICF e150—design, construction, and building products and technology of buildings for public use
ICF e155—design, construction, and building products and technology of buildings for private use

■ **Environmental Adaptations**
Products that make the built environment more accessible
Major Categories: indoor environment, furniture, outdoor environment, vertical accessibility, houses, specialties, lighting, signs

(Continued)

TABLE 6.1
AbleData's Categories of Assistive Technology Products Cross-Walked
With the ICF and ISO 9999 (*Continued*)

■ **Safety and Security**
Products to protect health and home
Major Categories: alarm and security systems, child proof devices, electric cords, lights, locks

Used with permission of AbleData.com

Information Network (EASTIN, http://www.eastin.info). Finally, a new ATD classification has been developed (Bauer, Elsaesser, & Arthanat, 2011) to provide consistency among the *ICF* and various other coding systems, which in the future may lead to increased consistency among classification systems, AT catalogs/directories, and AT websites.

Specific Product Groupings

In Chapter 5, *assistive technologies* or *devices* were described as products and re-sources for enhancing the capabilities of people who have functional limitations or disability. In the *ICF* classification of "Products and Technology," which is Chapter 1 of Environmental Factors (see Figure 5.4), are devices designed to enable people to engage fully in a range of activities and environments. The first row of categories in Figure 5.4 will be discussed in this chapter; the remaining four (buildings for public use, buildings for private use, land development, and assets) will be considered in subsequent chapters.

The categorization used by AbleData.com and ISO 9999 are presented because they are consistent with the *ICF*. In Table 6.1, the AbleData and ISO 9999 product classification areas are matched with the corresponding *ICF* classifications.

Fortunately, there are resources like AbleData that serve as an online catalog of these products. AbleData has hotlinks to device manufacturers and vendors, a section on books and other resources, and links to key orga-nizations working with AT.

Examples of ATs according to AbleData category are provided subse-quently. A cautionary note needs to be given, however, about examples of specific products provided. Although these devices are representative of what is on the market today, advances in technology may render them obsolete in the near future. Products come and go, and the key point of the following discussion is to present a broad enough range of available devices to stimulate ideas about the kinds of support most useful for any given person. The wisest course of action is to maintain contact with local experts, product suppliers, current print catalogs, and online resources to identify the most current option in an area of need.

■ **Blind and Low Vision**
Products for people with visual disability
Major Categories: computers, educational aids, health care, information storage, kitchen aids, labeling, magnification, office equipment, orientation and mobility, reading, recreation, sensors, telephones, time, tools, travel, typing, writing (Braille)

ATDs for blindness and low vision (above) are chiefly designed to help with reading, interpreting visual information, and safe travel. Magnifiers, Braille or voice output systems for reading, and canes for travel are examples of devices in this category.

Computer users with blindness and low vision require help with computer input, navigation, and output. Those who could benefit from computer screen magnification have several product choices, including the ZoomText Magnifier from Ai Squared (http://www.aisquared.com) that magnifies the screen up to 36 times without sacrificing image clarity. Synthesized speech output software, marketed as "screen readers," speaks the information on the screen (e.g., JAWS [http://www.freedomscientific. com] or Window-Eyes [http://www.gwmicro.com]). *Reading systems* are integrated software packages that include tools like text-to-speech, optical character recognition (OCR), and screen magnification to help people who have difficulties reading, processing, comprehending, and/or generating written information. These systems have a range of options, including text magnification, text highlighting, limited blocks of text on the screen, and so on, while synchronizing the visual output with aural output. They can also include word prediction and other enhancements to help with text generation. Examples are WYNN (http://www.freedomscientific.com) and Kurzweil 3000 (http://www.kurzweiledu.com).

Another device to help individuals with low vision see print material is a video magnification system, or closed-circuit television (CCTV). This device consists of a video camera that records information viewed on its surface and an attached monitor on which the information is displayed. One example of a CCTV is the Aladdin Rainbow Elite from Telesensory, which records and displays information in color as well as black and white. This device also has the unique ability to manipulate the colors of information to accommodate the vision needs of various users. For example, if a book is being viewed through the CCTV, the black text and white background can be converted to a high-contrast format such as yellow text on a blue background or green text on a black background. The unit has easy to use controls and magnifies up to 35 times. CCTVs can work with type, handwriting, and photos and illustrations. The user places a printed page, crossword puzzle, contract, labels, and so forth, on a table or plate and adjusts the magnification level and display colors to the desired level.

There are several options for those who would benefit from having books read to them, and this applies to not only those with low vision or blindness, but also those who best learn and retain information from multisensory input. The National Library Service for the Blind and Physically Handicapped, U.S. Library of Congress, has produced accessible versions of books for qualified individuals (available through your local library). Recording for the Blind & Dyslexic (http://www.rfbd.org) also has recordings of books, as does the American Printing House for the Blind, Inc. (APH; http://www.aph.org). The APH has produced the *APH Instructional Products Catalog*, which lists various accessible kits, aids, tools, and supplies useful for low vision needs at home, at work, or at school. This catalog is a complete listing of APH products, except for textbooks. In addition to low vision aids, they included talking computer software and electronic notetakers.

Other products originally designed for persons with low vision but which can be helpful to persons with various needs include talking alarm clocks, large button and digital talking watches, and portable CCTVs that are small and lightweight and can be worn around the neck to allow those with low vision to read the prices of items while shopping, reading menus, looking through phone books, and so on. Other portable options are reading pens that scan the words on can labels, receipts, and so on, and displays the words in large print or reads them aloud.

■ **Deaf and Hard of Hearing**
Products for people with hearing disability
Major Categories: amplification, driving, hearing aids, recreational electronics, sign language, signal switches, speech training, telephones, time

ATDs for people who are hard of hearing or deaf (above) are designed for sound amplification and concentration (amplified telephones, personal FM systems), access to information (captioned television, e-mail, text messaging), and alerting or signaling (vibrotactile pagers, flashing timers, and alarms). Products range from personal and portable devices to those that benefit multiple people at the same time and cover a large area.

The Pocketalker Ultra System is a personal amplification device for those who have difficulty hearing and understanding verbal communication. It does not require the use of hearing aids (http://www.teltex.com). An easy to use, discrete, portable system for one-on-one conversation and listening to TV that can also be used without hearing aids is the Comfort Contego. It can be placed in the center of a table to cover a group conversation (http://www.tecear.com).

For alerting the person to sounds, the KA1000 Alerting System is a wireless system for home or office that allows notifications to be received for various everyday alerts. It has a built-in clock, lamp outlet, telephone jack, bed shaker, and the ability to connect additional wireless transmitters that can be used to connect fire or smoke alarms, home security systems, videophones, and various other audible alarms (http://www.computty. com). Additional products are (a) the Telephone Signaler, which signals incoming calls by flashing a lamp on/off automatically, and (b) the Door Knocker 125, which can be placed above any door and its ultra bright LED indicator will flash repeatedly when someone is knocking.

■ **Communication**
Products to help people with disability related to speech, writing, and other methods of communication
Major Categories: augmentative and alternative communication (AAC), headwands, mouthsticks, signal systems, telephones, typing, writing

ATDs for communication (above) center on the ability to send and receive messages in spoken and written form. AAC devices, designed for those with speech and language production difficulties, are in this category. Augmentative communication products supplement the person's own communication abilities, including any residual speech, sounds, gestures, and signs. Alternative communication products are meant to provide speech when it is otherwise absent. AAC devices range from manual communication boards to computerized devices with synthesized speech output. Products are designed to serve the speech needs of persons of all ages. For adults who are in the hospital recovering from a traumatic or acquired brain injury, an 8 1/2 × 11 piece of cardboard with large print letters, key phrases, or illustrations, can be very useful in helping them convey their thoughts and feelings. As recovery progresses, but the production of speech remains difficult, more sophisticated devices may be needed.

An easy to learn option is the *ChatBox*, a portable communication device that holds 10 minutes of prerecorded messages that can be activated or spoken by a single-button press (http://www.saltillo.com). More sophisticated, computerized options include the Essence PRO, a communication device and Windows XP-based computer in one. It is simple to use and easy to access even as motor abilities change. There is a "one-touch" transition from computing to speech output, and it has large keys that make access easier for those with visual or motor challenges (http://www.prentrom.com).

For individuals who own an iPod, EZ Speech is an application that offers a quick and efficient communication platform for conversational speech in male or female voices (http://www.gusinc.com). EZ Speech organizes favorite phrases by topic for simplified conversation building.

A popular option for individuals who want help with spelling and grammar is the *Franklin Speaking Language Master—Special Edition* (http://www.franklin.com). It contains 300,000 words and definitions and a thesaurus with more than 500,000 words. It has an instant spell corrector, grammar guide, as well as educational word games. The dictionary pronounces every letter, word, definition, synonym, and more. Up to 26 messages can be stored for playback and used as an augmentative communication device. It also includes adjustable character size for easy reading, large user-friendly keyboard, press-on locator dots and orientation keys for easy navigation, headphones for private listening, and A/C adapter, as well as instructions on cassette tape and in printed format.

For individuals who want support for text entry or handwriting, there are many useful products. For example, the *NEO 2* is a low-cost, go-anywhere portable laptop with an instant on/off, one-button file access, and can store about 200 pages of text (http://www.renlearn.com/neo/NEO2). The *RinG-Pen Writing Instrument* is a writing aid designed for those with poor finger control and decreased ability to grasp (http://www.service.maddak.com).

■ **Aids for Daily Living**
Products to aid in activities of daily living
Major Categories: bathing, carrying, child care, clothing, dispenser aids, dressing, drinking, feeding, grooming/hygiene, handle padding, health care, holding, reaching, time, smoking, toileting, transfer

ATDs for personal and self-care (above) for those who have functional limitations in the fingers, hands, and arms enable independence in such fundamental areas as grooming, bathing, dressing, eating, and operating home appliances. Although these tasks may seem simple, success with small and simple tasks leads to success with larger and more complex ones. Who can go to work if they are unable to get dressed? Who can go to school if they are unable to bathe?

Low-tech options include nonslip placemats under dinner plates to prevent sliding of the plate, eating utensils that are angled or have a larger surface area for gripping, jar openers, long-handled sponges strapped across the back of the hand for bathing, Velcro closures instead of buttons on clothing, zipper pulls and special holders for pots and pans on the stove, and pistol-grip reachers that extend the ability to reach and grasp an item by squeezing a trigger on the handle to open and close two-pronged gripper.

Additional products range from lamps that turn on and off by touching them anywhere on their base to complex systems that allow several appliances to be controlled by voice. These complex systems are known as *electronic aids to daily living* or *environmental control systems*. Large-button telephones with speakerphone and abbreviated or quick-dialing capabilities are options that give persons with upper extremity limitations independence in calling and talking with other persons.

■ **Housekeeping**
Products to assist in cooking, cleaning, and other household activities, as well as adapted appliances
Major Categories: food preparation, housekeeping, general cleaning, ironing, laundry, shopping

ATDs for housekeeping (above) include adapted tools for cleaning and food preparation, carts on wheels, powered door openers, pull out trays, and lost item finders. There are many more devices in this category.

■ **Walking**
Products to aid people with disability who are able to walk or stand with assistance
Major Categories: canes, crutches, standing, walkers
■ **Wheeled Mobility**
Products and accessories that enable people with mobility disability to move freely indoors and outdoors
Major Categories: wheelchairs (manual, sport, and powered), wheelchair alternatives (scooters), wheelchair accessories, carts, transporters, stretchers
■ **Seating**
Products that assist people to sit comfortably and safely
Major Categories: seating systems, cushions, therapeutic seats

ATDs for walking and mobility (previous page) address getting around in one's environment and exercising choice over the environments one wishes to be in. Over half of all ATDs are designed for individuals with mobility disability. Low-tech products to facilitate mobility include basic canes and crutches. Canes can be made of wood or metal and can have a single "foot," or three or four "feet." A cane with four feet is referred to as a *quad cane*. They are useful for persons with weakness who desire assistance with their balance while walking.

Crutches, too, can be made of wood or metal. *Axillary crutches* support the person under the arm and require the hand to grip the crutch at around hip level. A *forearm crutch* has a cuff that goes around the arm to assist persons who do not have the hand strength for the use of an axillary crutch. These devices are more complex in design because they need to make up for more functional limitation. Another name for forearm crutches is *Lofstrand crutches*.

Like canes and crutches, *walkers* come in several styles depending on the person's functional need and preferences. Basically, a walker is a lightweight three-sided frame that extends in front of and on both sides of the person. Although walkers come in various sizes and shapes and have many different features, they all have four points of contact with the floor or ground. Walkers are usually adjustable in height so that the top is slightly below the user's waist, enabling the person to lean on it for support and balance while walking. A walker provides a wide base of support. It may have wheels, which are helpful on cement or linoleum, but not as useful on carpeting, and it may have built-in seats so that a person can stop and rest when needed.

Wheelchairs are used by persons who cannot walk unassisted and thus need more assistance with mobility than can be obtained from a walker. Wheelchairs are "chairs on wheels" and they are either manual (the wheels are manually propelled, or rotated, by the user or by someone pushing the wheelchair for the user) or battery powered or motorized. A joystick, a "sip-and-puff" tube, or a voice-activated interface controls the speed and direction of powered wheelchairs. Individuals using wheelchairs may need to have additional devices or products to ensure their comfort and safety. These include such things as tilt and recline features on the wheelchair itself, or *special support cushions and seating systems*.

Optional wheelchair equipment may involve adding a hydraulic mechanism to raise and lower the wheelchair seat and accessories such as wheelchair backpacks, baskets, lap trays, and cup holders. Wheelchair and scooter users also require ramps for accessing different levels of buildings and lifts for getting into vans and buses independently. Both manual and powered wheelchairs require special tie-down and restraint systems while riding in other vehicles such as buses or vans unless the person is able to transfer out of the chair and the chair can be folded or disassembled for transport. A person using a powered wheelchair who wishes to drive typically needs to have a van equipped with hand or head controls.

ATDs for culture, recreation, sport, and leisure have made most sports, recreational, and leisure activities accessible to persons with disability—from tethered sit-skiing to scuba diving, wheelchair basketball, sailing and card-shuffling. ATDs for child's play include adapted toys and switches for controlling electronic toys and games. In cases such as Ryan, he has simply needed to adapt to which sports suit him best. For example, playing on a basketball team after school allows him to release a lot of energy and make friends. However, competitive team sports often make him anxious. Thus, for competitive purposes, he prefers participating in individual sports such as tennis.

ATDs for education and the workplace focus on making educational and job materials accessible to the person with a disability as well as the worksite and school setting. Products include specialized workstations and adapted tools, as well as desirable modifications in the relevant environments. Ryan, in particular, benefits from having a Smart Board in his classroom where he can write answers to questions, allowing for a more interactive and hands-on learning experience.

Computer access can be made easier by alternate means of input. Examples of computer input options include the following (http://www .rjcooper.com):

- BIGGY—BIG cursors and more!
- CrossScanner—single switch method to completely control a computer
- ICanEmail—simple, talking, large print, e-mail program
- OnScreen—on-the-screen virtual keyboard
- Slo-Mo—FREE! (Mac only) Slows down all software so that it may become accessible (great for games)
- Thunder-RJ—Screen reader-on-a-stick! For blind, learning disability (LD), or early readers
- WordComplete—helper for slow typists, people with LD, poor spellers, and/or those that need word suggestions
- Mini-Keyboard/Trackpad —"Text" your text to your computer!
- Mouse Button-Box—Control the cursor, with buttons!
- Keys-U-See—super-bright, LARGE PRINT, keyboard with my Left/ Right Separator and a keyboard skin!
- BigKeys LARGE keyboards
- Magic Touch Screen—affordable and durable clip-on touch screens
- IntelliKeys—flat, customizable keyboard
- SAM—Switch-Adapted Mouse devices/switch interfaces
  - Trackball
  - Joysticks
- Foot Switch

Voice input is a popular choice for many individuals. For example, *Dragon NaturallySpeaking 11* is a speech recognition device that allows those with little or no arm use to create documents, send e-mail and instant messages, surf the Web, and more just by speaking the desired content (http://www.nuance.com).

AT products for the practice of religion and spirituality are adapted or specially designed products that are given or take on a symbolic meaning in the context of the practice of religion or spirituality. Examples of products include rosaries with large beads for those with poor dexterity, religious print materials in large print, adapted prayer mats, and special protection for wheelchair wheels when entering temples.

In summary, different people need different choices and adaptations. There may be 50 different types of communication devices or reading aids to help people of various ability levels. This chapter is not meant to be comprehensive but to provide a general idea of the range of assistance available for persons with cognitive disability in order to lead lives of independence and quality. For information on specific types of products, the reader is encouraged to visit the AbleData website at http://www .AbleData.com or other websites listed in Chapter 5. The next chapter will focus on ATs for cognition and its various elements (memory, thought, emotion, and so on) and how they can help an individual with a cognitive disability to be more independent, self-determining, and successful in performing activities and participating in desired life roles.

7

Assistive Technologies for Cognition

Thinking is easy, acting is difficult, and to put one's thoughts into action is the most difficult thing in the world.
—Johann Wolfgang von Goethe

*C*ognitive support technology (CST) is a special class of assistive products designed to increase, maintain, or improve functional capabilities for individuals whose cognitive changes limit their effective performance of daily activities. CSTs have become more commonplace and diverse (Bharucha et al., 2009; Braddock, Rizzolo, Thompson, & Bell, 2004; Depompei et al., 2008; Gillette & DePompei, 2004; Sablier, Stip, & Franck, 2009).

Broadly defined, CST could refer to very familiar, basic products used by people with and without disability to support memory, organization, or other cognitive functions, such as planner books, calendars, labels and Post-it notes placed strategically, wristwatches, and shopping lists. Simple and low-cost devices such as magnifying lenses, index cards, and timers/alarm clocks can promote independence and improve the individual's quality of life. Technologies supporting interaction with people or information (telecommunication technologies) are also important resources for individuals with cognitive disability, which include telephones, pagers, and the Internet.

There are also specialized devices designed expressly for use by individuals with cognitive disability and their caregivers. These specialty products have features that can

1. maintain, organize, and facilitate access to information;
2. present suggestions, instructions, or corrections to the user either on demand or at prescribed times;
3. assume responsibility for task components that have proven too complex for an individual to complete independently, so that

159

activities in which those components are embedded can be successfully completed;

4. provide more comprehensive, interactive guidance for tasks that are too difficult for the user to initiate or perform even with other types of modifications and compensatory strategies; and

5. monitor the quality of the user's task performance so errors can be tracked and the CST intervention subsequently modified in an attempt to reduce those errors (Scherer, Hart, Kirsch, & Schulthesis, 2005). Regardless of the sophistication of a device, the primary goal of CST interventions is to improve the performance of functional activities that are critical components of life-role fulfillment and participation in community activities, that contribute substantially to subjective well-being and quality of life, and that significantly reduce caregiver burden.

We saw in Figure 3.2 in Chapter 3 that when compared to persons with *a variety of* other diagnoses, stroke survivors' functioning was the worst. We also noted that people with bipolar disorder and traumatic brain injury (TBI) indicated significant environmental barriers to their optimal performance and participation. We can conclude, therefore, that these individuals in particular are in need of accommodating environments and supports for activities and participation.

According to Stiers, Perry, Kennedy, and Scherer (2011), meta-analyses have shown that some types of cognitive deficits respond better to restorative efforts to improve the underlying function, whereas other types of cognitive deficits respond better to compensatory efforts to accommodate the problem. Compensatory efforts include personal strategies and environmental accommodations, specialized technologies or CSTs, and the use of everyday technologies. We will discuss each in turn in this chapter and throughout the subsequent ones.

STRATEGIES

Strategies for optimizing the strengths and accommodating the needs of an individual with a cognitive disability are limited only by the ingenuity and resourcefulness of those working on deriving them. The following is an example of what one vocational rehabilitation counselor did to help a college student struggling to remain in school.

Helping Louisa Succeed in University

Louisa has been diagnosed with bipolar disorder and specific learning disability. She is a full-time student at university currently majoring in liberal studies. She is currently struggling in school and in danger of failing her classes.

Louisa received her associate of arts degree and transferred to university 1 year ago. However, going from community college to a 4-year university was not an easy transition for her, and she is currently on academic probation. Louisa's strengths are that she is very open and friendly and communicates well. However, some of her limitations are that she avoids dealing with any hardship and often withdraws and quits when things get tough. She is in her early 30s and trying to complete her bachelor's degree, but she has many barriers.

The matching person and technology (MPT) assessments were used to help identify strategies that may help Louisa. Through the MPT results, I was able to identify and narrow my focus to the areas where she needed the most assistance. A disincentive to using assistance is that Louisa may lack the discipline and motivation to actually use helpful tools.

We were able to identify that despite not having any difficulties with seeing, hearing, and use of her physical body, Louisa had great difficulties understanding and remembering. Louisa needs help with reading and having textbooks read to her. Additionally, she has difficulties in math and would benefit from a talking calculator to say the numbers out loud. She informed me that she also gets distracted in classrooms because of side conversations.

Suggestions made were to sit closer to the front where side conversations will be minimized and also to use reading software to have the textbooks and lecture notes read to her out loud. I called and spoke with the disability support services coordinator and the recommendation was to order audio textbooks for Louisa from the Recording for the Blind & Dyslexic (RFB&D). Audio textbooks would allow her to hear the text spoken as she read it. We also recommended the use of a yellow highlighter so she could emphasize key concepts as she read and listened. This would not only help her focus her attention, but would also facilitate later review for her exams. Finally, she should summarize what she has read and learned on index cards, sorted by topic for test preparation.

Louisa is currently taking psychotropic medications that may have impeded her learning. This fact, plus her distractibility and difficulties with attention and concentration, suggests that she needs help to stay focused during reading. Thus, recorded texts are a reasonable accommodation.

Follow-up with Louisa. As of this week, Louisa is passing all her classes. She has finals this week and she e-mailed me a few days ago that her current standing for spring quarter are two Cs—and one B. This is a drastic improvement from 12 weeks ago when she was placed on academic probation. Louisa reports that what really helped her was using the audio textbooks and being able to go over her notes for review. Louisa also said that she feels that she was able to be more successful this quarter because she felt a lot of support and understanding from me and her disability support services coordinator. Also, being placed on academic probation was a wake-up call that she must work harder than other students in the classroom.

Having useful strategies was important to Louisa's success. Just as valuable was the support she received and having someone derive those strategies for and with her. Another focus was on *minimizing distractions* by encouraging her to sit in front of the classroom or lecture hall (in other words, altering the environmental context). When the focus was on her reading, many things were done to aid her concentration and learning: The use of *multisensory presentation* of written information (text, audio, yellow highlight) involved her vision, hearing, and tactile senses. *Index cards, notebooks,* and *Post-it notes* are very inexpensive and easily obtained resources. They helped Louisa by having her *rewrite the information* she read and highlighted. The *written summaries* were useful in studying for her exams. Once she used these strategies and got into a routine for reading and studying, she improved her academic performance.

Other strategies could have involved the use of *color coding* with different colored highlighters, organizing her index cards into colored boxes or folders or envelopes, and the formation of a study or *discussion group* (as long as it could be organized to help her improve her focus and not be a further distraction). *Schedules, to-do lists,* and *pocket calendars* are useful for meeting deadlines for assignments and building in adequate time for studying. Caregivers can also provide compensatory supports such as verbal reminders, physical and verbal cues, or assistance with other organizational strategies.

Photos can be helpful in stimulating and maintaining a conversation. For individuals with memory loss, the addition of *pictures* can aid recall, as can *demonstrations and models, step-by-step guides, breaking tasks into small manageable parts,* and *the use of checklists and priority lists.* A portable *chalk* or *whiteboard* can be useful on the low-tech end of the spectrum, whereas small *voice recorders and video cameras, copy pens,* and *recording pens* can be used for those who can reliably remember to buy and change batteries. Table 7.3 provides 14 examples of the wide range of strategies and products useful for secondary and postsecondary students.

Many individuals with "mental, emotional, and behavioral disabilities" benefit from strategies and technologies, but when they have stress and anxiety, they may require accommodations in order to feel comfortable with use, such as added consistency and routine. There are evidence-based principles that lead to effective strategies for teaching or reteaching various skills and concepts to people with compromised learning (Sohlberg, Ehlhardt, & Kennedy, 2005). It is also helpful to exchange ideas with others for deriving creative ways to address the barriers faced by individuals with specific needs. For example, during their online course on assistive technology (AT) at San Diego State University (see Chapter 3 and Endnote 4), vocational rehabilitation counselors derived the following approaches and ideas. The discussion was initiated by one counselor who posted the following questions to the class:

> I work with the mental health population. They often have difficulties with organization, memory, and lack interpersonal skills. What types of devices have other counselors purchased to help with organization and memory? What about AT devices

to assist with stress and anxiety, like the ball you squeeze to let out stress? In terms of organization and memory, I have authorized palm pilots and voice recorders, but I find clients need even more. Any ideas?

These were the responses and ideas that were offered:

Consumers with psychiatric disability may have difficulty maintaining daily information. Accommodations can include allowing the individual the ability to tape record meetings, provide written documentation of counseling sessions and employment meetings, provide written instructions, allow additional time for training, and develop written checklists for task completion. Consumers with psychiatric disability may have cognitive limitations that impede their ability to complete job tasks on time or to employers' expectations. Accommodations in this area may include making a daily checklist of things that need to be done, use of a calendar to document meetings and deadlines, remind the consumer of important deadlines and meetings, utilize electronic organizers, divide big assignments into small tasks, and outline steps to completing a given project. Consumers with psychiatric disability may have cognitive limitations that impede their ability to remember tasks and sequences. They may also have cognitive limitations that impede their ability to concentrate on work details. Accommodations may include providing written job instructions; allowing time to take rest breaks to reorient; minimizing distractions with panels, cubicle walls, and doors that absorb sound, and with environmental sound machines; having an office that is not placed in a distracting environment; watch timers for prompting; and allowing the consumer the ability to have a headset to listen to music to help manage stress or anxiety. Consumers with psychiatric disability may have cognitive limitations that impede their ability to complete projects and meet deadlines. It is also imperative that consumers have the ability to take time off for medical appointments for mental health management. In addition, consumers should have the ability to call a close friend, counselor, or other individual to discuss employment issues. This gives the ability for the consumer to rebalance and vent frustration without creating a negative work environment.

When consumers see the contents of my own briefcase with my electronic organizer, calendars, brightly colored gel ink pens, ear plugs in case someone near me chews gum (that noise sets my teeth on edge), highlighters and tiny Post-it note pads, Dictaphone, and MP3 player, they might think I'm a bit geeky, especially with my ever-present Bluetooth flashing on my ear. But I doubt anyone who doesn't know me thinks I live with a serious mental illness and use all those tools to keep myself organized, calm, on track, and stable. My next purchase is a phone with Wii Internet where I can bring my Outlook calendar, electronic files, or access the Internet from anywhere. I can live without it because I have so far survived, but it will eliminate a lot of surplus weight from my briefcase and simplify my life quite a bit. For instance, I won't have to carry a printed copy of my things-to-do list on a clipboard all the time because I will be able to access it on my little screen (and I won't lose sleep at night thinking I will forget to add an item to my list or calendar the next day). Plus, I think my gadget will make me the envy of everyone who doesn't have one. It's quite the gorgeous little silver box. It helps me understand why people abandon AT that isn't mainstream and stylish even if it helps them perform certain tasks. I wouldn't carry around such an elaborate device if it bore the trademark symbol for a prescription medication on the side. But the phone I am getting is sleek and stylish. And best of all, I can ask my friends in the business community when the next or better model is coming out because I know everyone is getting one. "BlackBerry is here to stay but is so limited," they say. "Wait for the model that downloads MS Word and Excel perfectly," which is why I am waiting until my birthday to bag my new phone. And when I am working with my consumers needing similar accommodations, I can just pull mine out and demonstrate how it works or why it might be useful. No stigma. When I need to go low-tech for a client, I can explain that, too, of course. I was there before Outlook, which changed my life.

Speaking of low-tech, I guess I can think of one thing I didn't notice anyone else mentioning—a simple medication container with a box for each day of the week, the same thing my grandfather carried his heart medication around in. Here's a tip: Put the whole tube in a Ziploc bag before stashing it in your purse because those little doors can pop open. Not terribly stylish, but it keeps me from forgetting a dose, taking the wrong pill, and provides me with more routine, which I like (Sunday night I load my box for the week). Check. Then I can watch TV.

Everyone has mentioned most every device I could think of . . . except the yellow folder. One client could never remember the forms he needed or appointment times. We bought him a bright yellow folder with pockets. He puts his to-do list, forms to return, and appointment list in this. He is never without that folder now.

I feel that this is an area where the accommodations are very inexpensive but extremely important. Also, I think the simpler the accommodations, the better for the client. I always start with a "month at a glance" calendar and really talk to the clients about how to use it. Just because they have the calendar doesn't mean they will know how to use it effectively. I also talk to them about their commitments—how many, their typical schedule, and so on—right away so that I know what kind of time this person thinks will be enough to commit to a project, such as a job search and job, or if they are on their way to taking on too much. This is also a lead into the discussion about limiting stress (even good stress) and taking things one at a time. I regularly ask if these things are being worked through in their therapy.

Also, we can recommend that some clients make homemade labels for reminding. For instance, one can put a label on the stove to remember to turn off the burner after cooking.

Another device is called reminder messages. When a person enters or leaves his or her home, these gadgets activate a voice telling him or her to pick up the keys or lock the front door and so on. The messages can be recorded so that the voice is of someone he or she knows, such as a family member or even their own voice. Messages can also be recorded to remind the person of his or her daily appointments.

There is Planning and Execution Assistant and Training System (PEAT). PEAT is perfect for people with cognitive disorders due to brain injury, stroke, multiple sclerosis, autism, Alzheimer's disease, attention-deficit/hyperactivity disorder (ADHD), and so on. It is a personal planning assistant that provides help 24/7. It has automatic cues to start and stop activities such as the use of customized voice recordings, sounds, and pictures. It automatically monitors performance and corrects schedule problems when necessary. Finally, it can be personalized. The scripts can break large tasks into smaller steps and will guide the user through multistep procedures. It can also be customized for individual needs and preferences.

The QuickPad is a word processor and is easy to use. It works with just a point and press button. No software or cables to mess with. It allows students to focus on content, not on deciphering handwriting. It has a preinstalled Typing Tutor, and each program challenges every skill level from beginner to advanced students.

There is also an affordable ClaroRead Plus. This is a powerful reading and writing assistance with toolbars. It has flawless text-to-speech capabilities and is easy to use. Its features allow the users to quickly begin working with all the tools they need to be successful in today's school and work environments. It is compatible with Dragon Naturally Speaking Seamless Integration with Microsoft Office.

The value of posing questions to and obtaining ideas from colleagues cannot be overstated. Local and professional conferences provide opportunities for this as will team meetings and LISTSERVs. Even if one feels shy about posting such queries, the responses obtained will almost always yield good and useful information, and many others will also benefit from that information.

This section discussed a blend of strategies and technologies. Throughout this book, the term *cognitive support technology* or *CST* refers to (a) strategies; (b) no-tech, mechanical, or electronic devices designed to support memory, thought, or any of the *International Classification of Functioning, Disability and Health's* (ICF) specific mental functions; and (c) everyday technologies adopted by and/or adapted to the needs of persons with cognitive disability. Specialized technologies are the focus of the next section.

SPECIALIZED TECHNOLOGIES

Products designed to serve the needs of persons with cognitive disability are listed in Table 7.1., which follows the format set out in Chapter 4's Table 4.3 "ICF Body Functions and Structures" domains and categories with examples of behaviors and strategies.

In the relevant literature, we encounter yet another confusing array of terminology used to refer to specialized devices for cognitive needs. In addition to CST, they include

- cognitive orthotics or orthoses;
- cognitive AT;
- AT for cognition;
- cognitive aids; and
- memory aids.

Use of any of the aforementioned terms is absolutely fine because they are accurate and quite interchangeable. Different professions tend to pick one over the others, depending on the profession's core principles and practices, but the primary difference in terminology is because of preference and fashion versus substance.

Although the term *neural prosthetic devices* may also be found in the literature and added to the earlier list, it actually refers to devices that are "under the skin" or implanted in a person's body. Examples include cochlear implants,

TABLE 7.1

Difficulties That May Be Experienced by Individuals With Cognitive Disabilies and Examples of Relevant Support From Everyday and Specialized Technologies

ICF MENTAL FUNCTIONS—SPECIFIC	EXAMPLES OF BEHAVIORAL OBSERVATIONS	EXAMPLES OF WHAT MAY BE DIFFICULT	ISO 9999 CLASS	TECHNOLOGIES (LOW- TO HIGH-TECH) (NOTE: MANY FIT INTO MULTIPLE CATEGORIES)
Attention (b140) Specific mental functions of focusing on an external stimulus or internal experience for the required period	Will not focus or concentrate, distractible, cannot easily shift attention or continually shifts attention	Organizing step-by-step, performing a task to completion	05.12.09 Assistive products for training in attention	General alarms, white noise machines, personal FM systems (to amplify and focus sound), ChatterBlocker (http://chatterblocker.com), The Listening Program (http://www.thelisteningprogram.com), Visual Assistant (https://store.ablelinktech.com/store.php?crn=200&rn=339&action=show_detail), Community Integration Suite (https://store.ablelinktech.com/store.php?crn=200&rn=329&action=show_detail), Pocket Endeavor (https://store.ablelinktech.com/store.php?crn=200&rn=375&action=show_detail)
Memory (b144) Specific mental functions of registering and storing information and retrieving it as needed	Misses appointments, cannot locate items, forgets to take medication	Remembering things presented visually (right hemisphere injury) or verbally (left hemisphere injury)	05.12.03 Assistive products for memory training	Voice recorders; voice recorder software for iPod Touch, Windows Mobile, or Android; cue cards; colored index cards and Post-it notes; Google Calendar with SMS reminders sent to a cell phone; calvetica calendar for iPhone (http://calvetica.com), vibrating and talking alarm watches (http://forgettingthepill.com/), WatchMinder 2 (http://watchminder.com), (http://www.epill.com/medicalwatches.html); cueing devices such as Voice Cue (http://www.enablemart.com/Voice-Cue);

(Continued)

TABLE 7.1
Difficulties That May Be Experienced by Individuals With Cognitive Disabilities and Examples of Relevant Support From Everyday and Specialized Technologies (*Continued*)

ICF MENTAL FUNCTIONS—SPECIFIC	EXAMPLES OF BEHAVIORAL OBSERVATIONS	EXAMPLES OF WHAT MAY BE DIFFICULT	ISO 9999 CLASS	TECHNOLOGIES (LOW- TO HIGH-TECH) (NOTE: MANY FIT INTO MULTIPLE CATEGORIES)
				Invisible Clock (http://www.invisibleclock.com); Pocket Endeavor (https://store.abelinktech.com/store.php?crn=200&rn=375&action=show_detail); Community Integration Suite (https://store.abelinktech.com/store.php?crn=200&rn=329&action=show_detail); Visual Assistant (http://www.abelinktech.com/_handhelds/visual assistant.asp); Best Intentions and Memory Works for Names & Faces (http://www.thememoryworks.com/info); personal planning software to help build and manage schedules, Picture Planner 2.0. (www.cognitopia.com). See also technologies for *Higher level cognitive functions (b164)*.
Psychomotor (b147) Specific mental functions of control over both motor and psychological events at the body level	Agitation and restlessness, poor eye and hand coordination, slow speech, frequent and/or inappropriate gestures such as hand-wringing	Participating in social situations and conversations	05.18.21 Assistive products for training in sensory integration	SNOEZELEN Multi-Sensory Environment (http://www.snoezeleninfo.com); OneSwitch free computer games (http://www.oneswitch.org.uk), other computer games appropriate for persons with cognitive disability (www.nanogames.com)

Emotional (b152) Specific mental functions related to the feeling and affective components of the processes of the mind	Mood swings, temper outbursts, anxiety attacks	Socially expected and appropriate behaviors, has "meltdowns"	05.12.18 Assistive products for training in problem solving	Noise-canceling headphones, soft music players, alternative lights, vests that apply deep pressure. SNOEZELEN Multi-Sensory Environment (http://www.snoezeleninfo.com)
Perceptual (b156) Specific mental functions of recognizing and interpreting sensory stimuli	Inability to discriminate sounds, colors, shapes, smells, tastes, textures	Identify items in a grocery store, to make a meal, recognizing objects, faces and words; recognizing social cues (facial expressions, tone of voice)	04.36 Assistive products for perceptual training	Labels on objects, multisensory presentation of information; reduction of sensory load (e.g., using text chat for communication); scanning pens such as Quicktionary and Livescribe pen (http://www.livescribe.com/en-us)
Thought (b160) Specific mental functions related to the ideational component of the mind	Incoherent thoughts and delusions, illogical thinking	A sequence of tasks that require logic and planning, following through with a plan	05.12.06 Assistive products for training in sequencing; 05.12.12 concept development; 05.12.15 classification	Visual Assistant (https://store.ablelinktech.com/store.php?crn=200&rn=339&action=show_detail), Community Integration Suite (https://store.ablelinktech.com/store.php?crn=200&rn=329&action=show_detail), Pocket Endeavor (https://store.ablelinktech.com/store.php?crn=204&rn=375&action=show_detail), COGKNOW (http://www.cogknow.eu)

(Continued)

TABLE 7.1

Difficulties That May Be Experienced by Individuals With Cognitive Disabilities and Examples of Relevant Support From Everyday and Specialized Technologies (Continued)

ICF MENTAL FUNCTIONS—SPECIFIC	EXAMPLES OF BEHAVIORAL OBSERVATIONS	EXAMPLES OF WHAT MAY BE DIFFICULT	ISO 9999 CLASS	TECHNOLOGIES (LOW- TO HIGH-TECH) (NOTE: MANY FIT INTO MULTIPLE CATEGORIES)
Higher level cognitive functions (b164) Specific mental functions especially dependent on the frontal lobes of the brain, including complex goal-directed behaviors such as decision making, abstract thinking, planning and carrying out plans, mental flexibility, and deciding which behaviors are appropriate under what circumstances; often called executive functions	Poor decision making, stubbornness and fixation on an idea, poor insight into one's behavior, difficulty with novel situations, slow processing speed, rigid thinking, concrete interpretation, perfectionism, focus on the wrong details, difficulty with "if–then" thinking, overloaded easily	Time management, insight and judgment, cognitive flexibility, conceptual and abstract thinking	05.12.03 Assistive products for memory training; 05.12.06 training in sequencing; 05.12.15 classification; 05.15.09 understanding of time	Technologies to maintain and alert user of daily schedule and routines such as Schedule Assistant and Schedule Impact (http://www.ablelinktech.com/), Pocket Endeavor (https://store.ablelinktech.com/store.php?crn=200&rn=375&action=show_detail), PEAT (http://www.brainaid.com), Time Teacher (http://www.cyberbee.com/games/timeteacher.html), Picture Planner (http://www.cognitopia.com); TapMemo Voice Activated Personal Data Assistant (http://www.maxiaids.com)
			05.12.18 Assistive products for training in problem solving	Brainfood game (http://www.rinkworks.com/brainfood), WayFinder (https://store.ablelinktech.com/store.php?crn=200&rn=303&action=show_detail), COGS (http://www.abledata.com/abledata.cfm?pageid=19327&top=11225&productid=174868&trail=0&discontinued=0), The 4th R—Reasoning (http://www.abledata.com/abledata.cfm?pageid=19327&top=11225&productid=99802&trail=0&discontinued=0)

Language (b167) Specific mental functions of recognizing and using signs, symbols, and other components of language	Expression and word finding, comprehension of written or spoken language, repetitive or perseverative in conversations, gives odd verbal responses	Producing meaningful messages and communications, correctly interpreting what others are saying	22.30 Assistive products for reading; 05.06 training in alternative and augmentative communication; 05.03.03 voice and speech training; 05.03.06 developing reading skills; 05.03.09 developing writing skills	Software that allows users to input into a computer without using a keyboard; speech-to-text software (for example, Dragon Naturally Speaking); WordQ; reading assistance solutions (e-book readers, text-to-speech devices) such as Book Reader (www.lssproducts.com), Kurzweil, Kindle, and Nook; adaptations for web accessibility such as WevAdapt2Me, Web Trek (http://www.abelinktech.com); communication products such as Vantage Lite (http://www.prentrom.com), ChatBox (http://www.saltillo.com; https://store.prentrom.com), Minspeak (http://minspeak.com/), Endeavor Talker (www.abelinktech.com), Jive! (http://www.ablenetinc.com), Proloquo2Go (http://www.proloquo2go.com), DynaVox Xpress (http://www.dynavoxtech.com), AlphaSmart (http://www.alphasmart.com), Lingraphica for communicating with a vocabulary of picture icons (http://www.aphasia.com).
Calculation (b172) Specific mental functions of determination, approximation, and manipulation of mathematical symbols and processes	Overdraws checking account, confusion at store checkout areas, problems counting money	Correct payment of bills, managing a checking account	22.15 Assistive products for calculation	The Talking Checkbook (http://www.tfeinc.com/shop/index.php?_a=viewProd&productId=1526)

(Continued)

TABLE 7.1

Difficulties That May Be Experienced by Individuals With Cognitive Disabilies and Examples of Relevant Support From Everyday and Specialized Technologies (*Continued*)

ICF MENTAL FUNCTIONS—SPECIFIC	EXAMPLES OF BEHAVIORAL OBSERVATIONS	EXAMPLES OF WHAT MAY BE DIFFICULT	ISO 9999 CLASS	TECHNOLOGIES (LOW- TO HIGH-TECH) (NOTE: MANY FIT INTO MULTIPLE CATEGORIES)
Sequencing complex movements (b176) Specific mental functions of sequencing and coordinating complex, purposeful movements	Cannot prepare a meal correctly or organize one's grooming and dressing.	Doing things in the right order and completely	05.12.06 Assistive products for training in sequencing	Community Integration Suite, (http://www.ablelinktech.com), Visual Assistant (https://store.ablelinktech.com/store.php?crn=200&rn=339&action=show_detail), Pocket Endeavor (https://store.ablelinktech.com/store.php?crn=200&rn=375&action=show_detail)
Experience of self and time (b180) Specific mental functions related to the awareness of one's identity, one's body, and one's position in the reality of one's environment and of time	Altered view of one's size and weight, body schema, proprioception, kinesthesia, and phantom limb sensation	Correct identification of body parts, attention to tasks, appropriate selection and use of tools	04.36.06 Assistive products for training in perceptual coordination	Yoga, tai chi, balance boards, virtual reality training, Wii therapy games such as tennis or bowling (http://www.nintendo.com/games), robotic (exoskeleton) training (http://www.bkintechnologies.com)

visual prosthetics, peripheral nerve interfaces, functional electrical stimulation (FES) devices, cortical prosthesis, and spinal cord microstimulation. As we discussed earlier, *prosthetic* tends to refer to the replacement of lost function, whereas *orthotic* is related more to its strengthening. According to Stiers et al. (2011), cognitive orthoses may be *internal*, such as the use of contextual self-cueing to initiate behavior, mnemonics to organize behavior, associative memory to link behavioral steps, and repetition to develop procedural learning. Cognitive orthoses may also be *external*, and they include the use of timer alarms to cue behavioral initiation or cessation, calendars to organize and cue activities, and memory books to record and retrieve important information. One technological improvement in external prompting and guidance is the use of text messages delivered by cell phones or pagers at predetermined times. This can be done internally within some cell phones or personal digital assistants (PDAs) or by Internet computer services, which send specified messages at specified times. Finally, orthoses may be *environmental*, and in this sense, the term includes the use of visual flags to direct and engage attention, written labels to identify objects and locations, pill boxes to organize medications, and posting written instructions to guide task functioning.

Specific Devices for Cognition

Many people with cognitive disability, such as Down syndrome, TBI, dementia, autism, and learning disability, require help to maintain a schedule and stay on track. They often find it frustrating to have to depend on someone else to schedule activities and provide reminders when it's time to do something, yet they frequently fail to maintain their own schedules and remember key tasks. For example, Ryan becomes visibly agitated when he is reminded of homework assignments. However, when he is left on his own to complete and turn in assignments, he often fails to turn them in on time. Recently, Ryan has started to use his iPod to write his assignments down and set up alarms for later in the evening to cue him to begin his work.

The primary users of CSTs in many cases may be both individuals with cognitive disability and their caregivers (or teachers, job coaches, etc.). Individuals with cognitive disability often say that what bothers them the most is fatigue and second is being overwhelmed with information (Zeiner & Scherer, 2009). Caregivers are concerned about the time and energy required to master the use of a technology. It is, thus, very helpful to do what can be done to reduce the effort needed, simplify choices, and divide tasks into small steps. For a good number of individuals with cognitive disability and their caregivers, the interfaces on many electronic devices are too complex and the number of features are overwhelming (Davies, Stock, King, & Wehmeyer, 2008; Stock, Davies, Davies, & Wehmeyer, 2006). The balance needs to be found between giving users control over their activities and a sense of accomplishment from managing one's own schedule without cognitively exhausting them. Specialized technologies are products designed from the outset to be used by individuals with cognitive disability. Samples of these products are provided in Table 7.3, along with the manufacturers' websites to ensure that the most current product information, price, features, and so on can be obtained.

Not only are the designers, developers, and manufacturers knowledgeable about the needs of persons with cognitive disability and their caregivers, but they are also able to advise their customers about additional appropriate devices, where to receive training to maximize benefit from use of their products, and support groups composed of other users. They are also familiar with colleagues who develop products for individuals with other disabilities, such as blindness or deafness, and can make logical connections among devices that may be originally designed for one purpose but able to serve another. For example, a stroke survivor who wants a speech-clarifying device in addition to an electronic memory aid can be connected with an augmentative and alternative communication (AAC) manufacturer that would typically serve individuals with cerebral palsy or others who have lived with speech challenges since birth. For individuals with TBI, AbleLink Technologies has conducted research that has resulted in the Pocket Endeavor system that operates on Windows-based smartphones. Pocket Endeavor includes a suite of integrated applications to support executive functioning, including simplified utilities for creating an ongoing audio-based to-do list, recording meetings and classes, a multimedia scheduler, and a specialized picture-based cell phone.

Pocket Endeavor
Courtesy of AbleLink Technologies, Inc.

Accessing a computer can be a particularly difficult challenge for individuals with cognitive disability because of the prevalence of user interfaces that rely on capabilities assumed for the general population of users but that are often difficult for many individuals with cognitive limitations. For example, simple interface actions such as double-clicking, using scroll bars, or reading menu items and button labels can present barriers to use for these individuals. Cognitively accessible software can be used in these cases to provide easier access to programs, media, and web content. For example, the Endeavor Desktop Environment (AbleLink Technologies) sits on top of mainstream operating systems to provide a cognitively accessible environment for learning, accessing media or the web, or using the computer to communicate.

Endeavor Desktop Environment
Courtesy of AbleLink Technologies, Inc.

This system includes various accessibility options designed specifically for users with cognitive limitations, including

- *Web Trek.* A clean, visual web browser for accessing favorite websites and simplifying access to existing web-based resources used by schools for online learning.
- *Endeavor E-mail.* A picture-based address book and automated audio e-mail program that can be used as an alternative to written text for users with limited literacy skills.
- *Visual Media Player.* Pictures, video clips, movies, and audio recordings are played more easily using a built-in media player with controls that are customizable, straight-forward, and easy to navigate.

■ *Accessible RSS Reader.* The Endeavor News Reader provides information and pictures from RSS feeds with accessibility features that include text-to-speech and simplified, customizable controls.

■ *Step-by-Step Prompting with Visual Impact.* Computer-based, multimedia task prompting, using the AbleLink Instructional Media Standard (AIMS) learning system, which facilitates assembly and delivery of audio instructions, video clips, and pictures into instructional sequences that provide step-by-step instructions for nearly any task or activity.

Multisensory input can be very helpful for a person with a cognitive disability. Therefore, some products developed primarily for those who are blind or deaf can prove to be extremely useful. One example is *ClassInFocus*, a computerized system developed by a team of computer scientists (Cavender, Bigham, & Ladner, 2009) to help students who are deaf manage many visual sources of information (instructor, interpreter or captions, slides or whiteboard, classmates, and personal notes) by automatically notifying them of classroom changes, such as slide changes or new speakers. It is easy to make the connection to see how helpful this would be for students with cognitive disability in the area of attention.

There are various handheld computerized devices, such as Pocket Coach and Visual Assistant designed by AbleLink Technologies, to provide step-by-step guidance in completing a task.

Visual Assistant start page   Another page of the Visual Assistant
Courtesy of AbleLink Technologies, Inc.

Jott Voicemail, although an everyday technology, can be used to receive messages from caregivers, family, and friends that are then sent to the individual as reminders. Prompting devices, such as Pocket Coach or index cards, have been designed to cue individuals when to do a task (LoPresti, Simpson, Kirsch, Schreckenghost, & Hayashi, 2008) and even when to monitor their own behaviors (e.g., Kirsch, Shenton, & Rowan, 2004; Kirsch, Shenton, Spirl, et al., 2004; LoPresti, Bodine, & Lewis, 2008). There are GPS-based products to help with both navigation and to help locate a person prone to wandering. For example, AbleLink's WayFinder system provides a format to provide custom multimedia instructions for navigating municipal bus routes, and their Community Sidekick App for the iPhone or iPad allows caregivers to maintain continuous awareness of the location of a user in the community in real time.

WayFinder
Courtesy of AbleLink Technologies, Inc.

Smart Homes are being designed with the independent living needs of aging persons and those with cognitive disability in mind from the outset; they include built-in sensors and signaling systems to help the person locate objects, remember when to take medications, and so on.

Virtual reality games have also been shown to be useful for retraining cognitive skills and exercising weak muscles (Cherniack, 2011; King et al., 2010; Lewis, Woods, Rosie, & McPherson, 2011; Parker, Mountain, & Hammerton, 2011). *Virtual reality* (VR) refers to computer-created three-dimensional (3D), immersive environments that feature visual and auditory stimuli. The hippocampus was discussed in Chapter 3 as being responsible for the formation of sensory and emotional connections and integrated experiences from their respective locations throughout the brain. It functions in 3D and, therefore, can be stimulated by VR programs.

The number and variety of products are large and getting larger. As has been said repeatedly throughout this book, however, solution seeking has to begin with the needs and preferences of each unique individual with a disability. The following is an actual case that illustrates how important listening to the consumer is and how often the role of the professional is that of a creative team leader in the effort to match the person with the most appropriate solution, which will likely be a blend of strategies and appropriate technologies.

A Real-Life Solution-Seeking Example for Early Onset Alzheimer's Disease

All of the AT devices our team has been exploring are those to enhance short-term memory, and we discussed the following as having potential to help James: a PalmPilot, BlackBerry, iPhone, various calendars including a day planner book, notebooks (8.5 × 11 and 8.5 × 5.5), and a locator device for lost items.

I was able to borrow a PalmPilot Pre, BlackBerry, and iPhone from various close friends who have these items. Because I am not totally versed in the use of these items, I enlisted their help to work with us to see if James could learn to use them, feel comfortable with them, and could remember how to use them. James was not comfortable with any of these items. All three appeared to intimidate and overwhelm him. He found the BlackBerry and PalmPilot Pre particularly frustrating. The tiny keys for texting were particularly difficult and frustrating because his fingers kept hitting multiple keys. Of the three devices, the iPhone was the most user-friendly for him. Having the flat surface with the apps readily available with easily recognizable icons and the ease of accessing and moving the apps with the stroke of a finger appeared to lessen his anxiety; however, the next day, on the second attempt to use the iPhone, he could not remember how to manipulate the apps or even how to access the most basic commands of answering the phone, checking voice mail messages, making and retrieving notes/calendar notations, or accessing the Internet. It was as if he had never seen an iPhone before. He literally couldn't remember how to do any of the functions. James admitted that he was never very technologically savvy and has never fully embraced or kept abreast of computer technology development.

Because of James's diagnosis of early onset Alzheimer's disease resulting in difficulty learning and retrieving new information, the decision was made to delve more into items that were a part of his past as a younger man or child. This approach led to various types of paper/hard copy calendars and notebooks. He has now started using a basic wall calendar by the kitchen door that has simple, mostly unadorned squares where he has been writing his work schedule. He decided to only write the hours, such as 5–9 p.m., and leave the day blank if he is off. This minimizes the appearance of clutter for him, and he can tell at a glance whether or not he even works that day. Initially, he still had trouble figuring out which day it was, so he began crossing off the previous day first thing on the next morning. On days when he forgets to cross off the previous day and he is confused which day it is, I have been working with him to check the display on his cell phone, which clearly shows this information on the screen.

For use of a notebook, he chose a smaller notebook, which is 8.5 × 5.5 with a discrete black binder. Since this project began, he has had mixed success with this AT. He has not brought it to work with him and states that he doesn't feel it is necessary. At home, he readily writes things in it; but when he is cued to write something important, he doesn't always remember to check it. It has worked well for noting daily chores he has been asked to do. I thought by asking him to write down the chores, instead of someone else writing the information, it might stimulate his memory to do the chores, but this has not seemed to make a difference. His short-term memory function has deteriorated beyond the point where writing things down would make a difference. However, it has helped to just write things down and refer him to the list regardless of who makes the notations. He is also able to scratch off the chores as he completes them, giving him a great sense of accomplishment. He loves being able to throw away an entire sheet of paper with accomplished tasks. Another application for the notebook, which has met with less success on the initial tries, is writing down instructions for how to do things that are important to him. For instance, how to retrieve his voice mail messages from his cell phone and how to get rid of the little red light that is displayed on the cable TV box indicating the cable company has sent a message about a special offer—these are the two things that tend to agitate him until they are cleared. We sat down and I walked him through the steps for both of these as he wrote the directions down. After writing them down, he immediately tore the pages out of the notebook to go put them somewhere else. As I felt this was defeating the purpose of the notebook and heightened the likelihood that these pages would be thrown away as trash, he agreed to place these sheets in the pocket on the opposite inside cover of the notebook. This is the only time this AT application was tested (cable TV box red message light), but it did not work because he had indeed thrown away the instructions. He did write them down again and placed them in the pocket, but this time, he has written in large letters across the top of each sheet what the instructions are for: cell voice mail and cable TV box red message light.

I have also been working on modifying existing technology to fashion a locator device for smaller objects such as eyeglasses and a cell phone. The currently available products are based on a remote control locator that is synced with a receiver tag, about the size of a nickel or quarter, which can be hung on a key ring or attached with double-sided tape to a smoother surface like an eyeglass case. This has the potential to work fine if James remembers to replace his glasses in their case, which most of the time he doesn't. Both of these receiver devices are too large to attach to the actual eyeglass frames or too bulky to attach to a cell phone. In researching the currently available products, most got mixed reviews at best. The main problems were that the audible signal (beeping) wasn't loud enough or didn't work until you were within a couple of feet of the lost item (even when they were advertised to work within 25 feet), or the item was too complicated to program or set up. The engineer member of our team suggested and did some research on radio-frequency identification

(RFID) tag technology. This is the same system that is used in large department stores, such as Wal-Mart, to deter shoplifting. Inventory is tagged with an RFID label, which is deactivated by scanning during the checkout and what triggers the door alarm when the label isn't deactivated properly. This technology is promising for this application because the labels can be made very small; however, cost-effectiveness is an issue. The smallest labels are relatively inexpensive at less than $5 each, but they are made by a different company that makes the receivers, which can run as much as $20,000. We found a device that is versatile, reasonably priced, and has good reviews (http://www.ez-find.com/concept.html) but is still too large to attach to eyeglasses or a cell phone.

To summarize, the three products being implemented or explored include a wall calendar, a notebook, and a locator device. Clearly, the journey of matching person with technology (MPT) is not a linear one. The suitability of the person's match with a device can, and often does, change over time (e.g., as cognition declines), and hi-tech isn't always the best solution.

The evaluation of the impact of specialized technologies on daily activities and community participation, and measurement strategies for assessing these outcomes represent important domains of research (Arthanat, Nochajski, & Stone, 2004; Fuhrer, Jutai, Scherer, & DeRuyter, 2003; Lenker et al., 2010; Lenker, Scherer, Fuhrer, Jutai, & DeRuyter, 2005). The *ICF* framework provides an organizing scheme for many investigations, and the results of research performed to date have shown that many existing measures can be applied to the assessment of specialized technologies across *ICF* domains. We will discuss this in depth in a subsequent chapter.

EVERYDAY TECHNOLOGIES

People with cognitive disability and their caregivers have varying levels of knowledge about and interest in technology. Let us use two examples of what we think of as simple, everyday technologies—a wristwatch and the telephone. As shown in Table 7.3 for *memory*, some individuals with cognitive disability benefit from specialized products to alert and remind them of multiple events throughout the day—for example, when to take their medications. Specialized products include the e-pill alarm watch, but cell phone users can take advantage of Google Calendar with SMS reminders sent to the phone. Everyday wristwatches with alarms and reminding features can be just as effective for some, and they can be purchased in many department stores. Examples include Casio Databank and Timex Ironman watches. There are multiple models with varying numbers of alarms that can be set (daily, weekdays, or weekends), so one needs to actually see the watches in order to compare features.

Not that long ago (really!), a telephone was something we used in our homes or offices to connect us with another person in a different location. When you wanted a phone, you contacted your local telephone company and they came and installed it. The choices you had to make were pretty much limited to how many you wanted installed, where, and in what color. To make a local call, you used a phone that looked like the one in the picture shown below. You picked up the receiver (now called handset), turned a rotary dial punched with 10 holes to accommodate an average-sized finger (one hole each for the numbers 0–9), and dialed the unique string of seven numbers belonging to the person you wanted to reach. Although you still see this rotary, wired, analog, landline phone in some homes today, it is usually because an octogenarian is living there.

Rotary dial phone

Today, we have many choices in phones. One basic choice is selecting a fixed or a portable landline phone. Battery-operated, portable landline phones have replaced most fixed-in-place landline phones. A current and popular alternative is a cell (or mobile) phone, which can eliminate the need for a landline phone. If the user is capable, we probably want a cell phone for reasons of convenience and features— so that may be the option to pursue. Ah, but we've only begun making choices! We have to think about basic features and capabilities, special applications, and cost. Features can include cameras, calendars, note recorders, built-in GPS, and alarms. There may be a vibration mode, choice of screen size, and other options. If the individual benefits from photographs, video, and music, these are all possible to have as well. Many persons with brain injuries who experience agitation will remain

TABLE 7.2

List of Resources Providing Information on the Breadth of Assistive Technology Apps for Smartphones (e.g., iPhone and Google Android Phones) and Tablet Computers (e.g., iPad)

Tools, Apps, and Resources for TBI:
http://nolimitstolearning.blogspot.com/2011/02/tools-apps-and-resources-for-tbi.html

Products and Games for Seniors:
http://www.eldergadget.com

iPhone Apps for Disability and Vision Impairments:
http://www.disabled-world.com/assistivedevices/iphone-apps.php

There's an App for That: iPod/iPad 101
The Parent Advocacy Coalition for Educational Rights (PACER) Center's Simon Technology Center (STC) focuses on making technology more accessible to children and adults with disability. The aforementioned publication is available at www.pacer.org/stc/pubs/AllAboutAppsforEducationHandout.pdf

Google Search Results for AT Apps:
http://tinyurl.com/46e5tp5

iPad Assistive Technology/Disability Round-Up:
http://atmac.org/ipad-assistive-technology-disability-round-up

7 Assistive Communication Apps in the iPad App Store:
http://blog.friendshipcircle.org/2011/02/07/7-assistive-communication-apps-in-the-ipad-app-store/

iPhone, iPad and iPod touch Apps for (Special) Education Organized by Category:
http://www.scribd.com/doc/24470331/iPhone-iPad-and-iPod-touch-Apps-for-Special-Education

iPhone, IPod Touch—Accessibility Features & Apps:
http://abilitynet.wetpaint.com/page/iPhone,+Ipod+Touch+-+Accessibility+%26+Apps

quiet if engaged with a handheld gaming device, and games can be downloaded and added. A smartphone may include sophisticated web access capability, running applications (apps), and simultaneous e-mail and voice capability. Table 7.2 provides a list of resources with information on the breadth of AT apps for smartphones and tablet computers. Thousands of apps are available for the iPhone, iPod, and iPad. They offer a mainstream look and have built-in accessibility features. An iPhone app can be downloaded directly or downloaded to a computer and transferred to the phone. Apps provide several different functions, depending on the program. Some are meant to show news, sports, weather information, or provide maps. The apps can be purely for entertainment, including games, or serve a more practical function and are generally less than $2 (USD) per app. Before recommending an app, be sure to determine if there are any barriers to its use.

Now it is time to consider a choice of wireless carriers and the many competing products (iPhone, Android, BlackBerry, etc.), and it gives one a headache! But oh, no, we're not done yet. What about accessibility options? How is your dexterity? Your hearing? Do you want a Samsung Intrepid with voice-activated text? Do you have communication and speech difficulties? What's your budget?

Samsung and AT&T are two companies that have tried to be helpful by having a web page devoted to phone selection (see Figures 7.1 and 7.2).

FIGURE 7.1   Samsung phone comparison.
Courtesy of Samsung. Used with permission.

FIGURE 7.2 AT&T phones and selection guide.
Courtesy of AT&T Intellectual Property. Used with permission.

To access AT&T's site, you just need to go to http://www.att.com and select "Personal" from the top toolbar, then "Wireless," and "Shop All Phones." Then on the left side of the page, you'll see "Filter Phones/Devices" (shown below), which is a means of selecting the phone that will best match your preferences according to the criteria listed there.

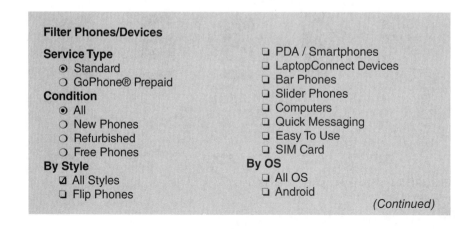

Filter Phones/Devices

Service Type
- ⦿ Standard
- ○ GoPhone® Prepaid

Condition
- ⦿ All
- ○ New Phones
- ○ Refurbished
- ○ Free Phones

By Style
- ☑ All Styles
- ❏ Flip Phones

- ❏ PDA / Smartphones
- ❏ LaptopConnect Devices
- ❏ Bar Phones
- ❏ Slider Phones
- ❏ Computers
- ❏ Quick Messaging
- ❏ Easy To Use
- ❏ SIM Card

By OS
- ❏ All OS
- ❏ Android

(Continued)

❏ Apple
❏ BlackBerry® (RIM)
❏ Palm
❏ Symbian
❏ Windows Phone
❏ Windows for PC
By Features
❏ Any Feature
❏ att.net
❏ 3G Network
❏ GPS/Navigation
❏ BLUETOOTH®
❏ Camera
❏ International
❏ Mobile Share
❏ Mobile TV
❏ Music
❏ Push To Talk
❏ Full Keyboard
❏ Touch Screen

❏ Video Share
❏ Wi-Fi
By Manufacturer
❏ All Manufacturers
❏ Acer
❏ Apple
❏ AT&T
❏ BlackBerry®
❏ Dell
❏ HP
❏ HTC
❏ LG
❏ Motorola
❏ Nokia
❏ Palm
❏ Pantech
❏ Samsung
❏ Sharp
❏ Sony Ericsson

Of course, a checklist like this requires a good deal of knowledge before it can even be completed. And it isn't giving a deaf person or one with limited movement of the hand and fingers the information he or she needs. Also, there is nothing quite as helpful as the opportunity to try products and compare them before making a purchase decision.

12 Questions to Ask Before Obtaining a Cell Phone

1. Is the phone the appropriate size and shape?
2. Are the device and its components (screen, keys, text/icons) of desired size?
3. Is there good contrast between the text and symbols and the keys and screen?
4. Is it easy to learn to use? In other words, is the cognitive load acceptable?
5. Is there a voice input option?
6. Is there speakerphone capability?
7. Is the volume adjustable? Is it loud enough? Quiet enough?
8. Does it have adequate battery life?
9. Can the battery be recharged quickly enough?
10. Is it easy to ignore or block unwanted features? How configurable is it?
11. Is access to the desired features easy and quick?
12. Does it have Internet and web access?

Tiny phones, small keys, and small screens are not always very useful to people with poor motor control and poor eyesight. And the demands on the user and cognitive load can be high (Paas, Renkl, & Sweller, 2003). Fortunately, there are even more choices available, including ones that favor those who have little interest in multiple features and complex operations. For the person who wants a mobile, small phone to just contact a few people and only in certain circumstances, one option is the Jitterbug phone available through GreatCall (http://www.greatcall.com). It is uncomplicated, good looking, and has many useful features for individuals with cognitive disability, including a powerful speaker, a bright screen with large text, large buttons, and a simple interface. The dial version has a larger keypad for dialing, but there is also the option for Yes/No action buttons ("no confusing icons"). There is even a OneTouch version to access 911 or to contact the GreatCall operator to place calls. Options include simple text messaging. Optional apps include

- *The Check-in Call*. Friendly automated calls up to six times per day. Questions relating to pain level, appetite, overall well-being, and sleep quality can be asked on each call based on your personal profile. If you reply that you need assistance or if you miss a call, GreatCall will send a notification for help to a friend or relative listed as a personal contact.

Jitterbug Phone
Reprinted from http://www.greatcall.com/assets with permission from GreatCall.

- *LiveNurse* for 24/7 access to registered nurses
- *Medication Reminder*
- *MyCalendar*

The Jitterbug has attracted users of all ages and with all degrees of technical sophistication. Jeff Lyons, founder of the satirical website, Used-Wigs, is a technically savvy person who wrote

> . . . When I'm away from my desk and my computer, I need the buzzing, the ringing and the key-tapping to cease. That is why I don't use my cell often or keep it on . . . [The Jitterbug] has barebones features and a complete lack of nonsense to interfere with making and receiving a call. It is the polar opposite of an iPhone. No frills, no nonsense, affordable, this phone was perfect for me. So join me, people. Simplify your lives by saying *no* to expensive, complex cell phones and plans and say *yes* to a larger, easier life. (Lyons, 2008)

Phones and watches are good examples of product types addressing memory, attention, and communication among other areas. Mainstream PDA training with mainstream software continues to be popular—for example, using the scheduling or task guidance software that comes with a Windows Mobile, iPod Touch, or Android PDA or that can be downloaded from a long list of mainstream apps. PDAs are more or less merging with smartphones, which is not insignificant, given the funding dilemma that comes with whether to provide a stand-alone PDA (given that a person with a cognitive disability will probably also need a cell phone) or provide a smartphone (problematic when the funder doesn't want to pay recurring data charges, and the person cannot afford it).

The list of appropriate everyday technologies is long and includes messaging and paging services (Fish, Manly, Emslie, Evans, & Wilson, 2008), television accessibility features (such as captioning), computer use for e-mail, accessing the Internet and World Wide Web, and performing writing tasks, mathematical calculations, and graphical/pictorial activities. Research has shown that individuals with TBI have a high interest in using and learning more about the Internet (e.g., Vaccaro, Hart, Whyte, & Buchhofer, 2007) in addition to portable electronic devices as memory and organizational aids (Hart, Buchhofer, & Vaccaro, 2004).

The 21st Century Communications and Video Accessibility Act of 2010 was passed to ensure that individuals with disability, including cognitive disability, have full access to everyday technologies—from TV or DVD menus to the web to smartphones. It establishes standards to accomplish the following:

- Enabling Americans who are blind to enjoy TV more fully through audible descriptions of the on-screen action

- Making TV program guides and selection menus accessible to people with vision loss
- Providing Americans who are deaf the ability to watch new TV programs online with the captions included
- Mandating that remote controls have a button or similar mechanism to easily access the closed captioning on broadcast and pay TV
- Requiring that telephone equipment used to make calls over the Internet is compatible with hearing aids
- For low-income Americans who are both deaf and blind, providing up to $10 million per year to purchase communications equipment to access the telephone system and the Internet so these individuals can more fully participate in society

There are also strategies that can be applied to computer and web pages to make them easy to navigate and understand. Although these may be especially appreciated by individuals with cognitive disability, they benefit all users. Some of these strategies are as follows:

- Break up text into smaller paragraphs or sections.
- Limit the number of choices and options.
- Provide key information in auditory and visual form and reinforce success.
- Minimize page distractions by eliminating unnecessary graphics, texts, and sounds.
- Make accessing information available in various ways such as the menu, site map use of the search option, well-identified icons, and designated graphic sections of the page.
- Provide an easy means to return to previous sections.

Individuals with cognitive disability may find a simplified e-mail interface more useful. In one study (Sohlberg, Ehlhardt, Fickas, & Sutcliffe, 2003) of eight individuals with acquired cognitive–linguistic impairment, errors made fell into two general categories: (a) computer usability (e.g., conceptual understanding of mouse/cursor operation) and (b) message composition (e.g., generating ideas for a message).

Easier access can be legislated and designed into technologies and information materials, but without computer skills, the individual is left at a disadvantage. Specialized software exists to assess an individual's computer skills (Koester, Lopresti, & Simpson, 2006), and assistance is available for those who would benefit from computer access technology (CAT), which allows people who have trouble using a standard computer keyboard, mouse, or monitor to access a computer (e.g., Simpson, Koester, & Lopresti, 2010). Many community centers and local educational facilities offer a diverse set of computer skills classes. Family members and friends can also be helpful in learning or improving skills.

We know from numerous research studies that many people with cognitive disability benefit from a particular technology or intervention (e.g., Bergman, 2002; Davies, Stock, Holloway, & Wehmeyer, 2010; de Joode, van Heugten, Verhey, & van Boxtel, 2010; Hart, Hawkey, & Whyte, 2002; Johnson, Bamer, Yorkston, & Amtmann, 2009; H. J. Kim, Burke, Dowds, Boone, & Park, 2000; Sablier et al., 2009; Sauer, Parks, & Heyn, 2010; Stock, Davies, Wehmeyer, & Palmer, 2008; Wennberg & Kjellberg, 2010; B. A. Wilson, Emslie, Quirk, Evans, & Watson, 2005). Yet, as we would expect, this is not uniformly the case. Several studies indicate that cognitive deficits often impede everyday technology use and increase perceived difficulties, and this may be particularly true for older adults with mild cognitive impairment and early stage dementia (Eek & Wressle, 2011; Nygård & Starkhammar, 2007; Rosenberg, Kottorp, Winblad, & Nygård, 2009).

Boman, Bartfai, Borell, Tham, and Hemmingsson (2010) stated that everyday devices can be too complex for some persons with disability to master, and that when new behaviors are forced on existing routines, there is often nonuse of the device. They highlight the need for individual assessments because it is crucial to match the person with the right solution. Device flexibility and adaptability is also a concern with everyday technologies because cognitive tasks will vary for any given person, and functioning well in one situation does not mean that the individual will function as well when the setting or tasks change. Just as important is the fact that many individuals will experience progressive cognitive loss (such as those with dementia), whereas others may be expected to improve (e.g., those with TBI), thus requiring the device to be adaptable.

Specific difficulties with the use of everyday technologies by those with acquired brain injury have been studied (Engström, Lexell, & Lund, 2010; Lindén, Lexell, & Lund, 2011; Lindén, Lexell, & Lund, 2010). A high rate of difficulties in using everyday technologies was found, which include the following;

- Struggling with fatigue that interfered with the use of technology
- Recognizing, finding, and using technology functions
  - Recognizing steps
  - Finding known functions
- Following sequences that the technology requires
  - Following the pace that the sequences require
  - Understanding and responding to the sequences required
  - Choosing an alternative among several
- Adjusting the technology
- Using manuals

Furthermore, these authors found that the presence of other persons negatively affected everyday technology use, perhaps because of stress and anxiety as they reported feeling pressured. The authors state that it is not possible to administer one technological solution to all clients, and they recommend the use of an individualized intervention process that involves the user with familiar everyday technology and tasks in daily life that the user prioritizes as most urgent to solve. They also point out that different kinds of technologies need to be used in interventions and it is important that professionals are ready to use various devices for supporting individuals with cognitive disability.

In summary, there is a need for a range of product choices from simple written notes to high-tech reminders, and Table 7.3 provides an example of both to help students, and perhaps some adults with job tasks. It is wise to keep the following relative advantages and disadvantages of everyday and specialized technologies in mind:

Advantages of Everyday Technologies

- User appears like everyone else, even "cool."
- They are usually less expensive than specialized technologies.
- Because they are cheaper than specialized technologies, they make an effective backup or secondary device.

Disadvantages of Everyday Technologies

- They most likely will not be paid for by health insurance or Centers for Medicare & Medicaid Services (CMS), which administers Medicaid, Medicare, and the Children's Health Insurance Program. The rationale is that they are not exclusive to medical needs.
- They are made for the "average user" and not those with individual, particular needs.

Advantages of Specialized Technologies

- They are likely to be paid for by health insurance or CMS.
- They tend to be very durable and can withstand being dropped, having moisture get inside, and so on.
- They have strong support services and warranties.
- They tend to work better for persons with complex needs.

Disadvantages of Specialized Technologies

- They may be large and heavy.
- Their cost may be high.

TABLE 7.3
Examples of the Wide Range of Products Useful for Secondary and Postsecondary Students

1. **Noise-cancelling headsets** allow students with attention problems or learning disability to block out background noise, thus increasing concentration.

2. A **digital voice recorder** assists students with visual impairments, learning disability, memory deficits, dyslexia, or disorders of written expression to concentrate in class without the worry of note taking. They can review the tapes as often as necessary and at their convenience to reinforce what was taught in class.

3. **Color overlays** can help students who have difficulty following lines of printed material or complain that the words "jump around" on the page.

4. A **bar magnifier** lies directly on printed page with a helpful red line to guide the eye. It helps students follow lines of written text.

5. A **talking calculator** will assist students to complete math assignments.

6. **ZoomText** magnifies any page and allows greater concentration for those overwhelmed by thousands of word on a page. ZoomText speaks all program controls, including menus, buttons, lists, and messages.

7. The **ReadingPen Basic Edition** allows the reader to scan unfamiliar words, which are then read aloud and defined. The **Pulse Smartpen** by Livescribe allows a person to make symbols of any size on the page, and when the symbol is clicked, it will play what was being said at the time the symbol was made.

8. The **Speaking Language Master Special Edition** is a handheld electronic spell checker that assists with spelling, pronunciation, and word definition. It is easier to use than print dictionaries because the user can make a guess at spelling. Although computers do spell checking, there is not a computer available to every student with a disability and many students do not have access to computers at home.

9. **Neo2** by AlphaSmart is a portable word processor designed specifically for writing. It is rugged, lightweight, and user-friendly. It turns on instantly to allow the user to record thoughts immediately. It also assists in alleviating hesitancy in writing.

10. **Dragon NaturallySpeaking** provides a fast and accurate way to turn speech into text. Users can dictate into virtually any Windows-based application at speeds up to 160 words per minute and achieve high levels of accuracy in creating documents, reports, e-mail messages, and more.

11. The **Pocket Talker Pro Amplifier—Deluxe Behind-the-Head Headphones** improve listening and attention by amplifying the instructor's voice and reducing background noise. It also assists in improving auditory discrimination and auditory attention.

12. **K-NFB Reader Mobile** gives access to print in a cell phone. It is a pocket-sized device that takes a picture of the printed material, processes the picture, finds the text, and reads it back out loud.

(Continued)

TABLE 7.3

Examples of the Wide Range of Products Useful for Secondary and Postsecondary Students (*Continued*)

13. The **Pocket Endeavor** is a bundle of software applications that run on Window's smartphones to support executive functioning for people with TBI and other cognitive disabilities. It includes a "to-do list" voice recorder, a utility for recording meetings and classes, a multimedia scheduler, and options for a cognitively accessible multimedia cell phone or quick-launch buttons for additional applications.

14. **WebAdapt2Me** is a large print voice output web browser.

Van Hulle and Hux (2006) studied three persons with TBI attempting to compensate for persistent memory deficits. The individuals used written reminders, the WatchMinder wristwatch, and a digital voice recorder and alarm system (Voicecraft). One individual showed no improvement, but two of the three individuals demonstrated increased independence in remembering to take medications, thus illustrating varying responses to compensatory interventions and AT devices. The authors state that professionals and caregivers need to recognize the uniqueness of each TBI survivor, adjust intervention programs accordingly, and persist in trying to increase functional independence repeatedly for many years postinjury.

Important aspects of products and technology selection are (a) knowing the settings in which they will be used and (b) addressing environmental factors and accommodations. Another key is AT service delivery, funding, and how to best match a particular individual with the most appropriate technology for his or her use. We will discuss these topics in the succeeding chapters.

8

Environmental Barriers And Enablers

The difference between animals and humans is that animals change
themselves for the environment, but humans change the environment
for themselves.
—Ayn Rand

As we know from reading the previous chapters, The *International Classification of Functioning, Disability and Health (ICF)* is not a classification of people, but rather of disability within the context of individualized life situations. If we think of an individual's life and living situation as being a snapshot in time, then the contextual factors form the background within which that person's life and living situation exist. The two components of this background are environmental and personal factors and their impact on the individual. According to the World Health Organization (WHO; 2001),

> Environmental factors make up the physical, social and attitudinal environment in which people live and conduct their lives. These factors are external to individuals and can have a positive or negative influence on the individual's performance as a member of society, on the individual's capacity to execute actions or tasks, or on the individual's body function or structure. (p. 16)

Environmental factors are organized on two levels: individual and social. On the individual level are the immediate environments the person encounters, and this includes home, school, and/or workplace. Also included are other people the individual comes in contact with such as family, teachers, employers, peers, and strangers.

On the societal level are the relevant informal and formal social structures, services, and overarching approaches or systems in the community or society as a whole that impact individuals. "This level includes organizations and services related to the work environment, community activities, government agencies, communication and transportation services, and informal social networks as well as laws, regulations, formal and informal rules, attitudes and ideologies" (WHO, 2001, p. 17).

Disability, thus, is not a characteristic of an individual but an outcome or result of a complex interrelationship among the individual's health condition, personal factors, and the external factors that represent the circumstances in which the individual lives. Disability is a situational and multidimensional phenomenon resulting from interactions within both physical and social environments. Thus, the same environment will have a varying impact on two different individuals, and different environments will impact the same individual in different ways. An environment with barriers (e.g., an intersection without curb cuts) is restrictive to a person who uses a wheelchair but may be facilitating for a person who is blind and new to using a cane for mobility. An environment with facilitators (e.g., ramps, elevators, Braille signage) will enhance a person's performance and participation whereas one with restrictions and barriers will not do so. Bickenbach (2008) notes that when an individual has the essential skills to succeed at a job but fails to accomplish what is expected, then this is an indication that there is a barrier in the environment such as the attitudes of a new boss, a change in policy, elimination or interruption of services, or new worksite features that are not accessible.

In the *ICF* framework, Environmental Factors consists of five chapters (see Figure 5.4) of which the first is "Products and Technology." We have discussed the first eight categories of "Products and Technology" in Chapters 5–7 as they concern technologies for direct personal use for various activities with a focus on devices that are used to achieve personal goals and to facilitate participation in desired life situations. These are the categories where assistive, specialized, and everyday technologies are included as important supports for individuals with disability.

The remaining four categories in Chapter 1, "Products and Technology," are a degree removed from the individual because they are external resources accessed or used by the person. The categories are buildings for public use, buildings for private use, land development, and assets (Figure 8.1).

International Classification of Functioning, Disability and Health

e ENVIRONMENTAL FACTORS

CHAPTER 1
PRODUCTS AND TECHNOLOGY

e1500
Design, construction and building products and technology for entering and exiting buildings for public use

e1501
Design, construction and building products and technology for gaining access to facilities inside buildings for public use

e1502
Design, construction and building products and technology for way finding, path routing and designation of locations in buildings for public use

e1550
Same for private use
Products and technology of entry and exit from the human-made environment that is planned, designed and constructed for (a) public or (b) private use, such as entries and exits, portable and stationary ramps, power-assisted doors, lever door handles and level door thresholds.

e1551
Same for private use
Products and technology related to design, building and construction inside buildings for (a) public or (b) private use, such as washroom facilities, telephones, audio loops, lifts or elevators, kitchen cabinets, appliances and electronic controls.

e1552
Same for private use
Indoor and outdoor products and technology in the design, building and construction of path routing, for (a) public or (b) private use, to assist people to find their way inside and immediately outside buildings and locate the places they want to go to, such as signage, in Braille or writing, size of corridors and floor surfaces.

e1600
Products and technology of rural land development

e1601
Same for suburban land

e1601
Same for urban land
Products and technology in land areas, as they affect an individual's outdoor environment through the implementation of land use policies, design, planning and development of space, such as pathways and signposting, curb cuts and street lighting and ramps.

e1650
Financial assets
Products, such as money and other financial instruments, which serve as a medium of exchange for labour, capital goods and services.

e1651
Tangible assets
Products or objects, such as houses and land, clothing, food and technical goods, which serve as a medium of exchange for labour, capital goods and services.

e1652
Intangible assets
Products, such as intellectual property, knowledge and skills, which serve as a medium of exchange for labour, capital goods and services.

FIGURE 8.1 ICF products and technology.
Source: World Health Organization.

THE CATEGORIES OF DESIGN, CONSTRUCTION, AND BUILDING PRODUCTS AND TECHNOLOGY IN THE *ICF*'S ENVIRONMENTAL FACTORS DOMAIN OF PRODUCTS AND TECHNOLOGY

Buildings for public and private use can be constructed at the outset to be accessible to persons with various disabilities or, if existing, have aspects and features that have been retrofitted to meet the needs of people with all levels of capabilities. Examples of retrofitting include adding ramps or elevators so that individuals with difficulty walking can avoid the use of stairs. In addition to accessible entrances and exits, facilities, and routing, retrofitting includes the installation of adequate lighting, signage, floor surfaces, and expanding the width of corridors. The inside of public and private buildings also requires accessible washroom facilities, telephones, appliances, entries and exits, portable and stationary ramps, power-assisted doors, lever door handles, level door thresholds and lifts or elevators. There are standards and guidelines specifying how accessibility can be achieved, one being the *Americans with Disabilities Act Accessibility Guidelines (ADAAG) Checklist for Buildings and Facilities* available at http://www.access-board.gov/adaag/checklist/a16.html. Products and technology for accessible buildings and facilities are included in ISO 9999 in the class "Assistive products for environmental improvement, and assessment" and within AbleData as "Environmental Adaptations."

Smart Homes

The focus of a *smart home* is on health maintenance and provision of care within the home to prevent social isolation, hospitalization, and institutionalization (Chan, Campo, Estève, & Fourniols, 2009). Smart homes are specifically designed and constructed to address the needs of persons with various limitations and are especially well suited to those with dementia and those having difficulties with mobility, memory, and health maintenance. Frisardi and Imbimbo (2011) define a "smart home" as a residence equipped with technology and "smart devices" that facilitate an individual's independence and quality of life while reducing the burden on family members and other caregivers. Smart devices include sensors, actuators, and/or biomedical monitors (e.g., blood pressure, blood glucose). Advances in smart devices, mobile wireless communications, sensor networks, pervasive computing, machine learning, middleware (or software that links programs) and agent technologies, and human computer interfaces have made workable smart homes possible (Roy, Roy, & Das, 2006; Schülke, Plischke, & Kohls, 2010).

Aldrich (2003) listed five types and levels of smart homes, from least to most advanced (and intrusive).

1. Homes with intelligent objects such as talking alarms, remote controls for home appliances, a missing object finder, and adapted telephones
2. Homes with intelligent objects that communicate. Devices include wearable monitors and sensors that detect and relay information about a person's health state. The devices are connected to a remote center that diagnoses the situation and initiates the provision of necessary assistance (e.g., paramedic attention). Other examples of devices in this level include carbon monoxide detectors, smoke and fire detectors, and so on. Care delivered remotely via telecommunications technologies (telehealth, telecare, and telemedicine) are introduced in this level of smart home.
3. Connected homes have both internal and remote control of what is in the home. For example, a caregiver can check and turn off appliances from a distance.
4. Learning homes address patterns of activity in the home and the data that are recorded and accumulated are used to anticipate the resident's needs and to control the environment. For example, turning up the heat an hour before the person gets up in the morning.
5. Attentive homes continuously monitor and register the activity and location of people and items within the home and this information is used to control the devices in anticipation of the resident's needs. This is known as *context-awareness* (e.g., Roy et al., 2006).

Family members and other caregivers who cannot provide consistent monitoring find smart home options appealing because they see this as a means of avoiding injuries, illnesses, and hospitalizations. However, the question always needs to be addressed regarding whose needs are truly being served. The value of such an examination cannot be overstated because there is a balance to be achieved between safety and security on the one hand and the loss of privacy, choice, and autonomy on the other. The more intrusive the intervention, the less privacy, choice, and autonomy exist. Although smart home technologies can positively impact residents' independence, instrumental activities of daily living (IADLs), socializing, and quality of life, there is scant evidence in the research literature that this, in fact, occurs (Brandt, Samuelsson, Töytäri, & Salminen, 2011).

Existing Home Environment Evaluation

Even though smart homes are an option, they are not as commonly used as making adjustments to an individual's existing residence. As noted by Gitlin et al. (2002), most persons with dementia and other forms of cognitive disability live in their current home and are cared for by family members or paid personal assistants and other caregivers. Certain physical features of the home environment, however, may be safety hazards or barriers to performing routine day-to-day activities. Therefore, recommending and implementing home modifications is considered a routine part of clinical practice in home care and rehabilitation. To help in determining needed changes, Gitlin et al. (2002) developed a checklist for evaluating the home environment of a person with dementia that can be applied to individuals who are aging in place or who have other disabilities. Areas assessed include the support of daily functioning or the performance of everyday tasks through the (a) removal of hazards, (b) physical adaptations (e.g., eliminating excess items and rearranging furniture), (c) the support of orientation through visual cues, and (d) comfort enhancement.

1. *Items addressing hazards*
   - Railings/handrails that are in good condition, installed securely, are the right height, and adequately cover all steps
   - External pathways are even, level, and constructed of quality materials.
   - Adequate lighting without shadows or glare
   - Interior flooring that is even, not slippery, and of good quality (no frayed carpeting or broken and loose tiles).
   - Items do not obstruct interior pathways.
   - Well maintained and quality electrical cords, switches, outlets, and so forth
   - Furniture that is strong and stable
   - Safe storage and adequate labeling of household chemicals, medications, and other ingestible substances

2. *Items addressing adaptation and use of assistive and cognitive support technologies*
   - Remote controls for TV and appliances
   - Special pillows, plastic covers, pads, and so forth
   - Monitoring devices, including intercoms, wandering devices
   - Adapted cooking and eating utensils
   - Adapted grooming and dressing aids
   - Childproof locks and latches
   - Colored tape to highlight stairs
   - Secure gates at top or bottom of staircase
   - Grab bars by toilet, sink, and tub/shower
   - Raised or adjusted toilet seat

■ Nonslip bath mat
■ Hot water adjusted to prevent scalding

3. *Items addressing visual cues and use of strategies to facilitate way finding, orientation, and awareness*
   ■ Instruction list for tasks
   ■ Daily schedule is provided
   ■ Grouping of objects on shelves, in a section of a room, and so forth.
   ■ Use of labels and pictures
   ■ Use of contrasting colors to highlight objects (e.g., red placemat and white dinner plate)

4. *Items addressing comfort*
   ■ Presence of meaningful photos and other objects of personal value
   ■ Ability to have privacy
   ■ Minimization of noise from radio, TV, neighborhood construction
   ■ Elimination of visual clutter

Gitlin, Winter, Dennis, Hodgson, and Hauck (2010) designed the Care of Persons with Dementia in their Environments (COPE) program in line with the aforementioned checklist. It targets the modification of environmental barriers and stressors to decrease sensory, physical, and cognitive demands. Results of their research showed that the program improved patient functioning, especially IADLs, patient engagement, and caregiver well-being and confidence.

Other researchers have also found that individuals who received functional-based assistive technologies (ATs) and environmental interventions showed significantly less functional decline (Mann, Ottenbacher, Fraas, Tomita, & Granger, 1999). In a study of older adults with cognitive impairments, primarily caused by Alzheimer's disease, devices to accommodate physical impairments were more readily adopted than those for cognitive impairments (e.g., memory aids, safety assists). However, once used, people were more satisfied with the cognitive devices (Lancioni et al., 2009; Mann, Karuza, Hurren, & Tomita, 1992).

The research discussed earlier focused on older individuals with dementia, but most of the findings and recommendations can be applied to others—of any age—who have a cognitive disability. When Hammel, Lai, and Heller (2002) studied the impact of AT and environmental interventions (AT-EI) on the functioning of older adults with developmental disability, they found many benefits for those living in the community and in institutional settings. However, for almost 10%, AT hindered rather than enhanced function because of the need for specialized devices to be set up carefully and caregivers not knowing how to do so or taking the time to do it properly. The authors note:

> People with developmental disabilities and proxies who pro-vided assistance both spoke of needing time to even accept and learn how to use the AT at first, especially with technology that was more advanced or represented a new skill area, such as a new communication device or wheelchair. It wasn't until months later that they were ready to learn new ways to incor-porate the AT-EI into more activities, to identify ways to adapt the technology or the environment to fit their needs better, or to consider adding additional technology given success with what they previously received. (p. 104)

Universal Design

Modifications to building interiors and exteriors target many of the same goals as ATs, and their combined use often is the most effective (Gitlin, 2002; Gitlin et al., 2002). *Universal design* (UD) ideally results in environments and products that are usable by everyone, and thus their relevance to and us-ability by persons with disability is assumed and is as invisible as possible.

UD is defined by the United Nations as "the design of products, en-vironments, programmes and services to be usable by all people, to the greatest extent possible, without the need for adaptation or specialized design" (United Nations General Assembly, 2007, p. 5). Table 8.1 lists the seven principles of UD developed in 1997 under the auspices of the Center for Universal Design at North Carolina State University. In contrast to UD, ATs tend to be products that are designed from the outset to enhance the individualized functional activities of persons with disability. The purpose of both is the same—to enable individuals to fully participate in all of life's activities regardless of capability or ability.

The principles of UD in Table 8.1 focus on universally usable design—not usability, which refers more to ease of and comfort with use. The late Knut Nordby (2003) developed a usability pyramid consisting of five levels of access for persons with disability. At the base, he represents (a) those who can use all goods and services directly. On the top of the base is the level representing (b) inclusive or UD. The next level up represents (c) those who can only access goods and services with some form of adaptation (e.g., tilting the head to hear in the better ear when at the checkout counter). The next level represents (d) those who require an AT to access goods and services (e.g., a personal amplification system to hear the cashier). The final and top level represents (e) those individuals who need assistance from one or more people to access goods and services (e.g., a sign language

TABLE 8.1
The Principles of Universal Design (Version 2.0)

PRINCIPLE ONE: Equitable Use

The design is useful and marketable to people with diverse abilities.

PRINCIPLE TWO: Flexibility in Use

The design accommodates a wide range of individual preferences and abilities.

PRINCIPLE THREE: Simple and Intuitive Use

Use of the design is easy to understand, regardless of the user's experience, knowledge, language skills, or current concentration level.

PRINCIPLE FOUR: Perceptible Information

The design communicates necessary information effectively to the user, regardless of ambient conditions or the user's sensory abilities.

PRINCIPLE FIVE: Tolerance for Error

The design minimizes hazards and the adverse consequences of accidental or unintended actions.

PRINCIPLE SIX: Low Physical Effort

The design can be used efficiently and comfortably and with a minimum of fatigue.

PRINCIPLE SEVEN: Size and Space for Approach and Use

Appropriate size and space is provided for approach, reach, manipulation, and use regardless of user's body size, posture, or mobility.

Source: Copyright 1997 NC State University, The Center for Universal Design. Available at: http://www.ncsu.edu/www/ncsu/design/sod5/cud/about_ud/udprinciplestext.htm

interpreter). The goal of UD is to expand as much as possible the bottom level consisting of those who can use all goods and services directly.

UD is an aspiration. In reality, it is not possible to fully achieve and, as stated by Bougie (2001), "Irrespective of the challenges and wide implementation of technology based on 'design for all', specific problems require assistive technology" (p. 13).

THE CATEGORY OF PRODUCTS AND TECHNOLOGY OF LAND DEVELOPMENT IN THE *ICF*'S ENVIRONMENTAL FACTORS DOMAIN OF PRODUCTS AND TECHNOLOGY

This category includes products and technology in rural, suburban, and urban land areas "as they affect an individual's outdoor environment through the implementation of land use policies, design, planning, and development of space, such as pathways and signposting, curb cuts and street lighting and ramps, signposting such as park signage and wildlife trails."

The Americans with Disabilities Act Accessibility Guidelines specify that accessible routes must have ground and floor surfaces that are stable, firm, and slip resistant. However, no existing standard test methods are capable of measuring the firmness and stability of surfaces found in outdoor environments. Beneficial Designs in Nevada endeavors to remedy this by developing recommendations for surface accessibility guidelines, which will improve access for all people, including those with mobility limitations, older adults, families with strollers, and others. Beneficial Designs is also a leader in the field on accessible trails, sidewalks, and shared use paths, as well as recreational and leisure technologies and ski area access (http://www.beneficialdesigns.com).

THE CATEGORY OF ASSETS (FINANCIAL, TANGIBLE, AND INTANGIBLE) IN THE *ICF*'S ENVIRONMENTAL FACTORS DOMAIN OF PRODUCTS AND TECHNOLOGY

In the *ICF*, assets are products, such as money and other financial instruments, which serve as a medium of exchange for labor, capital goods, and services. *Tangible assets* are products or objects, such as houses and land, clothing, food and technical goods, which serve as a medium of exchange for labor, capital goods, and services. *Intangible assets* include intellectual property, knowledge and skills, which serve as a medium of exchange for labor, capital goods, and services.

Assets are what an individual owns or has rights of use to procure goods and services and help in the achievement of goals. This is different from the Economic Life domain in Activities and Participation, which focuses more on the individual's control over achieving economic self-sufficiency (from private or public sources) and the capacity to engage in economic transactions. It is certainly the case in 2011 that most home accommodations made and ATs purchased are from funds out of the pockets of individuals. Therefore, the possession of or access to assets can be a strong determinant of who does and does not get assistive and cognitive support technologies.

CHAPTER 2 IN THE *ICF*'S ENVIRONMENTAL FACTORS COMPONENT: NATURAL ENVIRONMENT AND HUMAN-MADE CHANGES TO ENVIRONMENT

This domain addresses physical space and the characteristics that make it an identifiable entity—its natural and atmospheric features, terrain, altitude, climate, air quality, sounds, predominant plants and animals, as well as changes in these brought about by human behavior. These can be barriers or facilitators for persons with disability as they affect health and well-being. Many individuals with difficulty breathing cannot tolerate living at high altitudes. Most East Coast cities are at or near sea level, whereas Denver and Albuquerque, for example, are "mile high" cities where there is less oxygen. Breathing is also affected by the air quality where one lives as well as allergens from local flora and fauna (Figure 8.2).

International Classification of Functioning, Disability and Health

e ENVIRONMENTAL FACTORS

CHAPTER 1	CHAPTER 2	CHAPTER 3	CHAPTER 4	CHAPTER 5
PRODUCTS AND TECHNOLOGY	NATURAL ENVIRONMENT AND HUMAN-MADE CHANGES TO ENVIRONMENT	SUPPORT AND RELATIONSHIPS	ATTITUDES	SERVICES, SYSTEMS AND POLICIES

▼

e210	Physical geography	Features of land forms and bodies of water.
e215	Population	Groups of people living in a given environment who share the same pattern of environmental adaptation.
e220	Flora and fauna	Plants and animals.
e225	Climate	Meteorological features and events, such as the weather.
e230	Natural events	Geographic and atmospheric changes that cause disruption in an individual's physical environment, occurring regularly or irregularly, such as earthquakes and severe or violent weather conditions, e.g. tornadoes, hurricanes, typhoons, floods, forest fires and ice-storms.
e235	Human-caused events	Alterations or disturbances in the natural environment, caused by humans, that may result in the disruption of people's day-to-day lives, including events or conditions linked to conflict and wars, such as the displacement of people, destruction of social infrastructure, homes and lands, environmental disasters and land, water or air pollution (e.g. toxic spills).
e240	Light	Electromagnetic radiation by which things are made visible by either sunlight or artificial lighting (e.g. candles, oil or paraffin lamps, fires and electricity), and which may provide useful or distracting information about the world.
e245	Time-related changes	Natural, regular or predictable temporal change.
e250	Sound	A phenomenon that is or may be heard, such as banging, ringing, thumping, singing, whistling, yelling or buzzing, in any volume, timbre or tone, and that may provide useful or distracting information about the world.
e255	Vibration	Regular or irregular to and fro motion of an object or an individual caused by a physical disturbance, such as shaking, quivering, quick jerky movements of things, buildings or people caused by small or large equipment, aircraft and explosions.

FIGURE 8.2. ICF natural environment and human-made changes to environment. *(Continued)*
Source: World Health Organization

e260	Air quality	Characteristics of the atmosphere (outside buildings) or enclosed areas of air (inside buildings), and which may provide useful or distracting information about the world.
e298	Natural environment and human-made changes to environment, other specified	
e299	Natural environment and human-made changes to environment, unspecified	

FIGURE 8.2. *Continued*

CHAPTERS 3 AND 4 IN THE *ICF*'S ENVIRONMENTAL FACTORS COMPONENT: SUPPORT AND RELATIONSHIPS AND ATTITUDES

"Support and Relationships" has to do with those individuals who comprise a person's immediate and proximate circle of support, and "Attitudes" (see Figures 8.3 and 8.4) characterizes how they think and feel—that is, their values, opinions, and beliefs. "Attitudes" additionally addresses cultural and societal features that impact beliefs, values, and rules of people with disability as a group and specific individuals within the group—in other words, the social context that surrounds living a life with disability.

As shown in Figure 8.3, the *ICF* description of relevant support and relationships is very broad. An individual's circle of support includes not only family and friends, but also health care and other professionals and anyone that the individual may encounter in their various environments. Domestic animals are also included. As stated in Scherer (2005b):

> A person's social support network (family, friends, personal assistants, work colleagues, etc.) can greatly affect the *disability experience* and may even influence daily functioning and rehabilitation outcomes. Social support systems strongly influence how people with disabilities interpret their experiences and evaluate their options. (p. 97)

The opposite of social support is its absence, or even social conflict, and it is important to know how that affects the individual's psychological well-being, autonomy, and self-determination (e.g., Rook, 1984; Rook &

International Classification of Functioning, Disability and Health

e ENVIRONMENTAL FACTORS

CHAPTER 1	CHAPTER 2	CHAPTER 3	CHAPTER 4	CHAPTER 5
PRODUCTS AND TECHNOLOGY	NATURAL ENVIRONMENT AND HUMAN-MADE CHANGES TO ENVIRONMENT	SUPPORT AND RELATIONSHIPS	ATTITUDES	SERVICES, SYSTEMS AND POLICIES

▼

e310	Immediate family	Individuals related by birth, marriage or other relationship recognized by the culture as immediate family, such as spouses, partners, parents, siblings, children, foster parents, adoptive parents and grandparents.
e315	Extended family	Individuals related through family or marriage or other relationships recognized by the culture as extended family, such as aunts, uncles, nephews and nieces.
e320	Friends	Individuals who are close and ongoing participants in relationships characterized by trust and mutual support.
e325	Acquaintances, peers, colleagues, neighbors and community members	Individuals who are familiar to each other as acquaintances, peers, colleagues, neighbors, and community members, in situations of work, school, recreation, or other aspects of life, and who share demographic features such as age, gender, religious creed or ethnicity or pursue common interests.
e330	People in positions of authority	Individuals who have decision-making responsibilities for others and who have socially defined influence or power based on their social, economic, cultural or religious roles in society, such as teachers, employers, supervisors, religious leaders, substitute decision-makers, guardians or trustees.
e335	People in subordinate positions	Individuals whose day-to-day life is influenced by people in positions of authority in work, school or other settings, such as students, workers and members of a religious group.
e340	Personal care providers and personal assistants	Individuals who provide services as required to support individuals in their daily activities and maintenance of performance at work, education or other life situation, provided either through public or private funds, or else on a voluntary basis, such as providers of support for home-making and maintenance, personal assistants, transport assistants, paid help, nannies and others who function as primary caregivers.
e345	Strangers	Individuals who are unfamiliar and unrelated, or those who have not yet established a relationship or association, including persons unknown to the individual but who are sharing a life situation with them, such as substitute teachers, co-workers or care providers.

FIGURE 8.3.   ICF support and relationships. *(Continued)*
Source: World Health Organization

e350	Domesticated animals	Animals that provide physical, emotional, or psychological support, such as pets (dogs, cats, birds, fish, etc.) and animals for personal mobility and transportation.
e355	Health professionals	All service providers working within the context of the health system, such as doctors, nurses, physiotherapists, occupational therapists, speech therapists, audiologists, orthotist-prosthetists, medical social workers.
e360	Other professionals	All service providers working outside the health system, including lawyers, social workers, teachers, architects and designers.
e398	Support and relationships, other specified	
e399	Support and relationships, unspecified	

FIGURE 8.3.   *Continued*

International Classification of Functioning, Disability and Health

e ENVIRONMENTAL FACTORS

CHAPTER 1	CHAPTER 2	CHAPTER 3	CHAPTER 4	CHAPTER 5
PRODUCTS AND TECHNOLOGY	NATURAL ENVIRONMENT AND HUMAN-MADE CHANGES TO ENVIRONMENT	SUPPORT AND RELATIONSHIPS	ATTITUDES	SERVICES, SYSTEMS AND POLICIES

▼

e410	Individual attitudes of immediate family members	General or specific opinions and beliefs of immediate family members about the person or about other matters (e.g. social, political and economic issues), that influence individual behavior and actions.
e415	Individual attitudes of extended family members	General or specific opinions and beliefs of extended family members about the person or about other matters (e.g. social, political and economic issues), that influence individual behavior and actions.
e420	Individual attitudes of friends	General or specific opinions and beliefs of friends about the person or about other matters (e.g. social, political and economic issues), that influence individual behavior and actions.

FIGURE 8.4.   ICF attitudes. *(Continued)*
Source: World Health Organization

e425	Individual attitudes of acquaintances, peers, colleagues, neighbors and community members	General or specific opinions and beliefs of acquaintances, peers, colleagues, neighbors and community members about the person or about other matters (e.g. social, political and economic issues), that influence individual behavior and actions.
e430	Individual attitudes of people in positions of authority	General or specific opinions and beliefs of people in positions of authority about the person or about other matters (e.g. social, political and economic issues), that influence individual behavior and actions.
e435	Individual attitudes of people in subordinate positions	General or specific opinions and beliefs of people in subordinate positions about the person or about other matters (e.g. social, political and economic issues), that influence individual behavior and actions.
e440	Individual attitudes of personal care providers and personal assistants	General or specific opinions and beliefs of personal care providers and personal assistants about the person or about other matters (e.g. social, political and economic issues), that influence individual behavior and actions.
e445	Individual attitudes of strangers	General or specific opinions and beliefs of strangers about the person or about other matters (e.g. social, political and economic issues), that influence individual behavior and actions.
e450	Individual attitudes of health professionals	General or specific opinions and beliefs of health professionals about the person or about other matters (e.g. social, political and economic issues), that influence individual behavior and actions.
e455	Individual attitudes of health-related professionals	General or specific opinions and beliefs of health-related professionals about the person or about other matters (e.g. social, political and economic issues), that influence individual behavior and actions.
e460	Societal attitudes	General or specific opinions and beliefs generally held by people of a culture, society, subcultural or other social group about other individuals or about other social, political and economic issues, that influence group or individual behavior and actions.
e465	Social norms, practices and ideologies	Customs, practices, rules and abstract systems of values and normative beliefs (e.g. ideologies, normative world views and moral philosophies) that arise within social contexts and that affect or create societal and individual practices and behaviors, such as social norms of moral and religious behavior or etiquette; religious doctrine and resulting norms and practices; norms governing rituals or social gatherings.
e498	Attitudes, other specified	
e499	Attitudes, unspecified	

FIGURE 8.4. *Continued*

Pietromonaco, 1987). Thus, it is essential to determine not only an individual's actual social and material support (material support is referred to as *assets* in *ICF* terminology), but also how the individual perceives such support (e.g., Turner, Fleming, Ownsworth, & Cornwell, 2011; Wills & Shinar, 2000).

Support From Caregivers

The U.S. government has declared four key groups as vulnerable clinical research subjects: individuals with cognitive disability, children, pregnant women, and prisoners (e.g., Orticio, 2009). Children are considered a "vulnerable group" who require the protection of adults who have their best interests at heart. Additionally, as noted by Galvin and Donnell (2002)

> There are many situations in which family involvement is crucial to the success of the rehabilitation process. Indeed, the Individuals with Disabilities Education Act has given parents a critical role in the development of the child's individualized education plan. (p. 158)

For example, Ryan has an individualized education program (IEP) that monitors his progress in school, allows for input from him and his parents, and sets goals for his future. Every year, Ryan, his parents, and his teachers and counselors at school meet to discuss and update his IEP. This provides an opportunity to evaluate and improve services for Ryan that will enhance his ability to have a successful academic career.

The desirability of family involvement is just as true for adults with cognitive disability. According to the Family Center on Technology and Disability (FCTD), an educated and trained family is a key resource in the rehabilitation and community integration process. It is certainly the case that they have the most intimate and detailed knowledge of the person with a cognitive disability. For example, my mother lost her will to live when she was told during the team meeting that she would never walk again. They had meant to motivate her to literally get up and off her butt. But, had I been consulted about this, I would have told them how she would react.

A very important form of support for many persons with cognitive disability comes not only from family caregivers, but also from paid caregivers. Statistics from the National Alliance for Caregiving (NAC, 2009) reveal that caregivers comprise 29% of the U.S. adult population, or 65.7 million adults. Half of this number care for adult recipients and another 13% for both child and adult recipients. Family caregivers (also referred to as informal or unpaid caregivers) additionally provide care to spouses with disability, and child caregivers may provide assistance to their siblings, parents, or grandparents.

A 2004 national survey conducted by the NAC and the AARP defined five levels of caregiving. "Level 1" caregivers devoted relatively few hours each week (a mean of 3.5 hours per week) to providing care and provided no care in the form of help with activities of daily living (ADLs). "Level 5" caregivers were those with the heaviest burden (a mean of 87.2 hours per week), providing help with at least two ADLs and more than 40 hours of care each week. The intensity of care provided predicted several problems related to caregiver health status.

Rosalynn Carter, founder of the Rosalynn Carter Institute for Caregiving (2008, 2011), states that there is a caregiving crisis regardless whether the caregiver is a family member or a professional caregiver. Family caregivers provide a wide range of assistance, often including complex nursing care (e.g., respiratory care, medication management and dispensing, medical monitoring), cognitive support (e.g., management of delirium or agitation, ensuring safety), and care management, both in home (e.g., supervision) and out of home (e.g., arranging medical care appointments).

Research has consistently shown that family caregivers have concerns in five areas: (a) dealing with change, (b) managing competing responsibilities and stressors, (c) providing a broad spectrum of care, (d) finding and using resources, and (e) addressing emotional and physical responses to care. Feelings of anger while providing care, guilt for resenting the responsibility, and feeling unsupported are not uncommon.

Highway Mile Marker 387

Caregiver attitudes and feelings of fear, anger, and guilt are emotions I could relate to when it came to my mother, Marjorie. The 70-mile route to my mother's house at the highway's mile marker 387 went past a beautiful, well kept farm. The immaculate large white farmhouse sits about 20 yards from a beautiful big red barn, and together they form a scene right out of a Currier and Ives painting. In the heat of summer, the surrounding green fields and trees shading the house appeared to send out a cool refreshing breeze; in the depths of winter, especially when snow had fallen, the scene exuded warmth and shelter from the harshness of the outdoors. Regardless of the time of year, they gave off a sense of comfort, friendliness, and serenity. And regardless of the time of day or reason for my trip, I always made sure I looked over at the farm. It calmed me on those trips of uncertainty of what I would find at my destination, already looking forward to my return trip home past the farm: "See you in about 8 hours, farm." Then I made a resolve to be positive and as helpful as I could be to my mother.

Traveling to see my mother was rarely a trip filled with happy anticipation. I was always worried about what I would find when I got there, even back in the days when she was in relatively good health and was active. Would she be sober? Would she be okay? This, of course, says as much about me as it does anything about her. But even though she would turn out to be physically fine, there was always the worry about the emotionality of our time together. Then, as she got into her 90s, and her world became so small, it became difficult to tolerate the repetition of stories that I had heard hundreds of times before. Not just stories, but always the ones with a bitter recollection, a complaint, or other form of "negative thinking." Over time, when she needed me more, I found myself increasingly dreading those trips.

When the Caregiving Recipient Becomes a Caregiver

Another example of the effects of parental dementia on the family is found in the book, *Living in the State of Stuck* (Scherer, 2005b), which relates the lives and experiences of adults with spinal cord injuries or who were born with cerebral palsy. In the book, Butch, a young man who was a garbage truck driver before he received a spinal cord injury in a vehicular accident, talks about his father's Alzheimer's disease. Butch's spinal cord injury resulted in paralysis and the need to use a wheelchair for mobility. After his accident, he moved back in with his parents who helped care for him. Then he was placed in the role of a caregiver when his father developed Alzheimer's disease:

> He'll be talking about one thing and then he's talkin' about something from 60 years ago and then he's back talkin' about something else and he never finishes up. Ma and I have to watch him 24 hours a day. Now he'll get up and walk out the door and he don't even know he's out the door. Ma can't control him. She tells him to do somethin', he ignores her. I tell him to do somethin', he'll do what I tell him. We're just sittin' here stuck. I ain't been able to get out of the house to go for a ride or nothin'. It's bad enough being in this shape, now I'm trapped. There's nothin' else we can do. We can't put Pop in a nursing home or we'll lose the house. And we can't afford paid help. (p. 164)

After Butch's father died, his brother had an exacerbation of his psychiatric disability and moved back in with Butch and his mother who was now a frail old woman. Butch related his frustration:

> Now I'm just sittin' again. I've put on more than 100 pounds. I'll tell ya', this whole place [home] is so hard. I just stay up here in this room and watch TV. (p. 194)

In Butch's case, he had always taken great pride in his self-care and health after his spinal cord injury. But in addition to gaining weight, he had developed an ulcer in his foot. This was followed by a succession of ulcers and infections. He refused hospital care and debrided his wounds with his pocketknife. He didn't even want the visiting nurse to take his temperature saying, "Why bother?" The family was in poverty, and after Butch's death from systemic infection resulting from his ulcers, his mother went into a nursing home but, according to reports, died "because she didn't eat enough to stay alive." His brother remained in the house and was later involved in motorcycle accident that further exacerbated his disability.

Caregiver frustration, guilt, and anxiety are widespread and not usually openly acknowledged. This can lead to considerable stress and consequent health problems. A 25-year body of research shows that Butch and his family's experiences are not isolated ones and that family caregivers are at risk for a wide range of health and mental health problems. They are less apt to pursue such preventive health behaviors as exercising, eating regular meals, keeping medical appointments, and obtaining flu shots. When they do not avail of routine health care or undergo health screenings, they are at an increased risk for developing health problems that could have been avoided or forestalled.

Caregiver Distress and Needs

Approximately 20%–30% of caregivers are prone to depression, anxiety, and somatic symptoms, all of which likely have their roots in stress, exhaustion, and self-neglect (e.g.,Comans, Currin, Brauer, & Haines, 2011; Kreutzer et al., 2009). Dementia caregiving, according to Etters, Goodall, and Harrison (2008), has been associated with negative effects on caregiver health and early nursing home placement for dementia patients. They note that many factors influence caregiving experience, such as gender, relationship to the patient, culture, and personal characteristics. Regarding primary caregivers of persons with traumatic brain injury, researchers have found a high prevalence of psychological distress (e.g., Davis et al., 2009; Kreutzer, Gervasio, & Camplair, 1994a, 1994b; Sady et al., 2010). Schulz et al. (2004) report that spouses score higher on depression indices than parents do. When institutional care is sought, caregivers reported depressive symptoms and anxiety to be as high as they were while in-home caregivers. They state that this is especially difficult for spouses, and almost half visit the patient daily and continue to provide help with physical care during visits.

In summary, the needs of caregivers are personal, multifaceted, and quite complex but they have not gone unrecognized. Many excellent resources have been developed to guide professionals into helping caregivers (Niemeier & Karol, 2010a, 2010b; Sander, 2006).

Societal Attitudes As Well As Social Norms, Practices, and Ideologies

In the *ICF*, societal attitudes refer to "General or specific opinions and beliefs generally held by people of a culture, society, subcultural or other social group about other individuals or about other social, political and economic issues, that influence group or individual behavior and actions" (p. 191). Social norms, practices, and ideologies are defined as

> Customs, practices, rules and abstract systems of values and normative beliefs (e.g. ideologies, normative world views and moral philosophies) that arise within social contexts and that affect or create societal and individual practices and behaviors, such as social norms of moral and religious behavior or etiquette; religious doctrine and resulting norms and practices; norms governing rituals or social gatherings. (p. 191)

As indicated earlier, culture is viewed as the envelope in which individuals' attitudes, beliefs, values, behaviors, and communication patterns are formed. Culture affects views of disability, technology, support from caregivers, and support from professionals (Parette, Huer, & Scherer, 2004). When there is compatibility in perspectives, it is largely caused by having a shared culture.

There are many ways in which cultures have emerged, such as having a common physical location, religion, and even the same disability. Deaf culture, for example, has its own language and customs. One of those customs has traditionally been the rejection of technologies to restore hearing as their use is taken to mean a rejection of deafness and deaf culture (Scherer, 2004). Thus, one's identity as a member of deaf culture is related to the kinds of supports one accepts and uses.

There are cultural values attached to independence versus the reliance on caregivers and technologies. According to Ripat and Woodgate (2011), "Although health care cost savings are valued in Western society, if the family culture is to provide that assistance, [assistive technology] may represent a threat to the relationship and role of the family member as care provider" (p. 92). The authors further note that whereas individualistic societies value independence and autonomy, collectivist societies place more emphasis on community and interdependence and thus may not view some forms of AT favorably.

Stigma is something assigned to an individual by a society and culture. A deaf person may be stigmatized by deaf culture for receiving a cochlear implant. Thus, assistive and cognitive support technologies can assume symbolic status. Ripat and Woodgate (2011) give the example of the need for a wheelchair as indicative to many of disability and incapacity, whereas use of a walking stick or a cane rarely gets a second glance. When a person with a cognitive disability uses a computer or cell phone as forms of support, their commonplace use is not apt to draw much attention to the user. The influence of culture on the selection and use of technologies is strong and will be discussed again in Chapter 10 of this book.

Having a disability is no longer considered to be merely a reflection or result of an individual's developmental or medical condition, but a situation that arises from a societal perspective of what it means to have a limitation in one or more aspects of expected functioning. Therefore, societal (or social) and cultural views of disability as well as the personal meaning (or construction) of disability must equally be addressed.

CHAPTER 5 IN THE *ICF*'S ENVIRONMENTAL FACTORS COMPONENT: SERVICES, SYSTEMS, AND POLICIES

This domain in Environmental Factors has to do with the ways in which people with disability receive benefits (or not) in an organized and regulated manner. As indicated in Figure 8.5, this is the domain that focuses on the infrastructure for community service delivery as it is concerned with housing, transportation, health, education, employment, and so on, as well as the local and national laws and policies governing them.

Turner and colleagues (2011) found in their study of service and support needs during the transition from hospital to home following acquired brain injury that many individuals perceived service systems to be "complex, inconsistent, difficult to understand, bureaucratic and ultimately, impossible to work with" (p. 826). The authors' state,

> The present findings suggest that the complexity and rigidity of service systems can significantly impact upon transition success and amplify the difficulties individuals with [acquired brain injury] and their family caregivers experience with respect to adjustment and integration. (p. 828)

In *ICF* terms, complex and rigid service systems can serve as barriers to the community participation of individuals with cognitive disability as much as the absence of services. Facilitators, on the other hand, enhance accessibility and availability. As an example of a facilitator, a web-based videoconferencing training program for caregivers of adults with traumatic brain injury in rural areas was developed to help them with strategies for managing cognitive and behavioral changes in the person with the injury (Sander, Clark, Atchison, & Rueda, 2009).

The environments in which individuals live and work and in which supports are provided are greatly affected by legislation and health care policies. As detailed by Mendelsohn and Fox (2002), the development of the field of AT and rehabilitation has emerged in the context of civil rights,

International Classification of Functioning, Disability and Health

e ENVIRONMENTAL FACTORS

CHAPTER 1	CHAPTER 2	CHAPTER 3	CHAPTER 4	CHAPTER 5
PRODUCTS AND TECHNOLOGY	NATURAL ENVIRONMENT AND HUMAN-MADE CHANGES TO ENVIRONMENT	SUPPORT AND RELATIONSHIPS	ATTITUDES	SERVICES, SYSTEMS AND POLICIES

▼

e510	Services, systems and policies for the production of consumer goods	Services, systems and policies that govern and provide for the production of objects and products consumed or used by people.
e515	Architecture and construction services, systems and policies	Services, systems and policies for the design and construction of buildings, public and private.
e520	Open space planning services, systems and policies	Services, systems and policies for the planning, design, development and maintenance of public lands, (e.g. parks, forests, shorelines, wetlands) and private lands in the rural, suburban and urban context.
e525	Housing services, systems and policies	Services, systems and policies for the provision of shelters, dwellings or lodging for people.
e530	Utilities services, systems and policies	Services, systems and policies for publicly provided utilities, such as water, fuel, electricity, sanitation, public transportation and essential services.
e535	Communication services, systems and policies	Services, systems and policies for the transmission and exchange of information.
e540	Transportation services, systems and policies	Services, systems and policies for enabling people or goods to move or be moved from one location to another.
e545	Civil protection services, systems and policies	Services, systems and policies aimed at safeguarding people and property.
e550	Legal services, systems and policies	Services, systems and policies concerning the legislation and other law of a country.

FIGURE 8.5. ICF services, systems, and policies. (*Continued*)
Source: World Health Organization

e555	Associations and organizational services, systems and policies	Services, systems and policies relating to groups of people who have joined together in the pursuit of common, noncommercial interests, often with an associated membership structure.
e560	Media services, systems and policies	Services, systems and policies for the provision of mass communication through radio, television, newspapers and internet.
e565	Economic services, systems and policies	Services, systems and policies related to the overall system of production, distribution, consumption and use of goods and services.
e570	Social security services, systems and policies	Services, systems and policies aimed at providing income support to people who, because of age, poverty, unemployment, health condition or disability, require public assistance that is funded either by general tax revenues or contributory schemes.
e575	General social support services, systems and policies	Services, systems and policies aimed at providing support to those requiring assistance in areas such as shopping, housework, transport, self-care and care of others, in order to function more fully in society.
e580	Health services, systems and policies	Services, systems and policies for preventing and treating health problems, providing medical rehabilitation and promoting a healthy lifestyle.
e585	Education and training services, systems and policies	Services, systems and policies for the acquisition, maintenance and improvement of knowledge, expertise and vocational or artistic. skills. See UNESCO's International Standard Classification of Education (ISCED-1997)
e590	Labour and employment services, systems and policies	Services, systems and policies related to finding suitable work for persons who are unemployed or looking for different work, or to support individuals already employed who are seeking promotion.
e595	Political services, systems and policies	Services, systems and policies related to voting, elections and governance of countries, regions and communities, as well as international political organizations.
e598	Services, systems and policies, other specified	
e599	Services, systems and policies, unspecified	

FIGURE 8.5.   *Continued*

the removal of barriers in the built environment, shifting emphases in social policy, and various pieces of legislation such as the Rehabilitation Act of 1973, Individuals with Disabilities Education Act, Americans with Disabilities Act, and the Assistive Technology Act. Indeed, every piece of U.S. federal legislation enacted during the past 20 years regarding persons with disability has explicitly referred to AT devices and services, which were defined initially in the 1988 Technology Related Assistance for Individuals with Disabilities Act, known popularly as the "Tech Act." This legislation, as discussed in Chapter 5, defined AT devices and services for the first time. The Tech Act was reauthorized in 1994, 1998, and 2004. The 2004 reauthorization of the act is called The Improving Access to Assistive Technology for Individuals with Disabilities Act of 2004 (Public Law 108–364).

Another key U.S. law is the Americans with Disabilities Act, reauthorized in 2008 as the Americans with Disabilities Act Amendments Act (ADAAA). This legislation, along with the United Nations' Convention on the Rights of Persons with Disabilities and its Optional Protocol adopted in 2006, views the provision of AT devices and services as an important component of the human rights of persons with disability worldwide.

In summary, matching an individual with the most appropriate support for his or her use requires an understanding of the characteristics of that person's environments as made up of (a) physical and architectural elements; (b) a circle of support and the attitudes of those providing support; (c) cultural influences on the individual's values, attitudes, and beliefs toward AT; and (d) the availability of relevant services and supportive policies. For persons with physical disability, ATs help many to live independently and enter the workforce. Increases in the visibility of these devices have impacted community practices. For example, independent mobility by battery-powered wheelchair required the existence of accessible buildings and modified transportation systems. For persons with cognitive disability, the role of technology is no less important in supporting independence and the achievement of goals. How persons know about, select, and receive support from technologies is generally under the purview of the service delivery system—the topic of the next chapter.

9

Getting Support and Services

It is not the brains that matter most, but that which guides them—
the character, the heart, generous qualities, progressive ideas.
—Fyodor Dostoyevsky, Russian novelist

*T*he *International Classification of Functioning, Disability and Health*
(*ICF*) views disability and functioning as outcomes of interactions between *health conditions* (diseases, disorders, and injuries)
and *contextual factors*, which consist of external (environmental) and internal (personal) factors. Figure 9.1 takes the "Vitruvian Man" as drawn by
Leonardo da Vinci and expands him with bolder borders to indicate how
he is surrounded by these influences. Contained within the larger area,
the circle, are the environmental factors talked about in the last chapter:

- Availability of technologies and products for personal and community
  living (Chapter 1 in *ICF* Environmental Factors)
- Characteristics of one's living area including (a) the physical qualities
  of and access to one's community and its facilities and (b) the features
  of where one lives, whether it be in a private residence, group home,
  assisted living center, skilled nursing facility, and so on (Chapter 2 in
  ICF Environmental Factors)
- Support from key others, from family to health care providers to
  strangers (Chapter 3 in *ICF* Environmental Factors)
- The attitudes of and opportunities provided by others (Chapter 4 in
  ICF Environmental Factors)
- Available services, systems, and current policies and laws affecting
  people with cognitive disability (Chapter 5 in *ICF* Environmental Factors)

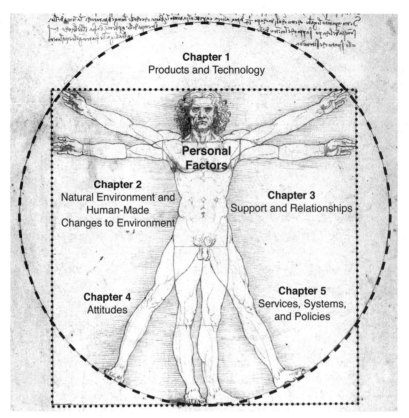

FIGURE 9.1   Contextual factors comprise the external context within which functioning of the WHOLE PERSON occurs.

When seeking help and treatment for a cognitive disability, all of the cited environmental factors influence what form that help and treatment will take. Also key are one's personal factors, which also surround the individual (think of the square area) and are influenced in large part by environmental factors. Within such a context, we have the individual's activities and participation according to the capacities afforded by that person's body functions and structures. Thus, and as this book has presented and as illustrated by the Vitruvian Man, any individual's health is viewed at the level of body or body part, the whole person, and the whole person in a personal and social context.

Although Marjorie, Theresa, Delmar, and Ryan can all benefit from cognitive support, they vary widely in the nature of their specific needs for support because of their particular cognitive disability and the capacities of their other body functions and structures. They similarly differ significantly in their personal factors. That is, their life course has been distinctive because of their individualized experiences, years living with disability, view of themselves, outlook for the future and goals, mood, motivation, and so on. For example, Marjorie's dementia, life experiences, and personality caused her to be more negative in outlook than Theresa, who is still pursuing opportunities and thus exhibits a freshness of life that comes with new experiences. Environmental factors also distinguish them because different laws and systems affect the services they receive and who provides them. For example, Delmar is a recipient of vocational rehabilitation services, whereas Ryan is a special education student and receives his supports from the public and private school systems. They also differ in the support they receive from others and the attitudes of those they encounter. An older adult female in the December of her life is not viewed by anyone as being similar to a young male in the April of his life.

SYSTEMS OF SERVICE DELIVERY

Cognitive rehabilitation has been shown to be effective (e.g., Cicerone et al., 2011) for persons with all types of cognitive disability, but it is not as widely available as is the need for it. Rarer yet are cognitive rehabilitation programs staffed by professionals skilled in assistive and cognitive support technology (CST) assessment and provision.

In Europe, the Horizontal European Activities in Rehabilitation Technology (HEART) study was conducted from 1993 to 1995 to survey assistive technology (AT) services in Europe and to propose positive future actions (HEART Consortium, 1995). Led by the Swedish Institute of Assistive Technology, the study team consisted of 21 institutions, organizations, and companies in 12 European countries. The HEART study defined six criteria for good service delivery systems:

1. *Accessibility* to those who need it. Accessibility is based on the needs of the individual; it means people know where to go for help, that the system is easy to understand, and that ample information about it is available. No one should be excluded regardless of where he or she lives or his or her ability to pay.
2. *Competence* of the people working in the service delivery system. This means that personnel have the knowledge, skills, and experience necessary to provide proper service to the users of the system.
3. *Coordination of the parts* into a cohesive whole
   - between the individual and all steps in the delivery process,
   - between the professionals working with service delivery, and
   - between the service delivery system and other sectors of society.

4. *Efficiency* in finding the best solutions for the greatest number of people, using available resources at the lowest cost in the shortest possible time.
5. *Flexibility* in responding to change and allowing for individual differences. Flexibility is vital for AT because of the diverse nature of disabilities and constant technological advances. Flexibility exists when
   - potential users can get devices that meet their needs whether or not those devices are on an approved list or are marketed in the countries where users live,
   - producer–importers can get a device tested at a reasonable cost, within a reasonable time, and
   - researchers and developers can get financial support for their work; cooperate and communicate with users, designers, and producers; and use new technology to meet needs.
6. *User influence* as indicated by
   - the presence and strength of user organizations,
   - the enforcement of user legal rights,
   - user involvement on the policy-making level,
   - frequent user consultation during the process, and
   - user influence in the decision-making process.

The HEART study's points were underscored in the 2007 report on *The Future of Disability in America* (Field & Jette, 2007). It appears, therefore, that many of the HEART criteria have both current and international applicability.

The 58th World Health Assembly in 2005 addressed disability prevention, management, and rehabilitation (World Health Organization [WHO], 2005). The report stated that there were approximately 600 million people globally living with disabilities of various types, and of that total, 80% live in low- and middle-income countries (LMIC); most are poor with limited or no access to basic services, including rehabilitation facilities and services. Limited access to information and services is a problem and, additionally, rehabilitation has not become a part of many health care systems worldwide because of many historical, cultural, political, and economic factors (Bricknell, 2003; Tinney, Chiodo, Haig, & Wiredu, 2007).

Cross-cultural studies of disability remain few in number for various reasons. Heterogeneous populations, research designs, and small numbers of study participants (yielding low statistical power) present significant challenges, as do differing cultural perspectives of such constructs as independence, autonomy, and psychological qualities like initiative and sense of control (e.g., Tamaru, McColl, & Yamasaki, 2007). Often, etiologies differ, making comparisons difficult. For example, in a study of individuals with spinal cord injuries (SCIs) in Columbia, South America, wounds from firearms are the largest cause of SCI, whereas in the United States and Canada, it is motor vehicle accidents (Lugo, Salinas, & García, 2007). Causes of brain injury (disease and infection, land mine explosions, vehicular accidents, etc.) have varying incidence rates from country to country.

As we have discussed, people with cognitive disability around the world live, work, play, and learn in widely varying situations or communities. The United Nations Convention on the Rights of Persons with Disabilities and its Optional Protocol must now be operationalized within a context of increasingly weak economies and infrastructures that result in barriers to the provision of assistive and cognitive support technologies to the individuals who would benefit from them.

In their article, "Providing Assistive Devices and Rehabilitation Services in Developing Countries," Øderud and Grann (1999) reflect on experiences from Scandinavia, Europe, and LMIC. They outline key elements for the effective provision of assistive devices, which emphasize the local availability of devices as well as their repair and maintenance. This requires competent providers and professionals as well as an effective service delivery system. The authors note that it is important to provide AT devices or ATDs to individual users in their local environments so as to ensure a match with the environment as well as the user. Effective use depends on local attitudes as well as local services. For example, some countries formerly under totalitarian regimes have followed the practice of institutionalization and exclusion of individuals with disability (Eldar et al., 2008).

In these countries, some professions such as social work do not exist, nor is there adequate training in human services professions; thus individuals do not receive information about available AT, not to mention the devices themselves. While recognizing local variation, the authors outline a structured service delivery system containing the following core elements (Øderud & Grann, 1999, p. 784):

1. Identifying potential users
2. Identifying user needs
3. Identifying potential ATD solutions
4. Individual matching of user and ATD
5. Training
6. Follow-up with users, personal assistants, caregivers, and families
7. Service and maintenance

Twelve years after Øderud and Grann published their article, the *World Report on Disability* (WHO, 2011) underscores the same points by highlighting the need to ensure that ATDs are appropriate, suit the environment and the user, and are of high quality with adequate follow-up to ensure safe and efficient use of the ATD. The term *appropriate technology* is used to mean "Assistive technology that meets people's needs, uses local skills, tools, and materials, and is simple, effective, affordable, and acceptable to its users" (p. 301).

The *World Report on Disability* documents widespread evidence of barriers to the achievement of this, including the following:

- **Lack of provision of services.** People with disabilities are particularly vulnerable to deficiencies in services such as health care, rehabilitation, or support and assistance.
- **Problems with service delivery.** Issues such as poor coordination among services, inadequate staffing, staff competencies, and training affect the quality and adequacy of services for persons with disabilities.
- **Inadequate funding.** Resources allocated to implementing policies and plans are often inadequate. Strategy papers on poverty reduction, for instance, may mention disability but without considering funding.
- **Lack of accessibility.** Built environments (including public accommodations) transport systems and information are often inaccessible. Lack of access to transport is a frequent reason for a person with a disability being discouraged from seeking work or prevented from accessing health care. Even in countries with laws on accessibility, compliance in public buildings is often very low. The communication needs of people with disabilities are often unmet. Information is frequently unavailable in accessible formats, and some people with disabilities are unable to access basic information and communication technologies such as telephones and television.
- **Lack of consultation and involvement.** Often people with disabilities are excluded from decision-making in matters directly affecting their lives. WHO states on page 96, "Educating people with disabilities is essential for developing knowledge and skills for self-help, care, management, and decision-making. People with disabilities and their families experience better health and functioning when they are partners in rehabilitation."
- **Lack of data and evidence.** A lack of rigorous and comparable data on disability and evidence on programmes that work often impedes understanding and action (WHO, 2011, pp. 262–263).

The localized approach to service delivery advocated by Øderud and Grann and in the *World Report on Disability* has been successfully used elsewhere for the training of professionals and providers (e.g., Christova, 1999 [Bulgaria]; Leonardi et al., 2005 in *ICF* training in Italy). In the case of ATDs, LOREWO (Local Rehabilitation Workshops; n.d.) emphasizes the identification of local materials and supplies as well as trained providers and technicians, information dissemination, individualized matching and adaptation of ATDs, and training and follow-up with users and families (e.g., Øderud, Brodtkorb, & Hotchkiss, 2004).

But, as noted in the *World Report on Disability*, many barriers remain. Although there are globally accessible information resources for ATDs such as AbleData, they often aren't available in the language of individuals in developing countries and, thus, their usability is limited. As an example of an effort to meet a global need for information on various ATDs using low-cost and local materials, the United Nations (1997) developed an excellent resource describing how to use local resources and materials to make prostheses and orthoses, Handicap International (HI) wooden wheelchairs, crutches, simple handgrips, stick reachers, swivel and pronged handles, spoons, special seating, and maintain hearing aids.

From Charity to Consumer Involvement and Empowerment

In the not-too-distant past, a charity model was the predominant service delivery system. Even today, nongovernmental organizations (NGOs) are a primary means of supplying and supporting ATDs in developing countries (e.g., Zongjie, Hong, Zhongxin, & Hui, 2007; Christova, 1999). Let us use for our example the first four elements in Øderud and Grann's structured service delivery system:

1. Identifying potential users
2. Identifying user needs
3. Identifying potential ATD solutions
4. Individual matching of user and ATD

People with disability in LMIC cannot typically afford ATs and may rely on a charity model for the devices and other supports they receive. However, taking donated wheelchairs and other devices, often used and refurbished, to other countries, albeit charitable, often results in an inappropriate match of person and device and waste when the device is found to be ineffective or inappropriate. Mukherjee and Samanta (2005) found that too often, wheelchairs are provided that are such a poor match with the user that they are rejected because of pain, fatigue and discomfort, and lack of habitat adaptability (i.e., they are difficult to maneuver under the local environmental conditions and architectural restraints). Mukherjee and Samanta (2005) conclude that wheelchairs (and other ATDs) should not be recommended without proper assessment of the user's needs, preferences, and priorities within their particular cultural and physical milieu.

The importance of the assessment of user needs and preferences was highlighted in an effort to design, fabricate, and provide low-height mobility devices for women living in rural and low-income India (Kim & Mulholland, 1999; Lysack et al., 1996). Mulholland et al. (2000) involved the end users in the process and derived a design that met their personal and environmental needs. The team found that the simpler the device, the greater the acceptance. Such design features as baskets and adjustable seating platforms were rejected because the users felt that they would hinder usability. The team also found that user feedback and professional opinion often did not match; users preferred simplicity even at the expense of a certain degree of functionality.

Populations are not static; take for example China. In spite of economic growth and advances in science and technology, rehabilitation services remain inadequate for the needs that exist (Z. Xu, personal communication, October 24, 2007; Zongjie et al., 2007). China is certainly not the only country with inadequate services for persons with disability.

In contrast, consider the example of neurorehabilitation services provided to children in Brazil. According to Lucia Braga (personal communication, October 30, 2007), the Brazilian SARAH Network sees 1.5 million children with brain injury, SCI, and other neurological problems each year. The SARAH Network consists of eight rehabilitation hospitals throughout Brazil with the aim to provide the most humanistic care possible, recruit the patient to be an active participant in his or her recovery, and respect the unique social settings that serve as the basis of each patient's life. The SARAH Network has a technology center that creates and manufactures devices and equipment for children with physical disability who lack independence in activities of daily living, or who have communication disability. Individuals in the SARAH Network are given all the necessary devices, tools, and equipment that they need at no cost. The network asks banks and other institutions to donate their unused or discarded computers, and SARAH repairs them and distributes them to individuals with disability, also at no cost. SARAH also provides them with the appropriate interfaces adapted to each patient's special needs so as to facilitate their use of the computer.

Although technologies continue to proliferate worldwide, and people who can afford to use electronic, computerized devices will hopefully get support when needed, there also remains a need for trained professionals. Economic investment needs to occur in personnel as well as in technology.

In the developed world, Ripat and Booth (2005) reviewed AT service delivery models in the province of Manitoba, Canada. They found that

> Variability exists with the availability of AT devices (e.g., types, choice and replacement of equipment for individuals with certain disabilities), the availability of AT services (e.g., professional assessment, training and follow-up), the referral and application process for AT, and the funder's knowledge of current applications of AT. (p. 1462)

As noted by Eggers et al. (2009), Ripat and Booth (2005), and others, ATDs and services fall under the purview of various public and private sector providers because of characteristics of the user (e.g., age, the nature of the injury, financial assets) and the setting in which the device(s) will be used (e.g., home, workplace, or educational setting). This variety results in a confusing and complex system of service delivery comprised of elements having their own policies and criteria for eligibility. There are also significant gaps such as the paucity of transitional services for individuals moving from child to adult services, school to work, and facility-based to home-based care.

In the context of such variety, there have been attempts to characterize the desired components of a quality AT service delivery process with most including an evaluation and training component, a device provision component, an education component, and a coordination and collaboration component. Based on the results of their study, Ripat and Booth (2005) derived fundamental recommendations for AT service delivery that include the following:

- Key services include evaluation, training, follow-up, and maintenance. Funds required for program evaluation, training users and caregivers, and providing maintenance and follow-up services must be considered as essential aspects of service delivery.
- The evaluation process should identify the unique individual's skills, abilities, needs, preferences, priorities, existing supports and resources, and context. The process should include the user throughout and emphasize current and desired functioning over diagnosis.
- Users of AT need the opportunity to try technology in the environments of use prior to making a commitment to a product. It is imperative that the AT be matched to the individual in context.
- Users of AT will have changing needs over time. Programs need to consider and be responsive to both current and future needs.
- AT will change over time. A better solution may be developed and available in the near future. Thus, users need continuing opportunities to try out and obtain what best meets their needs.

In the Republic of Ireland, a new AT service delivery model was formed by Client Technical Services, Central Remedial Clinic, Clontarf, Dublin (Craddock, 2002; Craddock & McCormack, 2002). A client-focused social and participatory service delivery model for AT was achieved, which included a local technical resource in the form of Technology Liaison Officers (TLOs). TLOs are people with physical disability who received training and certification in AT devices and services and who act as a liaison among professionals, users, and potential users of AT.

Because there are few standards regarding both ATDs and services, Elsaesser and Bauer (2011) outlined a standardized assistive technology service method (ATSM). They stated that ". . . irrespective of the context, service provider, disability and AT, all ATS [assistive technology services] share essential elements. These common elements comprise a transaction space for the exchange of knowledge across contexts, between professions, and for structuring and coordinating research" (p. 397).

Compatible with the *ICF*, the ATSM is a "standardized framework with a common language to facilitate communication for AT practice, education and policy activities" (Elsaesser & Bauer, 2011, p. 387).

In summary, international efforts to study and address AT services have many shared findings and recommendations. But no one has yet compared various and predominant existing models or examined the best from each that might be applied to the others. This is, in fact, in process by the Center on Effective Rehabilitation Technology (CERT) service delivery led by the Burton Blatt Institute (BBI) at Syracuse University and the Institute for Matching Person and Technology (IMPT), in collaboration with the Council of State Administrators of Vocational Rehabilitation (CSAVR), the Rehabilitation Engineering and Assistive Technology Society of North America (RESNA), the National Council on Independent Living (NCIL), and Rehabilitation Technology Associates. CERT's multidisciplinary research team will evaluate selected model employment and training programs to identify policies, procedures, and practices that result in the effective delivery of assistive technology and rehabilitation technology (AT/RT) to assist individuals with disability in achieving employment. Models studied are state vocational rehabilitation agencies, state Assistive Technology Act of 2004 projects, and Centers for Independent Living throughout the United States. Methods and criteria will be developed and refined to frame quality indicators of effective AT/RT service delivery. Effectiveness will be defined by quality indicators incorporating variables of structure, policy, decision-making processes and costs related to outcomes, and counselor and consumer satisfaction. The center will also analyze supports necessary for effective AT/RT delivery, including provider education, assessment tools and measures, information management, consumer education, quality assurance mechanisms, and public and private sector relationships. An additional objective is to identify, test, and develop strategies to support vocational rehabilitation counselors to make informed decisions, in concert with individuals with disability, to select the most appropriate AT/RT specific to employment objectives. This effort will result in a new validated instrument and system of measurement to improve AT/RT service delivery and reduce AT/RT nonuse and poor employment outcomes. The tool will be accompanied by an interactive training program for vocational rehabilitation counselors to build knowledge of AT/RT solutions and an improved assessment process, including a set of exemplars, tools, and guidance that agencies and programs can use to improve AT/RT service delivery. Information on the project can be tracked by visiting the homepage of the CERT at http://bbi.syr.edu/projects/cert/cert.htm. Separate research efforts by the BBI will expand this research protocol to the study of international service delivery models and contexts (Scherer, Adya, Samant, & Morris, 2011).

Service Delivery Outcomes

A recently published article on factors influencing consumer satisfaction with obtained ATDs found that there is a statistically significant relationship between being feeling informed and being satisfied with an ATD (Martin, Martin, Stumbo, & Morrill, 2011). The researchers found that being uninvolved in decision making and believing personal needs and preferences were not fully addressed were additional influences on low satisfaction and use.

This parallels the medical literature on treatment adherence and compliance (Scherer, Jutai, Fuhrer, Demers, & DeRuyter, 2007) and confirms the findings of other studies done over the past 30 years, which unfortunately means that not much improvement in the system of service delivery has occurred (e.g., Batavia & Hammer, 1990; Phillips & Zhao, 1993; Scherer & McKee, 1989).

Today, we strive for a model of service delivery that emphasizes the person and his or her empowerment and participation in (even more, contribution to) society at large, not merely that person's functional achievements, and the *ICF* presents an excellent example of just such a change. We have also moved from a philosophy of *normalization* (where the expectation was that persons with disability would strive to be like and do the same as nondisabled persons) to empowerment (persons with disability have the right to be self-determining and to make their own choices about their lives and to achieve the quality of life each believes is personally best).

We have often heard the medical and social models of disability discussed as dichotomous, and a common plea is to move away from the *medical model* of rehabilitation (with an emphasis on individual limitations) to a social model (with an emphasis on inclusion and participation and support for this through universal design, legislation, and societal attitudes of acceptance). Each of these models, however, has something to offer the consumer selecting technologies for support. Although the medical and social models each can advocate consumer inclusion and participation, extreme perspectives in each approach results in exclusion of individual preferences. Thus, it is most common today to see a blend of medical model and social model precepts. This has tremendous implications for all health care and rehabilitation professionals and the services they provide. According to the *ICF*,

> Disability is a complex phenomena that is both a problem at the level of a person's body, and a complex and primarily social phenomena. Disability is always an interaction between features of the person and features of the overall context in which the person lives, but some aspects of disability are almost entirely internal to the person, while another aspect is almost entirely external. (World Health Organization, 2002, p. 9)

Against a backdrop of individualization within various societies and service delivery models, we now focus on finding, funding, and receiving the necessary services to meet the needs, goals, and preferences of the unique individual. As a result, *assistive and cognitive support technology* selection will be more person centric.

A SUPPORT SELECTION FRAMEWORK

AT practice and research has been quite attentive to the outcomes of and satisfaction with technology use and its opposite—dissatisfied use, nonuse, and abandonment. This was essential when the field was in its early stages because it was through retrospective research that many influences on the outcomes of use or nonuse were identified (e.g., Phillips & Zhao, 1993; Scherer, 1993, 2002a, 2004, 2005b). Because of this knowledge, the field has advanced to a focus on getting the most appropriate match of person and technology at the outset. After all, when we obtain the right AT and CST for what the person wants and needs to do and where, then there is less need to worry about AT or CST abandonment or discard.

Studies in developed countries have consistently shown that the best match of person and technology occurs when the user is involved in the decision making and selection of the support to be used (e.g., Scherer, 2005b). For this to be successful, however, there must be an awareness of available options as well as trained professionals willing to involve the consumer and able to make the selected support available.

But just how does one help the person with a cognitive disability choose when to use support from technology, and when to seek assistance from another person? An emphasis needs to be placed on empowerment by working with the consumer to express needs and preferences as well as to discover that person's best blend of independence, interdependence, and often unavoidable dependence.

The support selection process is ideally person centric and based on a partnership of service provider and individual with a cognitive disability and/or caregiver. It occurs within a broader context and environment that serves to influence key personal factors of both the (a) individual with a cognitive disability/caregiver and (b) technology support provider(s). As the individual and provider meet for the purpose of support decision making and selection, they each bring to this process varying resources, levels of knowledge, expectations, preferences, and priorities. These in turn will affect the assessment of support needs both in terms of objective (e.g., functional evaluation) and subjective criteria (what is most desired).

The *ICF* is certainly relevant for the development of a framework for the selection of an assistive or cognitive support technology, but it does not pinpoint factors that influence that selection or outcome. Figure 9.2 depicts a *Support Selection Framework* (Scherer et al., 2007) that is compatible with the *ICF* framework and which summarizes in graphic form much of what has been presented in this book up to now. It, too, exists within a context of environmental and personal factors. Personal factors consist of resources (psychological, financial, etc.) that individuals (and/or their families and caregivers) bring to the process, as well as the skills, knowledge, and principles of the relevant service providers. Thus, there are environmental and personal factors associated with the consumer as well as environmental and personal factors associated with the provider that can influence the support selection process and outcome. Together, these environmental and personal factors create the context in which support decision making and device selection for a given individual occurs.

Environmental Factors

Individuals with disability and their caregivers, as well as service providers, live in a broad environment or milieu consisting of (a) legislation and policies impacting available services; (b) funding for supports, training, and education of both providers and consumers; (c) cultural priorities and values; and (d) attitudes of key others (including society/culture, person's family/significant others, etc.) toward ATs, personal assistance from family members, enhanced independence, and so on. These factors have an impact on the predispositions consumers (and service providers) have toward selecting and acquiring an AT.

The environment/milieu presents consumers with an array of resources within which supports will be recommended and procured such as finances and support from family and friends as well as peers. "Resources" in many cases is equated with options, informed choice, and a sense of empowerment and competence. Thus, resources are a key influence on what the consumer and providers are able to bring to the process of selecting support (be it AT, personal assistant, family help).

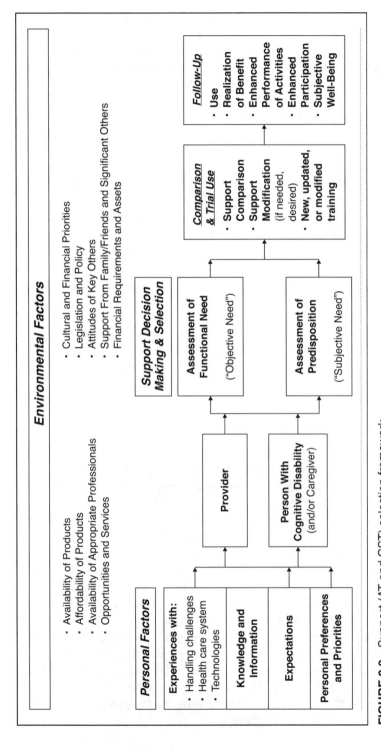

FIGURE 9.2 Support (AT and CST) selection framework.

Note. AT = assistive technology; CST = cognitive support technology. Adapted from Scherer, M., Jutai, J., Fuhrer, M., Demers, L., & DeRuyter, F. (2007). A framework for modelling the selection of assistive technology devices (ATDs). *Disability and Rehabilitation: Assistive Technology, 2*(1), 1–8.

Many individuals who could potentially benefit from AT may not be aware of who or what to ask, and that many of the professionals who are responsible for helping individuals navigate the rehabilitation process are not well-informed of the opportunities that AT offers in employment, education, transportation, and community integration (National Organization on Disability, 2004). Results from a 2001 survey of 1,414 persons with disability in the United States (Carlson, Ehrlich, Berland, & Bailey, 2002) showed that over half of the respondents (52%) participating in the survey reported receiving little or no information about AT, and 62% reported receiving little or no information about how to obtain AT. Only 20% of the respondents received help in the selection and purchase of AT and when they did, health care providers were reported to be the primary source of help and information (50%). One might expect that in the 10 years since this survey was conducted, these statistics would improve and that more people who could benefit from AT/CST would actually have them. Unfortunately, this is not the case. According to Sue Swenson, acting director of the National Institute on Disability and Rehabilitation Research, in February 2011, only 15% of people with disability have the technologies they want and need.

Persons with disability and family or household members pay for AT out of pocket in about 40% of the cases. The remainder are paid for by private health insurance, Medicare and Medicaid, and so on.

Devices that do not need personalized fitting or prescription are often purchased directly by the user from an appropriate store, catalog, or vendor. But some forms of technology support require careful personal fitting such as hearing aids, specialized vision technologies, wheelchairs, adapted seating systems, and augmentative and alternative communication (AAC) devices. Devices considered to be "medically necessary" and which may be paid for by Medicaid/Medicare usually require a prescription. Fitted and prescriptive devices need to be reviewed and recommended by experienced, and in some cases, licensed professionals, which include physicians, occupational and physical therapists, speech language pathologists, audiologists, and ophthalmologists. Vocational rehabilitation services conduct assessments for the purposes of job readiness and employment, whereas it is the responsibility of school districts to provide supports determined to be educationally necessary.

It is important that a professional or provider be located who has experience with and knowledge of the support under consideration, especially when selecting complex devices or systems. Rehabilitation engineers and AT providers are appropriate professionals to consult. Experienced peer users can be excellent resources, and they have been found to provide valuable assistance in an understaffed service delivery system. For example, in the Republic of Ireland, the group of peer users or TLOs described earlier in this chapter who received training in serving as the initial point of contact in each county, perform assessments of need, set up devices, and conduct follow-up evaluations (Craddock, 2002; Craddock & McCormack, 2002; Craddock & Scherer, 2002). Their involvement very quickly resulted in the service delivery system being more effective as well as efficient (e.g., the waiting list for an evaluation went from over a year to approximately a month).

We all live and work in a broad social environment consisting of expectations, priorities, and regulations that have resulted in large part from the enactment of laws and policy decisions at various levels of government. Laws and policies can affect the availability of supports (e.g., government standards for the approval of new products) and the ways in which they are made known and provided to consumers. Applicable financial policies and resources for products, professional training, and service provision are frequently aligned with legislative mandates.

A society that expects an individual with a disability to strive to be as functionally and financially independent as possible conveys that message to the consumer either directly or indirectly. When employed, expectations are placed on that person for a particular level of job performance and independence in performing tasks and meeting job requirements.

Cultural and subcultural values placed on functional support from ATs, as opposed to personal assistance from family members, and the value families place on enhanced independence can affect an individual's predisposition to use an ATD. For example, there may be family resistance to ATDs that call attention to the user, which is perceived as "spreading stigma" to the family. Families may agree to the use of an ATD in the home and community but fail to follow through on this agreement when stigmatizing effects are perceived by the family. Such attitudes are shaped by experiences with society in general, and they affect the willingness of individuals from culturally diverse backgrounds to work with ATD providers.

Additionally, culture affects the manner in which family members perceive and respond to providers and intervention efforts, and it exerts a strong influence on the way in which providers behave toward family members. Families can feel outnumbered by and distrustful of professionals (Talley & Crews, 2007), and when there is a lack of communication and understanding, poor treatment outcomes can result. For example, Sherer et al. (2007) note that greater discrepancies between family and clinician perspectives and ratings of "patient functioning" are associated with poorer therapeutic alliances of patient and provider and to poorer patient effort in therapies. They conclude that family perceptions and family functioning should be addressed to facilitate patient bonding with the rehabilitation program.

Inherent in ATD decision making is the assumption that partnerships among providers, family members, and the user are at least desirable, if not essential, in effectively identifying appropriate ATD solutions for use by persons with disability. These partnerships are more effective when consideration is given to cultural issues and to the characteristics and requirements of the milieu/environments where an ATD will be used.

The individual's comfort level with support use will be affected significantly by the environments of use because environmental factors will either facilitate use or serve as barriers to use. It often occurs that the device that worked so well in the rehabilitation facility is not working out in the home or the workplace. For example, the power wheelchair is tearing up the carpet or the communication device is not within reach when needed.

The perspectives and expectations of others in the environments of use can be influential, especially if the technology inconveniences others. In this fast-paced world, it is often easier for family members to just jump in and do a task for the person than to patiently step aside and watch the individual struggle to accomplish a task independently. Trials of equipment in actual settings of use and that involve everyone affected by the technology have proven to be cost effective in the long term because obstacles and barriers to optimal technology use are identified in time to derive solutions and alternatives.

Important resources for individuals with cognitive disability include emotional, physical, and material support from family as well as friends and other significant individuals. Support from others can promote such personal resources as enthusiasm, optimism, self-confidence, a sense of empowerment, and a readiness to try new approaches and products. Depending on the form and extent of support needed, an individual's financial assets become a key influence. In the United States, for example, many people who must pay out-of-pocket for the assistive and cognitive support technologies they need and want, go without them entirely or substitute an other type of support, or pay for them out of pocket.

The possession of resources in many cases is equated with options, informed choice, and a sense of empowerment and competence. Thus, resources are key to what the consumer is able to bring to the table during the selection of support.

Sample Questions to Answer About the Environments of Use

- Where will I use the support?
- How will each environment facilitate use?
- What are obstacles or barriers to my support use?
- Will I have the ongoing training and support I need to optimize use?
- How might my support use affect others?
- What resources are required?

Personal Factors and the Individual With a Cognitive Disability

Persons with cognitive disability differ as much personally as they do functionally. They and their caregivers bring expectations to the support selection process that are internal and external (Brown-Triolo, 2002; Scherer, 2005b). They carry the expectations of parents, spouses, employers, peers, and society in general that reflect varying values and cultural priorities. Individuals also place expectations on themselves that have evolved from their prior history with support use, the health care system, and so on. Their particular level of motivation, judgment, and outlook, and many other factors serve to combine in a way that defines each as a unique individual. Their expectations, combined with personality and temperament characteristics, such as the degree of self-determination and self-confidence or anxiety and depressed mood, serve to determine preferences and priorities. It is important to note that these influences interact and affect one another, and can change with the passage of time and accumulation of experience. Thus, at a given point in time, each person has a predisposition to view support use as being favorable or not for certain purposes and in particular settings or environments.

An important influence on a person's achievement of a rehabilitation goal is the character of the goal itself—specifically, to maximize the chance it will be achieved, the goal should be (a) explicit, (b) close to where the person's performance currently is, and (c) not too difficult. An additional influence, of course, is whether the experience of success or failure has accompanied the process of goal achievement in the past.

When the goal involves support from technologies, key factors to consider are motor skills, cognitive readiness, motivation, and psychological readiness for use. For many users of assistive and cognitive support technologies, their devices become an extension of the self, not just to themselves but also to other persons. The device, then, is incorporated into the individual's identity. But this process can be difficult for some, thus leading to underutilization or nonuse.

As discussed, persons with cognitive disability vary in their degree of knowledge and information about resources and opportunities as well as the means to obtain that information. For consumers and their family members and caregivers, access to peer support groups as well as the Internet can be key to being "connected" and in the information loop. Websites such as AbleData offer a wealth of information, as do blogs and online discussion groups. Online videos of product demonstrations are useful as are manufacturer and vendor webinars.

In the United States, support provided by independent living centers and through state projects funded by the Assistive Technology Act has made a crucial difference to many consumers and caregivers in having the knowledge and information they need to make informed choices.

Sample Questions to Answer About Preferences and Expectations: Person With a Cognitive Disability

- ■ How will use of the support fit with the way I usually do things?
- ■ How comfortable am I emotionally, cognitively, physically, and socially using this support?
- ■ Do I need additional capabilities to optimize use of this support?
- ■ Will this support use contribute to my quality of life?

Personal Factors and the Provider

Just as consumers differ in their environmental and personal resources, so do providers vary in the resources they bring to the service delivery process. Some are equipped with an advanced degree and certification or licensure. Some have a vast pool of contacts they can approach for help with complicated situations and questions or when confirmation is desired for a plan of action. Other providers may be more professionally isolated. Key resources for providers are those made available to them by their employers, the broader community, and what they obtained through their own creativity and initiative. Providers can benefit from conferences, professional literature and journals, and vendors to supply them with current and detailed technical information about available products. Providers who possess excellent resources also enjoy a sense of empowerment, competency, and confidence.

It is very common for providers to recommend only those supports that they are familiar with and, therefore, an important need exists for their ongoing training and education on assistive and cognitive support technologies. For example, O'Neil-Pirozzi, Kendrick, Goldstein, and Glenn (2004) studied the use of portable electronic memory devices in traumatic brain injury (TBI) rehabilitation and found that only 36% of clinicians reported familiarity. Clinician device training and confidence teaching patients device use were statistically associated with their use of such devices in TBI rehabilitation. They conclude that portable electronic memory devices may be underutilized with persons following TBI, and that there is a need for clinician training in the use of these devices for persons with TBI during their rehabilitation.

A recent survey of rehabilitation professionals with varied caseloads revealed that several respondents were not comfortable participating in the AT selection process with their clients and were not incorporating its precepts in their work (Barzegarian & Sax, 2011). Although AT was measured as important in the rehabilitation process, only a small percentage of individuals with disability were referred for an assessment or had AT recommended. Therefore, the professional must be given, and take advantage of, the time to gain knowledge, as well as the time to assess the individual, and understand how to match person and resources to achieve successful support selection.

The attitudes of providers and their expectations of the individual can have a profound influence on persons with cognitive disability and their expectations of themselves. What may seem to be a vital task to the individual may be given little attention by the provider and vice versa. Thus, to achieve a good match of person and technology, it is important that the potential technology user be paired with a well-informed and person-centered provider, and that the degree to which consumer and provider perspectives are shared is addressed.

Providers, too, have expectations of their own as well as those placed on them by their employers. Getting to know these expectations and openly sharing and discussing them will facilitate the selection of the most appropriate support for a given individual. Otherwise, the path to frustration, dissatisfaction, and nonuse of the support can begin early in the selection stage. In other words, the predisposing elements for support selection determine the outcomes achieved.

Sample Questions to Answer About Preferences and Expectations: Provider

- How comfortable am I discussing and recommending the use of assistive and cognitive support technologies?
- Do I need additional or updated information to confidently discuss a range of options for support use, including support from technologies?
- Am I given the time and resources to do a person-centered and comprehensive evaluation of various support options?

Objective and Subjective Need for Support

Personal factors lead to a predisposition to use support that defines the subjective need for that support, which may or may not match the *objective need* as determined by providers and measures of functional limitation. The predisposition to use and benefit from support can be characterized by assessing the individual's preferences and expectations and their influences (e.g., current level of subjective quality of life, self-esteem, mood, and attitudes of and support from others).

Providers must be especially cognizant of the impact of support use on individuals with new onset disability. The multiple issues that must be addressed by the individual can have an impact on that person's ability to understand the value of the support and gains that can be achieved from use of it. Given the importance of early support provision, individuals need to come to terms with living with a chronic illness or disability at the same time as they trying to learn and understand treatment issues and support use. Thus, the views of support use held by a young man with a new TBI are apt to be different from those of a child born with cerebral palsy or an aging person who is a recent stroke survivor. A highly positive outcome of the support decision-making process, therefore, is an individualized intervention that (a) considers the unique individual (including the nature of the disability, age at onset, etc., as well as objective and subjective need), (b) is minimally complex, and (c) is coupled with strategies for ongoing training for and encouragement and reinforcement of use as well as for the assessment of changing needs.

As we strive to help people with cognitive disability achieve their goals and include them in all aspects of community and society, it is imperative that personal preferences are addressed as early on as possible because they are correlated with the subsequent degree of and satisfaction with use of that support (e.g., Scherer, Sax, Vanbiervliet, Cushman, & Scherer, 2005). A comprehensive model of service delivery needs to also involve caregivers and families and match their needs to the support identified.

Support Comparison and Trial Use

Selecting the most appropriate support, with essential features included and nonessential ones left to consider later, is a complex process. Benefit from use should be achieved with minimum frustration and the shortest learning curve.

When a person in the process of being matched with a technology is involved in selecting it and encouraged to exercise choice regarding its features, the likelihood of the most appropriate technology being identified is enhanced, as is the probability of it being optimally used. However, many consumers may see only limited alternatives for themselves because they have not been exposed to sufficient options to make informed choices and express appropriate preferences.

An equally important issue is not presenting consumers with too many choices because that can often lead to confusion, feeling overwhelmed and anxious, and their resistance to making a choice (e.g., Schweizer, Kotouc, & Wagner, 2006). When comparing and choosing among competing AT or CST devices (i.e., the same basic device but with choice in degree of sophistication, style, size, etc.), three options will provide the person with the opportunity to exercise choice but not so many options that the person feels overwhelmed.

Individuals who have not yet come to terms with their disability and who may be depressed cannot be expected to exercise optimal judgment regarding technology selection. Additionally, depression may mask capabilities and capacities that would obviate the need for a technology.

Alternately, premature introduction of technologies may assume capacities and coping skills that in fact need to develop over time, which may result in the person feeling confused and frightened. For these reasons, it is always a wise course to have the individual try several support options in environments of actual use. This will give the individual the opportunity to exercise choice and will also give the provider information on what may need to be modified, added, or eliminated. It will also indicate where training for use needs to be concentrated.

Sohlberg, Ehlhardt, and Kennedy (2005) discuss instructional techniques effective in cognitive rehabilitation, when the individual needs to learn or relearn skills. For someone with a severe TBI or who has dementia, environmental accommodations may be the most useful support because it requires minimal training. Support that relies on paper and pencil, different colors, and labeling also requires comparatively little training when compared with many electronic and computerized supports. Therefore, when comparing supports, the individual should be provided a choice not only among competing styles, but also among different levels of complexity.

Options to compare and trial technologies may vary by the primary facility or agency coordinating the individual's treatment and rehabilitation. Most rehabilitation facilities have various technology options available, and manufacturers and vendors may be willing to loan or rent their products. Peer users of the same or similar technology are another potential resource.

When supports have been selected for trial use, such concerns as delivery time, warranties and guarantees, and so on should be discussed with vendors and manufacturers. If the individual finds use of the product too difficult, overwhelming, or otherwise dissatisfying, then the process of user training, consideration of environmental interventions and accommodations, and product modification are repeated.

Sample Questions to Answer: Support Comparison and Trialing

- Does use of this support reflect the individual's lifestyle, age, personality, priorities, and preferences?
- Have all available options been considered?
- How well does this support perform for the individual?
- Is this support easy to access, use, and maintain?
- Does this support fit with the other supports already being used?

Follow-Up

Periodic follow-up with individuals after they acquire their support will help to determine the success of the match and whether adjustments need to be made in the person's skills, environments of use, and/or support features. This also provides the opportunity to discuss the desirability of upgraded or additional supports. Professionals realize that follow-up evaluations of how well consumer needs are met need to become a regular part of the rehabilitation service delivery process because, increasingly, evidence is being requested regarding the quality of service delivery and the success of rehabilitation interventions.

Evans, Wilson, Needham, and Brentnall (2003) interviewed individuals with memory problems after acquired brain injury as well as their caregivers and found that the use of memory aids correlated with level of independence. The most important influence on an individual's use of the selected support is how well it actually serves that person. That is, how much it helps the individual accomplish desired goals and activities; fits with his or her lifestyle, routines, and preferences and does not result in stress and frustration; and enhances well-being. There are varied outcomes that can result from the technology selection process (Scherer, 2005b):

1. *optimal* use under all recommended conditions and situations;
2. *partial* use, where it is used in some situation but not others or part of the time;
3. *nonuse*, or "discontinued use" where the technology was once used but is set aside perhaps because it is no longer needed;
4. *avoidance* of use, where use is not even considered;
5. *reluctant* use, where the individual uses it but does so with displeasure; and
6. *abandonment*, or permanently giving up use usually out of frustration or annoyance.

The first three categories can be considered a successful outcome of the process if the individual with a cognitive disability reports realization of benefit from using or having used the technology. The last three categories, however, indicate a failure of the process to serve that individual.

Over time, and sometimes a short time, consumer capabilities and interests expand or evolve. This can be especially true when they have the most appropriate supports and, in *ICF* terminology, they are performing needed and desired activities, and are able to participate in various roles and events in varied settings where the lack of an appropriate device was a critical limiting factor for performance and participation. These are key outcomes, as are realized benefits from use of the selected support and the user's enhanced subjective well-being as a result of use. Unfortunately, such outcomes are not always achieved, and consumers abandon use of recommended technology supports.

Although some technologies are meant to be used for only a short time, premature nonuse and AT abandonment is costly both in terms of dollars as well as individual and provider time and resources. Outcome measures are used to demonstrate that particular goals established for an individual have been identified and then achieved. Without the use of outcome measures, the determination of intervention effectiveness can be impacted by incongruence in views held by consumers and therapists. For example, professionals tend to define the success of rehabilitation interventions in terms of gains in capabilities and functioning, whereas consumers more often equate success with social and personal gains. Outcomes vary among individuals, and one must obtain the consumer's perspectives of the most desired outcomes, which should be identified in the selection process when discussing expectations and priorities.

Sample Questions to Answer About the Outcomes of Support Use

- Have the individual's capabilities increased?
- Does the person report enhanced well-being?
- Is the individual participating more in desired roles, school or job, and the community?

CONCLUSION

When we think of the ultimate positive outcome of the service delivery process, we envision a consumer who is satisfied with their use of a recommended device and able to participate in various roles and events where the lack of an appropriate device had been a critical limiting factor. In other words, a positive outcome is where we know that the AT or CST and its use have empowered the individual with a cognitive disability. To achieve this is not difficult when four key points are kept in mind.

Support Selection Four Key Points

- Know the resources and where to get information.
- Identify not only needs but also expectations, preferences, and priorities.
- Use a process to guide and document decision making.
- Follow up.

The individual's life enhancement is the ultimate goal for most of us working in cognitive rehabilitation. We want individuals to be more capable, more independent, able to exercise more choice, and take advantage of a wide range of opportunities. Assistive and cognitive support technologies can play an important role in the achievement of such outcomes, but they will do so most effectively when the user is included in the process of selecting the technologies and is encouraged to express preferences regarding the device's features. It is also crucial that there be an "AT circle of support" in place. Dikter (2010) talks about an *AT Ecosystem*. It is the "circle of support" surrounding the successful selection and use of AT and CST. According to Dikter,

> The technology alone does not teach a child with significant learning difficulties. The technology alone cannot determine which AAC device and set up someone needs. Therefore, the ecosystem includes: the consumer or individual who will use the technology; parents and caregivers; professionals such as teachers, SLPs, vision specialists, rehab engineers, OTs and PTs; and IT companies who work with AT companies to ensure that technologies work together.

> There are also others that are involved in this ecosystem: government-national and state; the research community; non-profits and other agencies that support and build greater awareness not only to their communities but beyond. There is also the larger world of mainstream IT developers who need to understand accessibility for the corporate environment. Without all these constituent parts working together, AT and the power it provides can only do so much for any individual consumer. (Dikter, 2010)

When an AT and CST ecosystem or circle of support is in place, then the likelihood of the most appropriate AT being identified is enhanced, as is the probability of it being optimally used.

Efforts to classify outcomes of technology use (e.g., Jutai, Fuhrer, Demers, Scherer, & DeRuyter, 2005) and its predictors (e.g., Scherer, Sax, Vanbiervliet et al., 2005; Wielandt, Mckenna, Tooth, & Strong, 2006) underscore the need to understand how the selection framework may vary depending on the type of technology under consideration and the characteristics of the population addressed. But regardless of these factors, professionals, administrators, and funding sources acknowledge that consumers have a right to select the technologies and other resources they will be using and should, therefore, be involved in the processes of needs assessment, selection, and outcomes evaluation.

Quality service outcomes require that the rehabilitation service delivery process ensure that consumers receive a comprehensive and individualized evaluation by a qualified professional. It is crucial to apply a consumer-centered assessment approach when matching an individual with assistive and cognitive support technologies. Research on technology use has increasingly highlighted the fact that consumers are less likely to use recommended devices when their needs are neither fully addressed nor completely understood during the technology selection process.

The next chapter will focus on consumer-centered assessment and, in particular, the matching person and technology assessments as reliable and valid measures for selecting and evaluating technologies for use by individuals with cognitive disability.

10

Matching Person and Technology

What do we live for if not to make life less difficult for each other?
—George Eliot

*I*n the most straightforward conceptualization of the *International Classification of Functioning, Disability and Health (ICF)*, *body functions* and *body structures* can be considered the substrate that enables activities to occur, and, in turn, these activities enable participation in social, vocational, educational, civic, and other pursuits. Contextual factors (environmental and personal) facilitate or hinder participation. A comprehensive conceptualization of the *ICF* model recognizes the interconnectivity among all of these elements.

As an example, we will use a new product being developed under the auspices of the Rehabilitation Engineering Research Center for Advancing Cognitive Technologies (RERC-ACT) in Colorado. The product is a nonlinear prompting device. It is being developed because many individuals with acquired brain injury need cognitive prompts to habituate to their job tasks. Job coaches have typically performed this function, but it is difficult to find enough qualified job coaches. Current "coaching" or prompting devices are linear (i.e., they require the entire sequence of prompts each time the device is activated), and this has led to user frustration and product abandonment. The benefits of the new product are putting the user in control, eliminating frustration from having to go through an entire sequence, and increased independence and task performance.

Figure 10.1 takes the diagram of the *ICF* in Chapter 5 (Figure 5.2) and applies the example of the new nonlinear prompting device. This provides engineers and product designers with a fuller context to consider, as well as characteristics of the individual users.

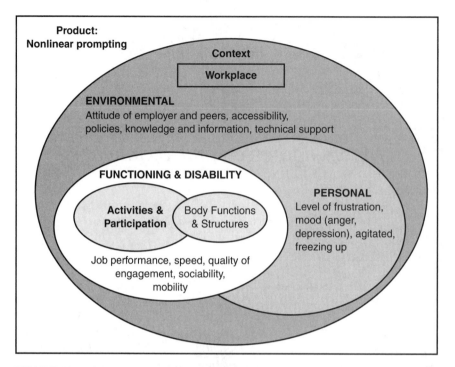

FIGURE 10.1 Diagram of the *ICF* with the example of the nonlinear prompting device.

Assistive technology/cognitive support technology (AT/CST) as an environmental factor could affect body functions and body structures as well as activities and participation. Activities and participation can affect body functions through the use of joints and muscles, acquisition of skills (and synaptic branching), and improvement of mood. Contextual factors likewise are dynamic. For example, considering personal factors, an individual may initially have negative attitudes toward a linear prompting device, but a positive experience with a well-matched nonlinear prompting device to perform desired activities may change those attitudes so that additional devices could more readily be considered. In a less successful example, a person with memory deficits (body functions) might have difficulties with activities and thus not ready to be employed (participation). A prompting device (environmental facilitator) can enable activities and job readiness. But other environmental factors might hinder its implementation, such as the attitudes of the employer toward technology use, or there might be financial limitations. Limits of the technology may prevent its successful use (i.e., it may not be well matched to the sensory and cognitive characteristics of the potential user, such that the prompt is too brief or the sound it emits is too distracting).

Support from appropriately selected technologies can make it possible to pursue employment, education, and involvement in community life.

Yet, individuals' views of the value of AT/CST in accomplishing these objectives and their predisposition to use one or more vary considerably. This is just as true if the primary user is the caregiver. In the previous chapter, a support selection process was outlined for optimally matching a technology with a particular person with a cognitive disability. An accompanying available model and assessment process to obtain information on the key elements of appropriate support selection is the subject of this chapter.

MATCHING PERSON AND TECHNOLOGY MODEL

The matching person and technology (MPT) model focuses on three primary areas that were found (Scherer, 1986) to most differentiate technology users and nonusers: (a) personal and psychosocial characteristics, needs, and preferences; (b) milieu/environmental factors; and (c) functions and features of the technology being evaluated. The MPT model was initially presented in 1989 (Scherer & McKee, 1989). The influences on technology use and nonuse as conceptualized in the MPT model have been used by several other AT researchers and authors (e.g., American Medical Association [1996] in *Guidelines for the Use of Assistive Technology*; Craddock [2002, 2006] and Craddock & McCormack [2002] for a new model of service delivery in Ireland; Demers, Weiss-Lambrou, & Ska [1996] for the development of the Quebec User Evaluation of Satisfaction with Assistive Technology [QUEST] assessment; Lasker & Bedrosian [2001] for the augmentative and alternative communication [AAC] acceptance model; and Zapf & Rough [2002] for the development of an instrument to match individuals with disability and service animals).

Elements within each of the three primary components—the *person*, the *milieu or environments* of use, and the *technology*—can contribute either a positive or a negative influence on technology selection and use. Too many negative influences will reduce the chance of technology adoption and use. In fact, the technology itself may appear perfect for a given need; but if it doesn't meet the person's priorities or preferences or does not receive needed environmental support, that perfect technology may go unused, or it may be used inappropriately and cause frustration and expense for those involved.

The model in Figure 10.2 is directed to the target of achieving a good match of person (individual with a cognitive disability and/or caregiver) and most appropriate AT and/or CST (it is equally applicable to the use of other supports by persons with disability) and is a companion to the support selection framework discussed in Chapter 9. The elements in the MPT model and the support selection framework have been shown to significantly influence the quality of the match of person and technology (Scherer, 1986, 1993a; Scherer, Sax, Vanbiervliet et al, 2005) and they have been subsequently validated by numerous others (e.g., Craddock, 2006; Eggers et al, 2009; Raskind, 2010; Riemer Reiss & Wacker, 2000; Steel, Gelderblom & de Witte, 2011; Strong, Jutai & Plotkin, 2011; Verza et al, 2006; Zapf & Rough, 2002).

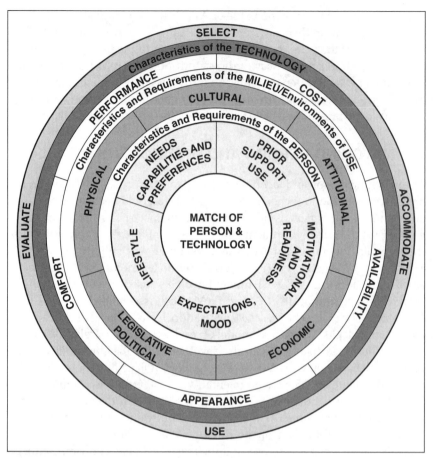

FIGURE 10.2 MPT model: Influences to consider when trying to achieve a good match of person and technology.
© Institute for Matching Person & Technology, Inc., 2002

Like the presentation of the *ICF* hierarchy in Chapter 4 of this book, the MPT model is best viewed from a gestalt perspective, where the whole is greater than the sum of its parts; a big picture beyond mere details, where one sees not only the forest but also the trees. In the current example, realization of benefit from the optimal match of person and technology is the forest. To achieve this, we address influences of the person, environment/milieu, and technology being considered (the trees). So that one "sees the forest," the MPT model is to be viewed as providing both a detailed description of an individual and a holistic view of that person so that the totality of person, environment/milieu, and technology influences are considered when selecting the optimal device.

1. The Person

Getting to know any given person requires a commitment to establishing rapport and exploring strengths, needs, and goals. Five examples of key areas to address are shown in Figure 10.2, but there are many others that could be added. Some key considerations regarding the characteristics and resources of the individual person include the following:

Body Functions, Body Structures, and Activities and Participation

Functional Needs
- Can the person participate in desired life areas? If not, what is getting in the way? What strategies, supports, or technologies might help?
- Does the person have the essential requisite skills to use the technology to maximum advantage? For example, does he or she have keyboard skills or the requisite ability to read?
- What are the person's strengths, interests, and priorities?
- Does the person prefer to have someone else help him or her because he or she desires that interpersonal contact?

Lifestyle
- What are the typical routines of the person?
- How much will use of the support affect typical routines? How much does that matter to the person?

Personal Factors

History of prior exposure to and experiences with technologies (and other supports)
- What is that person's receptivity or predisposition to the use of a technology?
- What is the person using or doing now?

Expectations, Mood
- What are the person's dreams and goals?
- Is the person generally content and able to manage typical periods of stress? Or is there generally a sad or anxious mood that might interfere with learning and using new technology?
- Does the person readily accept change or is change difficult to adjust to and accept?
- When faced with change, does the person generally approach it with a positive attitude, confidence, and self-determination, or with confusion, helplessness, and/or dependence on others?

Motivation and Readiness
- Does the person view technology (or other support) use as a desirable means of achieving dreams and goals?
- Does the person perceive a discrepancy between the current and desired situation?
- Does the person have appropriate trust in and respect for those who will be helping in support selection?

2. Milieu/Environment Factors Influencing Use

Moving outward from the center of the circle and beyond the characteristics of the person, considerations related to the characteristics and requirements of the environment(s)/milieu of use and their impact on the individual become crucial.

The word *milieu* is used because it connotes the *ICF* concept that our environment is not just a built one consisting of physical objects, but a place composed of people who have various attitudes and values. As we have discussed, attitudinal and cultural factors are important, as well as characteristics of the individual's built or physical environment. Within the *ICF*, the interface with the "built environment" for a person with disability or an older person with diminished physical or cognitive function is part of environmental factors. Resolving the environmental issues is a critical element in promoting independence. Mann, Ottenbacher, Fraas, Tomita, and Granger (1999) reported that making even minor modifications to the residence of frail older people produced more independence and allowed individuals to remain more functional in their homes rather than being institutionalized. This resulted in a slower rate of decline of the person's activities and reduced costs because of fewer nursing home placements.

We have discussed the move away from the medical model, where the focus is on individuals' limitations and the things they cannot do to a person's abilities, how we can strengthen those abilities, and how a technology can enhance activities and participation. What can we do in the physical or built environment to help this person function better and then what can we do to help that person develop a sense of belonging and connection?

People with disability vary in their desire for, or acceptance of, AT/CST versus personal assistance versus help from family members. Often, this is an outcome of one's culture and expectations as well as available resources. Family members may resent the use or presence of an AT/CST in the home. It may also be that they cannot take on the financial burden of obtaining the most appropriate supports. Financial limitations are a primary reason for individuals not getting the supports they need and want. For example, the public school that Ryan attended did not meet his educational and social needs, but in order to go to a school that had the appropriate resources, his family would have to pay private fees.

To use a truly idiographic, person-centered approach requires understanding such influences and pressures, level of program/professional trust, as well as language differences (a person who is deaf may require a sign language interpreter; a Native American may only communicate in his or her native language). Changes in the traditional family structure, cultural backgrounds, and linguistic heritages of families necessitate the need to develop skills in working with families from diverse backgrounds and understanding their perspectives regarding the selection and use of technology.

Sample considerations regarding the characteristics and requirements of the milieu/environments include

Cultural

- Within the person's familial culture, what have been his or her experiences and opportunities?
- Will the family encourage and support use of technology? Sometimes, caregivers and family members are primary users of these technologies. It's important to assess their perspectives as well as those of the person.
- Will associates (coworkers, friends, etc.) encourage and support use?

Attitudinal

- Do caregivers and the family have expectations and desires for the person different from those of the individual? Professionals?
- What are the predispositions of relevant others (employers, coworkers, teachers, etc.) to using a technology with this particular person?

Physical

- Are all of the necessary physical supports in place for this person to access and use the planned technology?
- If assistance is required for use of the technology, is it available?
- Do room settings need to be reorganized?
  - Is adequate space available in the room?
  - Is the lighting sufficient?
  - Will the person need to be near an electrical outlet?
  - Will the person require extra table/desk space for a device?
  - Will the person have clear access within the room?
- Will the person have physical access to all work, social, and lavatory facilities?
- If the device needs to be portable, is it sufficiently easy for the person to move and carry?

Legislative/Political
- Are the people in settings where AT/CST will be used familiar with all of the relevant legislation related to technology use?
- Have additional supportive/advocacy resources in the community been identified?

Economic
- What are the repair record and maintenance requirements of the technology, and how much do repairs or regular maintenance typically cost?
- Will the vendor provide services at the person's home or work location? At what cost?
- How often are upgrades available, and how much do they cost?
- Does funding exist to appropriately provide the device and ongoing support?
- Is a plan in place to upgrade or replace technologies that are no longer suitable?
- Have additional supports and assistance been considered and are they available if needed?

3. The Technology

Characteristics of the particular technology (or other support) being considered are the next concentric circle as we move outward from the center of the model. As discussed earlier, technology devices and technology services can be thought of as two halves of a whole, much like the yin-yang interconnectedness of Personal and Environmental Factors shown in Figure 5.3. There are many aspects of a technology to consider when beginning the process of narrowing down the available choices. Sample considerations regarding the characteristics of the technology include the following:

Availability
- How available is it? Can it be obtained in a timely fashion?
- Will it need adjustment or setup?

Appearance
- How compatible is the technology with desired social activities?
- Does the person feel self-conscious using it
  - Around family?
  - With friends?
  - At work or school?
  - Out in the community?

Comfort
- Does using the technology cause fatigue, strain, or pain?
- Is the technology easy for the person to use, transport, or set up?

- Does the individual have a sense of security with use?
- Is the person emotionally and socially comfortable with use?

Performance
- Does the technology support the person's varying needs and goals?
- Does the technology require considerable maintenance?
- How easily and quickly can servicing and repairs be done?
- For those with rapid developmental changes, how easily and quickly can upgrades be obtained?
- What is the impact of climate on this technology? How does it function in high humidity, heat, or cold?
- If the technology needs to be portable, is it?
- How durable is it and can it withstand a lot of wear and tear in going from place to place?
- How compatible is it with other technologies and supports being used or being considered for use?
- Is the person already using a device or number of devices, and will it interface well?
- Is a point of learning saturation and "cognitive overload" being reached? Are there simpler, less complex solutions?
- How accurate and fast is the device?
- Is training needed in order for the person to use this device and maximize benefit? How much training? Who will provide the training?
- Will using this device be distracting to other persons? For example, frequent beeping or loud clicking from keyboard entry.

Cost
- How much does it cost and who will pay for it? See Appendix C for options.
- What are the relative advantages to purchasing, leasing, or renting the technology?
- Are there effective alternatives that cost less?
- Is the cost reasonable in light of the expected gains?
- Can it be serviced locally or must it be shipped elsewhere?
- Are ongoing training, support, and upgrades built into the cost?

A technology must be adapted to the individual's needs and preferences; individuals should not have to adapt to a technology's features. Thirty years ago, it was common to have, for example, one style of wheelchair prescribed for many people (e.g., Scherer, 2002a, 2002b). Options and choices in wheelchairs and other assistive technologies, if they existed at all, certainly were not vast. Manufacturers of products or devices did not think it worth their while or cost-effective to uniquely shape devices or craft them to fit individual needs and preferences. Then in the late 1980s, different models became available (e.g., lightweight and sports wheelchairs) and in a range of colors and styles, which better suited individuals' unique needs and resulted in reduced health care and technology costs due to improper fit or use. It is precisely this need for the availability of varied choices in technologies that has led to the existence of the 38,000 products listed in AbleData. This is not to imply that every person with a disability is given a "wish list" of every item available. It does mean that there should be a process by which a person with a disability can receive the AT/CST that will allow availing of the opportunities that today's society has made available and will facilitate optimal health and well-being.

4. Cycle of Selection, Accommodation, Use, and Evaluation

The outermost ring in Figure 10.2 occurs when a technology has been chosen and its usability for the particular person is being addressed. *Usability* is actually the one word that best captures the essence, the sum total, of each preceding ring and element discussed earlier. It is important that AT/CST outcomes measurement focuses on the individual. Diversity among persons with disability is a central factor guiding the evaluation of whether technology is deemed usable or successful and should never be treated as "error" and "noise" to be ignored.

Both the first and last steps in achieving a good match of person and technology are to conduct a thorough assessment of person, milieu/environments, and proposed technology. After a trial period and any needed accommodations are made, after training has been provided, and the person has used the technology in actual situations and natural settings, feedback should be sought on how well the technology is performing for that person and how the person has changed in body functions or structures and/or activities and participation. This is using an *evidence-based* approach to technology evaluation and *measuring outcomes* of the technology as an integrated component of treatment.

This process may reveal that a person has stopped using a device when all it may require to become useful again is some small adjustment or modification or an upgrade to match the person's developmental changes (e.g., Scherer, 2005b). Consideration might be given to selecting additional devices or supports, making the necessary adjustments and upgrades and so on until the person finds the device *usable* again. Key considerations regarding the cycle of selection, accommodation, use, and evaluation include

Selection of the Technology
■ Once person, milieu, and environmental elements have been taken into account, what will best suit this person's current needs and preferences? A technology? Additional personal assistance? A combination?

- What is the most empowering choice for this person?
- Have the options been prioritized and has it been documented why one product or feature is preferable to another?

Accommodations
- Does the technology require customization or other adaptations to better match the person's needs and goals?

Use
- Has the technology been assembled correctly?
- Does the person have changing needs that need to be considered?
- Have there been changes in the settings of use?

Evaluation
- Has trial use occurred in the settings of use?
- Is the technology being used as intended?

It can at times appear that a particular device is ideal for a given person, only to find out later that the person stopped using it altogether, avoided use from the beginning, or used it only with reluctance. For example, if the person is supposed to use it 50% of the day but only uses it 25% of the day, then that needs to be addressed. Why is that happening?

In spite of the assistance and promise of independence offered by many technologies and the growth in AT/CST options, the rate of AT/CST nonuse, abandonment, and reluctant use remains high (e.g., Scherer, 2002a, 2005b). Studies reveal that on average, approximately 30% of all devices provided to individuals end up stored in the closet, basement, or drawer. Although many AT/CST products go into disuse because they are no longer needed, a lack of consumer involvement in selection is regarded by consumers themselves as an important reason devices are discovered to be inadequate (e.g., Scherer, 2002a, 2005b). This issue can be addressed appropriately by a comprehensive evaluation process. Individuals with disability who are involved in decisions in a meaningful way will generally be more satisfied with AT/CST services overall.

To reduce the likelihood of technology abandonment, the AT/CST evaluation should facilitate the judgment of how the person will respond to a given technology, what methods of teaching will facilitate the person's acceptance of it, or what alternative devices/resources might be better accepted and/or more appropriate. Some individuals may remain uninformed about alternative options available to them; others are not accustomed to being assertive and may hesitate to ask for the assistance to which they are entitled.

Follow-up in AT/CST service delivery provides the critical feedback that closes the loop for achieving the desired result. Without feedback, the whole effort of the AT/CST service provision may have been wasted. As stated previously, there is a 30% probability that the AT/CST may not meet the consumer's need and will go unused.

Based on earlier research (e.g., Scherer, 2005b), when the use of a device interfered with other activities or need satisfaction, it was discarded. According to a survey conducted in 1996, when the device itself was satisfactory, respondents often reported changed priorities or needs that led to the need to reinitiate the technology matching process, including the evaluation of the characteristics and resources of the person; the characteristics and requirements of the milieu/environments; the characteristics of the technology; and the technology selection, accommodation, and usability (Cushman & Scherer, 1996).

The available time for follow-up as well as thoughtful selection of technologies that considers the unique needs of the individual must be a priority. As the opening quote to this chapter implies, what better use of our time is there than to help a person with a cognitive disability achieve enhanced activities and participation, quality of life, and perhaps even beneficial change in body function or structure? The next section operationalizes the MPT model by discussing available assessments to help guide professionals into considering the key elements for support selection.

MATCHING PERSON AND TECHNOLOGY ASSESSMENT PROCESS

There should be advanced planning when an assistive device is being considered for (or by) a person with a disability to assist with activities and ultimately participation in social roles. Consideration must be given to the methods used by the therapist or other service providers to assess the match between the person and the device because these methods are critical to the successful adoption (or rejection) of the device (e.g., Gray, Quatrano, & Lieberman, 1998).

The key element in satisfied and successful AT/CST use is making sure there is a person-focused assessment with the individual with a disability or the responsible caregiver and that consumer-desired outcomes are identified (e.g., Scherer, Coombs, & Merbitz, 2004). This requires use of an assessment process, which helps uncover desired outcomes as well as both facilitators and barriers to the achievement of those outcomes. If the device meets the person's performance expectations, is easy and comfortable to use, and the person realizes benefit from use, then a good match of person and technology has been achieved. Thus, the driving force in device selection is the perspective of the user, not which technology the service provider thinks is best or which is most affordable or quickest to obtain. It is no longer acceptable to point to technological solutions before the prospective user's goals are fully defined and the individual's needs and preferences are known.

One means of assessing a consumer's "stake" or perspective is to have individuals rate their difficulties as well as prioritize their own desired outcomes and progress over time in achieving them. This is the system used in the MPT process (Scherer, 1998, 2005c), as well as other measures such as goal attainment scaling (e.g., Law et al., 1994; Malec, 1999; Wessels et al., 2002). In this way, outcomes are measured in terms of changes in the person's achievement of personal goals (e.g., being able to get to where the person wants to go) rather than merely by changes in the functional capability to do so. This is an idiographic approach (the person is the unit of analysis and serves as his or her own control) versus a nomothetic one (the person is compared to a group standard). For example, individuals with cognitive disability as a group may be characterized as needing memory aids; however, each individual person with a cognitive disability does not have precisely the same memory challenge and thus does not need the same identical memory aid. However, although individual needs may vary, it is possible to develop standard guidelines to ensure that individual needs and preferences are identified. The MPT assessment process offers one such standard approach. It emerged from a grounded theory research study (Scherer, 1986). To operationalize the model and theory, an assessment process consisting of several instruments was developed through participatory action research to capture the experiences of technology users and nonusers. Items emerged that differentiated characteristics of the actual experiences of users and nonusers, and they have held up well in additional research studies.

The MPT assessment forms are idiographic and person-focused. They can be used as an interview guide or the consumer can complete the forms independently on paper or on a computer. Assessments range from a quick screen, to specialized evaluations (completed in about 15 minutes), to a comprehensive evaluation (completed in about 45 minutes) by someone trained and experienced in their use. The specific steps, with accompanying measures for adults, are shown in Table 10.1 (separate forms and versions exist for children 0–5 and those in special education). Samples of the actual user forms can be found at http://matchingpersonandtechnology.com

Based on the results of research studies conducted to date, the Survey of Technology Use (SOTU), Assistive Technology Device Predisposition Assessment (ATD PA), and Educational Technology Predisposition Assessment (ETPA) have been shown to have good reliability and validity, and, thus, it can be concluded that they are useful measures both practically and in research (summarized in Scherer & Sax, 2010). The testing of the MPT model has determined that the model adequately represents the relevant influences on technology use and nonuse. A CD interactive program is available for training in the comprehensive MPT process (Scherer & Cushman, 2002). An option that is also available is computerized scoring with a printed report

TABLE 10.1
MPT Assesment Process and Forms*

Step 1: Initial worksheet for the matching person and technology process is organized by areas in which persons may experience loss of function (e.g., speech/communication, mobility, hearing, and eyesight) or have important strengths. It identifies initial goals and areas to strengthen through the use of a technology (or other support/strategy) or environmental accommodation. Potential interventions supportive of the goals are written in the space provided on the form. When a new technology is being introduced to a person, it is better to work from an area of strength. Each item should be addressed, regardless if a professional believes it's relevant for this individual or not. You never know what connection will be triggered or what information will be recollected that will impact later decision making.

Step 2: History of support use is used to identify supports used in the past, satisfaction with those supports, and why a new type of support may be better than alternatives. It is organized according to the same areas of functioning as the initial worksheet in Step 1.

Although Steps 1 and 2 do focus on the "separate parts" of the individual, as in the Vitruvian Man, it is believed that unless each area is addressed, key barriers to optimal technology use may be missed. For example, when you focus on communication and are about to recommend a device that requires very good vision, and that has not been assessed, there may be problems if the person does have significant vision loss or reports that their eyes tire easily. The goal is to emphasize the whole person and do a comprehensive assessment considering the whole person, environments of support use, and so on, but to achieve this is by considering in turn the many parts that comprise the whole and their relationship to one another.

Step 3: Specific technology matching. The individual (person with a cognitive disability, caregiver, or, ideally, both separately) completes his or her version of the appropriate form depending on the type of technology under consideration. The modular nature of the assessments allows the use of one, two, or more forms— and sections of forms as scales have their own reliability and validity data. The individual versions of the *Assistive Technology Device Predisposition Assessment* and *Cognitive Support Technology Device Predisposition Assessment* have the option for computerized scoring with interpretive guidelines (see Figure 10.3).

■ General:
  Survey of Technology Use—Individual
  Survey of Technology Use—Professional
  A 29-item checklist that inquires into the respondent's present experiences and feelings toward technologies. The questions ask individuals to list all the different technologies they use and feel comfortable using, the idea being that the introduction of a new technology should build and capitalize on existing comfort and skill. Individuals are also asked to provide information about areas regarding their general mood and preferences and social involvement that have been found in research to impact a favorable predisposition toward technology use. The professional version is identical to the individual version.

TABLE 10.1
MPT Assesment Process and Forms* (Continued)

■ Assistive:
Assistive Technology Device Predisposition Assessment (ATD PA)—
Individual
Assistive Technology Device Predisposition Assessment—Professional
The ATD PA inquires into individuals' subjective satisfaction with key body functions (9 items), asks individuals to prioritize aspects of their lives where they desire the most positive change (12 items), profiles individuals' personal factors and psychosocial characteristics (33 items), and asks for individuals' opinions regarding their expectations of the use of a particular type of assistive device (12 items). The scales are titled view of capabilities, subjective quality of life, and for personal factors/psychosocial characteristics they are family support, support from friends, mood and temperament, autonomy and self-determination, self-esteem, and readiness for technology use. The final scale allows for the comparison of competing devices or forms of support and rates the support and person match. The ATD PA (professional form) allows the professional to determine and evaluate incentives and disincentives to the use of the support by a particular person.

■ Cognitive Support:
Cognitive Support Technology Device Predisposition Assessment
(CST PA)—Individual
Cognitive Support Technology Device Predisposition Assessment—
Professional
The CST PA is structured like the ATD PA but has an additional 6 items in body functions focused on *specific mental functions:*
  ■ Paying attention, not getting distracted
  ■ Remembering information about people or events
  ■ Remembering where I put things
  ■ Managing appointments and doing things on time
  ■ Solving problems that come up in daily life
  ■ Reading

■ Educational:
Educational Technology Device Predisposition Assessment (ET PA)—Student
Educational Technology Device Predisposition Assessment—Teacher
The ET PA is a 43-item form designed to assess student and educator perspectives in four key areas: (a) educational goal and need, (b) particular educational technology under consideration, (c) psychosocial environments in which the technology will be used, and (d) student learning style and preferences.

■ Workplace:
Workplace Technology Device Predisposition Assessment (WT PA)—Employee
Workplace Technology Device Predisposition Assessment—Employer
The 28 items in the WT PA address key characteristics of the technology being proposed, the person or employee, and the workplace.

(Continued)

TABLE 10.1
MPT Assesment Process and Forms* (Continued)

■ Health Care:

Health Care Technology Device Predisposition Assessment (HCT PA)—Professional

The 42-item HCT PA is a checklist addressing characteristics of the particular health problem, health care technology, likely consequence of HCT use, personal issues, and attitudes of significant others toward the course of treatment.

Each of the individual forms may serve as a guide for an oral interview, if that seems more appropriate for the situation. The professional completes the professional version of the same form and identifies any discrepancies in perspective between the professional's and the individual's responses. These discrepancies then become a topic for discussion and counseling.

Step 4: The professional discusses with the individual those factors that may indicate problems with his or her acceptance or appropriate use of the technology.

Step 5: After problem areas (barriers, limitations) have been noted, the professional and individual work to identify specific intervention strategies and devise an action plan to address the problems.

Step 6: The strategies and action plans are committed to writing because experience has shown that plans that are merely verbalized are not implemented as frequently as written plans. Written plans also serve as documentation and can provide the justification for any subsequent actions such as requests for funding or release time for training.

Step 7: A follow-up assessment is conducted to determine any adjustments or accommodations needed to the technology and to inquire into realization of benefit, goal achievement, and whether the individual consumer has changed priorities. The measures in **Step Three: Specific Technology Matching** are used at baseline/initial assessment and then again at follow-up to determine change over time for a particular person.

* Measures for children are:
Ages 0–5, *Matching Assistive Technology & CHild (MATCH—Early Intervention)*
Ages 6–21, *Matching Assistive Technology & CHild (MATCH—School Version)*

(see Figure 10.3) designed to guide professionals into asking key questions in areas that appear to hinder optimal use of the selected device(s). Updated information about these resources, general developments with the MPT assessments, as well as sample portions of each of the assessment forms can be obtained from the website of the Institute for Matching Person & Technology at http://matchingpersonandtechnology.com

Although the assessment forms were created to provide a sequence of measures to inform professional practice, it is also appropriate to use any single measure alone. Additionally, each measure is composed of separate scales, and in some cases, single scales may be used as stand-alone measures when they have their own reliability and validity data. This is most often appropriate when a battery of multiple measures is used, and there is a need to document that particular factors were taken into consideration.

The forms are intended to be completed by consumers (individuals with cognitive disability and/or caregivers) and providers in partnership, thereby offering the opportunity to explore particular areas in more depth and to ensure the items have meaning consistent with consumers' primary language and cultural background (see Scherer, 2005b for an example of a rehabilitation professional's experiences with using the MPT process, illustrating the value of using an idiographic measure and adapting it to the consumer's culture and language).

Profiles derived from the results of the assessment and the process can be used to:

1. organize information about the needs of a particular consumer,
2. provide information regarding those factors that contribute, to, or detract from, the use of the desired technology,
3. help provide a rationale for funding and training, and
4. demonstrate improvement in skills over time.

With such information, the professional can identify potential or existing problem areas and intervene to better ensure that the use of the technology will enhance the consumer's quality of life as well as community, workplace, and educational experiences. A written summary of this information can specify what needs to be done, for whom, by whom, by when, and with what resources, thus equipping the professional with appropriate questions to ask technology providers and vendors. It can also serve as a "statement of need" that accompanies the individual to a new setting.

Subsequent steps in the assessment process will ideally include a trial use of the selected device or devices before committing to acquisition; an effort should be made to negotiate such terms with the vendor(s) if not already a component of a vendor's service or purchasing agreement. Periodic follow-up with users after they acquire their technologies will help to determine the success of the match and whether adjustments need to be made in the device. This also provides the opportunity to discuss the desirability of upgraded or additional supports. Follow-up versions of the MPT assessments exist to support this process. Rehabilitation professionals recognize that follow-up evaluations of how well consumer needs are met must become a regular part of the rehabilitation service delivery process as, increasingly, evidence is being required regarding the quality of services and the success of rehabilitation interventions provided.

AT practitioners and health care professionals acknowledge that people develop and change perspectives over time. A consumer who is not ready for technology use now may be ready in a few months. Professionals must raise the topic of technology again when it appears the consumer may be more receptive to considering alternative approaches.

Assistive Technology Device Predisposition Assessment and Cognitive Support Technology Predisposition Assessment to Assess Readiness for Use

The purpose for using the ATD PA or the Cognitive Support Technology Predisposition Assessment (CST PA) is to explore consumers' subjective ratings of

- body functions;
- subjective well-being/quality of life with an emphasis on current activities and participation;
- personal factors (such as self-esteem, mood, self-determination) and perceived support; and
- person–device match.

The assessments are designed to be used at the beginning of the AT/CST selection process so that consumer preferences and goals drive the matching process, obstacles to optimal AT/CST use and the need for additional supports/resources can be identified, and strategies for training in use can be implemented. After AT/CST acquisition and use, the assessments are administered again to obtain outcome data.

Ideally, the assessments are used for multiple or complex technologies and where a choice is available. The following is a description of how the assessments used by Delmar's rehabilitation team helped the process of selecting the most appropriate supports for him, in the team's own words.

Delmar

Delmar is a 39-year-old auto mechanic with a traumatic brain injury along with orthopedic and neurological damage to his right arm and hand. The first form that was used was the Initial Worksheet for the matching person and technology (MPT) process. The second form that was used was the History of Support Use (this is a very good form to help normalize or universalize the usage of assistive technology/cognitive support technology [AT/CST] devices). The third form that we used was the Survey of Technology Use (SOTU) and we administered the professional and consumer version. The fourth was the Assistive Technology Device Predisposition Assessment (ATD PA), professional and consumer version, and the device initial forms and follow-up process. We also used the Educational Technology Predisposition Assessment (ET PA) and the Health Care Technology Predisposition Assessment (HCT PA).

In completing the surveys, Delmar and his wife were involved, and we assisted with answering any questions that he had. We used the professional surveys ourselves. We did all the surveys at the breakfast table in Delmar's home, which we felt helped him realize that, as a culture, we use assistive devices all the time in our homes and office. This was also done so Delmar would feel much more relaxed in filling them out. After filling out all the surveys, we had him return to our office to view the technologies that we were talking about via the computer and going into our technology lab. He was shown pictures and descriptions of the devices that he was interested in. Then we went into the technology lab. Once we were able to assist Delmar to see the devices as just another thing to make life more manageable, he was more accepting of them.

The MPT surveys indicated that Delmar had a high probability of doing well with the top three devices selected and that he is open to the use of AT. The ATD PA scoring report (see Figure 10.3) noted that he had good family and peer support and has a high degree of coping ability, above-average autonomy and self-determination, and self-esteem. The survey stated that he would be comfortable seeking new challenges to improve his current level of activity and participation and will likely incorporate the device recommendations with no problems.

Evaluation

At this time, Delmar is very happy with the progress that he is making. We have really enjoyed working with him and his family. This has been a challenge for all of us. Delmar has been so willing and motivated that it just makes you want to find the absolutely best devices that are available. We feel that we will be working with him for at least another year.

He is currently trying out a one-handed keyboard like the one shown to him in our technology lab. If he likes it, we will purchase one. Some of the tools were already ordered, and we are working with an occupational therapist and a local machine shop to modify others. Vehicle modifications are in the works. After looking at several alternatives, Delmar chose a driving knob that attaches to the steering wheel. On this knob are several buttons that control all the functions.

Delmar has now seen the world of AT/CST that is out there so he does not feel as frustrated and angry as he said he was initially. Delmar feels that he will be able to assume the traditional role of breadwinner and head of household because of the technology and the training that he is receiving. His wife is very optimistic that her life will return to at least a semblance of normal in the future.

Delmar is hoping for a complete recovery, but realistically, because of the problems with his right hand and arm, he will always have to deal with the effects of the accident. Currently, it has been less than a year since his accident and he has already made great progress. Like so many other things, hard work and time may be the best healer.

When Delmar's rehabilitation team was selecting ATDs for his use, the ATD PA was a suitable form. For selecting CSTs, however, a more appropriate choice may be the CST PA. This is a relatively new assessment developed with funding from the National Institutes of Health[11] to help individuals select new and/or additional cognitive support technologies and achieve a good match of person and device. As shown in Tables 10.2A–D, the CST PA is divided into sections or scales and each item has been crosswalked to the *ICF*.

PAGE 1

Assistive Technology Device Predisposition Assessment
Consumer Version

DATA ENTRY FORM   (Fill out then e-mail to SchererMJ@aol.com)

Consumer: Delmar
Name of Interviewer: GML and CM
Device / System: One handed technology.   Gender (M/F): Male
Primary Goals (6 mos.): To be self employeed in in a custom firearms grip company   Ethnicity/race:

Primary Goals (1 Year): To be self employeed in in a custom firearms grip company

Note 1: The MPT Model assessments are designed to inform, not to replace professional judgment. They are screening tools whose purpose is to indicate areas in need of further assessment and intervention, their overarching assumption being that: (a) each match of person and technology is unique and requires individual attention, and (b) technologies are means for achieving goals, not ends in themselves. This assessment instrument is not meant to predict use or non-use of technology; it is designed to help identify obstacles to use and help reduce user frustration with use.

A unique situation or circumstance or the specific demands of a particular therapeutic relationship may render some of these guidelines unnecessary or even detrimental. Other circumstances may create a conflict between sections of these guidelines or between these guidelines and other guidelines or ethical imperatives. In such cases practitioners shall use their best professional judgment based on the information available to them at the time and guided by the standards of care in their community. - American Psychological Association

Please enter scores into the shaded areas that look like this:

NOTE: Hit the return key, not the arrow key, after each data entry EXCEPT for Section D (Device ratings) where the arrow key will be more efficient.

If sending to the Institute for scoring, please use a pseudonym or code number instead of the consumer's name.

Page 2 — Data Entry Area

Note: Please enter scores into this spreadsheet in the areas shaded like this:

Sections A & B: Assistive Technology Device Predisposition Assessment — INITIAL

FORM 4-1   Person

Section A Capabilities

	Question	1-5	+/-/o
Seeing	1	2	*
Hearing	2	3	0
Speech	3	2	*
Understanding/Remembering	4	1	*
Physical Strength/Stamina	5	1	*
Lower Body Use	6	2	*
Grasping and Use of Fingers	7	1	*
Upper Body Use	8	1	*
Mobility	9	2	*

Section B Subjective Quality Of Life

	Question	1-5	Importance	Obstacle (type E or PR)
Personal care/household activities	10	3	2	PR
Physical comfort & well-being	11	2		E
Overall health	12	1		E
Freedom to go where desired	13	2		E
Participation in desired activities	14	1	3	PR
Educational attainment	15	3		PR
Employment status/potential	16	1		PR
Family relationships	17	4		E
Close intimate relationships	18	4		E
Autonomy and self-determination	19	3	1	E
Fitting in, belonging, feeling connected	20	2		E
Emotional well-being	21	3		E

Section C: Psychosocial And Temperament Questions

Enter the number 1 for each item the consumer has circled. Otherwise, leave blank.

Question		Question		Question	
22.	1	33.		44.	1
23.	1	34.		45.	1
24.	1	35.	1	46.	1
25.	1	36.		47.	1
26.	1	37.	1	48.	1
27.	1	38.		49.	
28.		39.		50.	1
29.	1	40.	1	51.	1
30.	1	41.	1	52.	1
31.	1	42.	1	53.	1
32.		43.		54.	

Section D: Assistive Technology Device Predisposition Assessment

FORM 4-1   Device

(enter scores 1-5)	A	B	C	D	E	F	G	H	I	J	K	L
Device1= One handed Vehicle Controls	4	4	5	4	5	x	4	3	5	5	5	5
Device2= One handed Keyboard	4	3	5	5	3	3	4	2	5	5	5	4
Device3= Lighted Magnifying Mirror	4	2	5	x	4	4	4	2	5	5	5	4

FIGURE 10.3 The ATD PA scoring report for Delmar.

© 2005, Institute for Matching Person & Technology.

Page 3

Section A   Capability

Capability Score Interpretation

Note: A "-" in the table below indicates that the person believes his/her needs for support will decrease, and functioning will increase over time.

A "+" in the table below indicates that the person believes his/her needs for support will increase, and functioning will decrease over time.

A blank or "0" in the table below indicates the person believes his/her need for support and functioning will remain the same over time

Question	Score	+/-	Capability	Assessment	Need for Support
1	2	*	Seeing	Limitation	
2	3	0	Hearing	Average	
3	2	*	Speech	Limitation	
4	1	*	Understanding, remembering	Limitation	
5	1	*	Physical strength, stamina	Limitation	
6	2	*	Lower extremity use	Limitation	
7	1	*	Grasping and use of fingers	Limitation	
8	1	*	Upper extremity use	Limitation	
9	2	*	Mobility	Limitation	

Note: It is advisable to compare subjective capabilities and limitations with those provided by medical or rehabilitation
professionals in order to assess the degree to which perspectives match

Note: A score of 1 or 2 with an AT targeted to that area suggests AT use is likely. If no AT is currently targeted to
that area, it should be addressed, as the consumer indicates a limitation possibly requiring intervention.

Total Capability Score:	15
Total Capability Score Interpretation	

Sees more limitations than capabilities. If there are +'s, sees a need for more support and some functional decline.
Is likely a good candidate for AT use when the AT is targeted to areas of greatest limitation.

Page 4 | Section B | Subjective Quality of Life

Mean Score = 2.4

Subjective Quality Of Life Mean Score

The mean score is the average of the 12 questions. Possible scores are between 1.0 and 5.0
A mean score less than 3.0 indicates subjective quality of life is low; further psychological assessment is suggested.
A total mean score of 3.0 – 4.5 indicates subjective quality of life is generally within the average range.
A mean score higher than 4.5 indicates that subjective quality of life is high.

Subjective Quality Of Life Score Interpretation
Discussion Topics are provided where either an "E" or "PR" response was recorded

Question	Score	E/PR	Importance	Quality Of Life Category
10	3	PR	2	Personal care and household activities
				Specify constraints per task. Are pain and fatigue issues? Consider help with some tasks (PA, family) and a schedule with few tasks per day.
11	2	E	0	Physical comfort and well-being
				Can uncomfortable elements be eliminated, modified, bypassed? Activities be adapted? Is there adequate access to health-promoting activities?
12	1	E	0	Overall health
				Is there adequate and timely access to health care providers and facilities?
13	2	E	0	Freedom to go wherever desired
				If physical/architectural barriers exist, what are alternatives? What are the opportunities for advocacy?
14	1	PR	3	Participation in desired activities
				Is the key problem a lack of confidence? Explore he person's willingness to develop new skills, strategies and contacts.
15	3	PR	0	Educational attainment
				What are the goals, resource needs and timeline? Assess each step for feasibility. How can each step be facilitated?
16	1	PR	0	Employment status/potential
				How many hours? What accommodations are desirable? Identify a goal and create steps (with resources needed) to reach it.
17	4	E	0	Family relationships
				Is visitability a problem? What are creative alternatives to location, time, and so on?
18	4	E	0	Close, intimate relationships
				How can barriers to socializing be minimized? Barriers to intimacy? Is there a perceived lack of opportunities for meeting new people?
19	3	E	1	Autonomy and self-determination
				Are there specific obstacles that can be eliminated or modified? Are independent means available for getting around?
20	2	E	0	Fitting in, belonging, feeling connected
				Are there specific sites, groups or activities that cannot be accessed? Is appropriate transportation available? Could a peer support group help?
21	3	E	0	Emotional well-being
				Which environments are difficult? Is there access to resources that would decrease stress? Would counseling or a support group help?

Three Most Important Categories
Autonomy and self-determination
Personal care/household activities
Participation in desired activities

FIGURE 10.3 *Continued*

Page 5	Section C	Psychosocial and Temperament Characteristics

NOTES

Family Support

This individual's family support is likely much greater than average.

Positive Support From Friends

This individual indicates an average level of support from friends/peers.

Mood and Temperament

In this section especially, check for consistency of responses and a self presentation that may be overly positive (to favorably impress) OR negative (to appear needy).

This individual maintains a positive mood and may have above average psychological coping and adaptation skills/resources.

This individual is likely experiencing the following:

depressed mood.

angry mood

anxious mood

Psychological assessment, as well as counseling, is recommended due to the high level of psychological distress, especially if continued dialogue with this individual confirms this assessment. Consider an evaluation for suicidal thoughts.

Autonomy & Self-determination

This individual exhibits higher than average levels of self-determination and self-reliance and is likely a good self-advocate.

The individual also indicates an average to above average level of self-confidence

Self-esteem

This individual exhibits a higher than average level of self-esteem.

Readiness For Tech Use

This individual appears comfortable seeking new challenges to improve their current level of activity and participation, and will likely readily incorporate potential AT recommendations.

FIGURE 10.3   *Continued*

Page 7	Section D	Device Comparisons

The scores for all 12 items for each device are totaled. The highest possible score for a given device is 60, and scores between 50-60 indicate a good match of person and device. Scores below 50 indicate that there are areas where the match can be improved. If any items were scored 3 or less, there is a risk of device non-use or eventual abandonment. This risk will be even greater if the person has scored low on self-determination and motivation, and high on depression and anxiety. When comparing competing devices, the total score represents the most satisfactory device. However, review the three most important items circled to make sure the consumer's priorities are being met. For more device options, check the ABLEDATA website: www.abledata.com

Device 1 Score:	53	Interpret score based on the 3 most important items circled for this device (from Page 2 Section D above)
One handed Vehicle Controls		Items scored 1 or 2 indicate a possible problem with the AT selection, especially if they are circled as important.
		For every item scored 1 or 2, suggestions are provided for improving the match of person and AT.

ITEM A Score: Will help achieve goals	4	There is a good match of person and device on this item.
ITEM B Score: Will improve QOL	4	There is a good match of person and device on this item.
ITEM C Score: Knows how to use	5	There is a good match of person and device on this item.
ITEM D Score: Secure with use	4	There is a good match of person and device on this item.
ITEM E Score: Will fit with routine	5	There is a good match of person and device on this item.
ITEM F Score: Has capabilities for use	4	There is a good match of person and device on this item.
ITEM G Score: Supports exist for use	4	There is a good match of person and device on this item.
ITEM H Score: Will physically fit	3	There is an adequate match of person and device on this item. Is customization, modification needed?
ITEM I Score: Comfortable - family	5	There is a good match of person and device on this item.
ITEM J Score: Comfortable - friends	5	There is a good match of person and device on this item.
ITEM K Score: Comfortable - school/work	5	There is a good match of person and device on this item.
ITEM L Score: Comfortable - community	5	There is a good match of person and device on this item.

Device 2 Score:	48	Interpret score based on the three most important categories for this device from Page 2 Section D above
One handed Keyboard		Items scored 1 or 2 indicate a possible problem with the AT selection, especially if they are circled as important.
		For every item scored 1 or 2, suggestions are provided for improving the match of person and AT.
ITEM A Score: *Will help achieve goals*	4	There is a good match of person and device on this item.
ITEM B Score: *Will improve QOL*	3	There is an adequate match of person and device on this item. It would be useful to discuss other support options.
ITEM C Score: *Knows how to use*	5	There is a good match of person and device on this item.
ITEM D Score: *Secure with use*	5	There is a good match of person and device on this item.
ITEM E Score: *Will fit with routine*	3	There is an adequate match of person and device on this item. It would be useful to discuss device simplification.
ITEM F Score: *Has capabilities for use*	3	There is an adequate match of person and device on this item. It would be useful to discuss device simplification.
ITEM G Score: *Supports exist for use*	4	There is a good match of person and device on this item.
ITEM H Score: *Will physically fit*	2	Have all options been considered (AT style, manufacturer)? Is there a smaller, lighter model? Customization needed? What are the removable barriers in the environment? Are there extras on the AT that can be eliminated?
ITEM I Score: *Comfortable - family*	5	There is a good match of person and device on this item.
ITEM J Score: *Comfortable - friends*	5	There is a good match of person and device on this item.
ITEM K Score: *Comfortable - school/work*	5	There is a good match of person and device on this item.
ITEM L Score: *Comfortable - community*	4	There is a good match of person and device on this item.

FIGURE 10.3 *Continued*

Device 3 Score:	48	Interpret score based on the three most important categories for this device from Page 2 Section D above
Lighted Magnifying Mirror		Items scored 1 or 2 indicate a possible problem with the AT selection, especially if they are circled as important. For every item scored 1 or 2, suggestions are provided for improving the match of person and AT.
ITEM A Score: *Will help achieve goals*	4	There is a good match of person and device on this item.
ITEM B Score: *Will improve QOL*	2	A score of 1 or 2 on this item suggests a clear mismatch of this person and this AT. Explore other options for support such as a personal assistant, service animal, or a different type of AT.
ITEM C Score: *Knows how to use*	5	There is a good match of person and device on this item.
ITEM D Score: *Secure with use*	4	There is a good match of person and device on this item.
ITEM E Score: *Will fit with routine*	4	There is a good match of person and device on this item.
ITEM F Score: *Has capabilities for use*	4	There is a good match of person and device on this item.
ITEM G Score: *Supports exist for use*	4	There is a good match of person and device on this item.
ITEM H Score: *Will physically fit*	2	Have all options been considered (AT style, manufacturer)? Is there a smaller, lighter model? Customization needed? What are the removable barriers in the environment? Are there extras on the AT that can be eliminated?
ITEM I Score: *Comfortable - family*	5	There is a good match of person and device on this item.
ITEM J Score: *Comfortable - friends*	5	There is a good match of person and device on this item.
ITEM K Score: *Comfortable - school/work*	5	There is a good match of person and device on this item.
ITEM L Score: *Comfortable - community*	4	There is a good match of person and device on this item.

FIGURE 10.3 *Continued*

TABLE 10.2A
Items within the Four Scales/Sections of the CST PA and their Map to the *ICF*
Functioning

CST PA SECTION A: CAPABILITIES	*ICF* CLASSIFICATION: BODY FUNCTIONS (B)
Physical and Sensory	
1. Seeing	b210 Seeing functions
2. Hearing	b230 Hearing functions
3. Speech	b3 Voice and speech functions
4. Understanding	b164 Higher level cognitive functions; b1670 Reception of language
5. Physical strength/stamina	b730, b735, b740 Muscle functions
6. Lower body use	b760 Control of voluntary movement functions
7. Grasping and use of fingers	b760 Control of voluntary movement functions
8. Upper body use	b760 Control of voluntary movement functions
9. Mobility	b770 Gait pattern functions
Cognitive	
10. Paying attention, not getting distracted	b140 Attention functions
11. Remembering information about people or events	b144 Memory functions
12. Remembering where I put things	b144 Memory functions
13. Managing appointments and doing things on time	b1641 Organization and planning; b1642 Time management
14. Solving problems that come up in daily life	b164 Higher level cognitive functions
15. Reading	b16701 Reception of written language

TABLE 10.2B

Items within the Four Scales/Sections of the CST PA and their Map to the *ICF*
Subjective Well-Being

CST PA SECTION B. WELL-BEING, QUALITY OF LIFE	*ICF* CLASSIFICATION: ACTIVITIES AND PARTICIPATION (D)
1. Personal care, household activities	d5 Self-care; d630; d640 Household tasks
2. Physical comfort and well-being	b280 (Pain)
3. Overall health	b4, b5, b6, b8
4. Freedom to go wherever desired	d4 Mobility; d460 Moving around in different locations, d470, Using transportation; d475 Driving
5. Participation in desired activities	d2 General tasks and demands; d9 Community, social, and civic life
6. Educational attainment	d810–d839 Education
7. Employment status/potential	d840–d859 Work and employment
8. Family relationships	d760–e310 Family relationships
9. Close, intimate relationships	d770 Intimate relationships; e320 Friends
10. Autonomy, self-determination	d177 Making decisions
11. Fitting in, belonging	d7 Interpersonal interactions; d910 Community life
12. Emotional well-being	b152 Emotional functions; d240 Handling stress and other psychological demands

TABLE 10.2C

Items within the Four Scales/Sections of the CST PA and their Map to the *ICF*
Person Factors

CST PA SECTION C SUBSCALES	*ICF* CLASSIFICATION: CONTEXTUAL FACTORS
Attitudes and support from family, and friends	Support from family (e310, 410); Support from friends (e320,420)
Temperament	Personal, temperament, and personality (b126)
Mood	Emotional functions (b152)
Autonomy and self-determination	Making decisions (d177); Higher cognitive functions (b164); Attitudes (e4)
Self-esteem	Personal, emotional functions (b152)
Readiness for technology use	Incentive to act (b1301); Forming an opinion (b1645)

TABLE 10.2D
Items within the Four Scales/Sections of the CST PA and their Map to the *ICF* Characteristics of the *CST Device*

CST PA SECTION D. DEVICE MATCH	*ICF*: PRODUCTS AND TECHNOLOGY MATCHING (E115–E145)
Help achieve goals	General tasks and demands (d2)
Improve quality of life	All activities and participation (d); energy (b130); Sleep (b134); Emotional functions (b152)
Knows how to use	Learning and applying knowledge (d1); Support (training) from health professionals (e355)
Secure with use	Psychomotor function (b147); Emotional functions (b152)
Fits with routine	Carrying out daily routine (d230)
Capabilities for use	Specific mental functions (b140-bb180); Neuromusculoskeletal and movement–related functions (b7)
Supports for use	Support and relationships (e3)
Will physically fit	Moving around using equipment (d465); Domestic life (d6); Community life (d910), etc.
Comfort – family	Emotional function (b152); Family attitudes (e410)
Comfort – friends	Emotional function (b152); Friends attitudes (e420)
Comfort – school/work	Emotional function (b152); Peer attitudes (e425)
Comfort – community	Emotional function (b152); Stranger attitudes (e445)

Section D is designed to help in comparing up to three different options or forms of support. They may be three competing products by different manufacturers with different features. Or it may be the same basic product but representing a range from low- to high-tech.

It may even be three entirely different forms of support such as personal assistance versus a device versus some form of Internet-based support, or group/peer support intervention.

Ten stroke survivors receiving rehabilitation services provided by the University of Rochester Medical Center (males and females older than 60 years) completed the CST PA as did six individuals with traumatic brain injury (TBI; predominantly young males) receiving rehabilitation services provided by the Brain Injury Rehabilitation Program, Unity Health System in Rochester, New York (with five caregivers/family members). All participants with TBI and stroke were rated at Rancho Level VII–IX, meaning that they were

- consistently oriented to person and place, within highly familiar environments;
- able to attend to highly familiar tasks in a nondistracting environment for at least 30 minutes;
- able to initiate and carry out steps to complete familiar personal and household routines; and
- able to monitor accuracy and completeness of each step in routine personal and household activities of daily living (ADLs) and modify plans with minimal assistance.

The CST PA has five scales as listed in Table 10.3. Cronbach's α (alpha) coefficient of reliability (internal consistency) showed that the scales generally had good internal consistency/reliability with two exceptions. In general, psychometricians in the social sciences believe that alpha should be between .7 and .9 (Nunnally & Bernstein, 1994). The alpha for personal characteristics/factors is low, correctly suggesting that the items do not form a single scale. This 33-item scale comprised items addressing different constructs such as mood, perceived support, and so on. Thus, for example, when alpha is calculated for the mood subscale, it is .72.

Regarding the alpha for technology use and experiences, it is too high; this is likely caused by item redundancy. However, for the population being addressed and the primary purpose for administering the CST PA, redundancy can serve as a check on both the respondent's awareness and candidness.

TABLE 10.3
The Five Scales of the CST PA With Cronbach's α (alpha) Coefficient of Reliability (Internal Consistency)

- Subjective view of physical and sensory capabilities (9 items)
  – Reliability: Cronbach's α = .91
- Subjective view of cognitive functioning (6 items)
  – Reliability: Cronbach's α = .81
- Subjective well-being (14 items)
  – Reliability : Cronbach's α = .83
- Technology use and experiences (12 items)
  – Reliability : Cronbach's α = .98
- Personal characteristics (33 items)
  – Reliability: Cronbach's α = .61

Chi-square analyses identified differences among the respondent groups (stroke survivor, TBI survivor, TBI family caregiver). The results are shown in Figure 10.4. When addressing solely cognitive functioning, stroke consumers report higher attention and memory skills than do TBI consumers. TBI consumers see themselves as higher functioning than do their family/caregivers. This is consistent with other research findings. For example, K. R. Wilson, Donders, and Nguyen (2011) found differences in perspectives between adolescents with TBI and their parents in standardized

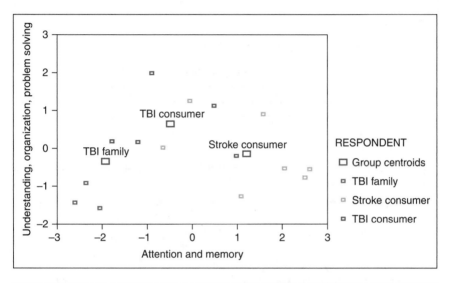

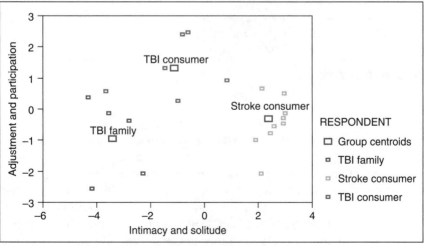

FIGURE 10.4 Differences among respondent groups on the Cognitive Support Technology Predisposition Assessment (CST PA). (*Continued*)

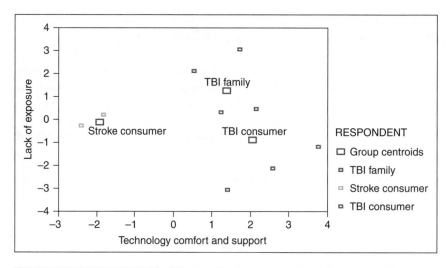

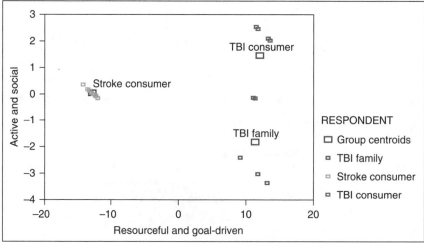

FIGURE 10.4 *Continued*

ratings of executive functioning. The parents generally identified more executive dysfunction than did the adolescents. The authors conclude that adolescents with more severe TBI may underestimate their executive dysfunction, particularly aspects of metacognitive abilities, possibly caused by impaired self-awareness. Another study also found impaired self-awareness in TBI patients with frontal lesions and executive function deficits (Spikman & van der Naalt, 2010), and the authors recommend seeking the judgment of relevant other persons about the individual's life functioning.

The three respondent groups also differed in views of the potential CST user's subjective well-being. Stroke survivors presented a more withdrawn profile. Compared to stroke survivors, the individuals with TBI reported more comfort with technologies and the support they receive for using them. They also characterized themselves as being more resourceful, goal-driven, active, and social than stroke survivors. TBI family/caregivers, however, see them as less active and social than the individuals with TBI viewed themselves.

It was also of interest to assess whether or not the CST PA distinguished among three categories of technology users: (a) sophisticated users (e.g., computers, smartphones, PDAs), (b) minimal users (e.g., cell phones, CD/DVD), and (c) nonusers (only microwave ovens, regular phone). Results are in Figure 10.5. For these analyses, stroke and TBI survivors were combined. Chi-square results showed no large differences among technology user groups on self-reported cognitive functioning, which suggests that perceived cognitive functioning/need may not be a strong influence on an individual's predisposition to use a CST. Many interpretations are possible, however, including impaired awareness.

Regarding other capabilities, technology nonusers self-reported more limitations (poor eyesight, hearing, strength, and grasping), thus indicating that they are precisely the ones who could benefit from support from technology. Perhaps unsurprisingly, the chi-square statistic is significant ($p < .01$) in differentiating the groups according to their current technology use. Sophisticated users report the most positive experiences with and support for technology use. Minimal users appear to use technology (such

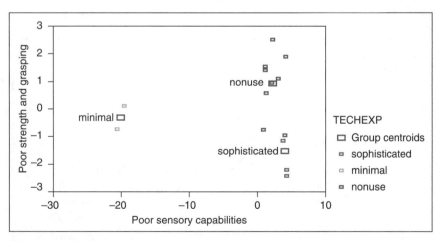

FIGURE 10.5 Differences among technology groups on the Cognitive Support Technology Predisposition Assessment (CST PA). (*Continued*)

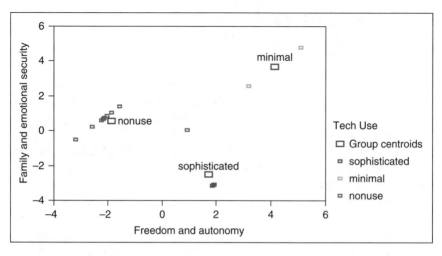

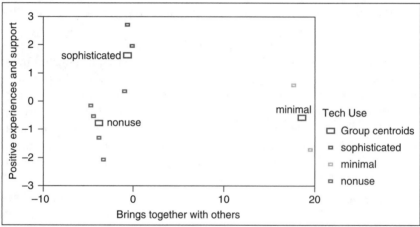

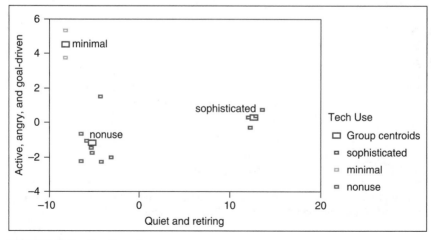

FIGURE 10.5 *Continued*

as cell phones) to connect with others. The groups also significantly differed ($p < .01$) in their personal characteristics, supporting the influence of this domain on the predisposition to use a new CST. On the subjective well-being scale, once again, there are clusters of respondents that have been identified by the CST PA. Sophisticated users tended to want more freedom/autonomy than did the nonusers.

Summary features of the CST PA are listed in Table 10.4. Most features also apply to the other MPT assessments and to the process as a whole.

In keeping with the support selection model in Chapter 9, as well as the importance of separating perceived functioning and needs from health status (see Chapter 4), and the consideration of personal factors and priorities, the MPT process and assessments provide a validated option for identifying potential mismatches of person and technology. When choosing any measure, however, it is important to ascertain that it meets the criteria for being a quality tool. Some questions to ask of every assessment or measure are as follows:

- Who developed it and for what purpose? Was it developed by someone trained in tests and measures, scale construction, scoring, and so on?
- Was it developed with the population you are assessing?
- Does its purpose match your use of it?
- Have others obtained reliable and useful information through the use of the assessment measure?
- Is the assessment continually being tested, validated, and, if necessary, revised?
- Do the items reflect current thinking and phrasing?

The MPT assessments were developed by the author specifically for the purpose for which they are used, and item content is based on the experiences of actual device users and nonusers. The assessments, which have been extensively used and tested, are periodically reviewed for the need to revise or update wording.

Regardless of which assessment is chosen, it will require time to administer, score, interpret, and translate into action, but it will be time very well spent. As we all know from making decisions about purchasing cars and houses, selecting a college, or searching for the "perfect first job," the investment of more time earlier in a decision-making process can save time, money, and frustration later on. This is greatly facilitated by conducting a comprehensive, upfront assessment of preferences, priorities, and needs. Ideally, an early and comprehensive assessment will proactively identify potential barriers that may have otherwise gone unrecognized and that, if left unaddressed, can result in frustration and a poor choice. It is precisely to this end that the MPT model and assessment process was developed.

TABLE 10.4
Features of the CST PA

Some Strengths:	Important Additional Considerations
■ Very individualized ■ Individual, caregiver, and professional perspectives can be compared ■ Enables prioritization of goals ■ Designed at the outset for support selection and outcome evaluation ■ Initial performance can be compared with performance following acquisition of the device. Useful to use retrospectively or pre test and posttest ■ Identifies potentially useful points for further exploration ■ Can be completed with paper and pencil, with a computer, in an interview, or by phone. ■ Suitable for a wide range of supports/ products, contexts of use, and user demographics ■ Effective as an intervention approach, therefore may increase consumer stake in the outcome ■ Good psychometric properties. Items are predictive of a match. ■ Sensitive to clinically significant changes in subjective functioning, well-being, personal factors, and realization of benefit from support use ■ It is not an add-on (another thing you have to do). It organizes information clinicians already need and use as part of good comprehensive rehabilitation ■ Outcome indicators are built in to the assessment process ■ Computerized scoring and interpretations available	■ Requires a commitment of at least 45 minutes to complete (longer if other forms are also used such as History of Support Use) and to involving the consumer or caregiver in the process ■ Many professionals are uncomfortable when consumers discuss personal factors. ■ Requires consumers to be able to identify their problems ■ Actual user performance with the support is not captured, therefore may need to use in conjunction with other tools or direct observation ■ Professional ratings of psychosocial incentives to use AT require knowing the user, which may be beyond the scope of a typical AT evaluation period and might need to rely on referring agency for some of the information ■ Possibility of interviewer bias ■ Specificity of goals to the end users circumstances hinders generalizability of results.

11

The Future Is Bright
But There Are Challenges

Life can only be understood backwards; but it must be lived forwards.
—Søren Kierkegaard

O ur brain can be injured at any point in our life span, and this can be caused by disease or trauma. The consequences depend on which areas of the brain have been affected and how severe is the damage. Not only are the consequences specific to each individual, but so too are the recovery process and outcomes. Important determinants of the outcome achieved are characteristics of the unique individual, the type and duration of medical intervention and rehabilitation, the supports received from others and technologies, and environmental resources and features, as well as accommodations.

These factors can be organized according to the World Health Organization's (WHO) *International Classification of Functioning, Disability and Health (ICF*; WHO, 2001). The *ICF* has been recognized as a framework that adequately describes various problems encountered by persons with traumatic brain injury (Svestkova, Angerova, Sladkova, Bickenbach, & Raggi, 2010) and dementia (Scherer et al., 2010). In keeping with the *ICF*, a *support selection model* has been discussed along with an assessment process and measures for guiding it.

In Chapter 4, it was recognized that people with disability, perhaps most especially those with cognitive disability, experience barriers to participation across many major life domains such as education and employment, a social life outside the family, family role functioning, and access to recreational and leisure activities. Such participation is what gives quality to life and a personal sense of well-being. An understanding of the individual and that person's needs, background, preferences, and priorities is the key to a successful rehabilitation process. This means identifying an experienced professional or team who can conduct a comprehensive assessment and provide a broad array of supports ranging from personal assistance to the selection of appropriate everyday technologies to matching the person with sophisticated, dedicated devices.

Providing technology solutions to meet individual needs is a complex process for which professionals require skills and strategies in addition to product information. There has been an international call for improved means of selecting technologies with the use of the matching person and technology (MPT) model as a means of achieving this (Bernd, Van Der Pijl, & de Witte, 2009; Bickenbach, 2008; Ripat & Booth, 2005; Steel, Gelderblom, & de Witte, 2010). However, there is a gap between theoretical agreement and actual practice and implementation.

Barbara Wilson, MRC Cognition and Brain Sciences Unit, England, addressed current challenges in (2006a) and for (2006b) neuropsychological rehabilitation. She highlights the need for more informed decisions when selecting treatments and improved ways of evaluating rehabilitation outcomes so that the real needs of individuals, their caregivers, and families are addressed.

Also in 2006, the U.S. Federal Interagency Committee on Disability Research and its Subcommittee on Technology sponsored a state of the art workshop on "Technology for Improving Cognitive Function" in Washington, DC. Presentations addressed individuals with learning disability, intellectual disability, psychiatric disability, and impaired memory because of aging or other causes (e.g., Alzheimer's disease, traumatic brain injury, and stroke). One of the themes that emerged concerned enhanced assessment as follows:

> Several presenters noted the importance of taking the time to discover consumer/user needs and how these may change over time. They articulated the necessity of conducting assessments of user needs early in the intervention planning process, but going beyond this to continually re-evaluate those needs as the individual's capabilities change. (Scherer & Bodine, 2006, p. 261)

In a related article on breakout session discussions (Bodine & Scherer, 2006), it was noted that cognitive demands in everyone's lives are increasing, but there is a wide variability in who can handle this increased demand and how much complexity can be contained within a device proposed for a particular individual's use. As noted by Holland, a cell phone today has more computing power than the Apollo space module. Cell phones, smartphones, the iPad, and many everyday technologies are getting so sophisticated, tiny, and multifunctional that people are challenged beyond their cognitive capabilities and, often, desires. Even those skilled in the design and operation of sophisticated technologies feel this way. For example, the Rehabilitation Engineering and Assistive Technology Society of North America (RESNA) has an excellent listserv where engineers and assistive technology providers as well as suppliers can exchange information. In response to one post about a new sophisticated product allowing full telecommunication capabilities in one's bathroom, the following are examples of comments made:

> "This is really cool but I really don't want the capability of responding to e-mail while brushing my teeth. Do the planners of tomorrow really think the average person wants this?"

> "Part of me was going 'Wow, that's really cool,' and the other part of me wanted to run away to a mountain cabin with a book and a flashlight."

> "I love new technology. However, after watching the video, my first thought was that if my daily life was like that I would need to increase my annual technology-free vacation by at least a week."

To operate an iPhone and all its applications requires the ability to sequence, make decisions and selections, and possess good dexterity and visual acuity—although there are accommodations for when these are lacking. In many ways, these devices add to the frustration of people with brain injuries. This needs to be fully acknowledged and addressed.

There can also be a tendency for some practitioners to overgeneralize solutions for divergent needs and to focus primarily on manifest symptoms. As one rehabilitation psychologist wrote on the listserv sponsored by the Rehabilitation Psychology Division of the American Psychological Association:

> Regarding the treatment of behavioral dysfunction . . . the challenge I often see is when folks try to treat the symptoms rather than the etiology. That is, for example, impulsivity can be driven by frustration, not getting needs met, confabulation, history of independence and "loner" type personality, high achievement and determination to be in control, etc. There are unlimited factors that contribute (organic injury, cognitive deficits, environmental factors, staff variables, emotional states, pre-onset psychosocial functioning, etc.). It may seem simple but I always recommend fully determining the cause of the behavior across all domains.

> I usually find treatment for behavior is easy once you are so famil-
> iar with etiological factors and their interplay that you can predict
> the person's responses. If one can predict behavior then design-
> ing an intervention that interferes with its occurrence or fails to
> stimulate its occurrence can proceed. [Note: See Karol, 2003]

The emotional, mental, social, communication, mobility and sensory capabilities, and priorities of individuals vary as much as their cognitive abilities. Importantly, all of these have to be addressed. This requires a comprehensive assessment to fully identify desirable features of the most appropriate solutions. Unfortunately, the resources to do this may not be available, and this needs to be given a priority if we hope to enable people with cognitive disability to lead lives of quality and participate in their desired life roles and activities.

In October 2010, another discussion on the listserv sponsored by the Rehabilitation Psychology Division of the American Psychological Association addressed the subject of "What is happening to psychologists in inpatient rehab?" One particularly poignant post is as follows:

> As a former Rehabilitation Psychologist (for 16 years) and
> now a Psychologist in private practice (last 4 years) who also
> provides psychology services to a rehabilitation unit, things
> have definitely changed! In my opinion, it has been a change for
> the worse with respect to the depth and breadth of psychology
> services available to the patient.
>
> Many of the services I formerly provided on a routine basis are
> NOT considered billable. I can no longer afford to spend hours
> in clinical staffings or in the rehabilitation gym consulting with
> the other disciplines about a patient's behavior or motivation
> for participation in the recovery process. Nor can I co-treat with
> an Occupational or Speech Therapist to assist with cognition or
> behavior. I can no longer pop into a patient's room for a friendly
> chat about how things are going while subtly providing a sup-
> portive outlet for the patient's frustration or discouragement.
> Many issues faced by rehabilitation patients just don't meet the
> "medical necessity rule" and therefore are not considered bill-
> able. Many hospitals don't want to deal with the billing issues
> and opt to allow psychologists to serve on the medical staff and
> bill themselves.
>
> In my opinion, rehabilitation patients are being short changed
> when psychology services are not considered an essential,
> routine part of the rehabilitation day.

What does this have to do with AT assessment? Those professionals, rehabilitation psychologists, and neuropsychologists, who typically provide assessment of cognitive functioning and who are also in a position to evaluate other domains of functioning needed for a comprehensive assessment, are increasingly excluded for "funding reasons" from rehabilitation teams and settings where assessments need to occur. Other professionals, for example occupational and physical therapists, can only bill for 45 minutes of time devoted to assessment.

Rehabilitation and neuropsychologists typically have multiple responsibilities but one key function is assessment of cognitive functioning, usually accomplished by administering a battery of tests such as those discussed in Chapter 4. Much of what is evaluated is not only, in *ICF* terminology, mental functions but also activities and participation, environmental factors (particularly support and relationships), and such personal factors as temperament, goals and preferences, lifestyle and ways of coping, and motivation. This information is provided to the rehabilitation team so that all disciplines share with one another to obtain as full a view as possible of the individual's status as well as potential future interests and needs.

Another form of essential assessment is that of results achieved. The Support Selection Framework in Chapter 9 emphasizes the following outcomes of a good match of person and technology:

■ Use of the selected support in relevant environments and situations
■ Realization of benefit from use
■ Enhanced performance of activities
■ Enhanced participation
■ Subjective well-being

As shown in Table 11.1, the influences found to most impact the quality (whether good or poor) of the match of person and technology can be organized as being characteristics of the person (the user), the milieu/environments of use, and the technology itself. Inherent in the items in the table are those relevant to activities and participation and subjective well-being.

Although the performance of activities can be observed in many cases, it is difficult to measure participation in a meaningful way beyond a mere frequency count of encounters or time spent in particular activities, and there is not always a direct correlation between frequency of activities and a person's perceived quality of participation in those activities. Personal preference needs to also be considered because a person can physically be in a place but not feel emotionally or socially connected, valued, or comfortable. For this same reason, accessible environmental features, freedom, choice, and equality are not totally satisfactory indicators.

TABLE 11.1
Influences on the Quality of the Match of Person and
Assistive Technology Device

	PERSON	MILIEU/ENVIRONMENT	TECHNOLOGY
Good Match	■ Comfort with using device ■ Motivated to use device ■ Technology use fits with lifestyle ■ Has the skills to use the device ■ Perceives discrepancy between desired and current situation ■ Realistic expectations of use	■ Support from key others ■ Realistic expectations of key others ■ Setting/environment both supports and rewards use ■ Availability of assistance for selection, maintenance, and repairs	■ No pain, fatigue, or stress with use ■ Compatible with/enhances the use of other supports ■ Is safe, reliable, easy to use, and maintain ■ Has the desired transportability ■ No better options currently available
Poor Match	■ Person doesn't want device ■ Does not experience benefits from use ■ Embarrassed to use device ■ Use requires many changes in routine/lifestyle ■ Does not have skills for use ■ Changes in priorities or needs	■ Lack of support from key others ■ Unrealistic expectations of others ■ Assistance not available ■ Setting/environment discourages or prevents use or makes it awkward ■ Lack of adequate training for use	■ Too much effort or discomfort with use ■ Requires a lot of setup ■ Device is inefficient ■ Perceived or determined to be incompatible with the use of other supports ■ Too expensive ■ Long delay for delivery ■ Is difficult to use ■ Repairs/service not timely or affordable ■ Other options are preferred

Source: Adapted from Scherer, M. J. (2005c). *The matching person & technology (MPT) model manual and assessments* (5th ed.). Webster, NY: The Institute for Matching Person & Technology.

Outcomes measurement generally serves best when it compares the results of different treatments (or treatment with no treatment) and outcomes across sites—for example, one type of technology versus another, or a person's capabilities with a device and then without it. It is also useful for tracking patient satisfaction with the care and services received and for planning the service mix to be offered by a center. Even then, it cannot be said that the map is the territory. That is, unless conditions are strictly controlled, there can be no great certainty that the outcomes achieved were primarily caused by the intervention.

What is less commonly done is using measures to guide decision making that both provide baseline and outcome data when repeated over time, or when used initially and at follow-up. That is when a more complete picture is obtained and is in keeping with a key theme of this book. Thus, it is much more useful to measure aspects of say, cognitive functioning, at the beginning and regularly after that, and use that information to help guide the match to the most appropriate interventions and supports and show progress and improvement over time in specific areas. As this chapter's opening quote by Søren Kierkegaard said, "Life can only be understood backwards; but it must be lived forwards." Assessments should be used to inform decisions and guide the selection of interventions that will affect the progression of life, not just summarize aspects of it as the person is going out the door.

Nevertheless, a quality assessment has the potential to do even more than that. By addressing key elements over time, it is possible not only to track progress (or the lack of it), but also to identify risk factors that may prevent progress.

A MODEL OF INJURY AND DISABILITY RISK REDUCTION THROUGH EARLY SELECTION AND PROVISION OF SUPPORTS

To assess the effects of biopsychosocial risk factors on medical treatment, Bruns and Disorbio (2009) sought to identify factors that influence outcomes from spinal surgery and spinal cord stimulation. They obtained data from 1,254 patients and community subjects from 106 sites in 36 U.S. states. Risk factors were identified using both subjective and objective criteria, and the authors offer recommendations for the use of biopsychosocial assessments to identify risks that could compromise a patient's ability to benefit from medical treatment. Once identified, they state, appropriate interventions could ameliorate the risks, or lead to the consideration of other treatments. Furthermore, Decullier et al. (2010) identified different falls and "faller profiles" and stated that the assessment of fall profiles could be helpful in developing fall prevention programs. Can *International Classification of Diseases (ICD)*, ICF, *Diagnostic and Statistical Manual of Disorders (DSM)*, and other codes be used to profile a candidate for support use? Can the same logic as Bruns and Disorbio used be applied to identifying risks because of the failure to consider and evaluate potential benefits from matching the individual with appropriate technologies and other supports?[12] Let us consider Marjorie as an example and refer to the schemata in Figures 11.1 and 11.2.

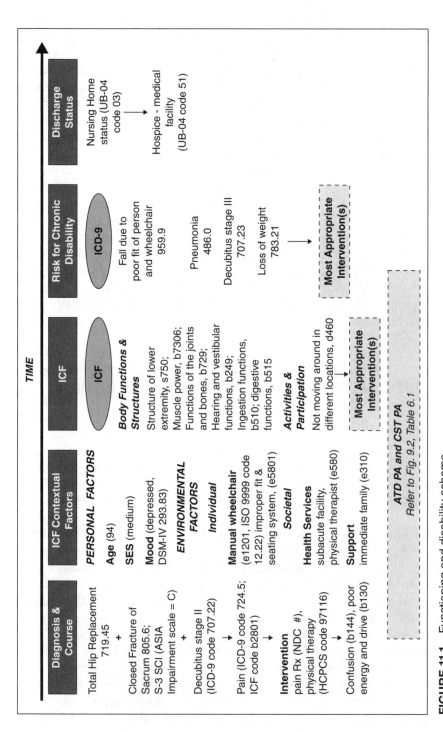

FIGURE 11.1   Functioning and disability schema.
Source: © Institute for Matching Person & Technology, Inc., 2011.

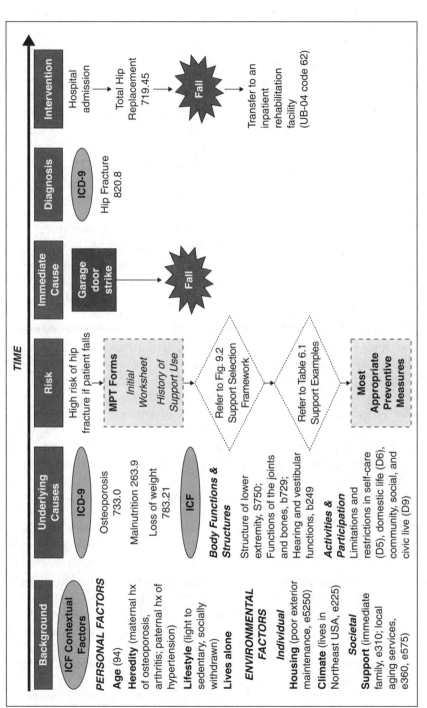

FIGURE 11.2 Disease/injury schema.

Source: © Institute for Matching Person & Technology, Inc., 2011.

Each figure is a schema consisting of various codes that classify Marjorie over a 6-month period from preinjury to hospice status. Under the U.S. Health Insurance Portability and Accountability Act (HIPAA), Department of Health and Human Services (HHS) was required to adopt standards for the electronic exchange of administrative and financial health care transactions to improve the efficiency and effectiveness of the health care system in the United States. Federal regulations adopted national standards for electronic health care transactions, code sets, and national identifiers for providers, health plans, and employers. HHS has adopted the following code sets as the standard medical data code sets: (a) *International Classification of Diseases, Ninth Revision, Clinical Modifications (ICD-9-CM)*, volumes 1, 2, and 3; (b) National Drug Codes (NDC) for Marjorie's pain medication; (c) Centers for Medicare and Medicaid Services Common Procedure Coding System (HCPCS) used for Marjorie's physical therapy (e.g., the code for gait training is 97116); (d) the American Medical Association's Current Procedural Terminology (CPT); and (e) *Code on Dental Procedures and Nomenclature*, second edition (CDT-2). Some of the following codes were discussed in Chapter 4: the *ICF*, the *ICD-9*, and the fourth edition with a text revision of the American Psychiatric Association's *Diagnostic and Statistical Manual of Mental Disorders* or *DSM-IV-TR*. The last coding used in Figure 11.2 is the Centers for Medicare & Medicaid Services' Uniform Billing (UB-04) Discharge Status Codes.

The appropriate codes are already collected for every individual in the medical system. By using these codes, we can organize the various data elements into a pattern that captures key information that would be indicative of risk for poor treatment outcomes. In addition to having such a pattern for each person, a benefit is that all of the data collection does not have to be done by one person. It just requires an overseer skilled in pattern recognition.

It is important to realize that creating an individualized schematic or pattern is *not* reducing the person to a collection of numbers. A key theme in this book is the need to focus on the person as a unique individual in a biopsychosocial context; seeing both the forest for the trees and the individual trees. As we increasingly move toward electronic health records (EHRs),[13] such a schematic can become another tool, a means of adding key details about the person to the EHR so that we can apply this knowledge to practice both the art and science of good health care and rehabilitation. For example, by collecting and synthesizing information about Ryan, his teachers, counselors, and doctors can help him and his family better make the most appropriate choices for Ryan that encompass multiple areas of his life, including education and social behavior.

In Figure 11.1, I characterize Marjorie's risk of injury from a fall by noting key features of Marjorie's background. I first use the *ICF* framework to highlight aspects of the context in which she lived. Personal factors include not only demographic information, but also family history and lifestyle. A medical history would typically reveal this information. Environmental factors list both individual and societal impacts on her life. An audit of her residence, according to the checklist discussed in Chapter 8 for evaluating the home environment of a person with dementia (Gitlin et al., 2002), would have indicated interior and exterior risks for tripping and falling. I also note relevant details according to the *ICD-9* and *ICF body functions and structures* and *activities and participation*. From the pattern obtained so far, it is obvious that Marjorie has a high risk for falling in or around her home. This triggers the need for supports and, in the box with the dashed line, an exploration of her needs and goals (*Initial Worksheet for the Matching Person and Technology Process*), as well as history of what has been used, to what extent, and with what results and obtained benefit (*History of Support Use*). The diamonds indicate further steps in the actual process of support selection. The supports then become the fall prevention measures. This is some of what I did for Marjorie, my mother, based on my data collection:

- I observed her going about her typical routines, including having her drive me to the local post office and grocery store (two of her typical trips) to evaluate her driving. She actually did very well by incorporating strategies such as right turns only, and going up and down stairs slowly and carefully.
- Had the local Aging Center come in on a regular basis to check in on her.
- Enrolled her in Meals on Wheels.
- Made sure telephones were easily accessible to her from her bed and in the places she spent the most amount of time.
- Removed as many environmental hazards as I could.

I could not anticipate or prepare for, however, the accident that did result in her fall and her diagnosis of hip fracture. The intervention, admission to the hospital and hip replacement surgery, is noted in the schematic as is her second fall postsurgery when she got up out of her hospital bed to go to the bathroom.

We now move from risk of disease and injury to risk for disability and long-term care. This is the schematic in Figure 11.2 where it is noted that her hospital stay resulted in hip replacement, a diagnosis of a sacral-level spinal cord injury, and a decubitus ulcer or pressure sore from lying in bed with little muscle or fat as protection. These medical conditions (*ICD-9* and ASIA codes) led her to experience pain for which she was given medication. She was placed in a subacute facility for rehabilitation, emphasizing physical therapy. At this point, the pain medication and after effects from the anesthesia and surgery left Marjorie with mental confusion and loss of energy and drive. She wasn't motivated to do her physical therapy exercises and complained of pain and being too weak and tired. Her context was now the acute rehabilitation facility and we add depressed mood to her personal factors. We also add the provision of a wheelchair that was selected based on it being available, not because of Marjorie's unique needs or preferences. Changes in her *ICF body functions and structures* and *activities and participation* indicate loss of muscle strength and inactivity, as well as difficulties with ingesting and digesting food.

Had they administered the *Assistive Technology Device Predisposition Assessment* or the *Cognitive Support Technology Predisposition Assessment* upon admission to physical therapy, her depression would have been apparent, as well as her feelings about the use of a wheelchair and what she liked and didn't like about it. Table 11.2 is the actual intervention plan I presented to her team, which I designed to call attention to not only her physical needs, but also her mood and nutritional needs. Notice that other than her wheelchair and seating, her supports and most appropriate interventions focused on strategies rather than technologies.

Then Marjorie slipped out her wheelchair one evening, as discussed earlier. It took this incident for her wheelchair and seating to be changed. One

TABLE 11.2
Marjorie's Intervention Plan

DAILY ACTIVITY LIST		
MOBILITY AND FUNCTIONING	**MOOD AND COGNITION**	**NUTRITION**
Provide physical exercise for strengthening arms and legs.	Ask Marjorie about her desires, but do what you know is best (e.g., she'll say she doesn't want to go to an activity but take her to it anyway, saying she can leave when she wants).	Marjorie needs to wear her dentures and glasses at all times. Have dentist address fit of dentures. Clean dentures daily: Remove old and apply new Fix-a-Dent
Have Tawny walk her even when Marjorie says she can't do it.	Involve her in every social activity.	Offer her food between meals.
	Put on Marjorie's favorite TV shows: ■ 4:00 *Oprah* ■ 6:00 *Special Report with Brit Hume* ■ 7:00 *Jeopardy* ■ Football games ■ Local news	

(Continued)

TABLE 11.2
Marjorie's Intervention Plan (*Continued*)

REGULAR ACTIVITY LIST		
MOBILITY AND FUNCTIONING	**MOOD AND COGNITION**	**NUTRITION**
Give Marjorie a change of locations.	Put on Marjorie's favorite TV shows: ■ 4:00 *Oprah* ■ 6:00 *Special Report with Brit Hume* ■ 7:00 *Jeopardy* ■ Football games ■ Local news	Try various locations for eating. (She doesn't mind wearing a bib.)
Take Marjorie to the atrium. She loves flowers and plants.	Play games/cards; do jigsaw puzzles.	

REEVALUATION AND ASSESSMENT ACTIVITIES		
MOBILITY AND FUNCTIONING	**MOOD AND COGNITION**	**NUTRITION**
Reevaluate the need for oxygen.		Review dietary restrictions: ■ Try soft, not pureed, foods and observe her while she eats. ■ Try enhanced flavors (spices) and various textures. ■ Marjorie loves chocolate.
Obtain a new wheelchair: ■ Improve seating/ positioning (with gel cushion) ■ Improve leg positioning and foot rests Continuously evaluate healing of pressure sores.		

evening at dinner, she aspirated some food with the outcome being pneumonia. She stayed in bed, which made her decubitus ulcer progress from Stage II to Stage III. She ate very little and continued to lose weight. Unable to participate in physical therapy and demonstrate progress, she was changed into a nursing home status where she continued to deteriorate. At this juncture, the most appropriate intervention was hospice care as it was clear that Marjorie's *body functions* and *body structures* were preparing for death (see discussion in Chapter 1). The items on the *Health Care Technology Predisposition Assessment* (HCT PA) indicated that the risks of artificial hydration and nutrition outweighed the benefits to be gained because they would only increase her pain and discomfort and increase the likelihood of infection.

The provision of the most appropriate support can have a direct, moderating, or mediating effect. A *moderator* variable is one that influences the direction or strength of a relationship between a predictor variable and a criterion variable, whereas a *mediator* variable is one that explains the relationship between the two variables. For example, with regard to the relation between hip fracture (predictor) and frequency of *emotional distress* as the criterion (anxiety, depression, anger), it is hypothesized that the most appropriate support is a moderator variable, in that the relation between hip fracture and emotional distress could be stronger for those who do not have or do not use an appropriate device for mobility and less strong for those who do. Similarly, it is hypothesized that appropriate supports strengthen one's *subjective well-being*. In keeping with the above comment: the type of support for mobility can also be a mediator variable when, as in this case, a poor match resulted in a subsequent fall. In this case, the fault was not with the product itself, but with the mismatch between person and technology; the level of support from the health professionals, (*ICF* code e355) who no doubt initially believed Marjorie would soon enough progress to use of a walker hen, when Marjorie did not progress, her team determined that the provision of a new wheelchair was not an economical intervention. This left Marjorie at risk.

Schemata such as we've discussed for Marjorie can serve the important purpose of identifying risk in time to assess for and select the most appropriate interventions, keeping in mind the crucial balance of need, personal preferences, and characteristics of the environments of use. Although Marjorie's example is that for a person at the end of life in a hospital and nursing environment, we could just as easily have created appropriate schemata for Delmar and his quest for remunerative employment in a workplace, for Ryan and his academic performance and social engagement in school, and for Theresa for her continued independence as she ages.

SOME SOLUTIONS TO CURRENT AND LIKELY ONGOING NEEDS

Undeniably, the use of a comprehensive assessment process yields a lot of information to assimilate, organize, and consolidate into a strategy for intervention or support, and this requires a commitment of time. We know that the payoff for devoting up-front time to a comprehensive assessment can be significant. Valuable information to guide next steps and intervene in potentially high-risk situations will be gained, as well as ideas for generating creative approaches and alternatives such as strategies for obtaining desired supports. Increasingly, however, and for various reasons, the time given to assessment may not be sufficient. An option is to do what has worked well in Ireland; that is, to partner with trained "graduates" of rehabilitation (and their family members/caregivers) to gather some of the initial information and query the person new to the rehabilitation journey on their needs and preferences. This not only gathers important information but also provides additional psychosocial support for the individual and family. It also allows those who have been through the rehabilitation process and system to give something back, and the rehabilitation facility to avail itself of the firsthand expertise these individuals have gained and are now willing to share.

Use a Guide for Planning

We have read in Chapter 4 that there is considerable choice in imaging and neuropsychological tests. What is less common are measures to guide support-selection decision making that both provide baseline and outcome data when repeated over time or when used initially and at follow-up. Use of such an assessment always results in a better outcome. By definition, shortcuts mean some information is missed. This may result in nonuse or less-than-satisfactory use and poor outcomes. Having to make too many adjustments and modifications represents costs in terms of money, professional time, and the individual with a cognitive disability having to do without the most appropriate support or, minimally, experiencing a delay in receiving it. The MPT assessment process and forms have been designed to guide the individual and professional in gathering the most useful information and can be repeated periodically to determine if needs have changed.

Trust Your Instincts and Use Common Sense

Technology is ubiquitous, and increasingly, so is our reliance and dependence on technology and view of it as holding the solution to our everyday problems and obstacles. According to Paul Schroeder of the American Foundation for the Blind,

> Technology is not a solution for every problem. It doesn't replace the need for quality teaching. It doesn't replace the need to teach social skills.

In many respects, we seem to have lost our capacity, or willingness, to rely on our own creativity and strategy finding. I recall watching a home improvement show on television around 2007 where the problem was having hot water take too long to flow out of the faucet in a second floor bathroom sink. The solution was the installation of an expensive device and some replumbing. I thought this was silly and for the life of me couldn't figure out why the home owners couldn't just go into the bathroom a minute earlier to start the water flow. It didn't have to be turned on to full force. It is precisely this kind of overreliance on devices that makes even technology experts long "to run away to a mountain cabin with a book and a flashlight."

As the health care system becomes more evidence based, we may see a de-emphasis on individualized intervention plans—what has traditionally been the hallmark of rehabilitation. But what makes sense statistically or epidemiologically may not make sense for the person you are working with clinically. A careful documentation of treatments chosen, the rationale for choosing them, and the outcomes achieved will hopefully serve the need for *proof of efficacy* in the future via aggregation of single-case studies that consider the uniqueness of each person. But professionals, families, caregivers, and individuals with cognitive disability themselves need to advocate for more choice, not less, more individualized solutions, not fewer. Otherwise, we risk a "one-size-fits-all" approach to service delivery, conformity in practice, and less experimentation and options in assistive and cognitive support technologies (e.g., Scherer, 2002b) that ultimately results in more expense and poorer outcomes. The same argument holds true for the current effort to create *minimum data sets* for the collection of information. They can well serve the need to compare data cross states and sites, but on an individual level, they are quite useless. Although epidemiologists know this, the concern is that facilities and practitioners will only collect and use what is required, and thus will shortchange consumers.

Keep Up With the Latest in Technologies for the Times When They Are the Solution

Support selection needs to start early, be constantly reevaluated, and evolve with the person as their needs change. Assistive and cognitive support technologies will be an important growth area into the future. If you have a picture of *assistive technology* as categories of thousands of products, you are correct, but only partially. The burgeoning growth of assistive technologies has formed areas of specialization dedicated to their design, development, manufacture, selection, and provision. Assistive technology is also a complex area of research.

Professionals who are enthusiastic about maximizing the potential of individuals with cognitive disability will benefit tremendously by obtaining a good working knowledge of the various products and services involved. Although this book has endeavored to provide a good, basic, working knowledge of the wide range of devices available today, products come and go. It is hoped, however, that the key resources and websites provided will stay current.

According to Russ Holland, former director of the Alliance for Technology Access (ATA), in an interview by the Family Center on Technology and Disability (2011):

> We once believed we could predict trends. Now, because technology is evolving faster and faster—and we have to adapt to technology rapidly—we're lucky if we can spot trends and describe them. . . . Families, AT users, practitioners and educators all face the same challenge: keeping up with the breakneck speed of technological change. . . . The field is now confronted with technology evolution on two fronts—AT and consumer technology—both of which are exerting considerable impact on families, children with disabilities, practitioners and educators. (p. 4)

To make sure you have knowledge of the very latest in devices, a frequent check of AbleData and manufacturer websites is a wise idea. But to actually see and try products, conferences and vendors are the best option. Other opportunities are webinars, online communities of practice, and organizational listservs.

Every U.S. state has an AT Act program that sponsors conferences, device demonstrations, and other educational opportunities. You can sign up for their e-mail list to keep informed of these and other events. You can find your AT Act program by visiting the RESNA Catalyst Project web page at http://resnaprojects.org/scripts/contacts.pl

Don't Forget the Value of Strategies

As helpful as assistive and cognitive support technologies are, they only work well in tandem with strategies designed with the individual's lifestyle, routine, and preferences in mind. For example, my mother certainly needed the right wheelchair, but what she needed the most to help her be motivated to use the wheelchair and progress in her rehabilitation was one-on-one attention to keep her more actively engaged—just a staff person to put on the television and help her start watching her favorite television programs. She, like others with advanced dementia, might have benefitted from a type of snoezelen room, which is designed to provide controlled multisensory stimulation through the use of lights, sounds, colors, and textures (e.g., Lancioni, Cuvo, & O'Reilly, 2002).

View the Rehabilitation Team as Mutual Support, Not Adversaries

My mother, Marjorie, had lived through 17 presidents, six wars, many disease epidemics, women gaining the right to vote, space exploration, and the Civil Rights Movement that was extended to those with disability.

In a mere 5 months, she went from what in retrospect was mild dementia to advanced dementia and death.

As for me, I went through initial denial, frustration, and anger—all had come into play, even though as a professional, I thought I knew what to expect and how to handle the various situations. At the end, the palliative care physician presented the options and what they would be like for my mother. After the decisions were made, I went outside for fresh air and just broke down and wept from the sheer progression and outcome of it all, the absolute hopelessness and helplessness I felt.

As discussed in Chapter 8, more attention needs to be paid to family members and their perspectives and experiences, as well as their stress and emotional needs. There are ways to make them feel part of the team without overwhelming them or, worse, treating them as nuisances and incapable of understanding their family member's true needs.

The Home Is the Place for the Future

The push to keep aging persons home and out of hospitals or nursing care facilities for as long as possible means that more health care and rehabilitation services will move into consumers' homes (e.g., Glueckauf, Whitton, & Nickelson, 2002). Future rehabilitation services will increasingly be delivered outside of rehabilitation facilities, and telecommunications technologies will play a role in the actual delivery of rehabilitation services, as discussed in Chapter 8. Although this will allow people to stay in their familiar environments, it may also mean that the burden on families and caregivers will increase. They will have to coordinate not only services for the individual with a cognitive disability, but also multiple products and systems of support.

For today's Marjories who are currently in nursing homes with dementia, future hope will primarily come in the form of new medications and the reversal of the disease or the ceasing of its progression, as well as increased focus on how to use evidenced-based psychological support, cognitive rehabilitation and assistive technology strategies to improve quality of life for as long as possible. But the Theresas, Delmars, and Ryans of today can look to a future full of opportunities for performing activities in all their chosen life areas. They have unprecedented possibilities for participating in all levels of education,[14] employment, and community life. This is due in no small part to advancements in technologies and their applications. Delmar can pursue his dream of making gun grips, Theresa can travel to even more faraway places like Uzbekistan and give speeches and advocate for others with Down syndrome. Ryan will go to college and pursue a career of his choosing. The key to their success will lie not in the availability of devices, but in their ability to obtain them and realize benefit from their use. It will also depend on their drive and motivation; their personal factors; the supportive relationships they have; and the kind of meaningful, rich, and autonomous lives they create—on their terms and as they define these concepts. As Neil Postman (1992), cultural critic and author of the book *Technopoly: The Surrender of Culture to Technology*, said, "We can make the trains run on time but if they are not going where we want them to go, why bother?" We can develop technologies, equip homes and other facilities with all kinds of devices and systems, and pass laws and regulate services, but unless they do for us what we want done and help us get to where we want to go, why bother?

Notes

Chapter One

1. An excellent overview of chronic obstructive pulmonary disease (COPD) can be obtained from the website of the National Heart, Lung, and Blood Institute of the National Institutes of Health at this URL: http://www.nhlbi.nih.gov/health/dci/Diseases/Copd/Copd_WhatIs.html

2. Leonardo da Vinci's *Vitruvian Man* is based on the work of Marcus Vitruvius Pollio, first century Roman architect, who wrote that the height of a well-proportioned man is equal to the span of his outstretched arms, these two equal measures yield a square which encompasses the whole body, while the hands and feet touch a circle centered upon the navel (Elam, 2001). It is a rendering in the golden ratio. Known by the Greek letter *phi* or Φ, the *golden ratio* is an irrational number expressed as 1:1.618. This ratio is found with surprising frequency in natural structures as well as man-made art and architecture. For further information on this, there are two fun websites for children (and when it comes to math, let's face it, many of us want this level of presentation!):
   a. http://www.mathsisfun.com/numbers/nature-golden-ratio-fibonacci.html
   b. http://mathforum.org/dr.math/faq/faq.golden.ratio.html

   Da Vinci's artistic side existed alongside a scientific and technical one, and he did many drawings of machines and anatomy. See Ganapati, P. (2010, April 15). This Day in Tech. April 15, 1452: It's the Renaissance, Man! *Wired*. Retrieved from http://www.wired.com/thisdayintech/2010/04/0415leonardo-davinci-born/

3. The *clock-drawing test* (CDT) is a screening test sensitive to executive function and it is used to assess spatial neglect (Palmer & Meldon, 2003; Samton et al., 2005). The individual is given a sheet of paper with a circle on it. Then the person is asked to draw the hands of the clock to represent the time "10 minutes after 11 o'clock."

Chapter Three

4. Vocational rehabilitation counselors employed by the state departments of rehabilitation have concurrently earned the Masters of Science degree in Rehabilitation Counseling, as required by the Comprehensive System of Personnel Development (Section 101[a] [7] of the Rehabilitation Act Amendments of 1992). Georgia State University, the University of North Texas, and San Diego State University formed a Consortium for Distance Education in Rehabilitation (CDER) to provide a Council on Rehabilitation Education (CORE)-accredited

Masters of Science in Rehabilitation Counseling through distance learning technology. One of the required courses in the program is *Applications of Rehabilitation Technology*, developed by Dr. Caren Sax, Professor and Chair, Department of Administration, Rehabilitation, & Postsecondary Education, San Diego State University Interwork Institute (Sax, 2002). The 12-week course is interactive, using mediated technology (e.g., discussion boards, web lectures, video, and audio streaming). The purpose of the course is to equip rehabilitation professionals with the knowledge and skills to support a consumer-driven process for assessing assistive technology (AT) needs. Course content includes research and resources on acquisition and funding of AT devices and services, and strategies for interdisciplinary and collaborative approaches for effectively integrating AT into the user's life. The major course project (representing over a third of the students' course grade) requires students to identify an individual who is interested in and may benefit from the use of AT and to help him or her make informed decisions on the AT devices that best fit his or her needs. The steps and components of the course project as described in the course syllabus include the following:

  a. Identification of an individual with a disability who is interested in and who may benefit from the use of AT
  b. Use of Marcia Scherer's Matching Person and Technology (MPT) assessments to interview the individual (and significant others as appropriate) to help identify a desired activity and to determine incentives and disincentives for using AT. All students obtain informed consent of the individual with whom they work, and permission to reproduce their work here has likewise been obtained.

5. *Asperger syndrome* is the term used by the National Institute of Neurological Disorders and Stroke, National Institutes of Health, and will be used in this book. However, Asperger's syndrome and Asperger's disorder are also used in the literature.

6. The number of civilians in the United States living with a long-term disability from traumatic brain injury (TBI) is now estimated to be 3.17 million, according to an article published in the *Journal of Head Trauma Rehabilitation* (Vol. 23, No. 6, pp. 394–400). The new prevalence estimate reflects the use of updated methodology and is not indicative of a reduction in the annual incidence of TBI, which remains at 1.4 million civilians in the United States.

Chapter Four

7. Medications can play an important and necessary role in the management of a patient with traumatic brain injury (TBI). However, the injured brain is considered more susceptible to medication effects, and medications with the potential to hinder cognitive recovery, promote confusion, or cause sedation are usually avoided. As much as possible, limiting the number of medications used is also important in order to decrease the risk of undesirable medical and cognitive effects. A lack of clear evidence regarding the benefits of specific medications means physicians vary in which they use. In their literature

review, Waldron-Perrine, Hanks, and Perinne (2008) discussed the side effects and contraindications of many medications.

8. The Joint Committee on Interprofessional Relations Between the American Speech–Language–Hearing Association and Division 40 (Clinical Neuropsychology) of the American Psychological Association have developed components of the rehabilitation process that facilitates the functioning of the interdisciplinary team for individuals with acquired brain injury (2008):
   a. Integration of information known to affect behavior and outcome
   b. Integration of specific discipline assessments and plans of care
   c. Development of an evidence-based plan of care
   d. Involvement of the patient and caregivers as integral members of the interdisciplinary team
   e. A measurement system for determining treatment outcomes

9. Frankel, Quill, and McDaniel (2003), faculty members at the University of Rochester Medical Center, have edited an excellent text on the biopsychosocial approach as applied to clinical practice, research, and education and administration. They reprint Engel's original 1997 article.

10. The American Psychiatric Association's current *Diagnostic and Statistical Manual of Mental Disorders*, text revision of the fourth edition (*DSM-IV-TR*) contains descriptions, symptoms, and other criteria for diagnosing and coding mental disorders. The goal, as with all coding systems discussed here, is to provide consistency among service providers. *DSM-IV-TR* diagnoses are linked to the diagnostic codes listed in the International Classification of Diseases and are used for research purposes as well as to report diagnoses to insurers for reimbursement and to public health authorities for causes of illness and death.

    The *DSM-IV-TR* is for diagnostic and coding purposes, and no information about treatment is included. Since it was introduced in 1952, it has been periodically reviewed and revised to capture new discoveries in neurology, imaging, genetics, and the behavioral sciences. The *DSM-V*, which is currently under preparation, will further alter the diagnostic criteria. Dimensional assessments will be a new addition in *DSM-V* (www.dsm5.org) and it will appear in 2012.

Chapter Ten

11. National Institutes of Health, National Institute of Child Health and Human Development, National Center for Medical Rehabilitation Research. Grant number HD052310 to The Institute for Matching Person & Technology, Inc., for the project, *Improving the Match of Person and Assistive Cognitive Technology*. 15 April 2006–31 March 2007.

Chapter Eleven

12. This idea emerged from a discussion that occurred during a meeting of the Academy Health Disability Research Interest Group in Chicago, 30 June 2009, as well as work with Rene Jahiel, MD, President, École Libre des Hautes Études (New York).

13. The electronic health record (EHR; also electronic patient record or computerized patient record) aggregates health-related information about individuals that typically includes demographic data, medical history, current medications, allergic reactions, laboratory test results, radiology images, vital signs, and billing information. A primary purpose of the EHR is to record all relevant health data to facilitate coordination of care among health care providers.

14. College programs exist for individuals with intellectual disability. There are also college programs specializing in the needs of persons with learning disability and traumatic and acquired brain injuries. For example, the Acquired Brain Injury (ABI) Program at Coastline Community College in California has a systematic curriculum to assist persons with ABI in learning to use technology as a compensatory strategy to assist in daily functional living. They also have a caregiver and professional boot camp that provides information, support, resources, and strategies for coping with the changes experienced after a client or family member sustains a brain injury.

References

Adler, P. A., & Adler, P. (2008). *Constructions of deviance: Social power, context, and interaction* (6th ed.). Belmont, CA: Wadsworth Publishing.

Agrawal, N., Johnston. S. C., Wu, Y. W., Sidney, S., & Fullerton, H. J. (2009). Imaging data reveal a higher pediatric stroke incidence than prior US estimates. *Stroke, 40*(11), 3415–3421.

Aldrich, F. K. (2003). Smart homes: Past, present and future. In R. Harper (Ed.), *Inside the smart home* (pp. 17–39). London, United Kingdom: Springer-Verlag.

Altman, I. M., Swick, S., Parrot, D., & Malec, J. F. (2010). Effectiveness of community-based rehabilitation after traumatic brain injury for 489 program completers compared with those precipitously discharged. *Archives of Physical Medicine and Rehabilitation, 91*(11), 1697–1704.

American Association of Neurological Surgeons. (2010). *Sports-related head injury.* Retrieved from http://www.aans.org/Patient%20Information/Conditions%20and%20Treatments/Sports-Related%20Head%20Injury.aspx

American College of Physicians. (1998). Death certificates. *Annals of Internal Medicine, 129*(2), 172.

American Medical Association. (1996). Primary care for persons with disabilities: Access to assistive technology. In *Guidelines for the use of assistive technology: Evaluation, referral, prescription* (p. 23). Chicago, IL: Author.

American Psychiatric Association. (2000). *Diagnostic and statistical manual of mental disorders* (4th ed., text rev.). Arlington, VA: Author.

American Stroke Association, American Heart Association. (2010). *Understanding risk.* Retrieved from http://www.strokeassociation.org/STROKEORG/AboutStroke/UnderstandingRisk/Understanding-Risk_UCM_308539_SubHomePage.jsp

Americans With Disabilities Act of 1990, Pub. L. No. 101-336, § 2, 104 Stat. 328 (1991).

Andersen, G., Vestergaard, K., Riis, J., & Lauritzen, L. (1994). Incidence of post-stroke depression during the first year in a large unselected stroke population determined using a valid standardized rating scale. *Acta Psychiatrica Scandinavica, 90*(3), 190–195.

Armstrong, C. L., & Morrow, L. (Eds.). (2010). *Handbook of medical neuropsychology: Applications of cognitive neuroscience.* New York, NY: Springer Publishing.

Arthanat, S., Nochajski, S. M., & Stone, J. (2004). The international classification of functioning, disability and health and its application to cognitive disorders. *Disability and Rehabilitation, 26*(4), 235–245.

Assistive Technology Act of 1998, Pub. L. No. 105-394, §§ 2 & 3 (1998).

Assistive Technology Act of 2004, Pub. L. No. 108-364, § 3 (2004). Retrieved from http://www.ataporg.org/atap/atact_law.pdf

Babirad, J., Scherer, M., Samant, D., Adya, M., Mendelsohn, S., Weber, A., ... McLane, B. (2010, June). *A comparison and contrast of leading taxonomies of assistive technology services and devices in use by state vocational rehabilitation agencies.* Poster session presented at the RESNA 2010 Annual Conference, Las Vegas, NV.

Barzegarian, B., & Sax, C. L. (2011). Rehabilitation counsellors: Incorporation of assistive technology device selection and referrals into professional practice. *Disability and Rehabilitation. Assistive Technology, 6*(5), 378–385.

Batavia, A. I., & Hammer, G. S. (1990). Toward the development of consumer-based criteria for the evaluation of assistive devices. *Journal of Rehabilitation Research and Development, 27*(4), 425–436.

Bauer, S. M., Elsaesser, L. J., & Arthanat, S. (2011). Assistive technology device classification based upon the World Health Organization's, International Classification of Functioning, Disability and Health (ICF). *Disability and Rehabilitation. Assistive Technology, 6*(3), 243–259.

Benedetti, F., Yeh, P. H., Bellani, M., Radaelli, D., Nicoletti, M. A., Poletti, S., ... Brambilla, P. (2011). Disruption of white matter integrity in bipolar depression as a possible structural marker of illness. *Biological Psychiatry, 69*(4), 309–317.

Bergman, M. M. (2002). The benefits of a cognitive orthotic in brain injury rehabilitation. *The Journal of Head Trauma Rehabilitation, 17*(5), 431–445.

Bernd, T., Van Der Pijl, D., & de Witte, L. P. (2009). Existing models and instruments for the selection of assistive technology in rehabilitation practice. *Scandinavian Journal of Occupational Therapy, 16*(3), 146–158.

Bharucha, A. J., Anand, V., Forlizzi, J., Dew, M. A., Reynolds, C. F., 3rd, Stevens, S., & Wactlar, H. (2009). Intelligent assistive technology applications to dementia care: Current capabilities, limitations, and future challenges. *The American Journal of Geriatric Psychiatry, 17*(2), 88–104.

Bickenbach, J. E. (2008). Assistive technology and the international classification of functioning, disability, and health. In S. Helal, M. Mokhtari, & B. Abdulrazak (Eds.), *The engineering handbook of smart technology for aging, disability, and independence* (pp. 81–99). Hoboken, NJ: John Wiley & Sons.

Bickenbach, J. E. (2009). Disability, culture and the U.N. convention. *Disability and Rehabilitation, 31*(14), 1111–1124.

Bigler, E. D. (2010). Neuroimaging. In R. G. Frank, M. Rosenthal, & B. Caplan (Eds.), *Handbook of rehabilitation psychology* (2nd ed., pp. 213–237). Washington, DC: American Psychological Association.

Bodine, C., & Scherer, M. J. (2006). Technology for improving cognitive function. A workshop sponsored by the US Interagency Committee on Disability Research (ICDR): Reports from working groups. *Disability and Rehabilitation, 28*(24), 1567–1571.

Bogousslavsky, J., & Caplan, L. (Eds.). (2008). *Uncommon causes of stroke* (2nd ed.). Cambridge, United Kingdom: Cambridge University Press.

Boman, I. L., Bartfai, A., Borell, L., Tham, K., & Hemmingsson, H. (2010). Support in everyday activities with a home-based electronic memory aid for persons with memory impairments. *Disability and Rehabilitation. Assistive Technology, 5*(5), 339–350.

Bougie, T. (2001, October 24). *Technology and persons with disabilities* (Full report P-SG[99] 35.5). Prepared for the committee of experts on the Impact of New

Technologies on the Quality of Life of Persons with Disabilities of the Council of Europe.

Bougie, T., & Heerkens, Y. F. (2010, August). Harmonization of terminology between ISO 9999 and the International Classification of Functioning, Disability and Health (ICF). Document number ISO/TC 173/SC 2 WG 11, N 141.

Bowen, A., McKenna, K., & Tallis, R. C. (1999). Reasons for variability in the reported rate of occurrence of unilateral spatial neglect after stroke. *Stroke*, *30*(6), 1196–1202.

Braddock, D. (2006, June 29). Cognitive technologies and consumer needs. Presentation for the Interagency Committee on Disability Research (ICDR), Interagency Subcommittee on Technology (IST), Technology for Improving Cognitive Function. Washington, DC. Retrieved from http://www.pptsearch.net/tag/cognitive-technologies-and-consumer-needs-david

Braddock, D., Rizzolo, M. C., Thompson, M., & Bell, R. (2004). Emerging technologies and cognitive disability. *Journal of Special Education Technology*, *19*(4), 1–14.

Braddom, R. L. (2006). *Physical medicine and rehabilitation* (3rd ed.). Philadelphia, PA: WB Saunders.

Brain Injury Association of America. (2011). *Mild brain injury and concussion.* Retrieved from http://www.biausa.org/mild-brain-injury.htm

Brain Injury Association of America Board of Directors. (1986, February 22). *Definition: Traumatic brain injury.* Retrieved from http://www.braininjurynetwork.org/thesurvivorsviewpoint/definitionofabiandtbi.html

Brain Injury Network. (2011). *Definitions of ABI and TBI.* Retrieved from http://www.braininjurynetwork.org/thesurvivorsviewpoint/definitionofabiandtbi.html

Brandt, A., Samuelsson, K., Töytäri, O., &, Salminen, A. L. (2011). Activity and participation, quality of life and user satisfaction outcomes of environmental control systems and smart home technology: A systematic review. *Disability and Rehabilitation. Assistive Technology*, *6*(3), 189–206.

Bricknell, S. (2003). *Disability: The use of AIDS and the role of the environment.* Disability Series. AIHW Cat. No. DIS 32. Canberra, Australia: Australian Institute of Health and Welfare.

Brown-Triolo, D. L. (2002). Understanding the person behind the technology. In M. J. Scherer (Ed.), *Assistive technology: Matching device and consumer for successful rehabilitation* (pp. 31–46). Washington, DC: American Psychological Association.

Bruns, D., & Disorbio, J. M. (2009). Assessment of biopsychosocial risk factors for medical treatment: A collaborative approach. *Journal of Clinical Psychology in Medical Settings*, *16*(2), 127–147. Retrieved from http://www.healthpsych.com/bhi/patient_selection.pdf

Butt, L., & Caplan, B. (2010). The rehabilitation team. In R. G. Frank, M. Rosenthal, & B. Caplan (Eds.), *Handbook of rehabilitation psychology* (2nd ed., pp. 451–457). Washington, DC: American Psychological Association.

Caplan, B. (2010). Rehabilitation psychology and neuropsychology with stroke survivors. In R. G. Frank, M. Rosenthal, & B. Caplan (Eds.), *Handbook of rehabilitation psychology* (2nd ed., pp. 63–94). Washington, DC: American Psychological Association.

Carlson, D., Ehrlich, N., Berland, B. J., & Bailey. N. (2002, April 12). *Highlights from the NIDRR/RESNA/University of Michigan Survey of Assistive Technology and*

Information Technology Use and Need by Persons with Disabilities in the United States. Retrieved from http://www.resnaprojects.org/nattap/library/bibl/highlights.html

Carter, R. (2011). Addressing the caregiving crisis. *Preventing Chronic Disease*, 5(1), A02. Retrieved from http://www.cdc.gov/pcd/issues/2008/jan/07_0162.htm

Cavender, A. C., Bigham, J. P., & Ladner, R. E. (2009). *ClassInFocus: Enabling improved visual attention strategies for deaf and hard of hearing students. Assets '09* (pp. 67–74). Proceedings of the 11th international ACM SIGACCESS conference on computers and accessibility. Pittsburgh, PA.

Centers for Disease Control and Prevention. (2007). Prevalence of autism spectrum disorders—autism and developmental disabilities monitoring network, 14 sites, United States, 2002. *MMWR Surveillance Summaries*, 56(1), 12–28.

Cerniauskaite, M., Quintas, R., Boldt, C., Raggi, A., Cieza, A., Bickenbach, J. E., & Leonardi, M. (2011). Systematic literature review on ICF from 2001 to 2009: Its use, implementation and operationalisation. *Disability and Rehabilitation*, 33(4), 281–309.

Chan, M., Campo, E., Estève, D., & Fourniols, J. Y. (2009). Smart homes—current features and future perspectives. *Maturitas*, 64(2), 90–97.

Cherniack, E. P. (2011). Not just fun and games: Applications of virtual reality in the identification and rehabilitation of cognitive disorders of the elderly. *Disability and Rehabilitation. Assistive Technology*, 6(4), 283–289.

Christova, C. (1999). Changes in the system for social services in Bulgaria concerning the use of assistive technical devices. In C. Bühler & H. Knops (Eds.), *Assistive technology on the threshold of the new millennium: Assistive technology research series* (pp. 787–790). Amsterdam, The Netherlands: IOS Press.

Chwalisz, K., & Dollinger, S. C. (2010). Evidence-based practice with family caregivers: Decision-making strategies based on research and clinical data. In R. G. Frank, M. Rosenthal, & B. Caplan (Eds.), *Handbook of rehabilitation psychology* (2nd ed., pp. 301–311). Washington, DC: American Psychological Association.

Cicerone, K. D., Dahlberg, C., Kalmar, K., Langenbahn, D. M., Malec, J. F., Bergquist, T. F., . . . Morse, P. A. (2000). Evidence-based cognitive rehabilitation: Recommendations for clinical practice. *Archives of Physical Medicine and Rehabilitation*, 81(12), 1596–1615.

Cicerone, K. D., Dahlberg, C., Malec, J. F., Langenbahn, D. M., Felicetti, T., Kneipp, S., . . . Catanese, J. (2005). Evidence-based cognitive rehabilitation: Updated review of the literature from 1998 through 2002. *Archives of Physical Medicine and Rehabilitation*, 86(8), 1681–1692.

Cicerone, K. D., Langenbahn, D. M., Braden, C., Malec, J. F., Kalmar, K., Fraas, M., . . . Ashman, T. (2011). Evidence-based cognitive rehabilitation: Updated review of the literature from 2003 through 2008. *Archives of Physical Medicine and Rehabilitation*, 92(4), 519–530.

Cicerone, K. D., Mott, T., Azulay, J., & Friel, J. C. (2004). Community integration and satisfaction with functioning after intensive cognitive rehabilitation for traumatic brain injury. *Archives of Physical Medicine and Rehabilitation*, 85(6), 943–950.

Coleman Institute, University of Colorado System. *Welcome to the Coleman Institute for Cognitive Disabilities website*. Retrieved from https://www.cu.edu/Coleman Institute/background.html

Comans, T. A., Currin, M. L., Brauer, S. G., & Haines, T. P. (2011). Factors associated with quality of life and caregiver strain amongst frail older adults referred to a community rehabilitation service: Implications for service delivery. *Disability and Rehabilitation, 33*(13–14), 1215–1221.

Craddock, G. (2002). Partnership and assistive technology in Ireland. In M. J. Scherer (Ed.), *Assistive technology: Matching device and consumer for successful rehabilitation* (pp. 253–266). Washington, DC: American Psychological Association.

Craddock, G. (2006). The AT continuum in education: Novice to power user. *Disability and Rehabilitation. Assistive Technology, 1*(1–2), 17–27.

Craddock, G., & McCormack, L. (2002). Delivering an AT service: A client-focused, social and participatory service delivery model in assistive technology in Ireland. *Disability and Rehabilitation, 24*(1–3), 160–170.

Craddock, G., & Scherer, M. J. (2002). Assessing individual needs for assistive technology. In C. L. Sax & C. A. Thoma (Eds.), *Transition assessment: Wise practices for quality lives* (pp. 87–101). Baltimore, MD: Paul H. Brookes Publishing.

Cushman, L. A., & Scherer, M. J. (1996). Measuring the relationship of assistive technology use, functional status over time, and consumer-therapist perceptions of ATs. *Assistive Technology, 8*(2), 103–109.

Davies, D. K., Stock, S. E., Holloway, S., & Wehmeyer, M. L. (2010). Evaluating a GPS-based transportation device to support independent bus travel by people with intellectual disability. *Intellectual and Developmental Disabilities, 48*(6), 454–463.

Davies, D. K., Stock, S. E., King, L. R., & Wehmeyer, M. L. (2008). "Moby-Dick is my favorite": Evaluating a cognitively accessible portable reading system for audiobooks for individuals with intellectual disability. *Intellectual and Developmental Disabilities, 46*(4), 290–298.

Davis, L. C., Sander, A. M., Struchen, M. A., Sherer, M., Nakase-Richardson, R., & Malec, J. F. (2009). Medical and psychosocial predictors of caregiver distress and perceived burden following traumatic brain injury. *The Journal of Head Trauma Rehabilitation, 24*(3), 145–154.

Deckter, D. (2010, November). Friends of ATIA Newsletter. *Assistive Technology Industry Association.* Retrieved from http://www.atia.org/files/Friends_of_ATIA_newsletter_-_Issue_4_Nov_2010.pdf

Decullier, E., Couris, C. M., Beauchet, O., Zamora, A., Annweiler, C., Dargent Molina, P., & Schott, A. M. (2010). Falls' and fallers' profiles. *The Journal of Nutrition, Health & Aging, 14*(7), 602–608.

de Joode, E., van Heugten, C., Verhey, F., & van Boxtel, M. (2010). Efficacy and usability of assistive technology for patients with cognitive deficits: A systematic review. *Clinical Rehabilitation, 24*(8), 701–714.

de Kleijn-de Vrankrijker, M. W., & Ten Napel, H. (2010, October). Harmonization of ICF environmental factors Chapter 1 and ISO9999 [Abstract]. WHO-FIC Collaborating Centre in the Netherlands. Toronto, Ontario, Canada.

Demers, L., Weiss-Lambrou, R., & Ska, B. (1996). Development of the Quebec User Evaluation of Satisfaction with Assistive Technology (QUEST). *Assistive Technology, 8*(1), 3–13.

Department of Veterans Affairs, & Department of Defense. (2009). *VA/DoD clinical practice guideline for management of concussion/mild traumatic brain injury (mTBI)*. Washington, DC: Author.

Depompei, R., Gillette, Y., Goetz, E., Xenopoulos-Oddsson, A., Bryen, D., & Dowds, M. (2008). Practical applications for use of PDAs and smartphones with children and adolescents who have traumatic brain injury. *NeuroRehabilitation, 23*(6), 487–499.

Dew, D. W., & Alan, G. M. (Eds.). (2007). *Rehabilitation of individuals with autism spectrum disorders* (Institute on Rehabilitation Issues Monograph No. 32). Washington, DC: The George Washington University, Center for Rehabilitation Counseling Research and Education.

Dikter, D. (2010). Editorial. *Friends of ATIA newsletter*. Retrieved http://www.atia. org/files/Friends_of_ATIA_newsletter_-_Issue_4_Nov_2010.pdf

Doig, E., Fleming, J., Cornwell, P., & Kuipers, P. (2011). Comparing the experience of outpatient therapy in home and day hospital settings after traumatic brain injury: Patient, significant other and therapist perspectives. *Disability and Rehabilitation, 33*(13–14), 1203–1214.

Dryden, D. M., Saunders, L. D., Rowe, B. H., May, L. A., Yiannakoulias, N., Svenson, L. W., . . . Voaklander, D. C. (2005). Depression following traumatic spinal cord injury. *Neuroepidemiology, 25*(2), 55–61.

Duhaime, A. C., Gean, A. D., Haacke, E. M., Hicks, R., Wintermark, M., Mukherjee, P., . . . Riedy, G. (2010). Common data elements in radiologic imaging of traumatic brain injury. *Archives of Physical Medicine and Rehabilitation, 91*(11), 1661–1666.

Economic and Social Commission for Asia and the Pacific. (2010). *Training manual on disability statistics*. Bangkok, Thailand. Retrieved from http://www.unescap. org/stat/disability/manual/Chapter2-Disability-Statistics.asp

Eek, M., & Wressle, E. (2011). Everyday technology and 86-year-old individuals in Sweden. *Disability and Rehabilitation. Assistive Technology, 6*(2), 123–129.

Eggers, S. L., Myaskovsky, L., Burkitt, K. H., Tolerico, M., Switzer, G. E., Fine, M. J., & Boninger, M. L. (2009). A preliminary model of wheelchair service delivery. *Archives of Physical Medicine and Rehabilitation, 90*(6), 1030–1038.

Eldar, R., Kullmann, L., Marincek, C., Sekelj-Kauzlaric, K., Svestkova, O., & Palat, M. (2008). Rehabilitation medicine in countries of Central/Eastern Europe. *Disability and Rehabilitation, 30*(2), 134–141.

Elsaesser, L. J., & Bauer, S. M. (2011). Provision of assistive technology services method (ATSM) according to evidence-based information and knowledge management. *Disability and Rehabilitation. Assistive Technology, 6*(5), 386–401.

Engel, G. L. (1977). The need for a new medical model: A challenge for biomedicine. *Science, 196*(4286), 129–136.

Engström, A. L., Lexell, J., & Lund M. L. (2010). Difficulties in using everyday technology after acquired brain injury: A qualitative analysis. *Scandinavian Journal of Occupational Therapy, 17*(3), 233–243.

Etters, L., Goodall, D., & Harrison, B. E. (2008). Caregiver burden among dementia patient caregivers: A review of the literature. *Journal of the American Academy of Nurse Practitioners, 20*(8), 423–428.

Eunice Kennedy Shriver National Institute of Child Health & Human Development, National Institute of Health, Department of Health and Human Services. (1997). Facts about Down syndrome (97-3402). Washington, DC: U.S. Government

Printing Office. Retrieved from http://www.nichd.nih.gov/publications/pubs_details.cfm?from=&pubs_id=24

Evans, J. J., Wilson, B. A., Needham, P., & Brentnall, S. (2003). Who makes good use of memory aids? Results of a survey of people with acquired brain injury. *Journal of the International Neuropsychological Society, 9*(6), 925–935.

Family Center on Technology and Disability. (2011). Can't stop the beat: The morphing of AT: An interview with Russ Holland. *FCTD Technology Voices*, (117), 4–11. Retrieved from http://www.fctd.info/assets/newsletters/pdfs/288/FCTD-TechVoices-Mar11.pdf?1302711915

Fann, J. R., Hart, T., & Schomer, K. G. (2009). Treatment for depression after traumatic brain injury: A systematic review. *Journal of Neurotrauma, 26*(12), 2383–2402.

Farmer, J. E., Kanne, S. M., Grisso, M. O., & Kemp, S. (2010). Pediatric neuropsychology in medical rehabilitation settings. In R. G. Frank, M. Rosenthal, & B. Caplan (Eds.), *Handbook of rehabilitation psychology* (2nd ed., pp. 315–328). Washington, DC: American Psychological Association.

Faul, M., Xu, L., Wald, M. M., & Coronado, V. G. (2010). *Traumatic brain injury in the United States: Emergency department visits, hospitalizations, and deaths 2002–2006*. Atlanta, GA: Centers for Disease Control and Prevention, National Center for Injury Prevention and Control.

Ferri, C. P., Ames, D., & Prince, M. (2004). Behavioral and psychological symptoms of dementia in developing countries. *International Psychogeriatrics, 16*(4), 441–459.

Ferri, C. P., Prince, M., Brayne, C., Brodaty, H., Fratiglioni, L., Ganguli, M., . . . Scazufca, M. (2005). Global prevalence of dementia: A Delphi consensus study. *Lancet, 366*(9503), 2112–2117.

Field, M. J., & Jette, A. M. (Eds.). (2007). *The future of disability in America*. Washington, DC: The National Academies Press.

Fish, J., Manly, T., Emslie, H., Evans, J. J., & Wilson, B. A. (2008). Compensatory strategies for acquired disorders of memory and planning: Differential effects of a paging system for patients with brain injury of traumatic versus cerebrovascular aetiology. *Journal of Neurology, Neurosurgery, and Psychiatry, 79*(8), 930–935.

Frankel, R. M., Quill, T. E., & McDaniel, S. H. (Eds.). (2003). *The biopsychosocial approach: Past, present, future*. Rochester, NY: University of Rochester Press.

Frisardi, V., & Imbimbo, B. P. (2011). Gerontechnology for demented patients: Smart homes for smart aging. *Journal of Alzheimer's Disease, 23*(1),143–146.

Fuhrer, M. J., Jutai, J. W., Scherer, M. J., & DeRuyter, F. (2003). A framework for the conceptual modelling of assistive technology device outcomes. *Disability and Rehabilitation, 25*(22), 1243–1251.

Galvin, J. C., & Donnell, C. M. (2002). Educating the consumer and caretaker on assistive technology. In M. J. Scherer (Ed.), *Assistive technology: Matching device and consumer for successful rehabilitation* (pp. 153–167). Washington, DC: American Psychological Association.

Geyh, S., Peter, C., Müller, R., Bickenbach, J. E., Kostanjsek, N., Ustün, B. T., . . . Cieza, A. (2010). The personal factors of the international classification of functioning, disability and health in the literature—a systematic review and content analysis. *Disability and Rehabilitation, 33*(13–14), 1089–1102.

Gillette, Y., & DePompei, R. (2004). The potential of electronic organizers as a tool in the cognitive rehabilitation of young people. *NeuroRehabilitation, 19*(3), 233–243.

Gitlin, L. N. (2002). Assistive technology in the home and community for older people: Psychological and social considerations. In M. J. Scherer (Ed.), *Assistive technology: Matching device and consumer for successful rehabilitation* (pp. 109–122). Washington, DC: American Psychological Association.

Gitlin, L. N., Schinfeld, S., Winter, L., Corcoran, M., Boyce, A. A., & Hauck, W. (2002). Evaluating home environments of persons with dementia: Interrater reliability and validity of the Home Environmental Assessment Protocol (HEAP). *Disability and Rehabilitation, 24*(1–3), 59–71.

Gitlin, L. N., Winter, L., Dennis, M. P., Hodgson, N., & Hauck, W. W. (2010). A biobehavioral home-based intervention and the well-being of patients with dementia and their caregivers: The COPE randomized trial. *The Journal of the American Medical Association, 304*(9), 983–991.

Glueckauf, R. L., Whitton, J. D., & Nickelson, D. W. (2002). Telehealth: The new frontier in rehabilitation and health care. In M. J. Scherer (Ed.), *Assistive technology: Matching device and consumer for successful rehabilitation* (pp. 197–213). Washington, DC: American Psychological Association.

Gray, D. B., Quatrano, L. A., & Lieberman, M. L. (Eds.). (1998). *Designing and using assistive technology: The human perspective*. Baltimore, MD: Paul H. Brookes Publishing.

Groenendaal, F., Termote, J. U., van der Heide-Jalving, M., van Haastert, I. C., & de Vries, L. S. (2010). Complications affecting preterm neonates from 1991 to 2006: What have we gained? *Acta Paediatrica, 99*(3), 354–358.

Haacke, E. M., Duhaime, A. C., Gean, A. D., Riedy, G., Wintermark, M., Mukherjee, P., . . . Smith, D. H. (2010). Common data elements in radiologic imaging of traumatic brain injury. *Journal of Magnetic Resonance Imaging, 32*(3), 516–543.

Hachinski, V. C., Iliff, L. D., Zilhka, E., Du Boulay, G. H., McAllister, V. L., Marshall, J., . . . Symon, L. (1975). Cerebral blood flow in dementia. *Archives of Neurology, 32*(9), 632–637. doi:10.1001/archneur.1975.00490510088009

Hackett, M. L., & Anderson, C. S. (2005). Predictors of depression after stroke: A systematic review of observational studies. *Stroke, 36*(10), 2296–2301.

Hackett, M. L., Yapa, C., Parag, V., & Anderson, C. S. (2005). Frequency of depression after stroke: A systematic review of observational studies. *Stroke, 36*(6), 1330–1340.

Hall, T., Krahn, G. L., Horner-Johnson, W., & Lamb, G. (2011). Examining functional content in widely used Health-Related Quality of Life scales. *Rehabilitation Psychology, 56*(2), 94–99.

Hammel, J., Lai, J. S., & Heller, T. (2002). The impact of assistive technology and environmental interventions on function and living situation status with people who are ageing with developmental disabilities. *Disability and Rehabilitation, 24*(1–3), 93–105.

Hart, T. (2010). Cognitive rehabilitation. In R. G. Frank, M. Rosenthal, & B. Caplan (Eds.), *Handbook of rehabilitation psychology* (2nd ed., pp. 285–300). Washington, DC: American Psychological Association.

Hart, T., Buchhofer, R., & Vaccaro, M. (2004). Portable electronic devices as memory and organizational aids after traumatic brain injury: A consumer survey study. *The Journal of Head Trauma Rehabilitation, 19*(5), 351–365.

Hart, T., Hawkey, K., & Whyte, J. (2002). Use of a portable voice organizer to remember therapy goals in traumatic brain injury rehabilitation: A within-subjects trial. *The Journal of Head Trauma Rehabilitation, 17*(6), 556–570.

HEART Consortium. (1995). *Improving service delivery systems for assistive technology—a European strategy: HEART study.* Stockholm, Sweden: Swedish Institute of Assistive Technology.

Heerkens, Y. F., Bougie, T., & de Kleijn-de Vrankrijker, M. W. (2010a, June). Assistive products [Abstract]. FDRG Meeting in Madrid, Spain.

Heerkens, Y. F., Bougie, T., & de Kleijn-de Vrankrijker, M. W. (2010b). Classification and terminology of assistive products. In J. H. Stone & M. Blouin (Eds.), *International encyclopedia of rehabilitation.* Retrieved from http://cirrie.buffalo.edu/encyclopedia/en/article/265/

Hibbard, M. R., & Tucson, A. Z. (2010, February). *Linking neurobehavioral challenges with violent behaviors post TBI.* Presentation for the Rehabilitation Psychology Conference.

High, W. M., Jr., Sander, A. M., Struchen, M. A., & Hart, K. A. (Eds.). (2005). *Rehabilitation for traumatic brain injury.* New York, NY: Oxford University Press.

Hoge, C. W., McGurk, D., Thomas, J. L., Cox, A. L., Engel, C. C., & Castro, C. A. (2008). Mild traumatic brain injury in U.S. soldiers returning from Iraq. *The New England Journal of Medicine, 358*(5), 453–463.

Holm, L., Cassidy, J. D., Carroll, L. J., & Borg, J. (2005). Summary of the WHO Collaborating Centre for Neurotrauma Task Force on Mild Traumatic Brain Injury. *Journal of Rehabilitation Medicine, 37*(3), 137–141.

Holtz, J. L. (2010). *Applied clinical neuropsychology: An introduction.* New York, NY: Springer Publishing.

Im, B., Scherer, M. J., Gaeta, R., & Elias, E. (2010, July). Traumatic brain injury. Inpatient rehabilitation. *EP Magazine,* 43–46.

Im, B., Trudel, T. M., Scherer, M. J., & Gaeta, R. (2010, March). The continuum of rehabilitation for persons with traumatic brain injury. *EP Magazine,* 37–40.

Individuals With Disabilities Education Improvement Act of 2004, 20 U.S.C. § 1400 *et seq.*

Institute of Medicine. (2011). *Cognitive rehabilitation therapy for traumatic brain injury: Evaluating the evidence.* Washington, DC: The National Academies Press.

Jiang, Q., Zhang, Z. G., & Chopp, M. (2010). MRI evaluation of white matter recovery after brain injury. *Stroke, 41*(Suppl. 10), S112–S113.

Johnson, K. L., Bamer, A. M., Yorkston, K. M., & Amtmann, D. (2009). Use of cognitive aids and other assistive technology by individuals with multiple sclerosis. *Disability and Rehabilitation. Assistive Technology, 4*(1), 1–8.

Joint Committee on Interprofessional Relations Between the American Speech–Language–Hearing Association and Division 40 (Clinical Neuropsychology) of the American Psychological Association. (2008). *Structure and function of an interdisciplinary team for persons with acquired brain injury* [Guidelines]. Retrieved from http://www.asha.org/policy

Joslyn, M. S. (1976). *A new kind of client paper.* Washington, DC: Alcohol, Drug Abuse, and Mental Health Administration.

Joslyn-Scherer, M. J. (1980). *Communication in the human services: A guide to therapeutic journalism (Sage Human Services Guides; V. 13).* Beverly Hills, CA: Sage Publications.

Jutai, J. W., Fuhrer, M. J., Demers, L., Scherer, M. J., & DeRuyter, F. (2005). Toward a taxonomy of assistive technology device outcomes. *American Journal of Physical Medicine and Rehabilitation, 84*(4), 294–302.

Karol, R. L. (2003). *Neuropsychosocial intervention: The practical treatment of severe behavioral dyscontrol after acquired brain injury.* New York, NY: CRC Press.

Katz, S., Ford, A. B., Moskowitz, R. W., Jackson, B. A., & Jaffe, M. W. (1963). Studies of illness in the aged. The index of ADL: a standardized measure of biological and psychosocial function. *The Journal of the American Medical Association, 185*(12), 914–919.

Kelly-Hayes, M, Robertson, J. T., Broderick, J. P., Duncan, P. W., Hershey, L. A., Roth, E. J., . . . Trombly, C. A. (1998). The American Heart Association Stroke Outcome Classification. *Stroke, 29*(6), 1274–1280.

Kim, H., & Colantonio, A. (2010). Effectiveness of rehabilitation in enhancing community integration after acute traumatic brain injury: A systematic review. *The American Journal of Occupational Therapy, 64*(5), 709–719.

Kim, H. J., Burke, D. T., Dowds, M. M., Jr., Boone, K. A., & Park, G. J. (2000). Electronic memory aids for outpatient brain injury: Follow-up findings. *Brain Injury, 14*(2), 187–196.

Kim, J., & Mulholland, S. J. (1999). Seating/wheelchair technology in the developing world: Need for a closer look. *Technology and Disability, 11*(1–2), 21–27.

King, M., Hale, L., Pekkari, A., Persson, M., Gregorsson, M., & Nilsson, M. (2010). An affordable, computerised, table-based exercise system for stroke survivors. *Disability and Rehabilitation. Assistive Technology, 5*(4), 288–293.

King's College London, & The London School of Economics. (2007). Dementia UK: A report to the Alzheimer's Society on the prevalence and economic cost of dementia in the UK. Retrieved from http://www.alzheimers.org.uk/News_and_Campaigns/Campaigning/PDF/Dementia_UK_Full_Report.pdf

Kirsch, N. L., & Scherer, M. J. (2010). Assistive technology for cognition and behavior. In R. G. Frank, M. Rosenthal, & B. Caplan (Eds.), *Handbook of rehabilitation psychology* (2nd ed., pp. 273–284). Washington, DC: American Psychological Association.

Kirsch, N. L., Shenton, M., & Rowan, J. (2004). A generic, "in-house", alphanumeric paging system for prospective activity impairments after traumatic brain injury. *Brain Injury, 18*(7), 725–734.

Kirsch, N. L., Shenton, M., Spirl, E., Simpson, R., Lopresti, E., & Schreckenghost, D. (2004). An assistive-technology intervention for verbose speech after traumatic brain injury: A single case study. *The Journal of Head Trauma Rehabilitation, 19*(5), 366–377.

Koester, H. H., Lopresti, E. F., & Simpson, R. C. (2006). *Measurement validity for compass assessment software.* Proceedings of the RESNA 29th Annual Conference. Atlanta, GA: RESNA. Retrieved from http://www.kpronline.com/files/compass validityresna2006.pdf

Koskinen, S., Hokkinen, E. M., Sarajuuri, J., & Alaranta, H. (2007). Applicability of the ICF checklist to traumatically brain-injured patients in post-acute rehabilitation settings. *Journal of Rehabilitation Medicine, 39*(6), 467–472.

Kou, Z., Wu, Z., Tong, K. A., Holshouser, B., Benson, R. R., Hu, J., & Haacke, E. M. (2010). The role of advanced MR imaging findings as biomarkers of traumatic brain injury. *The Journal of Head Trauma Rehabilitation, 25*(4), 267–282.

Kreutzer, J. S., Marwitz, J. H., Seel, R., & Serio, C. D. (1996). Validation of a neurobe-havioral functioning inventory for adults with traumatic brain injury. *Archives of Physical Medicine Rehabilitation, 77*(2), 116–24. Retrieved from http://www.ncbi.nlm.nih.gov/pubmed/8607734

Kreutzer, J. S., DeLuca, J., & Caplan, B. (Eds.). (2010). *Encyclopedia of clinical neuropsychology.* New York, NY: Springer Publishing.

Kreutzer, J. S., Gervasio, A. H., & Camplair, P. S. (1994a). Patient correlates of caregivers' distress and family functioning after traumatic brain injury. *Brain Injury, 8*(3), 211–230.

Kreutzer, J. S., Gervasio, A. H., & Camplair, P. S. (1994b). Primary caregivers' psychological status and family functioning after traumatic brain injury. *Brain Injury, 8*(3), 197–210.

Kreutzer, J. S., Rapport, L. J., Marwitz, J. H., Harrison-Felix, C., Hart, T., Glenn, M., & Hammond, F. (2009). Caregivers' well-being after traumatic brain injury: A multicenter prospective investigation. *Archives of Physical Medicine and Rehabilitation, 90*(6), 939–946.

Lancioni, G. E., Cuvo, A. J., & O'Reilly, M. F. (2002). Snoezelen: An overview of research with people with developmental disabilities and dementia. *Disability and Rehabilitation, 24*(4), 175–184.

Lancioni, G. E., Singh, N. N., O'Reilly, M. F., Sigafoos, J., Buonocunto, F., Sacco, V., . . . Addante, L. M. (2010). Persons with acquired brain injury and multiple disabilities access stimulation independently through microswitch-based technology. *Perceptual and Motor Skills, 111*(2), 485–495.

Lancioni, G. E., Singh, N. N., O'Reilly, M. F., Sigafoos, J., Pangrazio, M. T., Megna, M., . . . Minervini, M. G. (2009). Persons with moderate Alzheimer's disease improve activities and mood via instruction technology. *American Journal of Alzheimer's Disease and Other Dementias, 24*(3), 246–257.

Langa, K. M., Plassman, B. L., Wallace, R. B., Herzog, A. R., Heeringa, S. G., Ofstedal, M. B., . . . Willis, R. J. (2005). The aging, demographics, and memory study: Study design and methods. *Neuroepidemiology, 25*(4), 181–191.

Lasker, J., & Bedrosian, J. (2001). Promoting acceptance of augmentative and alternative communication by adults with acquired communication disorders. *Augmentative and Alternative Communication, 17*(3), 141–153.

Law, M., Baptiste, S., Carswell, A., McColl, M., Polatajko, H., & Pollock, N. (1994). *Canadian occupational performance measure* (2nd ed.). Toronto, ON: Canadian Association of Occupational Therapists.

Lawton, M. P., & Brody, E. M. (1969). Assessment of older people: Self-maintaining and instrumental activities of daily living. *The Gerontologist, 9*(3 Pt. 1), 179–186. doi:10.1093/geront/9.3_Part_1.179

LD OnLine. (2010). *What is a learning disability?* Retrieved from http://www.ldonline.org/ldbasics/whatisld

Lenker, J. A., Fuhrer, M. J., Jutai, J. W., Demers, L., Scherer, M. J., & DeRuyter, F. (2010). Treatment theory, intervention specification, and treatment fidelity in assistive technology outcomes research. *Assistive Technology, 22*(3), 129–138.

Lenker, J. A., Scherer, M. J., Fuhrer, M. J., Jutai, J. W., & DeRuyter, F. (2005). Psychometric and administrative properties of measures used in assistive technology device outcomes research. *Assistive Technology, 17*(1), 7–22.

Leonardi, M., Ayuso Mateos, J. L., Bickenbach, J., Raggi, A., Francescutti, C., Franco, M. G., . . . Chatterji, S. (2009). *MHADIE background document on disability prevalence across different diseases and EU countries.* Milan, Italy: Measuring Health and Disability in Europe.

Leonardi, M., Bickenbach, J., Raggi, A., Sala, M., Guzzon, P., Valsecchi, M. R., . . . Martinuzzi, A. (2005). Training on the International Classification of Functioning, Disability and Health (ICF): The ICF–DIN basic and the ICF–DIN advanced course developed by the Disability Italian Network. *The Journal of Headache and Pain, 6*(3), 159–164.

Lew, H. L. (2005). Rehabilitation needs of an increasing population of patients: Traumatic brain injury, polytrauma, and blast-related injuries. *Journal of Rehabilitation Research and Development, 42*(4), xiii–xvi.

Lewis, G. N., Woods, C., Rosie, J. A., & McPherson, K. M. (2011). Virtual reality games for rehabilitation of people with stroke: Perspectives from the users. *Disability and Rehabilitation. Assistive Technology, 6*(5), 453–463.

Lichtenberg, P. A., & Schneider, B. C. (2010). Psychological assessment and practice in geriatric rehabilitation. In R. G. Frank, M. Rosenthal, & B. Caplan (Eds.), *Handbook of rehabilitation psychology* (2nd ed., pp. 95–106). Washington, DC: American Psychological Association.

Lindén, A., Lexell, J., & Lund, M. L. (2010). Perceived difficulties using everyday technology after acquired brain injury: Influence on activity and participation. *Scandinavian Journal of Occupational Therapy, 17*(4), 267–275.

Lindén, A., Lexell, J., & Lund, M. L. (2011). Improvements of task performance in daily life after acquired brain injury using commonly available everyday technology. *Disability and Rehabilitation. Assistive Technology, 6*(3), 214–224.

LoPresti, E. F., Bodine, C., & Lewis, C. (2008). Assistive technology for cognition. *IEEE Engineering in Medicine and Biology Magazine, 27*(2), 29–39.

LoPresti, E. F., Simpson, R. C., Kirsch, N., Schreckenghost, D., & Hayashi, S. (2008). Distributed cognitive aid with scheduling and interactive task guidance. *Journal of Rehabilitation Research and Development, 45*(4), 505–521

LOREWO Local Rehabilitation Workshops. (n.d.). Retrieved from http://www .lorewo.com

Lugo, L. H., Salinas, F., & García, H. I. (2007). Out-patient rehabilitation programme for spinal cord injured patients: Evaluation of the results on motor FIM score. *Disability and Rehabilitation, 29*(11–12), 873–881.

Lyons, J. (2008). *Jitterbug: The anti-iPhone.* Retrieved from http://usedwigs.com/ jitterbug-the-anti-iphone/

Lysack, J. T., Mulholland, S. J., Panchal, V., Wyss, U. P., & Packer, T. L. (1996). Designing a short-range wheeled mobility device for women in India (p. 156). *Proceedings of the RESNA '96 Annual Conference, Salt Lake City, UT.*

Maas, A. I., Harrison-Felix, C. L., Menon, D., Adelson, P. D., Balkin, T., Bullock, R., . . . Schwab, K. (2010). Common data elements for traumatic brain injury: Recommendations from the interagency working group on demographics and clinical assessment. *Archives of Physical Medicine and Rehabilitation, 91*(11), 1641–1649.

Magasi, S. R., Heinemann, A. W., & Whiteneck, G. G. (2008). Participation following traumatic spinal cord injury: An evidence-based review for research. *The Journal of Spinal Cord Medicine, 31*(2), 145–146.

Malec, J. F. (1999). Goal attainment scaling in rehabilitation. *Neuropsychological Rehabilitation, 9*(3–4), 253–275.

Malia, K., Law, P., Sidebottom, L., Bewick, K., Danziger, S., Schold-Davis, E., . . . Vaidya, A. (2004). *Recommendations for best practice in cognitive rehabilitation therapy: Acquired brain injury.* Surrey, United Kingdom: Society for Cognitive Rehabilitation. Retrieved from http://societyforcognitiverehab.org/membership-and-certification/documents/EditedRecsBestPrac.pdf

Manley, G. T., Diaz-Arrastia, R., Brophy, M., Engel, D., Goodman, C., Gwinn, K., . . . Hayes, R. L. (2010). Common data elements for traumatic brain injury: Recommendations from the biospecimens and biomarkers working group. *Archives of Physical Medicine and Rehabilitation, 91*(11), 1667–1672.

Mann, W. C., Karuza, J., Hurren, D. M., & Tomita, M. (1992). Assistive devices for home-based elderly persons with cognitive impairments. *Topics in Geriatric Rehabilitation, 8*(2), 35–52.

Mann, W. C., Ottenbacher, K. J., Fraas, L., Tomita, M., & Granger, C. V. (1999). Effectiveness of assistive technology and environmental interventions in maintaining independence and reducing home care costs for the frail elderly: A randomized controlled trial. *Archives of Family Medicine, 8*(3), 210–217.

Martin, J. K., Martin, L. G., Stumbo, N. J., & Morrill, J. H. (2011). The impact of consumer involvement on satisfaction with and use of assistive technology. *Disability and Rehabilitation. Assistive Technology, 6*(3), 225–242.

Maryland Developmental Disabilities Council. (2010). *Federal definition of developmental disabilities.* Retrieved from http://www.md-council.org/resources/dd_definition.html

Maslow, A. H. (1954). *Motivation and personality.* New York, NY: Harper & Row.

McKee, A. C., Cantu, R. C., Nowinski, C. J., Hedley-Whyte, E. T., Gavett, B. E., Budson, A. E., . . . Stern, R. A. (2009). Chronic traumatic encephalopathy in athletes: Progressive tauopathy after repetitive head injury. *Journal of Neuropathology and Experimental Neurology, 68*(7), 709–735.

Mendelsohn, S., & Fox, H. R. (2002). Evolving legislation and public policy related to disability and assistive technology. In M. J. Scherer (Ed.), *Assistive technology: Matching device and consumer for successful rehabilitation* (pp. 17–28). Washington, DC: American Psychological Association.

Menon, D. K., Schwab, K., Wright, D. W., & Maas, A. I. (2010). Position statement: Definition of traumatic brain injury. *Archives of Physical Medicine and Rehabilitation, 91*(11), 1637–1640.

Mild Traumatic Brain Injury Committee of the Head Injury Interdisciplinary Special Interest Group of the American Congress of Rehabilitation Medicine. (1993). Definition of mild traumatic brain injury. *Journal of Head Trauma Rehabilitation, 8*(3), 86–87.

Mioshi, E., Dawson, K., Mitchell, J., Arnold, R., & Hodges, J. R. (2006). The Addenbrooke's Cognitive Examination Revised (ACE-R): A brief cognitive test battery for dementia screening. *International Journal of Geriatric Psychiatry, 21*(11), 1078–1085. doi:10.1002/gps.1610

Mitchell, S. L., Kiely, D. K., Hamel, M. B., Park, P. S., Morris, J. N., & Fries, B. E. (2004). Estimating prognosis for nursing home residents with advanced dementia. *The Journal of the American Medical Association, 291*(22), 2734–2740.

Mpofu, E., & Oakland, T. (Eds.). (2010a). *Assessment in rehabilitation and health.* Upper Saddle River, NJ: Merrill/Pearson.

Mpofu, E., & Oakland, T. (Eds.). (2010b). *Rehabilitation and health assessment: Applying ICF guidelines.* New York, NY: Springer Publishing.

Mukherjee, G., & Samanta, A. (2005). Wheelchair charity: A useless benevolence in community-based rehabilitation. *Disability and Rehabilitation, 27*(10), 591–596.

Mulholland, S. J., Packer, T. L., Laschinger, S. J., Lysack, J. T., Wyss, U. P., & Balaram, S. (2000). Evaluating a new mobility device: Feedback from women with disabilities in India. *Disability and Rehabilitation, 22*(3), 111–122.

National Alliance for Caregiving. (2009). *Executive summary: Caregiving in the U.S.* Retrieved from http://www.caregiving.org/pdf/research/Caregiving USAllAgesExecSum.pdf

National Alliance for Caregiving, & AARP. (2004). *Caregiving in the U.S.* Retrieved from http://www.caregiving.org/data/04finalreport.pdf

National Education Association. (2007). *Rankings and estimates: Rankings of the states 2006 and estimates of school statistics 2007.* Washington, DC: NEA Research.

National Institute of Neurological Disorders and Stroke, National Institutes of Health. (2010a). *Cerebral palsy: Hope through research.* Retrieved from http://www.ninds.nih.gov/disorders/cerebral_palsy/detail_cerebral_palsy.htm

National Institute of Neurological Disorders and Stroke, National Institutes of Health. (2010b). *NINDS learning disabilities information page.* Retrieved from http://www.ninds.nih.gov/disorders/learningdisabilities/learningdisabilities.htm

National Institute of Neurological Disorders and Stroke, National Institutes of Health. (2010c). *NINDS tardive dyskinesia information page.* Retrieved from http://www.ninds.nih.gov/disorders/tardive/tardive.htm

National Institute of Neurological Disorders and Stroke, National Institutes of Health. (2010d). *Stroke risk factors and symptoms.* Retrieved from http://www.ninds.nih.gov/disorders/stroke/stroke.htm

National Institute on Disability and Rehabilitation Research. (2010). *The traumatic brain injury model systems.* Retrieved from https://www.tbindsc.org/Documents/TBIModel%20SystemsBrochure2010.pdf

National Organization on Disability. (2004). *2004 NOD/Harris survey of Americans with disabilities.* Retrieved from http://www.nod.org/research_publications/nod_harris_survey/

National Research Council. (2011). *Health care comes home: The human factors.* Committee on the Role of Human Factors in Home Health Care, Board on Human-Systems Integration, Division of Behavioral and Social Sciences and Education. Washington, DC: The National Academies Press.

National Stroke Association. (2010). *Stroke 101 fact sheet.* Retrieved from http://www.stroke.org/site/DocServer/STROKE_101_Fact_Sheet.pdf?docID=4541.

Niemeier, J. P., & Karol, R. L. (2010a). *Overcoming grief and loss after brain injury.* New York, NY: Oxford University Press.

Niemeier, J. P., & Karol, R. L. (2010b). *Therapists' guide to overcoming grief and loss after brain injury.* New York, NY: Oxford University Press.

Nordby, K. (2003, March 27–28). *Design for all: Shaping the end-users' Tel-eEurope: ETSI's involvement in laying the foundation for an all-inclusive eEurope.* Paper presented at the CEN/CENELEC/ETSI Conference on Accessibility for All, Nice, France.

Novack, T. A., Scherer, M. J., & Penna, S. (2010). Neuropsychological practice in rehabilitation. In R. G. Frank, M. Rosenthal, & B. Caplan (Eds.), *Handbook of rehabilitation psychology* (2nd ed., pp. 165–178). Washington, DC: American Psychological Association.

Nunnally, J., & Bernstein, I. (1994). *Psychometric theory* (3rd ed.). New York, NY: McGraw-Hill.

Nygård, L., & Starkhammar, S. (2007). The use of everyday technology by people with dementia living alone: Mapping out the difficulties. *Aging & Mental Health, 11*(2), 144–155.

Øderud, T., Brodtkorb, S., & Hotchkiss, R. (2004). *Feasibility study on production and provision of wheelchairs and tricycles in Uganda.* Trondheim, Norway: SINTEF Health Research.

Øderud, T., & Grann, O. (1999). Providing assistive devices and rehabilitation services in developing countries. In C. Bühler & H. Knops (Eds.), *Assistive technology on the threshold of the new millenium: Assistive technology research series* (pp. 782–786). Amsterdam, The Netherlands: IOS Press.

Okawara, S., & Nibbelink, D. (1974). Vertebral artery occlusion following hyperextension and rotation of the head. *Stroke, 5*(5), 640–642.

Olesen, P. J., Gustafson, D. R., Simoni, M., Pantoni, L., Ostling, S., Guo, X., & Skoog, I. (2010). Temporal lobe atrophy and white matter lesions are related to major depression over 5 years in the elderly. *Neuropsychopharmacology, 35*(13), 2638–2645.

O'Neil-Pirozzi, T. M., Kendrick, H., Goldstein, R., & Glenn, M. (2004). Clinician influences on use of portable electronic memory devices in traumatic brain injury rehabilitation. *Brain Injury, 18*(2), 179–189.

Orticio, L. P. (2009). Protecting human subjects in research. *Insight, 34*(3), 14–16.

Ostir, G. V., Markides, K. S., Peek, M. K., & Goodwin, J. S. (2001). The association between emotional well-being and the incidence of stroke in older adults. *Psychosomatic Medicine, 63*(2), 210–215.

Paas, F., Renkl, A., & Sweller, J. (2003). Cognitive load theory: Instructional implications of the interaction between information structures and cognitive architecture. *Instructional Science, 32*(1–2), 1–8.

Palmer, R. M., & Meldon, S. W. (2003). Acute care. In W. R. Hazzard, J. P. Blass, J. B. Halter, J. G. Ouslander, & M. E. Tinetti (Eds.), *Principles of geriatric medicine & gerontology* (5th ed., pp. 157–168). New York, NY: McGraw-Hill.

Parette, H. P., Huer, M. B., & Scherer, M. (2004). Effects of acculturation on assistive technology service delivery. *Journal of Special Education Technology, 19*(2), 31–41.

Parker, J., Mountain, G., & Hammerton, J. (2011). A review of the evidence underpinning the use of visual and auditory feedback for computer technology in post-stroke upper-limb rehabilitation. *Disability and Rehabilitation. Assistive Technology, 6*(6), 465–472.

Peterson, D. B. (2010). *Psychological aspects of functioning, disability, and health.* New York, NY: Springer Publishing.

Phillips, B., & Zhao, H. (1993). Predictors of assistive technology abandonment. *Assistive Technology, 5*(1), 36–45.

Plassman, B. L., Langa, K. M., Fisher, G. G., Heeringa, S. G., Weir, D. R., Ofstedal, M. B., . . . Wallace, R. B. (2007). Prevalence of dementia in the United States: The aging, demographics, and memory study. *Neuroepidemiology, 29*(1–2), 125–132.

Plassman, B. L., Langa, K. M., Fisher, G. G., Heeringa, S. G., Weir, D. R., Of-stedal, M. B., . . . Wallace, R. B. (2008). Prevalence of cognitive impairment without dementia in the United States. *Annals of Internal Medicine, 148*(6), 427–434.

Pohjasvaara, T. I., Jokinen, H., Ylikoski, R., Kalska, H., Mäntylä, R., Kaste, M., & Erkinjuntti, T. (2007). White matter lesions are related to impaired instrumental activities of daily living poststroke. *Journal of Stroke and Cerebrovascular Diseases, 16*(6), 251–258.

Postman, N. (1992). *Technopoly: The surrender of culture to technology.* New York, NY: Knopf.

Prat, C. S., & Just, M. A. (2008). Brain bases of individual differences in cognition. *Psychological Science Agenda, 22*(5).

Randolph, C. (2010). The repeatable battery for the assessment of neuropsychological status (RBANS): Utility as an outcome measure in clinical trials for MCI and mild dementia. *Alzheimer's and Dementia, 6*(4), S486–S487.

Raskind, M. (2010). Matching assistive technology tools to individual needs. Retrieved from Great Schools website: http://www.greatschools.org/special-education/legal-rights/968-matching-assistive-technology-tools-to-individual-needs.gs?print=true&fromPage=1&page=1

Ricker, J. H. (2010). Traumatic brain injury in adults. In R. G. Frank, M. Rosenthal, & B. Caplan (Eds.), *Handbook of rehabilitation psychology* (2nd ed., pp. 43–62). Washington, DC: American Psychological Association.

Riemer-Reiss, M. L., & Wacker, R. R. (2000). Factors associated with assistive technology discontinuance among individuals with disabilities. *The Journal of Rehabilitation, 66*, 44–50.

Ripat, J., & Booth, A. (2005). Characteristics of assistive technology service delivery models: Stakeholder perspectives and preferences. *Disability and Rehabilitation, 27*(24), 1461–1470.

Ripat, J., & Woodgate, R. (2011). The intersection of culture, disability and assistive technology. *Disability and Rehabilitation. Assistive Technology, 6*(2), 87–96.

Rook, K. S. (1984). The negative side of social interaction: Impact on psychological well-being. *Journal of Personality and Social Psychology, 46*(5), 1097–1108.

Rook, K. S., & Pietromonaco, P. (1987). Close relationships: Ties that heal or ties that bind? In W. H. Jones & D. Perlman (Eds.), *Advances in personal relationships: A research annual* (Vol. 1, pp. 1–35). Greenwich, CT: JAI Press.

Rosalynn Carter Institute for Caregiving. (2010). *Averting the caregiving crisis: Why we must act now.* Retrieved from http://www.rosalynncarter.org/UserFiles/File/RCI_Position_Paper100310_Final.pdf

Rosalynn Carter Institute for Caregiving. (2011). *The case for caregiver support.* Retrieved from http://www.rosalynncarter.org/case_for_caregiver_support/

Rosenberg, L., Kottorp, A., Winblad, B., & Nygård, L. (2009). Perceived difficulty in everyday technology use among older adults with or without cognitive deficits. *Scandinavian Journal of Occupational Therapy, 16*(4), 216–226.

Roy, N., Roy, A., & Das, S. K. (2006). Context-aware resource management in multi-inhabitant smart homes: A Nash H-learning based approach. *Proceedings of the Fourth Annual IEEE International Conference on Pervasive Computing and Communications* (PerCom'06, pp. 148–158).

Russell, J. N., Hendershot, G. E., LeClere, F., Howie, L. J., & Adler, M. (1997). Trends and differential use of assistive technology devices: United States, 1994. *Advance Data*, (292), 1–9. Retrieved from http://www.cdc.gov/nchs/data/ad/ad292.pdf

Sablier, J., Stip, E., & Franck, N. (2009). Cognitive remediation and cognitive assistive technologies in schizophrenia. *L'Encéphale*, *35*(2), 160–167.

Sady, M. D., Sander, A. M., Clark A. N., Sherer, M., Nakase-Richardson, R., & Malec, J. F. (2010). Relationship of preinjury caregiver and family functioning to community integration in adults with traumatic brain injury. *Archives of Physical Medicine and Rehabilitation*, *91*(10), 1542–1550.

Salaycik, K. J., Kelly-Hayes, M., Beiser, A., Nguyen, A. H., Brady, S. M., Kase, C. S., & Wolf, P. A. (2007). Depressive symptoms and risk of stroke: The Framingham Study. *Stroke*, *38*(1), 16–21.

Samton, J. B., Ferrando, S. J., Sanelli, P., Karimi, S., Raiteri, V., & Barnhill, J. W. (2005). The clock drawing test: Diagnostic, functional, and neuroimaging correlates in older medically ill adults. *The Journal of Neuropsychiatry and Clinical Neurosciences*, *17*(4), 533–540.

Sander, A. M. (2006). A cognitive-behavioral intervention for family members of persons with TBI. In N. D. Zasler, D. I. Katz, & R. D. Zafonte (Eds.), *Brain injury medicine: Principles and practice* (pp. 1117–1130). New York, NY: Demos Medical.

Sander, A. M., Clark, A. N., Atchison, T. B., & Rueda, M. (2009). A web-based videoconferencing approach to training caregivers in rural areas to compensate for problems related to traumatic brain injury. *The Journal of Head Trauma Rehabilitation*, *24*(4), 248–261.

Sander, A. M., Clark, A., & Pappadis, M. R. (2010). What is community integration anyway? Defining meaning following traumatic brain injury. *The Journal of Head Trauma Rehabilitation*, *25*(2), 121–127.

Sauer, A. L., Parks, A., & Heyn, P. C. (2010). Assistive technology effects on the employment outcomes for people with cognitive disabilities: A systematic review. *Disability and Rehabilitation. Assistive Technology*, *5*(6), 377–391.

Sax, C. L. (2002). Assistive technology education: An online model for rehabilitation professionals. *Disability and Rehabilitation*, *24*(1–3), 144–151.

Sax, C. L., & Thoma, C. A. (Eds.). (2002). *Transition assessment: Wise practices for quality lives*. Baltimore, MD: Paul H. Brookes Publishing.

Scherer, M. J. (1986). *Values in the creation, prescription, and use of technological aids and assistive devices for people with physical disabilities* (Doctoral dissertation, University of Rochester, and final report to the National Science Foundation). *Dissertation Abstracts International*, *48*(01), 49A. (UMI No. ADG87-08247).

Scherer, M. J. (1993a). *Living in the state of stuck: How assistive technology impacts the lives of people with disabilities*. Cambridge, MA: Brookline Books.

Scherer, M. J. (1993b). What we know about women's technology use, avoidance, and abandonment. Co-published simultaneously in M. E. Willmuth & L. Holcomb (Eds.), *Women with disabilities: Found voices*. New York, NY: The Haworth Press and *Women & Therapy*, *14*(3/4), 117–132.

Scherer, M. J. (1998). *The matching person & technology (MPT) model manual* (Rev. ed.). Webster, NY: The Institute for Matching Person & Technology.

Scherer, M. J., & Cushman, L. A. (2000). Predicting satisfaction with assistive technology for a sample of adults with new spinal cord injuries. *Psychological Reports, 87*(3 Pt. 1), 981–987.

Scherer, M. J. (Ed.). (2002a). *Assistive technology: Matching device and consumer for successful rehabilitation.* Washington, DC: American Psychological Association.

Scherer, M. J. (2002b). The change in emphasis from people to person: Introduction to the special issue on assistive technology. *Disability and Rehabilitation, 24*(1–3), 1–4.

Scherer, M. J. (2004). *Connecting to learn: Educational and assistive technology for people with disabilities.* Washington, DC: American Psychological Association.

Scherer, M. J. (2005a). Assessing the benefits of using assistive technologies and other supports for thinking, remembering and learning. *Disability and Rehabilitation, 27*(13), 731–739.

Scherer, M. J. (2005b). *Living in the state of stuck: How assistive technology impacts the lives of people with disabilities* (4th ed.). Cambridge, MA: Brookline.

Scherer, M. J. (2005c). *The matching person & technology (MPT) model manual and assessments* (5th ed.). Webster, NY: The Institute for Matching Person & Technology.

Scherer, M. J. (2006). *Assistive technology assessment: Service provider concerns.* Presentation for the Interagency Committee on Disability Research (ICDR), Interagency Subcommittee on Technology (IST), Technology for Improving Cognitive Function. Washington, DC, June 29–30.

Scherer, M. J., Adya, M., Samant, D., & Morris, M. W. (n. d.). *Assistive/rehabilitation technology, disability, & prevalent international service delivery models.* Manuscript submitted for publication.

Scherer, M. J., & Bodine, C. (2006). Technology for improving cognitive function: Report on a workshop sponsored by the U.S. Interagency Committee on Disability Research. *Disability and Rehabilitation. Assistive Technology, 1*(4), 257–261.

Scherer, M. J., Coombs, F. K., & Merbitz, N. H. (2004). Garbage in, garbage out: The importance of initial assessments in achieving successful assistive technology outcomes. *American Occupational Therapy Association Technology Special Interest Section Quarterly, 14,* 1–4.

Scherer, M. J., Craddock, G., & Mackeogh, T. (2011). The relationship of personal factors and subjective well-being to the use of assistive technology devices. *Disability and Rehabilitation, 33*(10), 811–817.

Scherer, M. J., & Cushman, L. A. (2002). Determining the content for an interactive training programme and interpretive guidelines for the Assistive Technology Device Predisposition Assessment. *Disability and Rehabilitation, 24*(1–3), 126–130.

Scherer, M. J., Federici, S., Tiberio, L., Pigliautile, M., Corradi, F., & Meloni, F. (2010). ICF core set for matching older adults with dementia and technology. *Ageing International.* doi:10.1007/s12126-010-9093-9

Scherer, M. J., & Glueckauf, R. (2005). Assessing the benefits of assistive technologies for activities and participation. *Rehabilitation Psychology, 50*(2), 132–141.

Scherer, M. J., Hart, T., Kirsch, N., & Schulthesis, M. (2005). Assistive technologies for cognitive disabilities. *Critical Reviews in Physical and Rehabilitation Medicine, 17*(3), 195–215.

Scherer, M. J., Jutai, J., Fuhrer, M., Demers, L., & DeRuyter, F. (2007). A framework for modelling the selection of assistive technology devices (ATDs). *Disability and Rehabilitation. Assistive Technology, 2*(1), 1–8.

Scherer, M. J., & McKee, B. G. (1989). But will the assistive technology device be used? *Proceedings of the 12th Annual Conference: Technology for the Next Decade* (pp. 356–357). Washington, DC: RESNA.

Scherer, M. J., & Sax, C. (2010). Measures of assistive technology predisposition and use. In E. Mpofu & T. Oakland (Eds.), *Rehabilitation and health assessment: Applying ICF guidelines* (pp. 229–254). New York, NY: Springer Publishing.

Scherer, M. J., Sax, C. L., & Glueckauf, R. L. (2005). Activities and participation: The need to include assistive technology in rehabilitation counselor education. *Rehabilitation Education, 19*(2–3), 177–190.

Scherer, M. J., Sax, C., Vanbiervliet, A., Cushman, L. A., & Scherer, J. V. (2005). Predictors of assistive technology use: The importance of personal and psychosocial factors. *Disability and Rehabilitation, 27*(21), 1321–1331.

Schülke, A. M., Plischke, H., & Kohls, N. B. (2010). Ambient assistive technologies (AAT): Socio-technology as a powerful tool for facing the inevitable sociodemographic challenges. *Philosophy, Ethics, and Humanities in Medicine, 5*, 8. Retrieved from http://pubmedcentralcanada.ca/articlerender.cgi?tool=pubmed&pubmedid=20529272

Schulz, R., Belle, S. H., Czaja, S. J., McGinnis, K. A., Stevens, A., & Zhang, S. (2004). Long-term care placement of dementia patients and caregiver health and well-being. *The Journal of the American Medical Association, 292*(8), 961–967.

Schweizer, M., Kotouc, A. J., & Wagner, T. (2006). Scale development for consumer confusion. *Advances in Consumer Research, 33*(1), 184–190. Retrieved from http://www.acrwebsite.org/volumes/v33/v33_55.pdf

Seel, R. T., Kreutzer, J. S., Rosenthal, M., Hammond, F. M., Corrigan, J. D., & Black, K. (2003). Depression after traumatic brain injury: A National Institute on Disability and Rehabilitation Research Model Systems multicenter investigation. *Archives of Physical Medicine and Rehabilitation, 84*(2), 177–184.

Sherer, M., Evans, C. C., Leverenz, J., Stouter, J., Irby, J. W., Jr., Lee, J. E., & Yablon, S. A. (2007). Therapeutic alliance in post-acute brain injury rehabilitation: Predictors of strength of alliance and impact of alliance on outcome. *Brain Injury, 21*(7), 663–672.

Simpson, R., Koester, H. H., & Lopresti, E. (2010). Research in computer access assessment and intervention. *Physical Medicine and Rehabilitation Clinics of North America, 21*(1), 15–32.

Smith, D. L., Akhtar, A. J., & Garraway, W. M. (1983). Proprioception and spatial neglect after stroke. *Age and Ageing, 12*(1), 63–69.

Sohlberg, M. M. (2011). Assistive technology for cognition. *The ASHA Leader.* Retrieved from http://www.asha.org/Publications/leader/2011/110215/Assistive-Technology-for-Cognition.htm?sf1133475=1#2

Sohlberg, M. M., Ehlhardt, L. A., Fickas, S., & Sutcliffe, A. (2003). A pilot study exploring electronic (or e-mail) mail in users with acquired cognitive-linguistic impairments. *Brain Injury, 17*(7), 609–629.

Sohlberg, M. M., Ehlhardt, L., & Kennedy, M. (2005). Instructional techniques in cognitive rehabilitation: A preliminary report. *Seminars in Speech and Language*, *26*(4), 268–279.

Sohlberg, M. M., & Mateer, C. A. (2001). *Cognitive rehabilitation: An integrative neuropsychological approach*. New York, NY: The Guilford Press.

Sohlberg, M. M., McLaughlin, K. A., Todis, B., Larsen, J., & Glang, A. (2001). What does it take to collaborate with families affected by brain injury? A preliminary model. *The Journal of Head Trauma Rehabilitation*, *16*(5), 498–511.

Sohlberg, M. M., & Turkstra, L. S. (2011). *Optimizing cognitive rehabilitation: Effective instructional methods*. New York, NY: The Guilford Press.

Spikman, J. M., & van der Naalt, J. (2010). Indices of impaired self-awareness in traumatic brain injury patients with focal frontal lesions and executive deficits: Implications for outcome measurement. *Journal of Neurotrauma*, *27*(7), 1195–1202.

Steel, E., Gelderblom, G. J., & de Witte, L. (2010). Linking instruments and documenting decisions in service delivery guided by an ICF-based tool for assistive technology selection. In K. Miesenberger, J. Klaus, W. Zagler, & A. Karshmer (Eds.), *Computers helping people with special needs* (Lecture Notes in Computer Science 6179, pp. 537–543). Berlin, Germany: Springer-Verlag.

Steel, E., Gelderblom, G. J., & de Witte, L. P. (2011). Development of an AT selection tool using the ICF model. *Technology and Disability*, *23*, 1–6.

Steffens, D. C., Fisher, G. G., Langa, K. M., Potter, G. G., & Plassman, B. L. (2009). Prevalence of depression among older Americans: The aging, demographics and memory study. *International Psychogeriatrics*, *21*(5), 879–888.

Stiers, W., Perry, K. N., Kennedy, P., & Scherer, M. J. (2011). Rehabilitation psychology. In P. R. Martin, F. M. Cheung, M. Kyrios, L. Littlefield, M. Knowles, J. B.Overmier, & J. M. Prieto (Eds.), *IAAP handbook of applied psychology* (pp. 573–587). Oxford, England: Blackwell Publishing.

Stock, S. E., Davies, D. K., Davies, K. R., & Wehmeyer, M. L. (2006). Evaluation of an application for making palmtop computers accessible to individuals with intellectual disabilities. *Journal of Intellectual & Developmental Disability*, *31*(1), 39–46.

Stock, S. E., Davies, D. K., Wehmeyer, M. L., & Palmer, S. B. (2008). Evaluation of cognitively accessible software to increase independent access to cellphone technology for people with intellectual disability. *Journal of Intellectual Disability Research*, *52*(12), 1155–1164.

Strong, J. G., Jutai, J. W., & Plotkin, A. D. (2011). Competitive enablement: A client-centred conceptual model for device selections in low vision rehabilitation. In G. J. Gelderblom, M. Soede, L. Adriaens, & K. Miesenberger (Eds.), *Everyday technology for independence and care* (pp. 1033–1042). Amsterdam, The Netherlands: IOS Press.

Stuss, D. T., Winocur, G., & Robertson, I. H. (Eds.). (2010). *Cognitive neurorehabilitation: Evidence and application* (2nd ed.). Cambridge, United Kingdom: Cambridge University Press.

Surman, G., Hemming, K., Platt, M. J., Parkes, J., Green, A., Hutton, J., & Kurinczuk, J. J. (2009). Children with cerebral palsy: Severity and trends over time. *Paediatric and Perinatal Epidemiology*, *23*(6), 513–521.

Sutcliffe, A., Fickas, S., & Sohlberg, M. M. (2005). Personal and contextual requirements engineering. *Proceedings of the 13th IEEE International Conference on Requirements Engineering (RE'05).*

Svestkova, O., Angerova, Y., Sladkova, P., Bickenbach, J. E., & Raggi, A. (2010). Functioning and disability in traumatic brain injury. *Disability and Rehabilitation, 32*(Suppl. 1), S68–S77.

Swenson, S. (2011, February 15). *Statement to the Interagency Committee on Disability Research (ICDR).* Assistive Technology/Technology Forum, Washington, DC.

Talley, R. C., & Crews, J. E. (2007). Framing the public health of caregiving. *American Journal of Public Health, 97*(2), 224–228.

Tamaru, A., McColl, M. A., & Yamasaki, S. (2007). Understanding 'independence': Perspectives of occupational therapists. *Disability and Rehabilitation, 29*(13), 1021–1033.

Tham, M. W., Woon, P. S., Sum, M. Y., Lee, T. S., & Sim, K. (2011). White matter abnormalities in major depression: Evidence from post-mortem, neuroimaging and genetic studies. *Journal of Affective Disorders, 132*(1–2), 26–36.

Thomas, S. A., & Lincoln, N. B. (2008). Predictors of emotional distress after stroke. *Stroke, 39*(4), 1240–1245.

Thurmond, V. A., Hicks, R., Gleason, T., Miller, A. C., Szuflita, N., Orman, J., & Schwab, K. (2010). Advancing integrated research in psychological health and traumatic brain injury: Common data elements. *Archives of Physical Medicine and Rehabilitation, 91*(11), 1633–1636.

Tinetti, M. E. (1986). Performance-oriented assessment of mobility problems in elderly patients. *Journal of the American Geriatrics Society, 34*(2), 119–126.

Tinney, M. J., Chiodo, A., Haig, A., & Wiredu, E. (2007). Medical rehabilitation in Ghana. *Disability and Rehabilitation, 29*(11–12), 921–927.

Tonkonogy, J. M., & Puente, A. E. (2009). *Localization of clinical syndromes in neuropsychology and neuroscience.* New York, NY: Springer Publishing.

Traumatic Brain Injury Model Systems National Data and Statistical Center. (2011). *TBI model systems national database update.* Englewood, CO: Craig Hospital. Retrieved from http://www.tbindsc.org/

Trudel, T., Scherer, M. J., & Elias, E. (2009, October/November). Understanding traumatic brain injury. *EP Magazine,* 101–104.

Tsaousides, T., & Gordon, W. A. (2009). Cognitive rehabilitation following traumatic brain injury: Assessment to treatment. *The Mount Sinai Journal of Medicine, New York, 76*(2), 173–181.

Turner, B. J., Fleming, J., Ownsworth, T., & Cornwell, P. (2011). Perceived service and support needs during transition from hospital to home following acquired brain injury. *Disability and Rehabilitation, 33*(10), 818–829.

United Nations. (1997). *Economic and Social Commission for Asia and the Pacific: Production and distribution of assistive devices for people with disabilities: Supplement III: Technical Specifications.* Retrieved from http://www.unescap.org/esid/psis/disability/decade/publications/z15005s3/z1500505.htm

United Nations General Assembly. (2007). *Convention on the rights of persons with disabilities: Resolution/adopted by the General Assembly.* Retrieved from http://www.unhcr.org/refworld/docid/45f973632.html

U.S. Department of Education, Office of Special Education and Rehabilitative Services. (2003). *Twenty-fifth annual report to congress on the implementation of the Individuals with Disabilities Education Act*. Washington, DC: Author.

U.S. Department of Veterans Affairs, & U.S. Department of Defense. (2009). *Clinical practice guideline for management of concussion/mild traumatic brain injury*. Washington, DC: Author.

Uswatte, G., Taub, E., Mark, V. W., Perkins, C., & Gauthier, L. (2010). Central nervous system plasticity and rehabilitation. In R. G. Frank, M. Rosenthal, & B. Caplan (Eds.), *Handbook of rehabilitation psychology* (2nd ed., pp. 391–406). Washington, DC: American Psychological Association.

Vaccaro, M., Hart, T., Whyte, J., & Buchhofer, R. (2007). Internet use and interest among individuals with traumatic brain injury: A consumer survey. *Disability and Rehabilitation. Assistive Technology, 2*(2), 85–95.

Van Hulle, A., & Hux, K. (2006). Improvement patterns among survivors of brain injury: Three case examples documenting the effectiveness of memory compensation strategies. *Brain Injury, 20*(1), 101–109.

Verza, R., Carvalho, M. L., Battaglia, M. A., & Uccelli, M. M. (2006). An interdisciplinary approach to evaluating the need for assistive technology reduces equipment abandonment. *Multiple Sclerosis, 12*(1), 88–93.

Waldron-Perrine, B., Hanks, R. A., & Perinne, S. A. (2008). Pharmacotherapy for postacute traumatic brain injury: A literature review for guidance in psychological practice. *Rehabilitation Psychology, 53*(4), 426–444.

Wennberg, B., & Kjellberg, A. (2010). Participation when using cognitive assistive devices—from the perspective of people with intellectual disabilities. *Occupational Therapy International, 17*(4), 168–176.

Wessels, R., Persson, J., Lorentsen, Ø., Andrich, R., Ferrario, W., Oortwijn, W., . . . de Witte, L. (2002). IPPA: Individually prioritised problem assessment. *Technology and Disability, 14*, 141–145.

WHO Collaborating Centre for the FIC in the Netherlands. (2010). International Organization for Standardization: New features in the 2011 version of ISO 9999. *Newsletter on the WHO-FIC, 8*(2), 3–4.

Wielandt, T., Mckenna, K., Tooth, L., & Strong, J. (2006). Factors that predict the post-discharge use of recommended assistive technology (AT). *Disability and Rehabilitation. Assistive Technology, 1*(1–2), 29–40.

Wilde, E. A., Whiteneck, G. G., Bogner, J., Bushnik, T., Cifu, D. X., Dikmen, S., . . . von Steinbuechel, N. (2010). Recommendations for the use of common outcome measures in traumatic brain injury research. *Archives of Physical Medicine and Rehabilitation, 91*(11), 1650–1660.

Wilk, J. E., Thomas, J. L., McGurk, D. M., Riviere, L. A., Castro, C. A., & Hoge, C. W. (2010). Mild traumatic brain injury (concussion) during combat: Lack of association of blast mechanism with persistent postconcussive symptoms. *The Journal of Head Trauma Rehabilitation, 25*(1), 9–14.

Wills, T. A., & Shinar, O. (2000). Measuring perceived and received social support. In S. Cohen, L. G. Underwood, & B. H. Gottlieb (Eds.), *Social support measurement and intervention: A guide for health and social scientists* (pp. 86–135). New York, NY: Oxford University Press.

Wilson, B. A. (2006a). Current challenges for neuropsychological rehabilitation. *Brain Impairment, 7*(2), 151–165.

Wilson, B. A. (2006b). Recent developments in neuropsychological rehabilitation. *Higher Brain Function Research,* 1–8.

Wilson, B. A., Emslie, H., Quirk, K., Evans, J., & Watson, P. (2005). A randomized control trial to evaluate a paging system for people with traumatic brain injury. *Brain Injury, 19*(11), 891–894.

Wilson, K. R., Donders, J., & Nguyen, L. (2011). Self and parent ratings of executive functioning after adolescent traumatic brain injury. *Rehabilitation Psychology, 56*(2), 100–106.

World Health Organization. (2001). *International classification of functioning, disability and health.* Geneva, Switzerland: Author. Retrieved from http://www.who.int/classifications/icf/site/icftemplate.cfm?myurl=introduction.html%20&mytitle=Introduction

World Health Organization. (2002). *Towards a common language for functioning, disability and health ICF.* Retrieved from http://www.who.int/classifications/icf/training/icfbeginnersguide.pdf

World Health Organization. (2005). *Resolutions and decisions. Annex* (Wha58/2005/Rec/1). Paper presented at the Fifty-Eight World Health Assembly, Geneva, Switzerland.

World Health Organization. (2011). *World report on disability.* Geneva, Switzerland: Author. Retrieved from http://whqlibdoc.who.int/publications/2011/9789240685215_eng.pdf

Wright, B. A. (1960). *Physical disability: A psychological approach.* New York, NY: Harper & Row.

Zapf, S. A., & Rough, R. B. (2002). The development of an instrument to match individuals with disabilities and service animals. *Disability and Rehabilitation, 24*(1–3), 47–58.

Zeiner, H. K., & Scherer, M. J. (2009, February–March). *Devices: Cognitive support technologies.* Invited presentation, 2009 Rehabilitation Psychology Conference, Rehabilitation Psychology Division, American Psychological Association, Jacksonville, FL.

Ziermans, T. B., Schothorst, P. F., Schnack, H. G., Koolschijn, P. C., Kahn, R. S., van Engeland, H., & Durston, S. (2010). Progressive structural brain changes during development of psychosis. *Schizophrenia Bulletin.* 2010 Oct 7. Epub ahead of print.

Zongjie, Y., Hong, D., Zhongxin, X., & Hui, X. (2007). A research study into the requirements of disabled residents for rehabilitation services in Beijing. *Disability and Rehabilitation, 29*(10), 825–833.

Appendix A

GLOSSARY

accessibility*. Accessibility describes the degree to which an environment, service, or product allows access by as many people as possible, in particular, people with disability.

acquired disability. A disability acquired after the acquisition of language and after early socialization.

activities of daily living (ADLs). Those tasks that a person performs during a typical day (grooming, bathing, getting into and out of bed or a chair, etc.). Instrumental activities of daily living (IADLs) include doing household chores, doing necessary business, shopping, and getting around for other purposes.

advocacy services. Service provided to assist individuals with disability and their family members, guardians, advocates, and authorized representatives in accessing assistive technology devices and assistive technology services (Assistive Technology [AT] Act of 1998).

appropriate technology*. Assistive technology that meets people's needs; uses local skills, tools, and materials; and is simple, effective, affordable, and acceptable to its users.

Asperger syndrome. A neurobiological disorder characterized by normal intelligence and language development but autistic-like behaviors and marked deficiencies in social and communication skills.

assistive technology
> *Device:* Initially defined in the Technology-Related Assistance for Individuals with Disabilities Act of 1988 (P.L. 100–407): "any item, piece of equipment, or product system, whether acquired commercially off the shelf, modified, or customized, that is used to increase, maintain, or improve functional capabilities

---

*World Health Organization (WHO), 2011.

329

of individuals with disabilities." Such devices can be low tech (mechanical) or high tech (electromechanical or computerized), specialized or everyday technologies, and may compensate for sensory and functional losses by providing the means to move (e.g., wheelchairs, lifts), speak (e.g., communication devices), read (e.g., screen readers on computers for persons who are blind), hear (e.g., vibrotactile aids), or manage self-care tasks (e.g., automatic feeders, environmental control systems).

Service: Initially defined in the Technology-Related Assistance for Individuals with Disabilities Act of 1988 (P.L. 100–407): "any service that directly assists an individual with a disability in the selection, acquisition, or use of an assistive technology device."

Please see The Family Center on Technology and Disability (FCTD) *AT Fact Sheet Series: Assistive Technology Glossary* at http://www.fctd.info/show/glossary.

autism spectrum disorder. A developmental disability characterized by severe and pervasive impairment in thinking, feeling, language, and the ability to relate to others.

brain injury. Results from genetics, injury, and the effects of aging, as indicated in the subtitle of this book. It affects individuals from birth (intellectual disability, cerebral palsy, autism, Asperger syndrome, etc.), can be an outcome of disease and injury (stroke, traumatic brain injury, etc.), and can occur as a result of aging (dementia and Alzheimer's disease). It differs by type, cause, and level (mild, moderate, and severe). The chart that follows shows the types of brain injuries discussed in this book with examples of individuals who have been affected by them.

INFANCY	CHILDHOOD	OLDER AGE	ANY AGE
Intellectual disability including Down syndrome *Theresa* (Chapter 2)	Learning disability *Louisa* (Chapter 6)	Dementia, including Alzheimer's disease *Marjorie* (Chapter 1) *James* (Chapter 6)	Traumatic and acquired brain injury *Delmar* (Chapter 3)
Cerebral palsy *Maggie* (Chapter 2)	Asperger syndrome *Ryan* (Chapter 3)	Stroke *Marjorie* (Chapter 1)	Mental, emotional, and behavioral disabilities *Louisa* (Chapter 6)

The study and treatment of brain injury has its own specialized vocabulary. The following are examples of websites with glossaries:

http://www.biausa.org/
http://www.braininjury101.org/details/glossary
http://www.braininjurynetwork.org/
http://www.headinjury.com/tbiglossary.htm

The following government agencies have very relevant and useful websites:

Centers for Disease Control and Prevention: http://www.cdc.gov/
National Institute of Neurological Disorders and Stroke (NINDS), National Institutes of Health: http://www.ninds.nih.gov/

Centers for Medicare and Medicaid Services (CMS). A U.S. government agency that serves Medicare and Medicaid recipients by providing resources, outreach, and low-cost health insurance.

cognitive disability. Impairments in everyday capabilities and functioning of people with brain disorders that may involve any of the following: memory formation or retrieval, attention and concentration, reading and comprehension, learning, information processing, and problem solving.

cognitive support technology. A category of assistive technology that focuses on the needs of individuals with cognitive disability.

communication devices
> *AAC:* Augmentative and alternative communication devices ("aug comm devices"): technologies and techniques. Methods of communicating that supplement or replace speech and handwriting—for example, facial expressions, symbols, pictures, gestures, and signing. AAC devices range from word boards to computer-based devices with voice output.

developmental disability (DD). A chronic disability, either mental or physical, that manifests by age 22, is perpetuated throughout the life span, poses limitations in areas of basic functioning, and may require lifelong care.

Diagnostic and Statistical Manual of Mental Disorders, Fourth Edition, Text Revision (DSM-IV-TR). A manual published by the American Psychiatric Association that provides diagnostic criteria for the most common mental disorders. It also describes the disorder and includes information on diagnosis, treatment, and research findings.

durable medical equipment (DME). As defined in the Medicare statute, DME is an equipment that is expected to last for a substantial time, is subject to repeated use and not consumed by this use, is not needed by an individual in absence of a medical need, and is appropriate for use in the home.

early intervention*. Involves strategies that aim to intervene early in the life of a problem and provide individually tailored solutions. It typically focuses on populations at a higher risk for developing problems, or on families who are experiencing problems that have not yet become well established or entrenched.

education—inclusive*. Education that is based on the right of all learners to a quality education that meets basic learning needs and enriches lives. Focusing particularly on vulnerable and marginalized groups, it seeks to develop the full potential of every individual.

education—special*. Includes children with other needs—for example, through disadvantages resulting from gender, ethnicity, poverty, learning difficulties, or disability—related to their difficulty to learn or access education compared with other children of the same age. In high-income countries, this category can also include children identified as "gifted and talented." Also referred to as *special needs education* and *special education needs*.

environmental control system (ECS) or electronic aids to daily living (EADL). Activates various household appliances such as a coffee maker, TV, radio, lights, automatic dialing telephones, and intercoms through various alternative access methods such as switch or voice access.

frail older adult*. Older persons (usually older than 75 years old) who have a health condition that may interfere with the ability to independently perform ADLs.

incidence. The number of new cases during a specified period versus prevalence, which includes both new and old cases of an event, disease, or disability in a given population and time.

inclusive society*. One that freely accommodates any person with a disability without restrictions or limitations.

independent living. A philosophy advocating self-directed choice, self-determination, equal opportunities, and the ability to exercise as many free choices as possible.

individual education plan (IEP). A plan that identifies a student's specific learning expectations and outlines how the school will address these expectations through appropriate special education programs and services, including support from assistive and cognitive support technologies.

individualized plan for employment (IPE). A plan that identifies the job and lists the steps and services necessary to achieve employment, including support from assistive and cognitive support technologies.

Individuals with Disabilities and Education Act (IDEA). A U.S. law established to improve the quality of life for infants, toddlers, children, and youth with disability in achieving an appropriate education.

information technology. Information technology includes any product used to acquire, store, manipulate, or transmit information such as computers, multimedia, telecommunications, copy machines, and the Internet.

intellectual impairment*. A state of arrested or incomplete development of mind, which means that the person can have difficulties understanding, learning, and remembering new things and in applying that learning to new situations. Also known as intellectual disability, learning disability, learning difficulties, and formerly as mental retardation or mental handicap.

International Classification of Functioning, Disability and Health (ICF)*. The classification that provides a unified and standard language and framework for the description of health and health-related states. *ICF* is part of the "family" of international classifications developed by the WHO.

> *Activity*
> In the *ICF*, the execution of a task or action by an individual. It represents the individual perspective of functioning.
>
> *Activity limitations*
> In the *ICF*, difficulties an individual may have in executing activities. An activity limitation may range from a slight to a severe deviation in terms of quality or quantity in executing the activity in a manner or to the extent that is expected of people without the health condition.
>
> *Barriers*
> Factors in a person's environment that, through their absence or presence, limit functioning and create disability—for example, inaccessible physical environments, a lack of appropriate assistive technology, and negative attitudes toward disability.

Body functions

In the *ICF*, the physiological functions of body systems. *Body* refers to the human organism as a whole and this includes the brain. The *ICF* classifies body functions under several areas, including mental functions, sensory functions and pain, voice and speech functions, and neuromusculoskeletal and movement-related functions.

Body structures

In the *ICF*, the structural or anatomical parts of the body such as organs, limbs, and their components classified according to body systems.

Capacity

A construct within the *ICF* that indicates the highest probable level of functioning that a person may achieve, measured in a uniform or standard environment, and reflects the environmentally adjusted ability of the individual.

Contextual factors

Factors that together constitute the complete context of an individual's life and in particular the background against which health states are classified in the *ICF*. There are two components of contextual factors: environmental factors and personal factors.

Disability

In the *ICF*, an umbrella term for impairments, activity limitations, and participation restrictions denoting the negative aspects of the interaction between an individual (with a health condition) and that individual's contextual factors (environmental and personal factors).

Enabling environments

Environments that support participation by removing barriers and providing enablers.

Environmental factors

A component of contextual factors within the *ICF*, referring to the physical, social, and attitudinal environment in which people live and conduct their lives—for example, products and technology; the natural environment; support and relationships; attitudes; and services, systems, and policies.

Facilitators

Factors in a person's environment that, through their absence or presence, improve functioning and reduce disability—for example, an accessible environment, available assistive technology, inclusive attitudes, and legislation. Facilitators can prevent impairments or activity limitations from becoming participation restrictions because the actual performance of an action is enhanced, despite the person's problem with capacity.

Functioning
An umbrella term in the *ICF* for body functions, body structures, activities, and participation. It denotes the positive aspects of the interaction between an individual (with a health condition) and that individual's contextual factors (environmental and personal factors).

Health
A state of well-being, achieved through the interaction of an individual's physical, mental, emotional, and social states.

Health conditions
In the *ICF*, an umbrella term for disease (acute or chronic), disorder, injury, or trauma. A health condition may also include other circumstances such as pregnancy, ageing, stress, congenital anomaly, or genetic predisposition.

Impairment
In the ICF, loss or abnormality in body structure or physiological function (including mental functions), where abnormality means significant variation from established statistical norms.

Participation
In the *ICF*, a person's involvement in a life situation, representing the societal perspective of functioning.

Participation restrictions are problems an individual may experience in involvement in life situations.

Performance
A construct within the *ICF* that describes what individuals do in their current environment, including their involvement in life situations. The current environment is described using environmental factors.

Personal factors
A component of contextual factors within the *ICF* that relate to the individual—for example, age, gender, social status, and life experiences.

Quality of life/Subjective well-being
An individual's perception of their position in life in the context of the culture and value systems in which they live, and in relation to their goals, expectations, standards, and concerns. It is a broad-ranging concept, incorporating in a complex way the person's physical health, psychological state, level of independence, social relationships, personal beliefs, and relationship to environmental factors that affect them.

learning disability—specific*. Impairments in information processing resulting in difficulties in listening, reasoning, speaking, reading, writing, spelling, or doing mathematical calculations—for example, dyslexia.

mental health condition*. A health condition characterized by alterations in thinking, mood, or behavior associated with distress or interference with personal functions. Also known as mental illness, mental disorders, or psychosocial disability.

orthotic devices. Used to provide support for a weak part of the body (e.g., braces).

personal assistance. Care provided by individuals to help persons with disabilities with ADL and other activities. May be provided by family members, paid individuals, and so forth.

prevalence. All the new and old cases of an event, disease, or disability in a given population and time versus incidence, which is the number of new cases during a specified period.

prosthetic devices. Replaces or substitutes a part of the body (such as arms and legs).

reasonable accommodation*. Necessary and appropriate modification and adjustment not imposing a disproportionate or undue burden, where needed in a particular case, to ensure that persons with disability enjoy or exercise, on an equal basis with others, all human rights and fundamental freedoms.

rehabilitation. The working definition of "rehabilitation" used by most professionals in the field emphasizes the restoration of a person's physical, sensory, mental, emotional, social, vocational, and recreational capacities so the person can be as autonomous as possible and will be able to pursue an independent noninstitutional lifestyle.

rehabilitation disciplines as defined by WHO*

Occupational therapy
Promoting health and well-being through occupation. The primary goal of occupational therapy is to enable people to participate in the activities of everyday life. Occupational therapists achieve this outcome by enabling people to do things that will enhance their ability to participate or by modifying the environment to better support participation.

Physical and rehabilitation medicine doctors
Carry out services to diagnose health conditions, assess functioning, and prescribe medical and technological interventions that treat health conditions and optimize functional capacity. Also known as *physiatrists*.

Physical therapy/Physiotherapy
Provides services to individuals to develop, maintain, and maximize movement, potential, and functional ability throughout the life span.

Psychologist, neuropsychologist, rehabilitation psychologist
A professional specializing in diagnosing and treating diseases of the brain, emotional disturbance, and behavior problems, more often through therapy than medication.

Social worker
Professional social workers restore or enhance the capacity of individuals or groups to function well in society, and help society accommodate their needs.

Speech and language therapist
Aims to restore people's capacity to communicate effectively and to swallow safely and efficiently.

risk factor*. A risk factor is an attribute or exposure that is causally associated with an increased probability of a disease or injury.

schools—inclusive*. Children with disability attend regular classes with age-appropriate peers, learn the curriculum to the extent feasible, and are provided with additional resources and support depending on need.

schools—integrated*. Schools that provide separate classes and additional resources for children with disability, which are attached to mainstream schools.

sheltered employment*. Employment in an enterprise established specifically for the employment of persons with disability, but which may also employ nondisabled people.

state AT projects. By law, each state and territory in the United States receives federal monies to fund an Assistive Technology Act Project (ATAP). These projects provide services to persons with disability for their entire life span, as well as to their families or guardians, service providers, and agencies and other entities that are involved in providing services such as education and employment to persons with disability. To find your state's AT project, please visit the Association of Assistive Technology Act Programs website at http://www.ataporg.org/atap/

supported employment*. Supported job placements providing the opportunity for integration in the mainstream workforce.

universal design. Under the AT Act of 1998, *universal design* means a concept or philosophy for designing and delivering products and services that are usable by people with the widest possible range of functional capabilities. Examples of universally designed environments include buildings with ramps, curb cuts, and automatic doors. The WHO (2011) defines universal design as the design of products, environments, programs, and services to be usable by all people to the greatest extent possible, without the need for adaptation or specialized design.

vocational rehabilitation. This refers to programs conducted by state vocational rehabilitation agencies operating under the Rehabilitation Act of 1973 (and as reauthorized) to provide or arrange for a wide array of training, educational, medical, and other services individualized to the needs of persons with disability. The services are intended to help these persons acquire, reacquire, or maintain gainful employment. Most of the funding is provided by the federal government. Public Law 102–569, the *Rehabilitation Act Amendments of 1992*, increased access to assistive technology.

word prediction programs. Word prediction programs enable the user to select a desired word from an on-screen list located in the prediction window. This list, generated by the computer, predicts words from the first one or two letters typed by the user. The word may then be selected from the list and inserted into the text by typing a number, clicking the mouse, or scanning with a switch.

Appendix B

EXAMPLES OF ASSISTIVE TECHNOLOGY (AT) AND COGNITIVE SUPPORT TECHNOLOGY (CST) RESOURCES

A representative, but not comprehensive, sample of key resources for obtaining further information.

United States Organizations Focused on AT and CST

Alliance for Technology Access
1119 Old Humboldt Road
Jackson, TN 38305
Toll Free: 1 (800) 914-3017
Voice: (731) 554-5282
Fax: (731) 554-5283
TTY: (731) 554-5284
http://www.ataccess.org

Assistive Technology Industry Association (ATIA)
ATIA Headquarters
401 North Michigan Avenue
Chicago, IL 60611-4267
Toll-Free: 877-OUR-ATIA (687-2842)
Voice: 312-321-5172
Fax: 312-673-6659
E-mail: info@ATIA.org
http://www.atia.org

Rehabilitation Engineering and Assistive Technology Society of
North America (RESNA)
1700 N. Moore Street, Suite 1540
Arlington, VA 22209-1903
Phone: (703)- 524-6686
Fax: (703)-524-6630
TTY: (703)-524-6639
http://www.resna.org

Websites Relevant to Brain Injury, AT, and CST

AbleData
This site is a national database of information on thousands of products that are available for people with disability.
http://www.abledata.com

Acquired Brain Injury: A Web Portal for and by Brain Injury Survivors
Developed in collaboration with survivors of acquired brain injury (ABI),
this site provides information and resources for other survivors of ABI and
their families.
http://www.acquiredbraininjury.com

Alliance for Technology Access
A national network of community-based resource organizations to provide information and support to increase the access and use of assistive technology.
http://www.ataccess.org

Assistivetech.net
This National Assistive Technology Internet site provides up-to-date, thorough information on assistive technology devices and services, adaptive environments, and community resources. Users can search for AT devices by function or activity, keyword, vendor, or product type.
http://www.assistivetech.net

Assistive Technology Data Collection Project: An InfoUse Site
Provides links to AT-related government agencies, AT-related organizations, disability statistics agencies/organizations, and other disability-related organizations.
http://www.infouse.com/atdata/links.html

Brain Injury Association of America
Promotes awareness, understanding, and prevention of brain injury through education, advocacy, research grants, and community support services. State association locator, fact sheets (e.g., accessibility checklist for people with cognitive disability: What to look for when you're shopping for a cell phone or personal digital assistant [PDA]), marketplace, and other features.
http://www.biausa.org

Brain Injury Network (BIN)
The first international and U.S. national collective advocacy nonprofit organization operated for and by survivors of ABI.
http://www.braininjurynetwork.org

BrainLine.org
A WETA website funded by the Defense and Veterans Brain Injury Center.
http://www.brainline.org

Coleman Institute for Cognitive Disabilities
Established in 2001 to catalyze and integrate advances in science, engineering, and technology to promote the quality of life and independent living of people with cognitive disability.
http://www.colemaninstitute.org/index.php

Department of Defense Computer/Electronic Accommodations
Program (CAP)
Provides free assistive technology for federal employees with disability and wounded service members. CAP services are available to individuals with visual, hearing, dexterity, communication, and cognitive issues.
http://www.tricare.mil/cap

Disabilities, Opportunities, Internetworking, and Technology (DO-IT)
DO-IT provides resources on education, technology, accessibility, funding, and more.
http://www.washington.edu/doit

Disability.gov
This site organizes information and issues concerning disability into nine categories, listed as color-coded tabs at the top of every page. Simply select the tab of your desired category and links related to that topic will appear on the left.
http://www.disability.gov

Disabled Peoples' International
Searchable by country and very extensive.
http://www.dpi.org

Eldercare Locator Information on Assistive Technology Prepared Through the U.S. Administration on Aging
http://www.eldercare.gov/ELDERCARE.NET/Public/Resources/Factsheets/Assistive_Technology.aspx

Another website on assistive technology sponsored by the U.S. Administration on Aging is http://www.aoa.gov/AoAroot/Press_Room/Products_Materials/fact/pdf/Assistive_Technology.pdf

Equal Access to Software and Information (EASI)
EASI provides workshops, distance learning, webcasts, and other training on information technology. EASI's mission is to serve as a resource to the education community by providing information and guidance in the area of access-to-information technologies by individuals with disability.
http://easi.cc

European Assistive Technology Information Network
EASTIN is a network of databases from numerous European Union countries on assistive technology. It includes information on almost 70.000 assistive technology products available on the European market and over 5.000 manufacturers or suppliers; it also includes fact sheets and suggestions on assistive solutions for daily living problems.
http://www.eastin.info

The Family Center on Technology and Disability (FCTD)
A national center that offers free information resources on the subject of assistive technology for families, professionals, organizations, and programs that work with individuals with disability. Provides hundreds of assistive and instructional technology resource reviews that have been identified, reviewed, and annotated, as well as fact sheets (such as AT legislation), an AT glossary, AT resources CD, family information guide to assistive technology and transition planning, additional family guides, and newsletters. Supported by the Department of Education's Office of Special Education.
http://www.fctd.info

The International Brain Injury Association (IBIA)
IBIA is dedicated to the development and support of multidisciplinary medical and clinical professionals, advocates, policy makers, consumers and others who work to improve outcomes and opportunities for persons with brain injury. The IBIA strives to provide international leadership for creative solutions to the issues associated with brain injury.
http://www.internationalbrain.org

National Assistive Technology Advocacy Project
Sponsored by the Neighborhood Legal Services, provides an excellent clearinghouse of information on AT advocacy.
http://www.nls.org/natmain.htm

National Center for the Dissemination of Disability Research (NCDDR)
Disseminates information about disability research, including assistive technology.
http://www.ncddr.org

National Clearinghouse of Rehabilitation Training Materials
Funded by the Rehabilitation Services Administration, this site provides an extensive array of disability-related training resources.
https://ncrtm.org/moodle

National Library of Medicine
Listing of links related to assistive technology.
http://www.nlm.nih.gov/medlineplus/assistivedevices.html

National Rehabilitation Information Center
A library and information center on disability and rehabilitation.
http://www.naric.com

Rehabilitation Engineering Research Center for the Advancement of Cognitive Technologies (RERC-ACT)
Works to improve the lives of people with cognitive disability through the development and testing of cognitive support technologies.
http://www.rerc-act.org

Traveling With Assistive Devices and Mobility Aids
U.S. Transportation Security Administration.
http://www.tsa.gov/travelers/airtravel/specialneeds/editorial_1370.shtm

Accessibility Checklists for People With Cognitive Disability

Americans With Disabilities Act Accessibility Guidelines (ADAAG) Checklist for Buildings and Facilities
http://www.access-board.gov/adaag/checklist/a16.html

Information Technology in Education Accessibility Checklist
http://www.washington.edu/accessit/it-checklist

Instructional Materials Accessibility Checklist
For instructors preparing course materials on paper or on online.
http://www.csus.edu/accessibility/checklist.html

Software Accessibility Checklist
A tool for evaluating the extent to which software applications are accessible to most people with disability. This document is based on the U.S. Department of Education's "Requirements for Accessible Software Design."
http://www.justice.gov/crt/508/archive/oldsoftware.html

Web Content Accessibility Guidelines 1.0
http://www.w3.org/TR/1999/WAI-WEBCONTENT-19990505/

EXAMPLES OF RELEVANT COGNITIVE SUPPORT TECHNOLOGY MANUFACTURERS AND VENDORS

AbleLink Technologies
618 North Nevada
Colorado Springs, CO 80903
(719) 592-0347, fax: (719) 592-0348
info@ablelinktech.com
http://www.ablelinktech.com

AbleLink Technologies specializes in making technology easy to use. They take everyday technologies—like computers, the internet/email, PDA's and cellphones—and simplify the user interface so that it is intelligible and straightforward. Using the same design principles, they apply them to areas of need for people struggling with memory, organization and confusion.

AbleNet
2625 Patton Road
Roseville, MN 55113
(800) 322-0956, fax: (651) 294-2259
customerservice@ablenetinc.com
http://www.ablenetinc.com

AbleNet has designed practical products and creative solutions for individuals with disabilities for 25 years. They offer a complete line of assistive technology products, including communication aids, switches, environmental control, computer access, software, data management solutions and mounting devices. AbleNet also offers research-based special education curricula that meet state and federal mandates.

Attainment Co., Inc.
PO Box 930160
Verona, WI 53593
(800) 327-4269, fax: (800) 942-3865
info@attainmentcompany.com
http://www.attainmentcompany.com

Specializes in resources created for individuals with developmental, cognitive and communicative needs to help foster understanding, learning, and independence, plus encourages more active participation in classrooms, homes and communities. Products include Research Based Curriculum, Communication, Language Development, Literacy, Life Skills, Social Skills, Work/Vocational Skills, Mental Fitness, Dementia Care and more.

Cogent Systems, Inc.
Ft. Lauderdale, Florida
(888) 679-6378
info@cosys.us
http://www.cosys.us

This company is focused on the development and implementation of practical assistive technology that enables individuals with cognitive disabilities to achieve greater independence and self-sufficiency in all aspects of life. The company's currently released product is the ISAAC™ system, a small, fully individualized, battery powered and wearable cognitive prosthetic assistive technology system. Being fully individualized and very easy to use, ISAAC is appropriate for many individuals with cognitive disabilities such as developmental disabilities, traumatic brain injuries, and acquired brain injuries (including many stroke survivors and individuals with Alzheimer's disease).

Cognitopia Software
99 West 10th Ave., Ste. 397
Eugene, OR 97401
(541) 343-3384, fax: (541) 343-3384
tkeating@cognitopia.com
http://www.cognitopia.com

Cognitopia® Software features Picture Planner™, a visual calendaring application that provides a simple way to schedule and remember activities. Potential users include: children; individuals with autism, intellectual disabilities, or TBI; elders; or anyone with limited reading and writing proficiency. Easily create activity schedules using pictures with text to speech prompts. Schedules are printable and exportable to handheld devices. Compatible with Mac OS X, Windows XP and Vista.

Don Johnston Incorporated
26799 W. Commerce
Volo, IL 60073
(847) 740-0749, fax: (847) 740-7326
rcostion@donjohnston.com
http://www.donjohnston.com

Don Johnston empowers educators with supplemental instruction and intervention solutions to help the widest range of students build core literacy skills. Don Johnston's award-winning products build in physical accessibility, integrate validated research, capitalize on new discoveries in brain science, align to standards and are presented in multiple medias through engaging instructional models.

EnableMart
5353 S 960 East, Suite 200
Salt Lake City, UT 84117
(888) 640-1999, fax: (866) 487-0410
sales@enablemart.com
http://www.enablemart.com

EnableMart is a worldwide leader in assistive technology distribution. With customers in all 50 states and over 45 foreign countries, EnableMart provides over 3,000 assistive technology and assistive living devices from over 200 manufacturers. EnableMart's market leadership is the direct result of the goal to become an all inclusive source for assistive technology and assistive living devices.

Enabling Devices
50 Broadway
Hawthorne, NY 10532
(914) 747-3070, (800) 832-8697, fax: (914) 747-3480
http://www.enablingdevices.com

Founded in 1974 and originally known as Toys for Special Children, the company manufactures communicators, adapted toys, switches, adapted media, and sensory devices.

Ginger Software, Inc.
405 Waltham Street, #371
Lexington, MA 02421
(401) 243-5975, fax: (888) 658-6618
Josephm@gingersoftware.com
http://www.gingersoftware.com

Ginger Software is dedicated to empowering children and adults to write error-free texts independently. Ginger Software's revolutionary text correction tool uses context to automatically correct spelling mistakes, grammar errors and misused words. In a single click, whole sentences are corrected without changing the author's intent. Ginger tracks users' mistakes and progress, enabling educators to monitor students and personalize instruction in a positive writing environment.

Inclusive TLC Special Needs
2206 Legacy Oak Dr
Waxhaw, NC 28173
(704) 243-3622, fax: (704) 243-6323
info@inclusiveTLC.com
http://www.inclusivetlc.com

Inclusive TLC Special Needs aim to include all learners and enable them to take advantage of computer based education. Specializes in special needs software, switches and computer access devices, as well as simple communication aids and assistive technology for learners with a physical disability, sensory impairment or severe learning disability.

Laureate Learning Systems, Inc.
110 East Spring St.
Winooski, VT 05404
(802) 655-4755, fax: (802) 655-4757
info@laureatelearning.com
http://www.laureatelearning.com

For over 25 years, professionals and parents have relied on Laureate software to teach critical language, cognitive, and reading skills. Offers award-winning, research-based programs for children and adults with Autism, Developmental Disabilities, Language-Learning Disabilities, Aphasia, and TBI. Laureate software ensures success and makes learning a fun and rewarding experience.

Madentec Limited
4664-99 St. NW
Edmonton, AB T6E5H5
(780) 450-8926, fax: (780) 988-6182
nilam@madentec.com
http://www.madentec.com

Madentec Limited has been a leading supplier of assistive technology for people with physical disabilities for the past 20 years. Products include computer access or communication device 100% hands-free through use of Tracker products as well as an alternate keyboard or scanning access through the Discover product line. These products are ideally suited to people with severe physical disabilities, including: quadriplegia, cerebral palsy, multiple sclerosis, ALS and muscular dystrophy.

Monarch Teaching Technologies
20600 Chagrin Blvd, Suite 703
Shaker Heights, OH 44122
Sales: (800) 593-1934
Support: (800) 705-1382
steelea@bellefairejcb.org
http://www.monarchtt.com

MTT presents VizZle™. Web-based autism/special education software for quick and easy customized interactive visual lessons. Supports any IEP goal.

N2Y Inc
P.O. Box 550
Huron, OH 44839
(419) 433-9800, fax: (419) 433-9810
chrissy@news-2-you.com
http://www.n2yinc.com

N2Y, Inc. serves the special education community with a variety of products. News-2-You™ is an Internet newspaper published weekly in four levels.

Acquire a complete, standards-based special education curriculum with Unique Learning System™. There is a dynamic symbol set, SymbolStix©.

Perkins Products
175 North Beacon Street
Watertown, MA 02472
(617) 972-7308, fax: (617) 926-2027
perkinsproducts@perkins.org
http://www.perkinsproducts.org

Perkins Products provides low and high tech solutions for people with blindness, low vision, and learning disability around the world. From the Perkins Brailler to the Seika refreshable Braille display, and from hand held magnifiers to Dragon NaturallySpeaking, we make information access part of every person's daily life.

PointScribe
3595 East Fountain, E-2
Colorado Springs, CO 80910
(719) 685-7883, fax: (719) 685-7885
gmrichards@ultrathera.com
http://www.pointscribe.com

PointScribe teaches students of all abilities to handwrite. Interactive auditory, visual, and tactile lessons combine to create a highly motivational and successful method for teaching handwriting. Each lesson is reinforced with multi-sensory stimulation as the student hears the name of the shape, sees the shape, and is guided through writing each stroke of the shape. PointScribe captures, analyzes, and reports data essential for use in IEPs, progress reports, and true evidence-based teaching.

Prentke Romich Company
1022 Heyl Road
Wooster, OH 44691
(800) 262-1984, fax: (330) 263-4829
info@prentrom.com
http://www.prentrom.com

Has the new AAC Language Lab, a practical, easy-to-use resource for teaching language with AAC devices and Unity. Products include ECO2, ECOpoint, Vantage Lite and SpringBoard Lite.

Learning Ally (formerly Recording for the Blind and Dyslexic)
20 Roszel Road
Princeton, NJ 08540
(800) 221-4792, fax: (609) 987-8116
http://www.learningally.org

For 60 years, Recording for the Blind & Dyslexic® (RFB&D®), has been the leading producer of accessible audio textbooks for students with learning and print disabilities. For more information visit www.rfbd.org.

Rehabtool.com
P.O. Box 572190
Houston, Texas 77257
(281) 531-6106, Fax (281) 531-6406
http://www.rehabtool.com/at.html

Specializes in computer adaptations and builds custom software solutions for children and adults with disabilities. Our flagship product *Vocalize* is an innovative speech assistant that we developed with speech impaired persons to enable them to speak in a friendly human voice using standard computer equipment. We also offer free product searches.

RJ Cooper and Associates, Inc.
27601 Forbes Rd. #39
Laguna Niguel, CA 92677
(800) 752-6673, fax: (949) 582-3169
rjc@rjcooper.com
http://www.rjcooper.com

Considered a pioneer in the field of AT, RJ Cooper has been creating unique software, hardware, and electronic aids for special needs since 1983.

SAJE Technology
765 Dixon Ct.
Hoffman Estates, IL 60192
(847) 756-7603, fax: (847) 496-4515
sales@saje-tech.com
http://www.saje-tech.com

SAJE Technology is the premier manufacturer of adapted telephone products and environmental control units, promoting independence and accessibility for people facing aging or disability.

Saltillo Corporation
2143 Township Road #112
Millersburg, OH 44654
(800) 382-8622, fax: (330) 674-6726
aac@saltillo.com
http://www.saltillo.com

Saltillo Corporations manufactures and distributes augmentative communication (AAC) devices, specializing in portable communication products for ambulatory individuals. Saltillo's products come with pre-stored vocabulary pages for individuals with a wide variety of communication needs. The ChatPC and ALT-Chat products provide powerful, dynamic screen, communication capabilities in a small, portable package. The *SpeakOut* is a portable typing device with a double text display.

Slater Software, Inc.
351 Badger Circle
Guffey, CO 80820
(719) 479-2255, fax: (719) 479-2254
info@slatersoftware.com
http://www.slatersoftware.com

Slater Software, Inc., the leader in Picture-Assisted Literacy™ offers a variety of tools that promote literacy learning. The two highlighted software programs, Picture It and PixWriter™, effectively engage new and struggling readers and writers. Both software programs have been recently upgraded and utilize over 9,000 Literacy Support Pictures™ paired with words and voice output. Slater also offers ready-to-use Curriculum resources including 8 Simply Science™ Units and the Read and Tell™ Series.

Texthelp Systems
600 Unicorn Park Drive
Woburn, MA 01801
(888) 248-0652, fax: (866) 248-0652
u.s.info@texthelp.com
http://www.texthelp.com

Texthelp provides award-winning literacy software solutions. Read&Write GOLD's customizable toolbar integrates with mainstream applications to support individuals with reading and writing difficulties, learning disabilities or English Language Learners. Fluency Tutor, Texthelp's new offering, is an innovative online solution for developing and measuring oral reading fluency. Both products combine robust feature sets and options for school and home use to ensure that all students succeed.

Tobii ATI
333 Elm Street
Dedham, MA 02026
(781) 461-8200, fax: (781) 461-8213
customercare@tobiiati.com
http://www.tobiiati.com

AAC devices to give individuals with communication disabilities a voice and a way to live more fulfilled, integrated and independent lives.

Appendix C

FINDING AND FUNDING ASSISTIVE AND COGNITIVE SUPPORT TECHNOLOGIES

Finding and then financing technologies can be challenging for many individuals and families.

Finding: Examples of Resources for Finding Assistive Technology and Cognitive Support Technology Products

AbleData
http://AbleData.com

AgrAbility Assistive Technologies Database (U.S. Department of Agriculture)
http://fyi.uwex.edu/assistivetech

assistivetech.net National Public Website on Assistive Technology
Center for Assistive Technology and Environmental Access, Georgia Institute of Technology College of Architecture
http://assistivetech.net

Center for Assistive Technology & Environmental Access
http://assistivetech.net/search/products_for_disability.php

European Assistive Technology Information Network (EASTIN)
http://www.eastin.eu

EASTIN's member SIVA portal (Italy) is mapped to the ISO 9999:2011
http://www.portale.siva.it

Job Accommodation Network

Job Accommodation Network (JAN) is a free consulting service designed to increase the employability of people with disability by providing individualized worksite accommodation ideas, technical assistance regarding the Americans with Disability Act (ADA), and educating callers about self-employment options. JAN is a service of the Office of Disability Employment Policy, U.S. Department of Labor.
http://www.jan.wvu.edu

Funding

Once the appropriate technology has been identified through the *support selection process* and *Matching Person and Technology (MPT) assessments,* then consumers, families, and professionals can begin to identify funding sources and eligibility requirements. Because of the many types of funding sources available, and explicit qualification requirements, the following are general guidelines only.
http://matchingpersonandtechnology.com

Define and then document the individual's needs. The MPT forms will help with this step and show that a range of devices were compared. Then fill in the place on the form with information about the most appropriate device type, style, cost, and vendor. Be sure to note the results of the outcomes of product trials.

Determine if the device can be borrowed from a loan closet or within the community. Also, check to see if it can be covered by insurance. Many states have assistive technology (AT) recycling programs typically connected through the state AT Act projects. Contact:

National Assistive Technology Technical Assistance Partnership
1700 North Moore Street, Suite 1540
Arlington, VA 22209-1903
Phone: 703/524-6686
Fax: 703/524-6630
TTY: 703/524-6639
E-mail: resnaTA@resna.org
http://www.resnaprojects.org/nattap

Consider renting or leasing. It is sometimes possible to work directly with an individual vendor to arrange a loan or rent/lease a product. Many vendors will also help in researching potential funding.

For children, the primary funding options are the public school and Medicaid.

For adults of working age who need support to work, Vocational Rehabilitation Services should be contacted.

Other Resources

Assistive Technology Funding
Transcript of a conference held on October 21 to November 27, 2002
http://www.fctd.info/webboard/files/Funding.pdf

Living and Working With Disabilities: Tax Benefits and Credits (Internal Revenue Service)
http://www.irs.gov/pub/irs-pdf/p3966.pdf

Unmet Needs: Statistics on the Lack of Access to Assistive Devices, Technologies, and Related Services
http://www.itemcoalition.org/press/unmet.html

What Should Be in a Letter of Medical Necessity?
http://www.resnaprojects.org/nattap/goals/other/healthcare/mednec.html
Additionally, there are organizations worldwide that focus on serving specific populations of individuals such as those with the brain injuries discussed throughout this book (Down syndrome, Alzheimer's disease, Asperger syndrome, etc.). These organizations can be located by using a search engine. Many list resources helpful to finding and funding AT and cognitive support technology (CST).

Resources for Caregivers

Johns Hopkins Medicine Special Reports
Rabins, P. V., & Morrison, A. S. (2010). *Caring for a loved one with Alzheimer's disease: A guide for the home caregiver*. Baltimore, MD: Johns Hopkins Medicine Special Reports. Retrieved from http://www.johnshopkinshealthalerts. com/special_reports/memory_reports/HomeCaregiver_landing.html
This 134-page report discusses:

- When It's Time to Take Away the Car Keys
- Modifying the Home for People With Dementia
- Personal Care for the Dementia Patient

- Dealing with Alzheimer's Troubling Behavior Problems—Aggression, Agitation, Shouting, and Hallucinations
- Caregiving From Afar
- When Caring Takes Its Toll on the Dementia Caregiver
- Deciding to Move a Loved One into Residential Care includes
  - How do you know when the time is right?
  - What are your options?
  - What options exist to cover the cost of nursing home care?
  - What are the key questions you should ask when choosing a nursing home?

National Alliance for Caregiving
A nonprofit coalition of national organizations focusing on issues of family caregiving for children with special health care needs, veterans, and geriatric individuals.
http://www.caregiving.org

National Center on Caregiving Family Caregiver Alliance
Works to advance the development of high-quality, cost-effective policies and programs for caregivers in every state in the country. Uniting research, public policy, and services, the NCC serves as a central source of information on caregiving and long-term care issues for policy makers, service providers, media, funders, and family caregivers throughout the country.
http://www.caregiver.org

National Institute on Aging
Caring for a person with Alzheimer's disease: Your easy-to-use guide
http://www.nia.nih.gov/Alzheimers/Publications/caregiverguide.htm

Rosalynn Carter Institute for Caregiving at Georgia Southwestern State University in Americus, Georgia
This website includes caregiver resources and the Caregiver Intervention Database that gives detailed information on interventions that have been found to positively impact caregivers.
http://www.rosalynncarter.org

Professional Resources on Care Provision

Family Caregiver Briefcase
The American Psychological Association convened a task force in 2010 and charged them with the development of a user-friendly, online *Family*

Caregiver Briefcase to help psychologists and other health professionals assist family caregivers through individual and organizational practice, research, teaching, and community service. Information includes:

Facts about family caregiving
Common caregiving problems
How to identify and reach caregivers
Assessment tools and effective interventions
Educating and teaching about caregiving
Advocating for family caregivers
Resources for diverse populations and age groups

Available online:
http://www.apa.org/pi/about/publications/caregivers/index.aspx

Working With People With Traumatic Brain Injury

The Brain Injury Rehabilitation Unit, Liverpool Hospital, and Brain Injury Rehabilitation Directorate (BIRD), New South Wales Agency for Clinical Innovation, Sydney, Australia developed *Working With People With Traumatic Brain Injury*. Staff self-study modules include:

1. An Introduction to Traumatic Brain Injury
2. Communication
3. Promoting Skills for Independence
4. Understanding and Managing Cognitive Changes Following an TBI
5. Understanding and Managing Behavior Changes Following an TBI
6. Sexuality After an ABI: Issues and Strategies
7. Case Management
8. Supervising Staff/Managing Staff
9. Mobility

Available online: http://www.tbistafftraining.info

Family Caregivers, Patients, and Physicians: Ethical Guidance to Optimize Relationships

The American College of Physicians (ACP) issued a position paper on ethical guidance to physicians for developing mutually supportive patient–physician–caregiver relationships:

Mitnick, S., Leffler, C., & Hood V. L. (2010). Family caregivers, patients and physicians: Ethical guidance to optimize relationships. *Journal of General Internal Medicine, 25*(3), 255–260. doi:10.1007/s11606-009-1206-3

Available online:
http://www.acponline.org/running_practice/ethics/issues/policy/
caregivers.pdf

Health Care Comes Home: The Human Factors.
Committee on the Role of Human Factors in Home Health Care, Board
on Human-Systems Integration, Division of Behavioral and Social Sciences
and Education. Washington, DC: The National Academies Press, 2011.

Additional helpful information may be accessed on websites and listservs of professional and advocacy organizations (e.g., see http://www
.brainweb.ca in the Canadian province of Ontario).

Appendix D

ISO 9999 With *ICF* References for Code 05
Assistive Products for Training in Skills

Adapted from:

Working Document
A combined action of NEN (Dutch Normalisation Institute) and the Dutch WHO
FIC Collaborating Centre
December 2009
Theo Bougie & Yvonne Heerkens
Members of NEN/NC 303 072, FDRG7 and ISO/TC173/SC2/WG11
A revised version of N19rev
Based on ISO 9999, version 2007

05 ASSISTIVE PRODUCTS FOR TRAINING IN SKILLS

Devices that have a function other than training, but which may also be used for training, should be included in the class covering its principal function

05.03 Assistive products for communication therapy and training
Equipment for improving communication skills in written and spoken languages

05.03.03 Assistive products for voice and speech training
Equipment for training and developing the use of voice and speech,
   particularly in relation to the production and awareness of sounds
ICF-reference: Auditory perception (b1560)
ICF-reference: Voice and speech functions (b3)

05.03.06 Training materials for developing reading skills
Equipment for training and developing reading skills, particularly strategy,
   approach and performance
ICF-reference: Reception of written language (b16701)
ICF-reference: Learning to read (d140)
ICF-reference: Communicating with—receiving—written messages (d325)

05.03.09 Training materials for developing writing skills
Equipment for training and developing writing skills, particularly strategy,
   approach, performance and creativity
ICF-reference: Expression of written language (b16711)
ICF-reference: Learning to write (d145)
ICF-reference: Writing messages (d345)

(Continued)

ISO 9999 With *ICF* References for Code 05
Assistive Products for Training in Skills

05.06 Assistive products for training in alternative and augmentative communication

Assistive products for training alternative communication techniques and vocabulary to allow interpersonal communication

05.06.03 Assistive products for training in finger spelling

Equipment for training in, and learning, finger spelling, i.e. tactile
   communication for deaf blind people

ICF-reference: Reception of sign language (b16702)

ICF-reference: Expression of sign language (b16712)

ICF-reference: Integrative language functions (b1672)

ICF-reference: Basic learning (d130–d159)

ICF-reference: Communicating with—receiving—formal sign language
   messages (d320)

ICF-reference: Producing messages in formal sign language (d340)

ICF-reference: Using communication techniques (d3602)

05.06.06 Assistive products for training in sign language

Equipment for training in, and learning, sign languages, i.e. visual languages
   for deaf people

ICF-reference: Reception of sign language (b16702)

ICF-reference: Expression of sign language (b16712)

ICF-reference: Integrative language functions (b1672)

ICF-reference: Basic learning (d130–d159)

ICF-reference: Communicating with—receiving—formal sign language
   messages (d320)

ICF-reference: Producing messages in formal sign language (d340)

ICF-reference: Using communication techniques (d3602)

05.06.09 Assistive products for training in lip-reading

Equipment for training in, and learning lip-reading

ICF-reference: Reception of spoken language (b16700)

ICF-reference: Basic learning (d130–d159)

ICF-reference: Communicating with—receiving—spoken messages (d310)

ICF-reference: Communicating with—receiving—body gestures (d3150)

ICF-reference: Using communication techniques (d3602)

05.06.12 Assistive products for training in cued speech

Equipment for training and learning vocal language supplemented by signing

ICF-reference: Reception of spoken language (b16700)

ICF-reference: Reception of sign language (b16702)

ICF-reference: Basic learning (d130-d159)

ICF-reference: Communicating with—receiving—spoken messages (d310)

ICF-reference: Communicating with—receiving—formal sign language (d320)

ICF-reference: Using communication techniques (d3602)

(Continued)

ISO 9999 With *ICF* References for Code 05
Assistive Products for Training in Skills

05.06.15 Assistive products for Braille training

Equipment for training blind persons to read using the Braille code, which is a system of writing that uses characters made up of raised dots

ICF-reference: Reception of written language (b16701)
ICF-reference: Learning to read (d140)
ICF-reference: Learning to write (d145)
ICF-reference: Communicating with—receiving—written messages (d325)
ICF-reference: Writing messages (d345)
ICF-reference: Using communication devices and techniques (d360)

05.06.18 Assistive products for training in tactile symbols excluding Braille

ICF-reference: Visual perception (b1561)
ICF-reference: Reception of language (b1670)
ICF-reference: Expression of language (b1671)
ICF-reference: Learning to read (d140)
ICF-reference: Learning to write (d145)
ICF-reference: Using communication devices and techniques (d360)

05.06.21 Assistive products for training in icon symbols

Equipment for training and learning simplified and formalized pictures, that represent a message and/or information

ICF-reference: Reception of language (b1670)
ICF-reference: Expression of language (b1671)
ICF-reference: Basic learning (d130–d159)
ICF-reference: Communicating with—receiving—nonverbal messages (d315)
ICF-reference: Producing nonverbal messages (d335)
ICF-reference: Using communication devices and techniques (d360)

05.06.24 Assistive products for training in Blisscommunication

Equipment for training and learning communication with a special picture language called Bliss

ICF-reference: Reception of language (b1670)
ICF-reference: Expression of language (b1671)
ICF-reference: Learning to read (d140)
ICF-reference: Learning to write (d145)
ICF-reference: Communicating with—receiving— nonverbal messages (d315)
ICF-reference: Producing signs and symbols (d3351)
ICF-reference: Using communication devices and techniques (d360)

05.06.27 Assistive products for training in communication with pictures and drawings

Equipment for training and learning communication using pictures and drawings which illustrate the word or sentence to be communicated

ICF-reference: Reception of language (b1670)
ICF-reference: Expression of language (b1671)
ICF-reference: Basic learning (d130–d159)
ICF-reference: Communicating with—receiving—nonverbal messages (d315)
ICF-reference: Producing nonverbal messages (d335)
ICF-reference: Using communication devices and techniques (d360)

(Continued)

05.06.30 Assistive products for training in Morse communication

Equipment for teaching the Morse alphabet (a coded alphabet in which each
letter is represented by a specific sequence of sounds or of signals)
and training people to use it

ICF-reference: Reception of language (b1670)

ICF-reference: Expression of language (b1671)

ICF-reference: Learning to read (d140)

ICF-reference: Learning to write (d145)

ICF-reference: Communicating with - receiving - nonverbal messages (d315)

ICF-reference: Producing nonverbal messages (d335)

ICF-reference: Using communication devices and techniques (d360)

05.09 Assistive products for continence training

Devices to train a person to control the bladder and/or the intestine

05.09.03 Incontinence alarms

Devices that produce a signal when involuntary urination or defecation
takes place

ICF-reference: Urination functions (b620)

ICF-reference: Sensations associated with urinary functions (b630)

05.12 Assistive products for training in cognitive skills

Assistive products designed to enhance the abilities that underlie reasoning and
logical activities, e.g., memory, attention, concentration, conceptual and applied
thinking

05.12.03 Assistive products for memory training

ICF-reference: Memory functions (b144)

05.12.06 Assistive products for training in sequencing

Equipment for training a person to put words, actions, numbers, etc. in the
correct order

ICF-reference: Higher-level cognitive functions (b164)

ICF-reference: Calculation functions (b172)

ICF-reference: Mental function of sequencing complex movements (b176)

ICF-reference: Thinking (d163)

05.12.09 Assistive products for training in attention Equipment for developing concentration

ICF-reference: Attention functions (b140)

ICF-reference: Focusing attention (d160)

05.12.12 Assistive products for training in concept development

Equipment for training a person to understand concepts such as colour, size,
shape, etc.

ICF-reference: Abstraction (b1640)

ICF-reference: Mental functions of language (b167)

ICF-reference: Thinking (d163)

(Continued)

ISO 9999 With *ICF* References for Code 05
Assistive Products for Training in Skills

05.12.15 Assistive products for training in classification
Equipment for training a person to use the knowledge of concepts to group related things together
ICF-reference: Higher-level cognitive functions (b164)
ICF-reference: Mental functions of language (b167)
ICF-reference: Thinking (d163)

05.12.18 Assistive products for training in problem solving
ICF-reference: Problem-solving (b1646)
ICF-reference: Solving problems (d175)

05.12.21 Assistive products for training inductive/deductive reasoning
Equipment to train logical thinking when drawing conclusions from a set of facts and generalizing and
interpreting them
ICF-reference: Organisation and planning (b1641)
ICF-reference: Judgement (b1645)
ICF-reference: Problem solving (b1646)
ICF-reference: Solving problems (d175)

05.12.24 Assistive products for developing understanding of cause and effect
ICF-reference: Intellectual functions (b117)
ICF-reference: Solving problems (d175)

05.15 Assistive products for training in basic skills

05.15.03 Assistive products for early training in counting
Equipment designed to assist in the acquisition of the conceptual link between the number of objects,
figures and basic arithmetical operations
ICF-reference: Calculating functions (b172)
ICF-reference: Learning to calculate (d150)
ICF-reference: Calculating (d172)

05.15.06 Assistive products for coding and decoding written language
Equipment for training in the relationship between letters and their corresponding sounds
ICF-reference: Reception of written language (b16701)
ICF-reference: Expression of written language (b16711)
ICF-reference: Learning to read (d140)
ICF-reference: Learning to write (d145)

05.15.09 Assistive products for training in the understanding of time
Equipment for training in the concept and function of time
ICF-reference: Orientation to time (b1140)
ICF-reference: Higher-level cognitive functions (b164)

(Continued)

ISO 9999 With *ICF* References for Code 05
Assistive Products for Training in Skills

05.15.12 Assistive products for training in the understanding of money
Equipment for training in the basic concept and function of money
ICF-reference: Higher-level cognitive functions (b164)
ICF-reference: Basic economic transactions (d860)

05.15.15 Assistive products for training in understanding measures/capacity
Assistive products for the acquisition of the concept of units of measure (litres, metres) and its application to measurement of real things
ICF-reference: Visual perception (b1561)
ICF-reference: Higher-level cognitive functions (b164)

05.15.18 Assistive products for training in basic geometric skills
Assistive products for the acquisition of the main characteristics of geometric shapes acquiring basic abilities in their recognition, naming and comparison
ICF-reference: Visual perception (b1561)
ICF-reference: Visuospatial perception (b1565)
ICF-reference: Higher-level cognitive functions (b164)
ICF-reference: Thinking (d163)

05.18 Assistive products for training in various educational subjects

05.18.03 Assistive products for mother tongue training
Equipment for facilitating a person's ability to speak and understand the native language
ICF-reference: Mental functions of language (b167)
ICF-reference: Learning to read (d140)
ICF-reference: Learning to write (d145)
ICF-reference: Writing (d170)
ICF-reference: Speaking (d330)

05.18.06 Assistive products for foreign language training
ICF-reference: Mental functions of language (b167)
ICF-reference: Learning to read (d140)
ICF-reference: Learning to write (d145)
ICF-reference: Writing (d170)
ICF-reference: Speaking (d330)

05.18.09 Assistive products for training in humanistic subjects
Equipment for facilitating knowledge about humanistic subjects, e.g., history, philosophy and art
ICF-reference: School education (d820)

05.18.12 Assistive products for training in social subjects
Equipment for facilitating knowledge about social science subjects, e.g., sociology and psychology
ICF-reference: Interpersonal interactions and relationships (d7)
ICF-reference: School education (d820)

(Continued)

ISO 9999 With *ICF* References for Code 05
Assistive Products for Training in Skills

05.18.15 Assistive products for training in natural subjects

Equipment for facilitating knowledge about natural science subjects, e.g.,
biology, physics, mathematics and chemistry
ICF-reference: School education (d820)

05.18.18 Assistive products for training in occupational and commercial subjects

Equipment for facilitating knowledge about occupational-oriented subjects,
e.g., commerce and economics
ICF-reference: Vocational training (d825)

05.18.21 Assistive products for training in sensory integration

Equipment for facilitating the coordination of the incoming information from
different senses in the brain
ICF-reference: Psychomotor functions (b147)
ICF-reference: Seeing functions (b210)
ICF-reference: Hearing functions (b230)
ICF-reference: Vestibular functions (b235)
ICF-reference: Proprioceptive functions (b260)
ICF-reference: Touch function (b265)
ICF-reference: Sensory functions related to temperature and other stimuli (b270)

05.21 Assistive products for vocational training

05.21.03 Assistive products for vocational guidance

Equipment for training and learning about vocational guidance
ICF-reference: Vocational training (d825)
ICF-reference: Work and employment (d840-d859)

05.21.06 Assistive products for general job training

Equipment for acquiring the basic skills required in a broad spectrum of jobs
ICF-reference: Vocational training (d825)
ICF-reference: Work and employment (d840-d859)

05.21.09 Assistive products for training in office and business functions

Equipment for acquiring basic office and business skills
ICF-reference: Vocational training (d825)

05.21.12 Assistive products for training in programming and informatics

Equipment for acquiring computing skills
ICF-reference: Vocational training (d825)

05.21.15 Assistive products for training in telecommunication

Equipment for acquiring basic telecommunications skills
ICF-reference: Using communication devices and techniques (d360)

05.24 Assistive products for training in the arts

Assistive products for the acquisition of, and the exercise of, functional abilities
and/or tools allowing artistic expression in a range of fields

(Continued)

05.24.03 Assistive products for training in musical skills
Equipment used for learning about general music theory, how to play a
   specific instrument and how to sing
ICF-reference: Production of notes (b3400)
ICF-reference: Arts and culture including playing a musical instrument (d9202)

05.24.06 Assistive products for training in drawing skills
Equipment used for learning about drawing and painting techniques
ICF-reference: Producing drawings and photographs (d3352)

05.24.09 Assistive products for training in drama and dance
ICF-reference: Arts and culture (d9202)

05.27 Assistive products for training in social skills
Devices and material for helping to learn how to interact with the outside world,
both in terms of individual social integration and relationships with others

05.27.03 Assistive products for training in recreational activities
Equipment for training to take part in leisure activities
ICF-reference: Recreation and leisure (d920)

05.27.06 Assistive products for training in social behaviour
Equipment used for training to interact and live in harmony with other individuals
ICF-reference: Basic interpersonal interactions (d710)
ICF-reference: Complex interpersonal interactions (d720)

05.27.09 Assistive products for personal safety training
Equipment used for training in identification of external dangers and
   dangerous personal behaviour
ICF-reference: Looking after one's health (d570)

05.27.12 Assistive products for travel training
Equipment for training to travel, e.g., use of public transport, maps, timetables
ICF-reference: Using transportation; (d470)
ICF-reference: Recreation and leisure (d920)

05.30 Assistive products for training in control of input units and handling products and goods

05.30.03 Assistive products for training in mouse control
ICF-reference: Acquiring skills (d155)
ICF-reference: Using writing machines (d3601)

05.30.06 Assistive products for training in joystick control
ICF-reference: Acquiring skills (d155)
ICF-reference: Using writing machines (d3601)

05.30.09 Assistive products for training in switch control
ICF-reference: Acquiring skills (d155)
ICF-reference: Using writing machines (d3601)

05.30.12 Assistive products for training in keyboards skills
ICF-reference: Acquiring skills (d155)
ICF-reference: Using writing machines (d3601)

(Continued)

ISO 9999 With *ICF* References for Code 05
Assistive Products for Training in Skills

05.30.15 Assistive products for training in selection techniques
ICF-reference: Acquiring skills (d155)

05.33 Assistive products for training in daily living activities

05.33.03 Assistive products for training to use orthoses and prostheses
ICF-reference: Acquiring skills (d155)
ICF-reference: Mobility (d4)

05.33.06 Assistive products for training in everyday personal activities
ICF-reference: Acquiring skills (d155)
ICF-reference: Self-care (d5)

05.33.09 Assistive products for training in personal mobility
ICF-reference: Acquiring skills (d155)
ICF-reference: Mobility (d4)

05.33.12 Assistive products for training in housekeeping
ICF-reference: Acquiring skills (d155)
ICF-reference: Domestic life (d6)

Retrieved August 9, 2011 from: http://www.rivm.nl/who-fic/in/ISO9999withICFreferences.pdf

Index

AAC. *See* augmentative and alternative communication

AANS. *See* American Association of Neurological Surgeons

abandonment outcome, technology selection, 239

ABI. *See* acquired brain injury

AbleData
database, 124, 145–146
product categories, 146, 147–150*t*

Academy Health Disability Research Interest Group, 303

acceptance, community, cognitive rehabilitation, 115–119

accessibility
buildings, facilities, 196–198, 200–201, 201*t*
checklists, cognitive disability, 343–344
computer, 175–177

accommodation, matching person and technology, 252–254

acquired brain injury (ABI)
defined, causes, 33–34
rehabilitation, interdisciplinary team functioning, 303
treating, 59–63

Acquired Brain Injury (ABI) Program, Coastline Community College in California, 304

ACRM. *See* American Congress of Rehabilitation Medicine

activities, limitations, cognitive rehabilitation, 110, 110*t*

activities of daily living (ADLs). *See also* assistive technology devices (ATDs)
caregiver support levels, 208–209
products aiding, categories, 154

acute inpatient rehabilitation, 62

ADAAA. *See* Americans with Disabilities Act, Amendments Act

ADAMS. See Aging, Demographics, and Memory Study

ADHD. *See* attention deficit/hyperactivity disorder

ADI-R. *See* Autism Diagnostic Interview–Revised

ADLs. *See* activities of daily living

ADOS. *See* Autism Diagnostic Observation Schedule

adults. *See* older adults, dementia, cognitive rehabilitation

aging brain. *See also* dementia
case study (Marjorie), 1–3
medical history, 3–4, 5–17
psychosocial history, life course, 4–5
deterioration, mental, 9–10
stroke (brain attack), 5–9, 6*f*, 7*f*

Aging, Demographics, and Memory Study (ADAMS), 11

AgrAbility Project, 144

Alliance for Technology Access (ATA), 297

Alzheimer's disease, 11–12
early onset, case study, cognitive support technology (CST), 178–180

American Association of Neurological Surgeons (AANS), 34–35

American College of Physicians, 16–17

American Congress of Rehabilitation Medicine, 61

American Medical Association, Current Procedural Terminology (CPT), 290

American Printing House for the Blind, Inc. (APH), 152

American Psychiatric Association, 37

American Stroke Association, 5

Americans with Disabilities Act, 216
Accessibility Guidelines (ADAAG), Checklist for Buildings and Facilities, 196
Amendments Act (ADAAA), 216